HOPE IS OF A DIFFERENT COLOR:
FROM THE GLOBAL SOUTH
TO THE ŁÓDŹ FILM SCHOOL

T0364853

BOOKS
Nº19
The MUSEUM UNDER CONSTRUCTION book series
We are building a Museum of Modern Art in Warsaw
We are writing a new history of art

HOPE IS OF A DIFFERENT COLOR: FROM THE GLOBAL SOUTH TO THE ŁÓDŹ FILM SCHOOL

EDITED BY
MAGDA LIPSKA
MONIKA TALARCZYK

MUSEUM OF MODERN ART
IN WARSAW
LODZ FILM SCHOOL 2021

BOOKS
N°19

MAGDA LIPSKA, MONIKA TALARCZYK
Introduction: From International Solidarity
to a New Color Curtain   9

I   Students from the Global South at the Łódź Film
           School, 1948–89:
           Biographies   29
           Extant List, Enrolled Students   33
           Selected Film Stills   34

II   CONSTANTIN KATSAKIORIS
           Effective Solidarity with the Postcolonial World:
           Cold-War Educational Assistance from the Socialist
           Countries   59

           MATTHIEU GILLABERT
           Students of Color and State Socialism: Can Double
           Exoticism Be Endured in Public Space?   79

           MONIKA BOBAKO
           The Jew, the Arab, the Pole: March 1968 in Poland
           and the History of an Alliance Between the Second
           and Third Worlds   99

           BEATA KOWALSKA, INGA HAJDAROWICZ
           Unwanted Legacy, as Told by Its Witnesses: Arab
           Students in People's Poland   121

           BOLAJI BALOGUN
           Cold War Internationalism: The Myth of Race-Blind
           Eastern Europe
                                                          143
           BARTOSZ NOWICKI
           Representing Africans in The Polish Review:
           A Projection of the PRL as Racism-Free   165

III

GABRIELLE CHOMENTOWSKI
The Training of Third-World Filmmakers in Eastern
Bloc Schools before 1991 **191**

MONIKA TALARCZYK
WE WANT THE SUN! Short Films by Łódź Students from
the Global South, Compared with Models from Polish
Art Cinema **209**

KATARZYNA MĄKA-MALATYŃSKA
The Familiar, the Strange: Works by Students from
the Global South in the Context of the Polish School
of Documentary Film **231**

MARIE PIERRE-BOUTHIER
Podróż to Poland: In Search of a Potential Moroccan
Cinema **251**

OLIVIER HADOUCHI
Voices and Faces from the Third World **271**

RACHAEL DIANG'A
Sao Gamba's Creative Legacy in Kenya **289**

IV

JAKUB BARUA
"The Documentary Film in Eastern Africa: Sao
Gamba's Secret Legacy"
(2009) **307**

JOHN ALEX MAINA KARANJA
"The Cinema and I (A Black Filmmaker)"
(July 1986) **317**

LÉA MORIN
Lesson 41: Going to Poland to Become a Moroccan
Filmmaker **329**

Filmography: Student Shorts   368

Index   372

Magda Lipska is a curator and art theorist currently working at the Museum of Modern Art in Warsaw, where she has curated and cocurated exhibitions including *Niepodległe: Women and the National Discourse* (2018), *Danwen Xing: A Personal Diary* (2017), and *Lest the Two Seas Meet* (2015, with Tarek Abou el Fetouh), as well as film and public programs. She edited the exhibition catalog *Niepodległe: Kobiety a dyskurs narodowy* and has contributed to publications including *Points of Convergence: Alternative Views on Performance* (2017), *Historie filmu awangardowego: Od dadaizmu do postinternetu* (2020), and *Pawlenski* (2016). She is currently working on the post-conference publication *What Are Our Genealogies? Realism, Socialist Realism, and Soc-Modernism in a Global Perspective* (forthcoming, with Piotr Słodkowski).

Monika Talarczyk is a film scholar and associate professor at the Łódź Film School. She is the author of *Wanda Jakubowska: Revisited* (forthcoming in 2022), *Biały mazur: Kino kobiet w polskiej kinematografii* (2013, *The White Mazur: Polish Women's Cinema*), *Wszystko o Ewie: Filmy Barbary Sass a kino kobiet w drugiej połowie XX wieku* (2013, *All about Eve: Barbara Sass's Film and Women's Cinema in the Later Twentieth Century*) and publications about women film directors including the *Pantoptikum* issue "Women in Cinema" (2022, no. 23), and the collection *(Nie)widzialne kobiety kina* (2018, *(Non)visible Women in Film*), edited with Małgorzata Radkiewicz. Talarczyk's major research field is Minor Cinema (women's cinema, minorities in film culture). In 2014, she received the Polish Film Institute Award. A member of the European Women's Audiovisual Network (EWA), the Polish Women of Film society, and FIPRESCI (the International Federation of Film Critics). Currently developing the research project about Jerzy Toeplitz's activity in the international network of film schools and film archives in the twentieth century.

MAGDA LIPSKA
MONIKA TALARCZYK

INTRODUCTION: FROM INTERNATIONAL SOLIDARITY TO A NEW COLOR CURTAIN

" I always dreamed of coming to Poland and now the nightmare has come true"—this statement, by an unnamed student from an African country, comes from a volume edited by Ewa Nowicka and Sławomir Łodziński focused on adaptation issues that students from the Global South faced while on scholarship in Poland.[1] And while the respondent was quick to add that he did not intend to speak badly of his host country, when one reads the results of a survey conducted between 1985 and 1988 among a group of students at the School of Polish for Foreign Students at the University of Łódź (SJPdC)—where every foreign citizen who had earned a scholarship attended mandatory intensive language courses—one can hardly resist the impression that the turn of phrase was a Freudian slip. As such, it reveals a reality that has been assiduously papered over ever since with declarations of transnational fraternity and internationalist solidarity.

1   Grażyna Zarzycka-Suliga, "Pierwsze kontakty studentów zagranicznych z Polską: Relacja z łódzkiej 'Wieży Babel,'" in Gość w dom: Studenci z krajów Trzeciego Świata w Polsce, ed. Ewa Nowicka and Sławomir Łodziński (Warsaw: Oficyna Naukowa, 1993), 47.

Eastern European scholarship programs for what were then termed Third World[2] countries were introduced as part of a wider agenda of assistance for developing countries that the United Nations appealed for in the mid-1950s, during the de-Stalinization period.[3] In 1960, Nikita Khrushchev inaugurated a university for students from those countries in Moscow, soon renamed after Patrice Lumumba, the Congolese independence leader who had just been assassinated. Educating Global South elites was not just a way of promoting socialism, but also a strategic move, aimed at striking political and economic alliances and circumventing Western domination. More broadly, it was an attempt to build an "alternative global modernity" based on the values of anti-colonial internationalism "committed to anti-imperialist politics and non-capitalist development."[4]

This belief that a different world is possible began to wane in the early 1970s. Set in motion by the Helsinki Process,[5] the détente between the Soviet bloc and the West meant that European countries adopted a more continental focus in foreign policy. Contacts with Third World countries grew weaker. Internationalism's ideological foundations gradually eroded, too. It was increasingly seen

---

2   We use the term Third World in its original meaning; that is, to describe those countries (mostly postcolonial) that despite their socialist leanings did not wish to comply with either the West (capitalism) or the East (communism) and instead pursued a third way beyond imperial paradigms.

3   The advanced educations of film students from the Global South at Eastern-bloc schools is a topic that receives growing attention through film-historical research and curatorial practices. See Tereza Stejskalová, ed., *Filmmakers of the World, Unite! Forgotten Internationalism, Czechoslovak Film and the Third World* (Prague: Transit.cz, 2017); Rasha Salti, ed., with Gabrielle Chomentowski, *Saving Bruce Lee: African and Arab Cinema in the Era of Soviet Cultural Diplomacy* (Berlin: Haus der Kulturen der Welt, 2018).

4   James Mark, Bogdan C. Iacob, Tobias Rupprecht, and Ljubica Spaskovska, eds., *1989: A Global History of Eastern Europe* (Cambridge: Cambridge University Press, 2019), 130.

5   A joint declaration on principles was adopted for the first time during the Cold War on August 1, 1975, at the closing meeting of the third phase of the Conference on Security and Cooperation in Europe. The consensus among the thirty-five participating states—all of Europe except Albania and Andorra, along with the United States and Canada—would guide relations between them.

as a waste of money—money that could and should be spent at home, especially during the 1980s' economic crises, felt acutely by all Eastern bloc countries.[6]

After Khrushchev's declaration of an "opening up toward Africa and the Third World," made at the Twentieth Congress of the Soviet Communist Party in 1956, it became a priority of cultural policy among Soviet bloc countries to educate fledgling experts from the Global South, especially those who identified with socialism and communism. The purpose was to produce a left-leaning international elite. While economic and military aspects played a role as well, these student-scholarship programs are among the elements of diplomacy that are worth reexploring from a humanities perspective as a revealing cultural form activated during the Cold War era.

A Transnational People's Poland?

The concept of transnational cinema emerged in the late twentieth century, conceived in response to a new order of film culture that, as a result of globalization processes and new flows of film production, was unhindered by economic and political boundaries of the Cold War period. As the scholars Elizabeth Ezra and Terry Rowden explain in their *Transnational Cinema*, the concept serves to recognize global forces connecting the people and institutions of film beyond national borders while acknowledging that the category of nationality has grown less and less pertinent as a regulator of world cinema.[7]

But can this also be applied to studies of Cold War–era student film? Before trying to answer that question, we must return to historical concepts used to describe world cinema as well as cinemas of the First, Second, and Third Worlds. The term Second World, as a synonym for the Eastern bloc and its allies, first appeared in an essay published in *L'Observateur* in 1952 by the French anthropologist

6   The generation that had arrived two decades earlier perceived their stays in Poland in quite different terms. See Beata Kowalska and Inga Hajdarowicz, "Unwanted Legacy, as Told by Its Witnesses: Arab Students in People's Poland," in this book.

7   Elizabeth Ezra, Terry Rowden, eds., *Transnational Cinema: The Film Reader* (London: Routledge, 2006), 1.

and demographer Alfred Sauvy, who wrote: "We speak readily of two worlds in confrontation, of their possible war, of their coexistence, etc., forgetting all too often that there is a third—the most important and, in fact, the first world in the chronological sense."[8] Moreover, Sauvy suggested that the Third World was the raison d'être of the Cold War, with the global powers vying, if not to conquer it, at least to bring it under their sway.

That division, along with the table of the "worlds," left a trace in film culture in the manifesto "Toward a Third Cinema" (1970) by the Argentine filmmakers Fernando Solanas and Octavio Getino, dealing with the phenomenon of new South American cinema. Translated into cinema paradigms, the geopolitical nomenclature resulted in their analysis in a split into "First Cinema," as the cinema of global Hollywood, where "man is viewed as a consumer of ideology, not as the creator of ideology," and "Second Cinema," that is, auteur cinema, where a director searches for their own language and exposes ideologies, but remains caught in the trap of individualism. "Third Cinema," according to Solanas and Getino, promises liberation through collective struggle against the system of capitalist domination—now widely understood to be inherently racist.[9]

Short films completed by Global South students while studying at the Łódź Film School during the Cold War are striking evidence that these filmmakers matured within a film milieu that had been nationalized[10] in 1945, which would then give rise to the Polish film school (auteur cinema) and the Polish documentary-film school (auteur documentary) a decade or so later. Within the bounds of student film, this shaping of a nationalized cinema and the Polish film "brand" on the international scene was accompanied by a cinema project that transgressed not only national boundaries but also those of the Eastern bloc. The term "socialist cinema" can be found

8   As quoted in Carl E. Pletsch, "The Three Worlds or Division of Social Scientific Labour circa 1950–76," *Comparative Studies in Society and History* 23, no. 4 (1981): 569.
9   Fernando Solanas and Octavio Getino, "Toward a Third Cinema," *Cineaste* 4, no. 3 (1970–71): 1–10.
10   In the sense of being owned and managed by the state, typical for the Eastern bloc economies.

13 INTRODUCTION: FROM INTERNATIONAL SOLIDARITY TO A NEW
COLOR CURTAIN

in the era's literature and journalism.[11] Far from being a monolithic bloc isolated from outside influence, this cinema even organized institutional paths of internal flows through student exchange. Boundaries were defined by ideology rather than the map. This allows us to use the category of "transnationality" in analyzing the global project of socialist cinema within world cinema of the second half of the twentieth century.

This "transnational People's Poland"—as film scholars Sebastian Jagielski and Magdalena Podsiadło explain—encompassed various ways of internationalizing cinematography beyond the Iron Curtain, whether through attempts to open it up to the West or by integrating it with the greater organism of the Soviet sphere.[12] Those in charge of Eastern bloc cinematographies signed and implemented cooperation agreements, while controlling incidental examples of Western coproduction. Film schools in the Eastern bloc participated in the greater project, under the patronage of the Soviet Union, of internationalizing socialist cinema. As the cultural historian Marsha Siefert has written, the purpose of collective projects was to establish a socialist film elite through educational and formal associations: educating filmmakers sensitive to social issues in non-socialist countries, while establishing a transnational network of financial and technological support for like-minded filmmakers.

In short, it was Soviet-style cinematic internationalism.[13] Along with three forms that Siefert mentions of cultivating this internationalism—those being the Moscow Film Festival, annual meetings of Eastern bloc filmmakers, and Soviet coproductions—systematic work was being pursued by Central and Eastern European film schools. We can thus speak of a global socialist cinema organ-

11 Jerzy Toeplitz, *Historia sztuki filmowej*, vols. 1–5 (Warsaw: Filmowa Agencja Wydawnicza, 1955), passim; Bolesław Michałek, "Historia kina socjalistycznego: Po ankiecie historycznej," *Kino*, no. 9 (1979): 48–49; Rafał Marszałek, "Historia kina socjalistycznego: Między historią i krytyką," *Kino*, no. 5 (1979): 47–51.
12 Sebastian Jagielski and Magdalena Podsiadło, eds., *Kino polskie jako kino transnarodowe* (Kraków: Universitas, 2017), 18.
13 Marsha Siefert, "Soviet Cinematic Internationalism and Socialist Film Making, 1955–1972," in *Socialist Internationalism in the Cold War: Exploring the Second World*, ed. Patryk Babiracki and Austin Jersild (London: Palgrave Macmillan, 2016), 161–93.

ized around schools, festivals, Eastern bloc coproductions, and cooperation with the developing South, with the core idea of this Soviet cinematic internationalism.

A Continental School

The Łódź Film School (today the Leon Schiller National Film, Television, and Theater School; PWSFTviT) has been described in the literature as a paragon of the continental film school during the postwar development of national cinematographies.[14] Shortly after the war, filmmakers were training at the Film Institute in Kraków, then in Łódź at the Film Department of the Fine Arts College, directed by Marian Wimmer. The Łódź Film School was launched in 1948, run by a generation of instructors including Eugeniusz Cękalski and Jerzy Toeplitz who traced roots to a committed group of prewar cinephiles. In the 1930s, they had been striving to elevate film culture in Poland and directing their own attempts to advance Polish cinema artistically. For five years, as members of the START Association of Art Film Enthusiasts (founded in 1930), they animated film culture in Warsaw and Łódź, organizing screenings and discussions, shooting artistic shorts (impressionistic, ethnographic, documentary), and lobbying public institutions and state authorities to create conditions for the production and distribution of films for more discerning viewers.

14   Duncan Petrie, Rod Stoneman, *Educating Film-makers: Past, Present, and Future* (Bristol: Intellect Ltd., 2014), 27. The Soviet Union became a leader in cinematic internationalism not only for political reasons, but also due to its pioneering role in educating filmmakers, including the first film school, the All-Union State Institute of Cinematography (VGIK), founded in Moscow in 1919. Film-education historians see three phases in the founding of film schools. First, they are conceived as tools of new political regimes, as with VGIK, set up after the 1917 Bolshevik Revolution, and the Centro Sperimentale di Cinematografia, started by Italy's fascist regime as the first such school in Western Europe. In the second phase, after the Second World War, film schools became institutions of national cinema, such as the Film and Television School of the Academy of Performing Arts in Prague (FAMU, 1946), the Łódź Film School (1948), and the Konrad Wolf Film University in Potsdam-Babelsberg, East Germany (founded in 1954 as the German Academy of Film Art). The third phase, after the fall of Communism, saw the emergence of schools training professionals for the free-market film industry (Petrie, Stoneman, *Educating Film-makers*, 4). This list includes the Institut des Hautes Études Cinematographiques (IDHEC), founded during the Second World War in France, which would play a major role in educating students from postcolonial countries.

After the war, these STARTers received the first top awards for Polish film at international festivals: Wanda Jakubowska for *Ostatni etap* (*The Last Stage*; Crystal Globe at the Karlovy Vary IFF, 1948); Jerzy Bossak with Wacław Kaźmierczak for *Powódź* (*Flood*; Grand Prix for Best Documentary Short at the Cannes IFF, 1947). From their group came the Łódź Film School's first rector: Jerzy Toeplitz, a cinema historian and film critic.

Toeplitz had already been deeply involved in organizing film education in Poland as secretary of the prewar Film Industry Supreme Council's Committee for Film Training, tasked with establishing a national Film Institute.[15]

Shortly after the war, he joined an international network of cooperation for film culture, which led to his presidency of the International Federation of Film Archives (1948–72), and to the Łódź Film School's inclusion in the CILECT International Association of Film and Television Schools (1955), and to European cinema masters including Vsevolod Pudovkin and Joris Ivens visiting Łódź, as well as theoreticians including Béla Balázs and Umberto Barbaro.[16] After Toeplitz was dismissed as rector in 1968 in the midst of Party-led "anti-Zionist" purges instigated that March, his stature on the inter-

15   Jerzy Toeplitz, "O talentach i wykształceniu filmowem," *Pion*, no. 4 (1935).
16   Toeplitz's characterization of socialist cinema, published for the English-speaking public in 1968, may be considered authoritative, particularly given his international standing: "There are three elements which seem to me characteristic and really decisive for the character of east European cinema in all the countries I am speaking of[:] the Soviet Union, Poland, Czechoslovakia, Hungary, R[o]mania, Bulgaria, Yugoslavia. First, they are all state owned cinemas. The state takes on the task of financing film production, running the theatres, and also controlling distribution of films in foreign countries and the importation of foreign films into these countries. The second thing common to all these countries is that the rank of the cinema in the hierarchy of the arts is much higher than in the western states. There is a feeling that it is the duty of the state to take care of cinema, that the cinema is an important part of art—not entertainment, not industry, but art. The reason is quite clear. All the Marxists in all these countries have read the famous statement by Lenin that 'of all the arts the cinema is the most important for us.' The third common denominator in all these countries is the idea of the film school as nursery for future film makers. I think this is of the greatest importance because there is a natural influx of new people with fresh ideas coming out of the schools into film production. Production could hardly exist without the schools. Producers do not have to search for people who might be useful to them. There is a regular channel for young people interested in film and seeing film as a career leading them from school into the profession." Jerzy Toeplitz, "Cinema in Eastern Europe," *Cinema Journal* 8, no. 1 (1968): 3–4.

national scene would be reconfirmed when he was hired to coorganize the Australian Film, Television, and Radio School (AFTRS) in Sydney. Toeplitz had accepted an invitation from La Trobe University in Melbourne to deliver a year-long lecture series on cinema history, then was appointed AFTRS's founding director, a position he held for six years (1973–79), just as the Australian New Wave was being fomented.

Immediately after the war, Łódź, Poland's third largest city and the nearest one to the shattered capital where the urban fabric had survived, was being transformed into an academic hub, a process that included the founding of the film school. In the late nineteenth century, the city had rapidly grown into a major manufacturing center; in the twentieth, just as the postwar period began, into a city of higher education, film culture, and nationalized industry. A key principle in the film-education project was joining theory and practice in parallel with humanities training. The declared model was, of course, Moscow's VGIK, although sources show that the new school's statute was also consulted with an IDHEC professor in France.[17]

Practical training required unique infrastructure that was developed alongside the reborn domestic cinematographic industry as a whole. Early on, students used equipment and soundstages of the Wytwórnia Filmów Fabularnych studios, founded in Łódź in 1949. In 1955, the school inaugurated its own film-production center, Szkolny Ośrodek Produkcji Filmów, fully equipped for shooting, lighting, sound recording, and editing. As part of their curriculum, directing students were required to submit an editing exercise, a production exercise, two documentary shorts, two feature shorts, and a TV show. For cinematography students, requirements included exercises in black-and-white and color in various footage lengths and film-stock types (16 mm, 35 mm). Two full shooting crews could work at once, and the technical staff was almost the size of the teaching staff (the latter numbered nearly one hundred). Due to

17   Note on the Statute typescript, Jerzy Toeplitz Archive, Łódź Museum of Cinematography. Both educational models are discussed by Gabrielle Chomentowski in her essay, "The Training of Third-World Filmmakers in Eastern Bloc Schools before 1991," in this book.

capacity issues and budget shortages—funds allocated usually fell
short of what had been applied for—Polish graduate students were
allowed, per an ordinance from the minister of culture and art, to
produce the practical part of their master's projects with the professional Zespoły Filmowe state film studios.[18] This did not hold for
foreign students, whose graduation films were made at the school's
production center. The sole exception is the Iranian Kaweh Pur
Rahnama's war drama, No Way Back, Johnny (1969), which Rahnama's
supervisor recommended for production at Zespoły Filmowe's
"Vector" studio.

Films from the Tower of Babel

Students from the Global South began arriving at the
Łódź Film School at the end of the 1950s; the first were two cinematography students from India in 1959. These early candidates had
either already studied at art schools at home or—this applies to
advanced classes—had already studied on other scholarships for
students from postcolonial countries (greatly facilitated by knowing
a host country's language, as with those from former French colonies applying to study at IDHEC).

Film schools in the Eastern bloc required foreign students to complete a year-long language course. Classes took place
in international groups, as yet undivided into disciplines, and often
at a distance from the main academic centers, sometimes in the
countryside. In Poland, these language courses were initiated in
1952 at the Preparatory College for Schools of Higher Learning,
renamed the School of Polish for Foreign Students (SJPdC), at the
University of Łódź in 1957. Until the late 1970s, SJPdC was the sole
such institution in the country.[19] Łódź, therefore, was the hub for
adaptation and transfer for students with diverse aims from all over
the world.[20] SJPdC course participants went from 132 in 1952 to a

18	Danuta Wódz, "Produkcja filmów szkolnych w Państwowej Wyższej Szkole Filmowej, Telewizyjnej i Teatralnej im. Leona Schillera" (MA diss., Łódź Film School, 1981), Łódź Film School Library.
19	See Matthieu Gillabert, "Students of Color and State Socialism: Can Double Exoticism Be Endured in Public Space?" in this book.
20	Universities in Warsaw and Kraków offered short courses and summer schools.

record 653 in 1989.[21] Alumni would then usually go on to study for degrees in technology, economics, and medicine; far fewer attended film or theater schools.[22]

    Among 170 foreign students from 1948 to 1989 at the Łódź Film School, sixty-three came from countries of the Global South,[23] almost exactly a third of the total. The proportions are somewhat different than for SJPdC and the language program with which students began: most came from Africa (nineteen from North Africa, nine from Sub-Saharan Africa), then from Latin America (twenty-three), the Middle East (six), Asia (five), and the Caribbean (one). Demand peaked in the 1960s for film studies and the scholarship program, when there were a total of thirty students from developing countries, compared with a few in the 1970s and fewer in the 1980s. Within these numbers, in the 1960s there were larger groups of Moroccans and South Americans, while a group of Algerians attended in the 1980s. Figures for students from the Global South indicate that the 1960s had been a "golden decade" for the overseas scholarship program.[24]

Forced Adjustments and Adaptations

    From the perspective of gender studies, in the case of students from the Global South, studying at the Łódź Film School proved an almost exclusively male experience. This seems specific to the Łódź Film School, as VGIK in Moscow, FAMU in Prague, and the Konrad Wolf Film University in Potsdam-Babelsberg all had women students from three continents. It is as yet unclear whether this was

21   Dorota Wielkiewicz-Jałmużna, "Studium Języka Polskiego dla Cudzoziemców Uniwersytetu Łódzkiego w latach 1952–2002," *Acta Universitatis Lodziensis: Kształcenie Polonistyczne Cudzoziemców*, no. 15 (2008): 25.

22   Wielkiewicz-Jałmużna, "Studium Języka Polskiego," 77.

23   About one hundred attended FAMU in Prague during the same period; see Stejskalová, *Filmmakers of the World, Unite!*, 17.

24   Based on data cited during *Les Ecoles de Cinema au XXe siècle: Objet d'étude privilègie pour histoire institutionale des circulations artistiques et politiques*, organized online by Dr. Gabrielle Chomentowski on November 24, 2020. An exception was the Konrad Wolf Film University in Potsdam-Babelsberg, East Germany, where the program was intensified in the 1970s by the new rector, Peter Ulbrich; see Ilka Brombach, "Filme ausländischer Student*innen an der Hochschule für Film und Fernsehen 'Konrad Wolf,'" August 31, 2018, *bpb*, http://www.bpb.de/gesellschaft/bildung/filmbildung/274740/filme-auslaendischer-studentinnen-an-der-hochschule-fuer-film-und-fernsehen-konrad-wolf.

a recruitment bias at the Łódź Film School or due to decisions at the Ministry of Foreign Affairs. During the Cold War, the only woman from the Global South to study direction was Beverly Joan Marcus (1978–82), from the Republic of South Africa. Nancy Cárdenas—a Mexican poet, playwright, filmmaker, and pioneering lesbian activist—studied at SJPdC and intended to enroll at the Łódź Film School, but never did. Students from the Global South managed to avoid androcentrism, choosing to work with cinematographers including Tatiana Dębska, Ewa Strzałka, Jolanta Dylewska, and Katarzyna Remin, and focusing on women's issues in their documentary shorts (including *Marta, Elżbieta K., Zofia and Ludmiła, Aleksander*). This was an effect of the the cultural offer of the Polish People's Republic (PRL), both in the recruitment of women into the Faculty of Cinematography and in trends in Polish documentary film, with working women as a frequent theme. It was also symptomatic of scholarship-program participants identifying with less-privileged peoples' experiences of alienation, linguistic uprootedness, disabilities and alterity.

The film shorts made by these scholarship students reflect the development over time of two phenomena: the gradual diminishment from utopian enthusiasm to disappointment if not disillusionment, along with an empowerment among the protagonists, their growing ambivalence and postcolonial awareness. Initially welcomed with considerable fervor from both hosts and participants, the student-exchange project then generated issues of adaptation, racist incidents, security-police surveillance, and revealing exposure to real-existing socialism across the decades, all of which were felt in eventual assessments of the program as an educational experiment.

March 1968 brought a rough halt to internationalist aspirations. Participant numbers still looked impressive, but any age of innocence was over. Students from the Global South identified with the contexts of 1968 that were French and North African (*Shadow among Others*; *Somewhere, Someday*), Middle Eastern (*Report: September 1969*), and South American (*Che*; *Guerrilla*; *Without Requiem*), rather than with the anti-Zionist campaign that then raged in Poland. Francophone students were likely familiar with Frantz Fanon's *Black Skin, White Masks* (1952), where the political philosopher drew a close connection between his concept of negrophobia—which today is termed anti-Black racism—and anti-Semitism. This would have aroused real concern among them, even fear, as half of Poland's remaining Jews were having their citizenships revoked to be permitted to emigrate. Meanwhile, their fellow students and professors were leaving their studies and being dismissed from their positions, including Jerzy Bossak, Aleksander Ford, and Jerzy Toeplitz, the long-serving rector and a founder of the school. The scholarship students, in their turn, were being tailed by security agents and being encouraged or pressured to turn informants.

Nomadism and Its End

This student-scholarship program was the second moment in history when people of color traveled to Eastern Europe. A first wave of such focused arrivals had followed the Bolshevik revolution of 1917, attracting mainly Afro-American and Afro-Caribbean activists including Claude McKay, George Padmore, Langston Hughes, and W.E.B. Du Bois, who traveled across Eastern Europe on their way to the newly created Soviet Union, seeking alternatives to Western racism and in the hope of new models from a classless, post-racial society.[25]

The second wave of migration to Eastern Europe took place in the postwar period and involved mainly people from the Global South, citizens of newly decolonized countries whose motivations for going to the Eastern bloc were completely different. As mentioned before, despite many having pro-communist sympathies, most weren't planning to stay in Europe and were focused on getting a higher education and acquiring specialist knowledge, much prized and often unavailable at home. Of great significance were the scholarships granted by socialist countries, which also allowed young

---

25   See Kate A. Baldwin, *Beyond the Color Line and the Iron Curtain: Reading Encounters Between Black and Red, 1922–1963* (Durham: Duke University Press, 2002).

people from lower-income families to go to university. Their motivations, therefore, were more pragmatic than the broader social aims of the previous generation.

Both these waves, as the historian Maxim Matusevich points out, prove the insufficiency of the race theorist Paul Gilroy's argument, posited in the latter's book *The Black Atlantic: Modernity and Double-Consciousness*, that modernity is geographically bound up with the Atlantic slave trade between Africa and the Americas by way of Western European shipping concerns, and a result of the material and cultural absorption it affected.[26] As argued by Matusevich and Monica Popescu, a scholar of African literatures, this genealogy should be expanded to include the Cold War–era experience of intellectuals from the Global South, mainly continental Africa: "An African diaspora in the Eastern bloc," Popescu writes, "is not of the same order of magnitude as the diaspora shaped by interaction with western cultures; yet... it is not negligible either."[27] In her research on South African literature, Popescu emphasizes that for an entire generation of writers and activists of the apartheid era, from Lewis Nkosi and Alexa La Guma to Mandla Langa, Chris Hani, and Ronnie Kasrils, their time in Eastern Europe proved a formative experience.[28]

This influence was mutual. Arriving in the insulated countries of the Eastern bloc, students from Africa, Asia, and South America confirmed ideological foundations of the socialist state and they also, as Matusevich points out, challenged them. Thanks to the freedom of travel they enjoyed,[29] they brought hard currency as well lively and unfamiliar clothes and fashion sensibilities, books, and music, implanting in socialist societies where they were aspects of "Western lifestyle" that may have been official condemned but overtly and appealingly reflected more global ways of thinking and being. Thus, by their presences in an "insulated socialist society," these

26   Maxim Matusevich, "Expanding the Boundaries of the Black Atlantic:
      African Students as Soviet Moderns," *Ab Imperio*, no. 2 (2012): 325–50.
27   Monica Popescu, "Lewis Nkosi in Warsaw: Translating Eastern European
      Experiences for an African Audience," *Journal of Postcolonial Writing* 48, no. 2
      (2012): 177.
28   Popescu, "Lewis Nkosi in Warsaw," 177.
29   Unlike their Polish colleagues, foreign students were allowed to travel
      abroad twice a year, also to Western countries. See Patryk Pleskot, ed.,
      Cudzoziemcy w Warszawie 1945–1989 (Warsaw: IPN, 2012).

"modern nomads [...] often served as conduits to the outside world and in this capacity played an ideologically ambiguous and clearly modernizing role,"[30] as Matusevich writes.

This then came to an abrupt halt in 1989. What in Central and Eastern Europe was being hailed as an "opening out," "unification," and a "return to Europe" became for many Third World intellectuals a change freighted with treason, menace, and a closure. "Some non-European anti-imperialists," as it is argued in *1989: A Global History of Eastern Europe*, "understood 1989 as a story of deglobalization through which Eastern Europe had sought a civilizational realignment to the white world and the racialized privileges this would afford them."[31]

Consequently, if we interpret 1989 as a radical redefinition of Eastern Europe's relations with Africa and Asia, then the Iron Curtain was not so much lifted as redeployed across the south, toward the Mediterranean Sea separating Europe from Africa. It is a moment that, following the novelist Richard Wright's book-length report on the Bandung Conference in 1955, could be called a restoration of the color curtain. The fall of the Berlin Wall has set off building processes for other walls around Europe, as clearly indicated in 2015 by the migration crisis from the south and east, and the severing of migration paths that until then had remained viable for those from the Global South.

Like the communist past in general, the project of Soviet-era socialist internationalism, founded on ideas of equality, cooperation, and international solidarity that were being deployed in contradistinction to Western racial realities, was marginalized after 1989 and repressed from collective memory. Today, when the world again needs an alternative to global capitalism in its rapacious reliance on human and planetary resources, the ideals of that era are taking on a renewed significance. This book serves as a reminder that the pre-1989 reality and its values are part of our heritage.

30   Maxim Matusevich, "Journeys of Hope: African Diaspora in the Soviet
            Society," *African Diaspora* 1 (2008): 55.
31   Mark et al., *1989*, 9.

In order to portray the scholarship project in its breadth of potential and its implementation structure, we have decided across the present volume to highlight it from four angles. First, drawing from the Łódź Film School archive, we present capsule biographies of eighteen alumni whose experiences and filmographies have informed the research completed on this subject, a definitive list of enrolled students from the period 1948–89, and a selection of film stills from that same time frame, providing a glimpse of the visual character of the films discussed in various detail throughout.

Second, through discussing student-scholarship programs with Third World countries in a broad international context, and presenting the historical and political background against which internationalist solidarity was then being built (essays by Constantin Katsakioris, Matthieu Gillabert). One often-denied issue of the period was racism, a daily experience for many foreign students in the Eastern bloc. The essays by Beata Kowalska and Inga Hajdarowicz, Bolaji Balogun, and Bartosz Nowicki question any assumption of Eastern European exceptionalism on the subject of race relations. In her essay, Monika Bobako shows how Jew-Arab-Pole relations, contextualized by the events of the Six-Day War and March 1968's anti-Semitic events in Poland, became the beginning of the end of the internationalist project in the PRL.

Third, we will follow the trajectories of foreigners studying in film schools of the Eastern bloc (Gabrielle Chomentowski), along with the aesthetics and politics of their short works. In their essays, Marie Pierre-Bouthier, Olivier Hadouchi, Rachael Diang'a, Katarzyna Mąka-Malatyńska, and Monika Talarczyk discuss how student filmmakers' experiences of studying in the Eastern bloc impacted their subsequent careers. Finally, by way of selected source materials, we want to give voice to the book's protagonists— that is, to overseas scholarship students and alumni of the Łódź Film School. This section includes John Alex Maina Karanja's master's thesis in the directing department, "The Cinema and I (A Black Filmmaker)." Jakub Barua, a Polish-Kenyan director, shares reflections on Sao Gamba, his mentor and friend, who was also a Łódź Film

School student. Léa Morin has collected reminiscences from the Moroccan and Algerian alumni Mostafa Derkaoui and Abdelkrim Derkaoui, Abdelkader Lagtaa, Ahmed Lallem, and their Costa Rican friend Miguel Sobrado, who played protagonists in their student shorts.

This book's title, as with that of the film program we presented in late 2019 at the Museum of Modern Art in Warsaw, comes from a poem, "Point d'interrogation," written by Abdelkader Lagtaa in Łódź in 1972 (see the insert to this book). This phrase is also the title of Lagtaa's short student film in which he critically examines how Poles relate to their Roma neighbors. In the all-but monoethnic Polish society of the Cold War era—an abrupt, terribly costly legacy of the Second World War—Lagtaa sought ruptures providing glimpses behind the polished screen of socialist reality. Colorfulness brought into that reality by students from the Global South offered hope that a differing reality was possible. It's a hope we need today, as well.

Translated from the Polish by Marcin Wawrzyńczak.

27

PART I

Jakub (Jacob) Barua (b. 1967), a Polish-born Kenyan, studied in the Film and TV Direction Department of the Łódź Film School (1989–94) before earning a degree in film and literature from Warwick University. Director of the student shorts *This-That* (1989), *Sabou* (1990), *The Welcome* (1990), *The Rider* (1990), and *Shine* (1992). Director of the ethnographic film *Forgotten Places* (1994), the first Swahili-language film in 35mm format, produced by Studio Filmowe Kronika–TVP– PWSFTviT. Director of the educational films *Polish Hues* (1999) about Polish-African relations from earlier eras to the present day, a TVP production, and *My Daddy Was an Uhlan* (2006) about the last member of a group of child refugees who had been brought to Kenya during the Second World War. Codirector and coproducer of the documentary *No Limits: Amelia Earhart's Last Flight* (US, 1997). Author of essays, scholarly and newspaper articles, contributor to *Time Frames: Conservation Policies for Twentieth-Century Architectural Heritage* (Ugo Carughi and Massimo Visone, eds., London: Routledge 2017), among other publications. Art director of Telewizja Niepokalanów (1997–2000), director of the Zanzibar International Film Festival in Tanzania (2005–06), lecturer at Don Bosco Utume College in Nairobi, curator of exhibitions at the National Museum of Kenya in Nairobi.

Stanisław (Stan) Barua (b. 1965), a Polish-born Kenyan, is a graduate of the Direction of Photography and TV Production Department of the Łódź Film School (1986–90). His master's thesis, "An Interpretation of Being," was written under the supervision of Jerzy Wójcik. Director of photography for the student shorts *Scent of Islam* (1989), *Aureliano* (1989), *The Welcome* (1990), *The Rider* (1990), for the features *Forgotten Places* (1994), *Polish Hues* (1999), *My Daddy Was an Uhlan* (2006), *Polish Jerusalem* (2020), as well as numerous documentaries for cinema and television. Member of the Canadian Society of Cinematogra-

phers, the Academy of Canadian Cinema & Television, and the International Cinematographers Guild. Nominated for and recipient of numerous awards for cinematography in Europe, Africa, the United States, and Canada.

Hamid Bensaïd (Mohamed Ben Said) (b. 1948, Morocco), is a graduate of the Film and TV Direction Department of the Łódź Film School (1968–73). In France, actor and assistant for Noël Burch and Jean-Andre Fiesch of the *Cahiers du Cinéma* circle. Director of the student shorts *Pensioners' House* (1969), *Zofia and Ludmiła* (1971), *To Serve Twice* (1973), with script and dialogue cowritten by Ewa Strzałka, based on Julio Cortazar's short story "Servicio." For *Zofia and Ludmiła*, he received the Jury Special Award at the Nyon International Film Festival (1973), an honorary mention at the Łódź Film School Student Shorts Festival in Warsaw, and first prize at the Student Shorts Festival in Łódź (1972). His master's thesis was "The Function of the Object in Film." He made a cameo appearance (as the Turkish man at the hotel) in the Polish cult comedy *What Will You Do When You Catch Me?* (1978, dir. Stanisław Bareja).

Abdelkrim Derkaoui (b. 1945, Morocco), is a graduate of the Direction of Photography and TV Production Department of the Łódź Film School (1966–70). Director of cinematography for the student shorts *Amghar* (1968), **THE ADOPTION** (1968), **CELLAR PEOPLE** (1969), **SHADOW AMONG OTHERS** (1969), **SOMEWHERE, SOMEDAY** (1971), and the New Wave feature *About Some Meaningless Events* (1974). Director of and cinematographer for *Le Jour du forain* (1982), *Rue le Caire* (1994), *Les griffes du passé* (2015), among other productions.

Mostafa Derkaoui (b. 1941, Morocco) studied at the International University of Rabat and at IDHEC in Paris before graduating from the Film and TV Direction Department of the Łódź Film School (1966– 72). His master's thesis, "The Role of Film in the Process of Transforming and Raising Consciousness," was written under the supervision of Henryk Kluba. Director of the student shorts *Amghar* (1968), **THE ADOPTION** (1968), **CELLAR PEOPLE** (1969), and **SOMEWHERE, SOMEDAY** (1971), the New Wave feature *About Some Meaningless Events* (1974, re-premiered at Berlinale 2019), the films *Les cendres du clos* (1976) and *Les beaux jours de Chahrazade* (1982), author of the scripts for *Le Jour du forain* (1982), *Titre provisoire* (1984), and *La femme rurale au Maroc* (1988), coauthor of the documentaries *The Gulf War, What's Next?* (1993), *Le doux murmure du vent après l'orage* (1993), *Les amours de haj Mokhtar Soldi* (2000), *Casablanca by Night* (2003), *Casablanca Daylight* (2004).

José Luis di Zeo (b. 1933, Argentina), is a graduate of the Acting Department of the Art School of Teatro Popular Independiente in Buenos Aires and of the Film and TV Direction Department of the Łódź Film School (1964–68), and a member of the Communist Party of Argentina. Director of the student shorts *Letter to the Children* (1964), *Wake* (1965), *The Meeting* (1968). His short *Guerrilla* (1966) received the Grand Prix at the International Student Film Festival in Amsterdam (1967). His master's thesis was "The Evolution of the National-Popular Theme in Argentine Film." He worked as the second-unit director for Grzegorz Królikiewicz's *Permanent Objections* (1974) and Mieczysław Waśkowski's *Her Portrait* (1974). Director of the documentary *Borges: Un destino sudamericano* (1975) and author of *Borges: Cuenta Buenos Aires* (with Carlos Greco, 2010).

Abdellah Drissi (born in Morocco) is a graduate of the Superior School of Dramatic Arts of the National Theater of Strasbourg and the Film and TV Direction Department of the Łódź Film School (1964–69). Director of the student shorts *The Register 4105* (1970) and *Lesson 41* (1966), which received the Warsaw Documentary Film Studios Award at the Łódź Film School Student Shorts Festival. His master's thesis was "From the Brothers Lumière to Godard:

Foreign Cinematography in Morocco." Former assistant director at the Jaracz Theater in Łódź. Director of UNESCO-commissioned documentaries about North Africa and newsreels for CCM.

Sao Gamba (Seraphinus Otieno) (1940–2004), was a Ugandan-born and Kenyan-based graduate of the Direction of Photography and TV Production Department at the Łódź Film School (1965–71), the first student from sub-Saharan Africa enrolled as part of the school's international scholarship program. Director of the student short **THE MOON CHILDREN** (1970), and cinematographer for the student shorts *Post-Accident* and *Confrontation* (both dir. Paweł Wyrzykowski, 1968). After his studies, Gamba was forced to document the life of Idi Amin, the president of Uganda from 1971 to 1979. Following his escape from Uganda to Kenya, he made documentary and feature films. Director of the documentary *The Maasai Heritage (Imaashoi El Maasai*, aka *People of the Red Ocher*, Kenyan Broadcasting Corporation, 1978, 45') and the feature film *Kolormask*, the first film shot with a full Kenyan cast and crew, produced with government funds (Kenya Film Corporation, 1986). Later in life, he eschewed filmmaking for painting and sculpture, practiced at the Hippo Valley Inn, a home/studio/hotel he founded on the edge of the Nairobi National Park. Author of the self-published book *Revival of African Myths and Legends: Concept and Meaning of Various African Cultural and Traditional Rituals, Written and Reflected in Art Form by Sao Gamba*.

Fayçal Hassaïri (H'saïri Ben Khemaïes Faïcal) (b. 1961, Tunisia) is a graduate of the Higher Institute of Dramatic Arts of the University of Tunis and the Film and TV Direction Department of the Łódź Film School (1987–91). Director of the student shorts **RESERVED FOR FOREIGNERS** (1988), *Hope* (1989), *North-South* (1990, master's project, supervision: Kazimierz Karabasz). His master's thesis was "The Position and Functioning of Cinema in the Cultural Policy of Tunisia." He made a cameo appearance in *Kroll* (1991, dir.

Władysław Pasikowski). After his studies, he worked as director and producer for a Rome-based Arab TV network, then for Al Jazeera in Doha. An associate of the Palestinian director and actor Mohammed Bakri, he was assistant director for the documentary *Jenin, Jenin* (2002) and coproducer of *Ajsheen, Still Alive in Gaza* (2010). Director and producer of shows for Arab TV networks, coproducer of the feature films *A Son* (2019, dir. Mehdi Barsaoui), *The Man Who Sold His Skin* (2020, dir. Kaouther Ben Hania), and *200 Metres* (2002, dir. Ameen Nayeh).

Idriss Karim (1936–2008), a Moroccan, was a graduate of the International Theater Institute in Paris and the Film and TV Direction Department of the Łódź Film School (1967–73). Director of the student shorts *Marta* (1969), *Elżbieta K.* (1973), **SONG FOR THE DEATHS OF THE YOUNG** (1973). Recipient of the Jury Special Award at the Nyon International Film Festival (1973). President of the Polish Branch of the Moroccan Student Union. His master's thesis was "Traditions of the British School: The Influence of the Documentary School on Free Cinema." He worked as Jerzy Grzegorzewski's assistant at the Jaracz Theater in Łódź and as assistant director at the W. Horzyca Theater in Toruń.

John Alex Maina (JAM) Karanja (1956–2002), a Kenyan, was a graduate of the Kenyan Institute of Mass Communication and the Film and TV Direction Department of the Łódź Film School (1981–86). Director of the student shorts **BORN IN CHAINS** (1983) and *The Trap* (1986). His master's thesis was "The Cinema and I (A Black Filmmaker)," written under the supervision of Jerzy Bossak. Upon his return to Kenya, Karanja was an activist for human rights and the rights of disabled persons.

Abdelkader Lagtaa (b. 1948, Morocco) is a graduate of the Film and TV Direction Department of the Łódź Film School (1967–71). His master's thesis was devoted to the phenomenon of direct cinema. Director of the student shorts *Wacław A.* (1969), **SHADOW AMONG OTHERS** (1969), **BUT HOPE IS OF A DIFFERENT**

COLOR (1972), *Voyage* (1975). A conceptual poet, he collaborated with Ewa and Andrzej Partum. Director of the feature films *Love in Casablanca* (1991), *Les Casablancais* (1999), *Face á face* (2003), *La Moitié du Ciel* (2015).

Ahmed Lallem (1940–2009), an Algerian, was an intern with Yugoslavian TV in Belgrade, graduate of IDHEC, student at the Film and TV Direction Department of the Łódź Film School (1964–66), war reporter on the Tunisian-Algerian border, activist with the National Liberation Front (FLN). Director of the student short *The Lost One*, the documentary films *Elles* (1966) and *Algierennes 30 ans après* (1995), the feature film *Zone interdite* (1974), among other works.

Chaouki Mejeri (1961–2019), a Tunisian, was a graduate of the Film and TV Direction Department of the Łódź Film School (1987–94). Director of the student shorts *Scheherazade* (1988), *Scent of Islam* (1989), and *Aureliano* (1989). Often worked with the director Fayçal Hassaïri. Mejeri spent most of his career working for TV in Syria and Egypt. His feature film *The Kingdom of Ants* (2012), about the history of a Palestinian family against the backdrop of the Palestinian-Israeli conflict, earned him much renown. Recipient of the Tunisian Order of Merit (2019).

Kaweh Pur Rahnama (1933–2012) was a Polish-based Iranian who published in Polish, graduate of the directing departments of the Krastyo Sarafov National Academy for Theater and Film Arts in Sofia, Bulgaria, and the Łódź Film School (1964–69), member of the Tudeh Party of Iran, writer and second-language acquisition scholar, longtime employee of the Institute of Oriental Studies of the University of Warsaw, author of books for Farsi-language learners as well as the Polish-language novels *Ten Iranians and a Corpse in Warsaw* (2006), *The Name of Love Is Sufi* (1998), *Mitra* (1988). Director of the documentary student short *Evening-Class Test* (1966), the feature short *The Wallet* (1966), and, as his graduation project, the feature-length *No Way Back, Johnny* (1969). His master's thesis, "An Analysis of Technical Issues in the Film

No Way Back, Johnny," was written under the supervision of Wanda Jakubowska.

Eduardo Coronado Quiroga (b. 1952, Peru), studied literature and film at the Universidad San Marcos de Lima before graduating from the Film and TV Direction Department of the Łódź Film School (1976–83). Director of the student shorts *The Prologue* (1979), *Chronica anonyma* (1980), *Cinequan* (1981), *Face to Face* (1983). His master's thesis, "The Poetics of Pedagogic Film," styled as a poetic-academic essay, was written under the supervision of Maria Kornatowska. *Face to Face* received the Łódź City Award.

Rupen Vosgimorukian (b. 1943), a Lebanese-born Armenian, is a graduate of the Direction of Photography and TV Production Department of the Łódź Film School (1965–70) and director of the student short *Report: September 1969* (1970). After his studies, he started working for ABC News in the US. A longtime coworker with the broadcast journalist Peter Jennings, they were stationed in Beirut in the 1970s, filing reports from Africa and the Middle East. Vosgimorukian later moved to Paris, traveling around the world from there. Received an Emmy Award for cinematography for documentary films. Fluent in several languages.

Raul Saucedo Zermeño (b. 1939, Mexico), graduated from the School of Theater Arts at Teatro Popular de Belles Arts in Mexico City and the Film and TV Direction Department of the Łódź Film School (1968–72). Director of the student shorts *Mea culpa* (1968), **WITHOUT REQUIEM** (1969), *About-Face* (1970). His master's thesis analyzed the work of Luis Buñuel. Director of the Współczesny Theater in Wrocław (1972–74), he also worked with theaters in Poznań and Słupsk, as well as with Polish TV Theater.

Translated from the Polish by Marcin Wawrzyńczak.

1959
Chander Malhotra (India), cin.
1960
Toufigue Kitchlew (India), cin.
Abdul Khalik (Iraq), dir.
1961
Mohamed Mobarak (Iraq), dir.
1962
Mohamed Ben Soude (Morocco), dir.
Cend Namzhil (Mongolia), cin.
Khelil Siala (Tunisia), dir.
Bator Sugarzhav (Mongolia), cin.
Manuel Torres (Mexico), dir.
1963
José Luis di Zeo (Argentina), dir.
1964
Abdellah Drissi (Morocco), dir.
Ahmed Lallem (Algeria), dir.
Kaweh Pur Rahnama (Iran), dir.
1965
Djamel Bourtel (Algeria), dir.
Fausto Fuser (Brazil), dir.
Oscar Gamardo (Argentina), dir.
Sao Gamba (Uganda), cin.
Achene Madani (Algeria), dir.
Eliel Lopez (Mexico), dir.
Rupen Vosgimorukian (Lebanon), cin.
1966
Abdelkrim Derkaoui (Morocco), cin.
Mostafa Derkaoui (Morocco), dir.
José María Sánchez Ariza (Mexico), dir.
Eduardo Mancera (Venezuela), dir.
Raul Saucedo Zermeño (Mexico), dir.
1967
Abdelkader Lagtaa (Morocco), dir.
Salah Riza (Tunisia), dir.
Antonio Rodriguez (Brazil), dir.
1968
Idriss Karim (Morocco), dir.
Hamid Bensaïd (Morocco), dir.
Roland Paret (Haiti), dir.
1970
Lorenzo Pineda (Mexico), dir.
Vasco Shienetar (Venezuela), cin.
1972
Hyacinthe Mienandi (Congo), cin.
Luc Siassia (Congo), cin.

1973
Ali Abdel Chayoum (Sudan), dir.
Gilbert Nsangata (Congo), dir.
1976
Armando Nadrin de Urioste (Bolivia), cin.
Rolando Loewenstein (Venezuela), cin.
Syed Ali Haider Rizvi (Bangladesh), dir.
1978
Beverly Joan Marcus (South Africa), dir.
Eduardo Coronado Quiroga (Peru), dir.
1980
Djamel Benkhaled (Algeria), dir.
Abdelcelem Boutellaa (Algeria), dir.
Laredj Khader (Algeria), dir.
Abdesselam Mezerreg (Algeria), dir.
1981
Nestor Cabrera (Venezuela), dir.
Juan Caicedo (Colombia) dir.
John Alex Maina Karanja (Kenya), dir.
Ntougela Masilela (South Africa), dir.
Saer Mussa (Syria), dir.
1982
Samir Zedan (Iraq), dir.
1983
Erasmo Gill (Venezuela), dir.
Ricardo Torres Ramírez (Colombia), cin.
1984
Rafael Tinoco (Venezuela), cin.
1985
Sergio Vega (Mexico), dir.
José Morales Perez (Mexico), dir.
1986
Ruben Balderas Salas (Mexico), dir.
Stanisław Barua (Kenya), cin.
Leonardo Palleja (Argentina), dir.
1987
Fayçal Hassaïri (Tunisia), dir.
Chaouki Mejeri (Tunisia), dir.
1989
Jakub Barua (Kenya), dir.

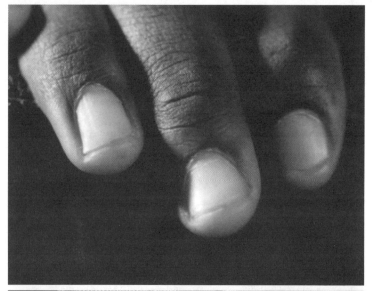

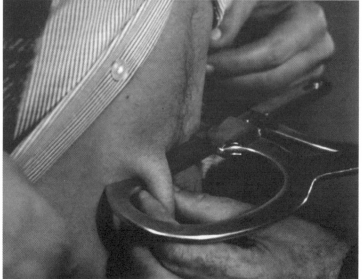

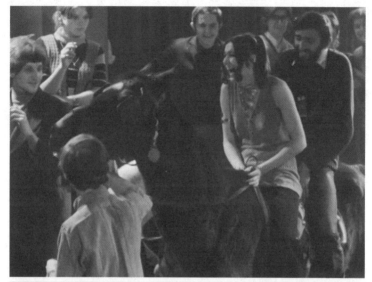

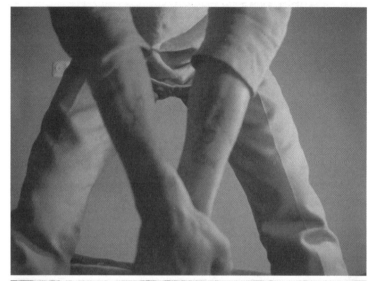

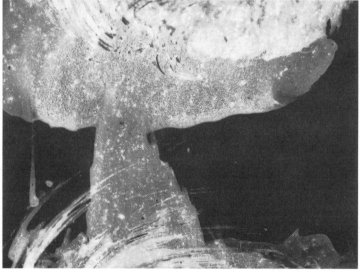

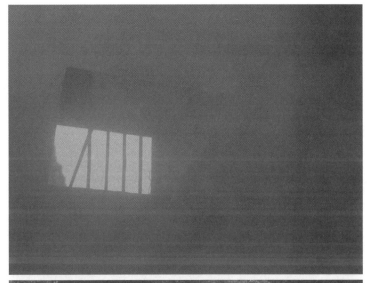

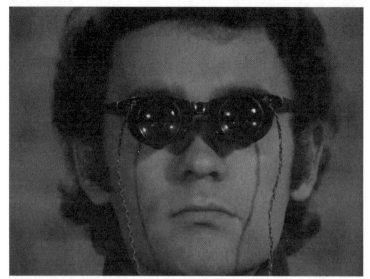

57   PART II

Constantin Katsakioris holds a PhD in contemporary history from the École des hautes études en sciences sociales in Paris (2015). He is a Senior Researcher—PRIMUS Fellow (PRIMUS/21/HUM/011) in the Institute of World History at Charles University in Prague. His research work focuses on the relations between the Eastern bloc, Africa, and the Middle East, international communism, African socialism, and the history of federalism.

EFFECTIVE SOLIDARITY WITH THE POSTCOLONIAL WORLD: COLD-WAR EDUCATIONAL ASSISTANCE FROM THE SOCIALIST COUNTRIES

" The golden days of diverse scholarships for African students to study in Moscow, Prague, Warsaw, Budapest, and Belgrade seem to be almost over and rival scholarships to study in Western countries have been drastically reduced," wrote Ali Mazrui, the prominent Kenyan-American political scientist, in 1999. "The golden days of Czech, Hungarian, and Polish professors teaching at African universities are almost over and resources for Western visiting professors have been drastically reduced."[1]

That may sound like an exercise in nostalgia, yet Mazrui's statement does capture the direct and indirect importance of educational assistance provided by the socialist countries to Africa and, more broadly, to the Third World from the 1950s to the end of the Cold War. Major educational institutions were established across the globe with Soviet and East European aid, and hundreds of professors from socialist countries worked in the postcolonial world. Over a hundred thousand "ordinary" students from Africa, Asia, and Latin America came and trained in Eastern Europe, the Soviet Union,

1   Ali Mazrui, "From Slave Ship to Space Ship: African Between Marginalization and Globalization," *African Studies Quarterly* 2, no. 4 (1999): 9.

and Cuba, the vast majority on scholarships granted by their host countries.[2] The East and the West competed increasingly in training postcolonial elites, to the benefit of the recipient countries.

It remains noteworthy that two schools in the Soviet Union and Czechoslovakia were created specifically for Third World students. The Peoples' Friendship University was established in Moscow in 1960, then renamed the following year in honor of Patrice Lumumba after the Congolese leader had been assassinated. In 1961, November 17 University was founded in Prague, modeled on Lumumba University, and trained students until 1974.[3] Still, as Fafali Koudawo, the prominent Togolese political scientist, rightly observed in referring to the latter university, that institution was "the tree hiding the forest."[4] For the forest included dozens of universities, professional-technical institutes, and art schools across the Soviet Union and Eastern Europe, and its contribution to the training of international students was of enormous importance. One institution playing a key role during this era was the Łódź Film School.

This essay looks back at the training of Third World students across the former socialist countries. It examines who those students were and how they reached Eastern Europe, explores the variety and evolution of the training programs, and refers to those programs' effects in terms of educating a scientific-technical and creative intelligentsia for the postcolonial world. First, however, it focuses on the international context and the political and ideological premises that lay behind this story of educational assistance. It is essential to sketch out the background against which relations between Eastern Europe and what is now termed the Global South took hold, and to highlight why education became a crucial channel of exchange.

2   In distinction from these "ordinary" students, short-term trainees and
           students at political or military schools are not included in this estimate.
3   Constantin Katsakioris, "The Lumumba University in Moscow: Higher
           Education for a Soviet–Third World Alliance, 1960–91," *Journal of Global
           History* 14, no. 2 (2019): 281–300; Marta Edith Holečková, "Konfliktní lekce
           z internacionalismu: Studenti z 'třetího světa' a jejich konfrontace s
           českým prostředím (1961–1974)," *Soudobé Dějiny* 20, nos. 1/2 (2013): 158–76.
4   Fafali Koudawo, *La formation des cadres africains en Europe de l'Est depuis 1918:
           Des nègres rouges aux russotiques* (Paris: L'Harmattan, 1992), 128.

Europe's division between East and West and the Communists' victory in China in 1949 weren't the only major geopolitical developments following the Second World War. The demise of European empires in Asia and Africa and the emergence of a plethora of independent states that followed the colonial collapse were dramatically changing the world's political geography. Beginning shortly after the war in the Middle East and Asia, decolonization culminated around 1960 when seventeen African countries transitioned peacefully to independence. In the meantime, wars of national independence were fought in Vietnam, Algeria, and elsewhere. African liberation movements would pursue their struggles against Portuguese colonial rule and white-minority regimes until the end of the Cold War. Thus, if one major postwar development was the expansion of the socialist camp, largely under Soviet tutelage, the other was the emergence of Asian and African countries resentful of Western imperialism and seeking to build modern nation-states.

While Stalin was alive, there was little overlap between these two developments. As colonial countries gained independence, including India in 1947 and Indonesia in 1949, or were transitioning to independence, as with Ghana and Nigeria in the 1950s, they were often dismissed as "bourgeois nationalist" regimes—that is, as capitalist-oriented, pro-Western countries. The Eastern bloc's internationalist solidarity was reserved for countries and movements that had espoused communism as their ideology, as with China, North Vietnam, and North Korea, and the National Liberation Front during the Greek Civil War (postwar phase, 1946–49). This solidarity was also expressed through educational assistance. North Korean and Greek orphans were schooled in Poland, Romania, Czechoslovakia, Hungary, and East Germany. Chinese, Korean, and Vietnamese students attended universities in the Soviet Union along with other students from Eastern Europe.

Until the mid-1950s, however, it had been rare that ordinary students from the Global South were provided that same chance. In 1951, a handful of Nigerian students whose families were involved in the labor movement were granted scholarships to study in East Germany. This gesture of solidarity was decided on after the massacre in 1949 of twenty-one striking workers at the Iva Valley coal mine in Enugu.[5] In 1953, the first three students from French West Africa were enrolled in the Department of Medicine at the University of Bucharest. Among them was Majhemout Diop, the future leader of the African Independence Party (PAI), the Senegalese Marxist-Leninist party, who also attended classes in Marxism-Leninism under the auspices of the Romanian Union of Communist Youth.[6]

The policy of socialist countries toward the emerging non-communist South underwent dramatic changes from 1953, after Stalin's death and with Nikita Khrushchev's rise to power. The Third World, once dismissed, was now considered a region with huge political and economic potential, and a prospective ally of the socialist camp. Developments across the Southern Hemisphere and international events including the Afro-Asian Conference held in Bandung in 1955 could not be ignored.[7] During the Suez Crisis in 1956, for example, Egypt was supported by the Eastern bloc. Meeting in Moscow in November 1957, communist leaders and heads of workers' parties issued a Common Declaration stressing that standing alongside "the invincible camp of socialist countries" were "the Asian and African nationalist governments [that] maintained an anti-imperialist stance."[8] If the Suez Crisis had marked a turning point, the Common Declaration sealed the turn toward a new internationalism. This internationalism was no longer confined to the broad communist movement but open to "nations oppressed by imperialism," as Lenin had originally advocated. The East-South rapprochement that was established in the second half of the 1950s was hailed as a return to his grand vision for an alliance between the communist and nationalist movements in the colonial and nonindustrialized countries.

5   Sara Pugach, "Eleven Nigerian Students in Cold War East Germany: Visions of Science, Modernity, and Decolonization," *Journal of Contemporary History* 54, no. 3 (2019): 551–72.

6   Majhemout Diop, *Mémoires de luttes: Textes pour servir à l'histoire du Parti Africain de l'Indépendance* (Paris: Présence Africaine, 2007), 28–29.

7   James Mark, Artemy M. Kalinovsky, and Steffi Marung, eds., *Alternative Globalizations: Eastern Europe and the Postcolonial World* (Bloomington: Indiana University Press, 2020).

8   Draft of the Common Declaration prepared by the Soviet and the Chinese Communist parties, November 10, 1957. See the entire text in Aleksander A. Fursenko, ed., *Presidium TsK KPSS, Postanovleniia 1954–1964* (Moscow: ROSSPEN, 2006), vol. 2, 723.

This turn had major effects in terms of international cooperation and internationalist solidarity. To begin with, numerous nationalist and Marxist-inspired African liberation movements would benefit from Eastern bloc military aid. Furthermore, countries received substantial Soviet assistance, with India and Egypt building the Bhilai Steel Plant and the Aswan Dam, respectively. Experts from the Eastern bloc were involved in industrial, agricultural, and urban development projects, and assisted Third World countries in the founding of medical facilities and educational institutions. Provision of scholarships and training of students also became a major component of the Eastern bloc's international cooperation and solidarity with the Third World. This was the beginning of that era Ali Mazrui would characterize as a golden one.

In the postcolonial world, training students was extremely important for many good reasons. Most of these countries had a terrible lack of trained experts and were heavily reliant on Western specialists, and their dependence on the West needed to be reduced or at least counterbalanced. A domestic educated elite was required for expanding state administrations and services, developing economies and education systems, and promoting national cultures. Foreign aid was indispensable and welcome, and some of these countries looked to the Eastern bloc for both aid and inspiration.

Ghana, Guinea, and Mali, the three West African states that opted for socialism in the early 1960s, sent hundreds of students to study in socialist countries. Once home, they were then expected to contribute to their countries' developments along socialist lines. Likewise, in the Republic of the Congo (also referred to as Congo-Brazzaville to distinguish it from its large neighbor, the Democratic Republic of the Congo), which in 1968 opted for scientific socialism, President Marien Ngouabi affirmed that it was in the interests of his country and its government to train national elites who would be both "red and experts." Subsequently, the Republic of the Congo relied on cooperation with the Eastern bloc.[9] At the same time, even countries not claiming to follow a socialist path of development and

9   Patrice Yengo, "Former des cadres 'rouges et experts': Mouvement étudiant congolais en URSS et parti unique," *Cahiers d'Études africaines* 226, no. 2 (2017): 313–29.

remaining close to the West—Ethiopia under Emperor Haile Selassie, the Kingdom of Morocco, Tunisia, and others—were also very willing to receive the Eastern bloc's educational assistance. The socialist countries, eager to cultivate friendly ties and expand their influence, offered thousands of scholarships to three groups of beneficiaries. The vast majority of scholarships were provided to African and Asian states, which in turn selected the students who studied in the Soviet Union and Eastern Europe. Most state scholarships went to countries that embarked on a socialist-development path: examples are Ghana under President Kwame Nkrumah, South Yemen, and Ethiopia after the revolution of 1974. Western-oriented countries, however, were also offered state scholarships in the name of peoples' friendship and within the framework of the Eastern bloc's international-development assistance. The second group of beneficiaries, by contrast, comprised radical opposition parties, anti-imperialist and communist organizations, and trade and youth unions active in Western-oriented or nonaligned Third World countries. These "political scholarships" were granted to this group by the Eastern bloc's non-state organizations, including the International Union of Students in Prague, the East German and the Soviet Afro-Asian Solidarity committees, and trade unions, primarily on the basis of political and ideological criteria. Latin American and Middle Eastern communist parties were among the primary beneficiaries in this group, along with a vast array of radical African organizations, among them the PAI in Senegal, the Socialist Workers and Farmers Party of Nigeria (SWAFP), the National Union of Moroccan Students (UNEM), and the Sawaba party in Niger.[10]

Last but not least was the group of liberation movements still fighting colonialism or white-minority regimes. Among the first to study in socialist countries were supporters of the Algerian National Liberation Front (FLN) during the Algerian War of Independence (1954–62). Two prominent Algerian filmmakers, Mohammed Lakhdar-Hamina and Boubaker Adjali, had received training in

10   See, for instance, Maxim Matusevich, *No Easy Row for a Russian Hoe: Ideology and Pragmatism in Nigerian–Soviet Relations, 1960–1991* (Trenton: Africa World Press, 2003); Klaas van Walraven, *The Yearning for Relief: A History of the Sawaba Movement in Niger* (Leiden: Brill, 2013); Tobias Rupprecht, *Soviet Internationalism after Stalin: Interaction and Exchange between the USSR and Latin America during the Cold War* (Cambridge: Cambridge University Press, 2015).

Czechoslovakia in the late 1950s, along with other peers from home.[11] Along with Algeria, this specific group of beneficiaries included the Popular Movement for the Liberation of Angola (MPLA), the African Party for the Independence of Guinea and Cape Verde (PAIGC), the Mozambique Liberation Front (Frelimo), the Zimbabwe African People's Union (ZAPU), the African National Congress (ANC), the South African Communist Party (SACP), as well as the South West Africa People's Organization (SWAPO) in Namibia. Libertine Inaviposa Amathila, a SWAPO activist who studied at the Medical University of Warsaw, became the first female minister in independent Namibia.[12]

As the number of beneficiaries and students expanded, so did the range of student destinations across the socialist world. Cuba, a country that was sending students abroad after the 1959 revolution, with thousands of specialists trained in the Soviet Union and Eastern Europe, emerged over time as a host country. Along with members of many other liberation movements, Cuba hosted hundreds of Sahrawi students, supporters of the Polisario Front, which was fighting a war against Morocco's annexation of Western Sahara. Most Third World students in Cuba first received secondary education in "friendship schools" established on the Isle of Youth (Isla de la Juventud) before pursuing their studies in higher education on Cuban government scholarships.[13] The Cuban example inspired East Germany to create the School of Friendship (Schule der Freundschaft) in Staßfurt in 1982 for students from Mozambique. Until the end of the 1980s, the school provided nearly nine hundred Mozambicans with professional-technical educations.[14]

11   Olivier Hadouchi, "Mohammed Lakhdar-Hamina and Boubaker Adjali: The Careers of Two Algerian Filmmakers Who Attended FAMU," in *Filmmakers of the World, Unite! Forgotten Internationalism, Czechoslovak Film and the Third World*, ed. Tereza Stejskalová (Prague: Tranzit.cz, 2017), 123–36.
12   Libertine Inaviposa Amathila, *Making a Difference* (Windhoek: University of Namibia Press, 2012).
13   Elena Fiddian-Qasmiyeh, "Representing Sahrawi Refugees' 'Educational Displacement' to Cuba: Self-Sufficient Agents or Manipulated Victims in Conflict?" *Journal of Refugee Studies* 22, no. 3 (2009): 323–50.
14   Tanja R. Müller, *Legacies of Socialist Solidarity: East Germany in Mozambique* (Lanham: Lexington Books, 2014); Marcia C. Schenck, "Small Strangers at the School of Friendship: Memories of Mozambican School Students of the German Democratic Republic," *German Historical Institute Bulletin*, supplement 15 (2020): 41–60.

Still, the overwhelming majority of Third World students studying in the socialist countries attended higher-education institutions. As a rule, they spent the first year learning the language of the host country and taking remedial courses related to their specialization. In East Germany, international students studied German at the University of Leipzig's Herder Institute. In Bulgaria, they attended the University of Sofia's Institute for Foreign Students, named for Gamal Abdel Nasser, the Egyptian president. At Lumumba University in Moscow during the 1960s, students who had yet to complete secondary-level education could attend the preparatory department for up to three years and earn a degree providing access to higher education. The University of Leipzig's Workers' and Peasants' Faculty (ABF) offered a similar option. This path to higher education was conceived for youth from lower-class backgrounds, in the tradition of workers' faculties first established by the Bolsheviks after the October Revolution.[15] It is fair to argue that these institutions practiced class-based affirmative action at the international level. At the same time, all educational aid offered to the Third World as solidarity to nations oppressed by imperialism constituted a form of nation-based affirmative action at an international level. This however did not apply to sending countries, most notably a few from the Middle East that financed their nationals' studies abroad.

At the level of the Eastern bloc's organization known as Comecon, the Council for Mutual Economic Assistance, there was a keen interest in educational cooperation. According to Comecon statistics compiled in 1963 and covering all member states, 37.3 percent of Third World students pursued studies in the engineering, transport, and industrial and communication technologies fields, 33.2 percent studied economy or law, 17.7 percent medicine and medical specializations, and 5.6 percent agronomy. The remaining 6.2 percent enrolled in programs of humanities and arts, from archeology and literature to theater and cinema.[16] The rather high proportion of students in economics and law was largely due to Latin Americans and

15   Ingrid Miethe et al., eds., *Globalization of an Educational Idea: Workers' Faculties in Eastern Germany, Vietnam, Cuba and Mozambique* (Munich: De Gruyter Oldenbourg, 2019).
16   Documents found in the files of the Soviet Ministry of Education at the State Archive of the Russian Federation (GARF). See collection 9606, inventory 2, file 134, page 105.

Africans. However, according to data from the Soviet Union, which was the biggest host country, this proportion fell over time. By contrast, the percentage of students studying engineering reached more than 50 percent, and that of medical students nearly 20 percent.[17]

For the great majority of students, earning a scholarship to study in the Eastern bloc was a unique chance to pursue higher education, live a student life without material concerns, and pave the way for a good professional career. Ahmed Mahi had come up in a poor Algerian family and joined the FLN during the war, mostly serving in refugee camps on the border with Morocco. Reaching East Germany in 1959 completely changed Mahi's life. He studied Marxism-Leninism and became a leader in the Algerian student union and the communist movement. After completing his studies at the Technical Institute of Dresden, he returned to Algeria with his East German wife to manage state enterprises and economic institutions.[18]

His compatriot, Boubaker Adjali, after being wounded in a wartime engagement and receiving medical treatment, attended the prestigious Film and Television School of the Academy of Performing Arts (FAMU) in Prague to study filmmaking. He later put this knowledge into practice in South Africa, East Timor, and Lebanon, to mention only a few countries he worked in as a filmmaker of liberation movements and a war correspondent.[19] Thousands of Palestinian refugees from Jordan and Lebanon were granted scholarships by socialist countries who otherwise would never have had the chance to pursue studies in tertiary education. The same is true for Kurdish youth whose communities suffered massacres and discrimination. It was actually to the Soviet Union that Izzeddin Resul and Maruf Khaznadar—later prominent scholars of Kurdish literature and history—came from Iraqi Kurdistan to receive training during the 1960s.[20]

17   Data compiled and published in Constantin Katsakioris, "Creating a Socialist Intelligentsia: Soviet Educational Aid and Its Impact on Africa," Cahiers d'Études africaines 2, no. 226 (2017): 259–88.
18   See his memoirs, Ahmed Mahi, De l'UGÉMA à l'UNÉA: Témoignage sur le mouvement étudiant (1959–1965) (Algiers: INAS Éditions, 2014).
19   Hadouchi, "Mohammed Lakhdar-Hamina and Boubaker Adjali."
20   Michiel Leezenberg, "Soviet Kurdology and Kurdish Orientalism," in The Heritage of Soviet Oriental Studies, ed. Michael Kemper and Stephan Kornemann (London: Routledge, 2011), 95–96.

The 1950s and 1960s were an era of high expectations, in contrast to the 1980s, when the Eastern bloc deteriorated and Third World socialism met its demise. Even though the suppression of the Hungarian uprising in 1956 and of the Prague Spring in 1968 dealt a blow to these expectations within and with regards to the Eastern bloc, the rise of the Third World and the Cuban revolution sustained the hope of socialism shifting the center of gravity toward the Global South.[21] On the one hand, a number of states from Algeria to Tanzania sought to build socialism, taking into account national aspirations and realities. On the other hand, communism and leftist nationalism had a huge appeal among the younger population. Heated political and ideological debates took place at student conferences and international youth festivals hosted by the socialist countries. Powerful organizations, such as the Union of African Students in Europe, which was founded in Belgrade in 1962, had their strongholds in the East. For Third World students, moreover, mobility was possible not only within the Eastern bloc but also across the East-West divide.

However, as the historian Eric Burton has shown, numerous of these students seized the opportunity to immigrate to the West.[22] If some had a plan in place from the beginning, Western countries were also enticing many Third World students, securing scholarships for them and placements at universities. Job opportunities were undeniably a decisive factor, especially since, one after the next, most sending countries sank into economic crisis. Political reasons also forced students who were active in opposition movements either to prolong their stays in the East or to immigrate to the West. A combination of these factors was common among students sent abroad by a government who would then, as a consequence of a coup d'état at home, have to return to live under a new, often hostile regime. War at home was certainly a major cause behind

21   James Mark and Péter Apor, "Socialism Goes Global: Decolonization and the Making of a New Culture of Internationalism in Socialist Hungary, 1956–1989," Journal of Modern History 87, no. 4 (2015): 852–91.

22   Eric Burton, "Decolonization, the Cold War, and Africans' Routes to Higher Education Overseas, 1957–65," Journal of Global History 15, no. 1 (2020): 169–91.

decisions to remain abroad, as with hundreds of Lebanese during the civil war in Lebanon (1975–90). East Berlin constituted the most important gate to the West long after the Wall went up in August 1961. Some students who immigrated to the West cited additional causes, including racism, indoctrination, and poor living conditions in the Eastern bloc, as did others who returned home. To be sure, lack of both space in dormitories and goods in markets was common. Nevertheless, for the majority of students not coming from well-to-do backgrounds, living standards were clearly not a problem. The same is true regarding indoctrination and courses with political and ideological content, cited as a cause of frustration mostly in accounts published in the West by some former students. It may be safely stated, however, that for faculty members in all these schools, teaching mainstream scientific courses remained by far the most important task. According to most reliable sources and accounts, students were very much more concerned with concentrating on their major subjects, rather than with the few required ideological courses they had to take.[23]

By contrast, various sources including oral testimonies, memoirs, literature, and archival material testify to the presence of xenophobia and racism, in particular for students from sub-Saharan Africa. In some cases, the deaths under mysterious circumstances of Black students in the Soviet Union and East Germany triggered mass protests and led students to drop out of their programs.[24] Incidents of verbal and physical violence against Africans were reported in the early 1960s, when the first sizable contingents of students arrived, and during the late 1980s, as state socialism collapsed. Third World students were often blamed for living at the expense of the host countries, filling needed places in schools and dormitories, and enjoying benefits that they did not deserve.

23   See various testimonies in Monique de Saint Martin et al., eds., *Étudier à l'Est: Trajectoires d'étudiants africains et arabes en URSS et dans les pays d'Europe de l'Est* (Paris: Karthala, 2015).
24   Müller, *Legacies of Socialist Solidarity*; Julie Hessler, "Death of an African Student in Moscow: Race, Politics, and the Cold War," *Cahiers du Monde russe* 47, nos. 1/2 (2006): 33–64; Maxim Matusevich, "Journeys of Hope: African Diaspora and the Soviet Society," *African Diaspora* 1 (2008), 53–85; Constantin Katsakioris, "Burden or Allies? Third World Students and Internationalist Duty through Soviet Eyes," *Kritika: Explorations in Russian and Eurasian History* 18, no. 3 (2017): 539–67.

While such reactions were typically xenophobic, verbal and physical attacks against Black students were explicitly racist. In all, the oft-repeated claim that racism had been eliminated in the classless societies of socialist countries was not true, unfortunately. The relations of foreign students with local women of the host country often lit the fuse of such xenophobic reactions and conflicts.

Fiction published by former students has captured these realities. *Un African dans un iceberg: Impossible amour à Saint-Petersbourg* (*An African in an Iceberg: An Impossible Love Story in Saint Petersburg*) is a novel written by Zounga Bongolo when he was a student from the Republic of the Congo in Leningrad (Saint Petersburg) in the early 1980s. Published in 2006, the novel is based on the author's love story with a fellow student who was his peer at the Herzen Institute of Pedagogy. Natasha, who plays that role in the novel, comes from a peasant family and used to live on a collective farm. Jan, the novel's Congolese student, is the first Black person Natasha ever met. The two fall in love, share moments of passion, and plan their marriage. But Natasha's family and organizers from Komsomol (the communist youth movement) at the institute make every effort to separate her from Jan. Constantly blackmailed and harassed, they are forced to divorce and Natasha eventually commits suicide.[25]

Another source that sheds light on the experiences of mixed couples and international students is the novel *Ludmila ou le violon à la mort lente* (*Ludmila or the Violin of Slow Death*) by Anouar Benmalek. Benmalek, an outstanding Algerian intellectual and writer hailed as the "Faulkner of the Mediterranean," wrote his PhD at the Kiev Institute of Mathematics in the early 1980s. *Ludmila*, published in Algiers in 1986 but then censored by the Algerian socialist regime, tells the story of Nasser, an Algerian student who falls in love with Ludmila, his Ukrainian peer. As with Natasha in Bongolo's novel, Ludmila comes under attack by university officials because of her relationship with a foreigner. After Ludmila becomes pregnant, Nasser arranges for her a covert visit to a doctor to have an abortion.

25   Zounga Bongolo, *Un African dans un iceberg: Impossible amour à Saint-Petersbourg* (Paris: Editions Paari, 2006).

Written with an elegant style and humor, this tragic story castigates xenophobia in the Soviet Union and illustrates political and social contradictions in the Soviet system.[26]

At the same time, Benmalek draws a picture of conviviality and friendship between students from different countries who share rooms in the dormitories, and refers to the excellent relations Nasser has with his PhD supervisor. These two aspects were integral parts of the students' experiences in socialist countries. These foreign students were active in their departments' friendship committees and highly esteemed by their European peers. International friendships were created in the mixed dormitories and forged through shared classes and vacations. Some international student brigades crossed Siberia to work in construction sites. International music and theater groups performed on many stages, while national bands played in competitions with Latin Americans, winning prizes and plaudits. In addition, mixed couples were created and marriages registered, despite xenophobic and racist reactions. The secure argument remains that those women and many families in the host countries demonstrated remarkable openness toward foreigners. These facts are highlighted in *Un roman algéro-soviétique (An Algerian-Soviet Novel)* by Mustapha Negadi, who studied medicine in Moscow in the late 1950s.[27]

Likewise, even the most critical accounts acknowledge the merits of the education systems and pay tribute to superbly committed faculty members. Professors were available for discussions and students in need could attend remedial courses. Systematic work began in preparatory departments where international students learned the language. Practical training was part of the curriculum from the early semesters, constituting a major advantage of programs in socialist countries compared to the West. Along with Lumumba University in Moscow and the November 17 University in Prague, other institutions including the prestigious Institute of Civil Aviation Engineering in Kiev and the Higher School of Economics

26   Anouar Benmalek, *Ludmila ou le violon à la mort lente* (Algiers: Entreprise
         nationale du livre, 1986).
27   Mustapha Negadi, *Un roman algéro-soviétique: Aux origines de l'UGEMA* (Algiers:
         Dar El Adib, 2014).

(Hochschule für Ökonomie) in East Berlin played huge roles in training people who were badly needed in the developing countries. The same is true for art schools, at which a rather liberal atmosphere reigned, allowing students to experiment with techniques and combine national themes with various international influences. The outcome in terms of training a scientific-technical and creative intelligentsia was impressive.

Indeed, plenty of postcolonial countries were able to staff their administrations, hospitals, and educational institutions with students returning from Eastern Europe and the Soviet Union, and many graduates became influential politicians, prominent scientists, artists, and intellectuals. A glimpse to several African countries testifies to this importance of elites educated in the Eastern bloc. One example is Ghana, where the celebrated poet and distinguished academic Atukwei Okai, who served for many years as secretary general of the Pan-African Writers' Association, was one of the students Kwame Nkrumah, the socialist president, had sent to the Soviet Union in the first half of the 1960s. That cohort produced prominent physicists who became university professors and leading scientists on Ghana's Atomic Energy Commission. Through 2014, over 10 percent of Ghana's doctors registered with the National Medical and Dental Council had trained in the Soviet Union.[28]

In Nigeria, which never embarked on a socialist development path, graduates returning from the Eastern bloc became distinguished scholars and public intellectuals. The three most important examples may be Eskor Toyo, Festus Iyayi, and Segun Osoba. Toyo, a University of Calabar economics professor, wrote his PhD at Warsaw's Central School of Planning and Statistics (SGPiS).[29] He was a prominent and widely published Trotskyist thinker, as well as an indefatigable activist in leftist politics. Festus Iyayi, Toyo's likeminded colleague, was a graduate of the Kyiv Institute of National

28   Jeremy Holt, Samuel Newhouse, and Daria Ukhova, "Scholarships and the Healthcare Human Resources Crisis: A Case Study of Soviet and Russian Scholarships for Medical Students from Ghana," *Oxfam Case Study* (Oxfam International, 2014), 13; Abena Dove Osseo-Asare, *Atomic Junction: Nuclear Power in Africa after Independence* (Cambridge: Cambridge University Press, 2019).

29   Toyo's PhD was published as *Marks i Keynes: Analiza porównawcza metodologii makroekonomicznej* (Warsaw: Państwowe Wydawnictwo Naukowe, 1976).

Economy (KINE). Along with his important academic career, Iyayi was an award-winning novelist writing in the style of socialist realism. Segun Osoba, finally, who attended Moscow State University, was a preeminent Marxist historian and taught significant Nigerian scholars. He was also coauthor of the radical 1978 Minority Report, a proposal for reforming the Nigerian constitution largely inspired by the socialist countries.[30]

In Mali, another historian rose to prominence: Alpha Oumar Konaré, who wrote his PhD at Warsaw University between 1971 and 1975. A founding member of scientific organizations and an activist in the leftist opposition to the regime of Moussa Traoré, Konaré was one of the architects of Mali's democratic transition and became the country's first elected president in 1992. He later served as chairperson of the African Union Commission. Three other returning graduates left their imprint on Mali's culture and art education. The filmmaker Souleymane Cissé attended the All-Union State Institute of Cinematography (VGIK) in Moscow in the mid 1960s. He is the director of films including *Finyé* (*The Wind*, 1982) and *Yeelen* (*Brightness*, 1987), which assail social injustice and deplore the corruption of the single-party state. The award-winning writer Gaoussou Diawara, who attended the Maxim Gorky Literature Institute in Moscow and later studied theater with Bertolt Brecht's Berliner Ensemble in East Berlin, served as a professor of drama at the National Institute of Arts in Bamako. The painter Mamadou Somé Coulibaly was that institute's director until 1987, and had attended the prestigious Vasily Surikov Academy of Art in Moscow.[31]

In Algeria, along with Lakhdar-Hamina and Adjali, the two Prague-educated filmmakers cited above, the list is very long of returning graduates who rose to prominence and made important careers. Artists on it include the sculptor Mustapha Adane, who

30   See Adam Mayer, *Naija Marxisms: Revolutionary Thought in Nigeria* (London: Pluto Press, 2016).
31   Paul Davis, "'Coulibaly' Cosmopolitanism in Moscow: Mamadou Somé Coulibaly and the Surikov Academy Paintings, 1960s–1970s," in *Africa in Europe: Studies in Transnational Practice in the Long Twentieth Century*, ed. Eve Rosenhaft and Robbie Aitken (Liverpool: Liverpool University Press), 142–61; Gabrielle Chomentowski, "Filmmakers from Africa and the Middle East at VGIK during the Cold War," *Studies in Russian and Soviet Cinema* 13, no. 2 (2019): 189–98.

attended the Academy of Fine Arts in Leipzig having served as a teacher in an orphans' center during the Algerian War for independence from France. Adane became a distinguished artist as well as a theorist of art. He was a coauthor of the 1967 Aouchem Manifesto, which advocated for Algerian art returning to sources that reject the Western Orientalist canon. Adane would also reject socialist realism and decry the subordination of artists to dictates of single-party states.[32] Around the same time, the filmmaker Djafar Damardji, known for his critical views on the Algerian elite, studied at the University of Leipzig's Department of Theater Studies.[33]

In the 1960s, another now-prominent Algerian filmmaker sought education in Eastern Europe. Ahmed Lallem, who had served as a reporter during the war and made traineeships in Belgrade and Paris, was granted a Polish scholarship to attend the Łódź Film School between 1963 and 1966. The year of his graduation, he directed *Elles* (*The Women*, 1966), a major documentary film studying the aspirations of female students in postwar Algeria.[34] The tradition of Algerian filmmakers who received training in socialist countries continued with Rabah Bouberras, Jean-Pierre Lledo, and Azzedine Meddour, all of whom studied at VGIK between the late 1960s and the 1970s. Meddour's *La montagne de Baya* (*Baya's Mountain*), released in 1997, depicts the resistance of a Kabyle village to colonial expropriation and has become a classic of Kabyle-Berber cinema.[35] Other young artists spent time in socialist countries on short-term programs in art education and production. The great Algerian painter M'hamed Issiakhem, who had previously received training in Algiers and Paris, also attended the Academy of Fine Arts in Leipzig.[36] The

32   See Hamid Tahri, "Mustapha Adane," in *El Watan*, March 30, 2017, article reedited at https://www.founoune.com/index.php/adane-mustapha-hamid-tahri/.

33   On Damardji and his well-known film *Les bonnes familles* (*The Good Families*, 1972), see Patricia Caillé, "On the Shifting Significance of 'Algerian Cinema' as a Category of Analysis," in *Algeria Revisited: History, Culture and Identity*, ed. Rabah Aissaoui and Claire Eldridge (London: Bloomsbury, 2017), 162.

34   See Olivier Hadouchi, "Voices and Faces from the Third World," in this book.

35   Frédérique Devaux Yahi, *De la naissance du cinéma kabyle au cinéma amazigh* (Paris: L'Harmattan, 2016).

36   See a short biography of Issiakhem by Djafar Inal, in *M'hamed Issiakhem: Exposition hommage* (Algiers: Ministère de la culture, 2010), 8–13.

same is true for Ahmed Cherkaoui, one of Morocco's greatest painters, who studied for a year at the Academy of Fine Arts in Warsaw and was deeply influenced by the Polish School of Posters. Beyond the field of arts, returning students worked in academia and became leaders in ministries, state enterprises, and economic institutions.

While examples of students who would then make brilliant careers are common in most sending countries, it is even more important to recall the thousands of comparatively anonymous graduates who served as doctors and nurses, teachers, and engineers, often under very difficult circumstances. Even if sending countries never became a promised land of socialism, the host countries did hold to their promise to contribute to the developmental efforts of the Third World, providing scholarships and educational aid in various forms. Educational assistance was therefore an expression of internationalism toward countries long subjected to foreign exploitation and a particularly effective form of solidarity, as evidenced by its remarkable effects. Thousands of young people without the means to study at a university were the primary beneficiaries of this aid. Their experiences in socialist countries, the skills they acquired, and the friendships and families they created changed their lives forever.

The crisis and collapse of state socialism in the late 1980s and the dismantling of the Eastern bloc brought this chapter of history to an end. Across the Global South, those dramatic developments fostered or accelerated change in terms of establishing democratic rule and simultaneously pushing through neoliberal economic reforms. While many observers decried the demise of a bloc that provided precious support and counterbalanced the influence of the West, others blamed socialism for a whole range of political and economic ills. However, few then remembered that educational assistance was a vital component in socialist countries' policies toward Africa, Asia, and Latin America. Ali Mazrui's "golden age" of education assistance fell into oblivion.

Faced with oblivion, it is essential to revisit these educational and cultural connections, to highlight the contribution of numerous institutes and schools including the Łódź Film School, to retrace the trajectories and recover the experiences of the students who attended them. As this essay has sought to argue, the task is not overly complicated, for the legacies of these educational connections are manifold and remarkable. Still, it is a task of extreme significance, calling attention to a history of internationalism and friendship among peoples. Ultimately, this history shows that people arriving from distant countries and differing cultural and social backgrounds may share similar visions and the commitment to solidarity and friendship. As such, it is a history that challenges mainstream theories of Orientalism and any "clash of civilizations."

Matthieu Gillabert is senior lecturer in contemporary history at the University of Fribourg (Switzerland). As a specialist in the history of Swiss cultural diplomacy (*Dans les coulisses de la diplomatie culturelle helvétique*, Alphil, 2013), he has focused his research on trans-bloc cultural relations. He has published an illustrated monograph on the history of Warsaw (*Varsovie métropole 1865 à nos jours*, Noir sur Blanc, 2016). Since 2014, he has developed projects on student mobilities and student movements in the Cold War era, especially in the Eastern bloc, with a postcolonial approach. His post-doctoral thesis, "From the Internationalization of the University to Student Internationalism: Student Migration in Europe at the Time of University Massification (1945–1980)" was defended in 2021.

STUDENTS OF COLOR AND STATE SOCIALISM: CAN DOUBLE EXOTICISM BE ENDURED IN PUBLIC SPACE?

In the Museum of Warsaw's portrait gallery, a painting of the jazz drummer August Agboola O'Brown, who lived in Warsaw and fought in the Warsaw Uprising of 1944, hangs next to one of Bolesław Bierut, the Stalinist-era president of the Polish People's Republic (PRL). This conjunction is complex, and deconstructing it reveals a dual exoticism, a distancing doubled by the surprise effect.

The visitor may be astonished at first by the large format of the Bierut portrait, when no trace of the former president remains in Warsaw's public space. The painting's imposing format in this gallery of Warsaw-makers seems to be reminding us that he shouldn't be forgotten. Indirectly, this presence of Bierut focuses on our forgetfulness of that revolutionary period, which now appears to us strange and unfamiliar.

This rapprochement between the two portraits then aims to remind us that Polish history is entangled with the colonial world and the Third World. With O'Brown positioned from bare chest up before a sharp red-white backdrop—the colors of Poland's flag—this image of a Black person in this white museum and urban environment creates that surprise effect for the visitor, which in a way reinforces the distance from him and, more broadly, from a globally connected history of Poland. Strangeness and distance are components of exoticism, which is a social construction of the Other. In the Polish case, this otherness concerns both time and space. From one perspective, the otherness is that of the complex past: Poland under communist rule, often repressed and therefore more distant from our present.[1] From another, the Other is the person from the colonial world who is bound in a complex "system of representations."[2] As the historians Christoph Kamissek and Jonas Kreienbaum argue, Poland, although not directly involved in the overseas colonial enterprise, participated in the "imperial cloud,"[3] sharing and propagating knowledge and representations about the colonial world. This insertion of Poland into those colonial relations modifies a widespread representation of an Eastern bloc periphery colonized by the Soviet Union. Thus Poland participates in the exotic character of a past that is believed to be known and limited to the nation yet appears unknown and global. Assuming that exoticism can be a collective phenomenon,[4] a social imaginary,[5] we must question how it emerged, especially by utilizing the example of Third World scholarship students.

The visitor's experience at the Museum of Warsaw combines a double exoticism, facing both the socialist past and racialized otherness. It may be particularly pertinent to articulate them through the following hypothesis. This form of exoticism of Black people in public space can be explained at least in part by the fall of Communism. The PRL would indeed fit into the Eastern bloc's global space, which increased its Black presence through thousands of exchanges,

1   Andrzej Leder, Prześniona rewolucja: Ćwiczenie z logiki historycznej (Warsaw: Wydawnictwo Krytyki Politycznej, 2014).
2   Serge Moscovici, "Des représentations collectives aux représentations sociales: Éléments pour une histoire," in Les représentations sociales, ed. Denise Jodelet (Paris: PUF, 2003), 79–103.
3   Christoph Kamissek and Jonas Kreienbaum, "An Imperial Cloud? Conceptualising Interimperial Connections and Transimperial Knowledge," Journal of Modern European History 14, no. 2 (2017): 164–82.
4   Anaïs Fléchet, "L'exotisme comme objet d'histoire," Hypotheses 11, no. 1 (2008): 15–26.
5   Charles Taylor, A Secular Age (Cambridge, MA: Harvard University Press, 2007).

particularly academic, between Poland and the Third World. The fall of Communism became an interruption of those contacts. In Eastern European countries with state-socialist regimes during the Cold War, foreign students were among the few people from the colonial and postcolonial worlds whom local citizens were encountering. The second wave of such encounters came in 2015 with the arrival in Europe of around one million refugees. At that time, some observers noted the persistence of an East-West divide in the perception (and reception) of refugees.[6] They pointed to the difference in attitudes toward foreigners between Western Europe and former Eastern bloc countries. In Eastern Europe, the absence of an overseas colonial and immigration past may explain the difficulty of confronting racialized otherness. While the most broad and consequential exchanges with the Third World—the presence of Black students in Polish urban space—took place during the PRL period, that came to be forgotten after 1989 and the political transition. Is this omission linked to a distancing from the communist past? Or to a distancing of those exchanges within countries considered subordinate to Western Europe?

This raises the question of a specific legacy from communism that has developed an anti-racist discourse[7] while maintaining power relations with the Third World in policies aimed at modernization. Before the pressures with migration in 2015, the previous encounter with non-European foreigners goes back to the era of sociopolitical thaw—especially with foreign students coming from the socialist-leaning countries and movements of the Global South.

After 1989, in Eastern Europe, one could trace a similar move from participation in the global socialist bloc toward European integration. There were very few encounters with foreigners from the developing world. In higher education, Eastern countries

6   See André Liebich, "Mais pourquoi donc l'Europe de l'Est refuse-t-elle d'accueillir les réfugiés?" *Le Temps*, September 15, 2015; Rick Lyman, "Eastern Bloc's Resistance to Refugees Highlights Europe's Cultural and Political Division," *New York Times*, September 12, 2015.

7   Ian Law and Nikolay Zakharov, "Race and Racism in Eastern Europe: Becoming White, Becoming Western," in *Relating Worlds of Racism: Dehumanisation, Belonging, and the Normativity of European Whiteness*, ed. Philomena Essed, Karen Farquharson, Kathryn Pillay, and Elisa Joy White (London: Palgrave Macmillan, 2009), 113–39.

have in large part adapted their universities to the European system and created an array of private institutions. The number of foreign students has dropped, while a large number of Central European students have opted for mobility in Western Europe, thanks specifically to Erasmus programs. Since 2000, the number of students arriving has increased again, though their origin has been Europeanized: in 2017, 80 percent of foreign students came from Europe. Thus, for student mobility in Poland, the fall of Communism corresponds to a renewed European whiteness.

Today, retracing this exchange within the Eastern bloc becomes an archeology of its history with postcolonial otherness. In turn, that otherness sheds light on relations with otherness in the present day. This essay is part of a larger project utilizing student movements in Poland to better understand how Eastern-bloc participation led local populations into specific forms of globalization.

By studying two levels of distancing, the present essay turns to this history of colonial and postcolonial students' presence in Poland. It will analyze forms of instrumentalizing those academic exchanges by the communist authorities, from a top-down perspective. These students' presence, through the example of the School of Polish for Foreign Students (SJPdC) in Łódź, allows the link of the PRL's political situation within the bloc to be shown, along with the wider developmental context that favored higher education of the nascent business and political elite of the Global South, in both the East and the West. This problem will then be approached from the bottom up, by analyzing local peoples' everyday encounters with the scholarship students in Łódź's urban space. SJPdC's establishment at the University of Łódź explains the city's choice as the space of investigation.

Toward a Global, Postcolonial History of State Socialism

This essay is part of a broad, multidisciplinary, deconstructivist history of the Cold War. It first postulates that the Iron

FIG. 1
SJPdC, UNIVERSITY OF ŁÓDŹ, 1970, © ZBIGNIEW WDOWIŃSKI/PAP

Curtain is far from a hermetic border[8]—a point of view that is now widely agreed upon and the subject of extensive research. However, the Cold War is not an entirely fluid transnational space. While the Iron Curtain remains an obstacle, it is not an insurmountable one.

For student mobility, the criterion of belonging to the Eastern bloc and to former imperial powers is paramount. In France, the number of students from former African colonies grew steadily during the 1960s. Meanwhile, foreign students arriving in Poland in the same period came mostly from countries in the Council for Mutual Economic Assistance or from the nonaligned movement. For example, in 1969, 25 percent of students came from Comecon countries including Cuba and Mongolia. Another significant proportion—15 percent—came from Arab countries under Ba'athist regimes (Iraq, Syria) and other socialist-oriented regimes (Algeria, Egypt, Sudan). The origin of students from sub-Saharan Africa is less politically defined and more diversified, as Constantin Katsakioris notes.[9] Ethiopia, Ghana, and Nigeria were the countries sending the most students from Africa to Poland in the late 1960s.[10] These multiple and indeterminate trajectories attest to the Iron Curtain's porosity and to multiple factors behind early-career choices those students were making.

The focus will then progress to global exchanges in the academic field within the Eastern bloc. The international opening among state-socialist regimes is linked to their economic, scientific, and cultural investment in the Third World in the wake of the Khrushchev-era USSR. Historians have shown the main reasons for this.

8   Simo Mikkonen, Giles Scott-Smith, and Jari Parkkinen, eds., *Entangled East and West: Cultural Diplomacy and Artistic Interaction during the Cold War* (Berlin: De Gruyter Oldenbourg, 2019); György Péteri, "Nylon Curtain—Transnational And Transsystemic Tendencies in the Cultural Life of State-Socialist Russia and East-Central Europe," *Slavonica* 10, no. 2 (2004): 113–23; Michael David-Fox, "Iron Curtain as Semipermeable Membrane: Origins and Demise of the Stalinist Superiority Complex," in *Cold War Crossings: International Travel and Exchange across the Soviet Bloc, 1940s–1960s*, ed. Patryk Babiracki and Kenyon Zimmer (College Station: Texas A&M University Press, 2014), 14–39.

9   Constantin Katsakioris, "Creating a Socialist Intelligentsia: Soviet Educational Aid and Its Impact on Africa (1960–1991)," *Cahiers d'Études africaines* 2, no. 226 (2017): 259–88.

10   Statistics based on UNESCO data. See UNESCO, *Statistics of Students Abroad: 1969–1973: Statistical Reports and Studies / Rapports et études statistiques* 21 (Paris: UNESCO, 1976).

On the one hand, socialism appears as an alternative to the capitalism that was synonymous with imperialism. On the other hand, rivalries—between the traditional blocs of the Cold War, between the USSR and China—increase the participation of the main actors.[11] The Cold War thus reveals its multipolar complexity. The "third ways" pursued by particular Third World leaders wanting to break with Cold War ideological rigidity[12] also offered popular democracies the possibility of acting on a global scale according to their own interests.[13] In Poland, connections with Arab countries—North African and Middle Eastern—and China have been highlighted, in large part.[14]

Such multiple networks attest to a degree of autonomy for communist states in developing their agenda according to their own interests and specializations. In Łukasz Stanek's recent book, *Architecture in Global Socialism*, the architecture historian shows how the experience of reconstructing postwar Warsaw established Polish urbanists' profiles for renovating the urban fabric of Baghdad, to give one example.[15] This was strengthened in Poland where the Sovietization of universities was never brought about fully.[16] Technical cooperation and education weren't the sole factors in the globaliza-

11   James Mark et al., "'We Are with You, Vietnam': Transnational Solidarities in Socialist Hungary, Poland and Yugoslavia," *Journal of Contemporary History* 50, no. 3 (2015): 439–64; Sara Lorenzini, "The Socialist Camp and the Challenge of Economic Modernization in the Third World," in *The Cambridge History of Communism: The Socialist Camp and World Power 1941–1960s*, ed. Norman Naimark, Silvio Pons, and Sophie Quinn-Judge (Cambridge: Cambridge University Press, 2017), 341–63.

12   Michael E. Latham, "The Cold War in the Third World, 1963–1975," in *The Cambridge History of the Cold War*, ed. Melvyn P. Leffler and Odd Arne Westad (Cambridge: Cambridge University Press, 2010), 258–80, 259.

13   Albert Manke and Kateřina Březinová, eds., *Kleinstaaten und sekundäre Akteure im Kalten Krieg: Politische, wirtschaftliche, militärische und kulturelle Wechselbeziehungen zwischen Europa und Lateinamerika* (Bielefeld: Transcript Verlag, 2016), 11–33; Theodora Dragostinova and Małgorzata Fidelis, "Introduction," *Slavic Review* 77, no. 3 (2018): 577–87, 582.

14   Margaret K. Gnoinska, "Poland and the Cold War in East and Southeast Asia, 1949–1965" (PhD diss., George Washington University, 2010), https://scholarspace.library.gwu.edu/etd/8s45q888c; Przemysław Gasztold-Seń, Massimiliano Trentin, and Jan Adamec, *Syria during the Cold War: The East European Connection* (Fife: University of St. Andrews Centre for Syrian Studies, 2014).

15   Łukasz Stanek, *Architecture in Global Socialism: Eastern Europe, West Africa, and the Middle East in the Cold War* (Princeton: Princeton University Press, 2019), 182–95.

16   John Connelly, *Captive University: The Sovietization of East German, Czech, and Polish Higher Education, 1945–1956* (Chapel Hill: University of North Carolina Press, 2000).

tion of student exchange. Along with networks and numerous conferences developed by the International Union of Students, the Youth Festivals were peak experiences of encounter between local people and Third World delegations. Such mega-events reinforced the exoticism of Black students, thus relations of domination. At the 1955 festival in Warsaw, the local leader of a Łódź delegation of young Poles reported that they were mainly interested in "people from exotic countries."[17]

The third theoretical level goes beyond the Cold War conflict and shows that this presence of Third World students reveals symbolic boundaries other than those of ideology. Pioneering studies on the perception of foreigners and more recently on media representations of African students demonstrate that migration within and between blocs creates new frontiers.[18] From one viewpoint, exoticism reveals the extent to which Poland was entangled in those colonial relations. Recent research has highlighted that knowledge and representations about the colonial world and imperialism in Poland date back to the late nineteenth century, when initial emigrant settlements projected a possible new Polish state in Brazil.[19] This conception then extended during the interwar period, in particular through the Polish Maritime and Colonial League.[20] Once the socialist offensive in the Third World was launched by Khrushchev, such colonial conceptions infused relations with the Third World, as

17   Note by Regina Cierakowska [Festival secretary], June 9, 1955, Warsaw, 2/1533,14, Polish Central Archives of Modern Records, Warsaw, Poland; Matthieu Gillabert, "Varsovie 1955 et la Guerre froide globale / L'internationalisation de l'Europe centrale au prisme du 5e Festival mondial de la jeunesse et des étudiants," Monde(s), no. 18 (2020): 51–72; Pia Koivunen, "Performing Peace and Friendship—The World Youth Festival as a Tool of Soviet Cultural Diplomacy, 1947–1957" (PhD diss., University of Tampere, 2013).

18   Jerzy Kochanowski, ed., Warszawiacy nie z tej ziemi: Cudzoziemscy mieszkańcy stolicy 1945–1989 (Warsaw: Dom Spotkań z Historią, 2013); Bartosz Nowicki, "Representations of Africans in Polish Press Photography: 1955–1989" (PhD diss., Ulster University, 2020), https://pure.ulster.ac.uk/en/studentTheses/representations-of-africans-in-polish-press-photography-1955-1989.

19   Lenny A. Ureña Valerio, Colonial Fantasies, Imperial Realities: Race Science and the Making of Polishness on the Fringes of the German Empire, 1840–1920 (Athens: Ohio University Press, 2019).

20   Taras Hunczak, "Polish Colonial Ambitions in the Inter-War Period," Slavic Review 26, no. 4 (1967): 648–56.

the historian Małgorzata Mazurek shows in the case of the economist Oskar Lange, who claimed that Poland's past was India's present and Poland's present was India's future.[21]

From another viewpoint, these academic policies modify the peripheral perception and self-perception of Poland. By attracting students to Łódź from around the world, the country became a center for diffusing modernity. Racial and modernity distinctions then became as important as classic ideological borders. By "racial," I refer to the sociologist Stuart Hall's proposal of seeing race as a cultural and discursive otherness based on different types of knowledge.[22] This investment in the education of Third World students was based on knowledge and convictions linked to modernization. Such investment therefore aimed to mark a form of cultural and racial distinction characterized by recurrent representations of indistinct "African" students having difficulty in adapting. As the language school's director stated in 1984, SJPdC was not a place of teaching, but of education.[23]

Socialist Investment in Training Foreign Cadres: The Example of the School of Polish for Foreign Students in Łódź

Student migration to Poland followed a pattern found in other Eastern bloc countries. Around the 1960s, increasing numbers of scholarship recipients arrived from the Third World. This trend continued until the end of the 1970s. These decades correspond to the culmination of a developmentalist promise that was

21   Małgorzata Mazurek, "Polish Economists in Nehru's India," *Slavic Review* 77, no. 3 (2018): 588–610, 595.
22   Stuart Hall, *The Fateful Triangle: Race, Ethnicity, Nation* (Cambridge, MA: Harvard University Press, 2017).
23   "A przecież praca tutaj to nie tylko nauczanie, to także sprawy wychowawcze, socjalno-bytowe i wiele innych." [And yet working here is not only about teaching, it is also about educational, social, and care matters, and many others.] Jerzy Barski, "Łódzka 'Wieża Babel,'" *Dziennik Łódzki*, February 10, 1984, 3.

shared by a large part of industrialized countries and that was realized mostly through education and training. In Poland, interest in educating cadres continued even until the end of the Cold War.[24]

In some countries, this education policy was visible in public space. In Moscow, the Peoples' Friendship University was built in 1961 then renamed for Patrice Lumumba.[25] In Prague in the same year, the campus of the November 17 University was specially built for foreign students.[26] From the end of the Second World War, the Czechoslovak capital developed into a very important crossroads; at first for political exiles, then for students from the Third World, as it hosted the International Union of Students headquarters. A building dedicated to that association was built in 1974. There is no such monumental structure in Poland. The most renowned international institution, SJPdC, was founded in Łódź in 1957, before Lumumba University. Its main building was erected in 1963 at 16 Kopcińskiego Street, but did not have the impact on the urban landscape of its Soviet and Czechoslovak counterparts.

SJPdC was launched in the context of the Polish opening to the Third World, following the lead of the USSR. Poland had been regularly welcoming foreign students since the end of the Second World War, but in limited numbers. During the Korean War, a first contingent of 132 North Korean students had arrived in Łódź. The choice of city is not clear, and two explanations are offered. The first posits that Łódź was far enough from Warsaw to circumvent embassies from interfering too much in the lives of their students or engaging them for espionage purposes. In the second explanation, the University of Łódź was built in 1945 and considered a

24   Minister of Higher Education, "Report on Foreign Cooperation in the Field of Science and Higher Education Conducted by Higher Education Institutions in 1987," OLCAPSW-1, University of Łódź Archives (UŁ), Łódź, Poland.

25   Constantin Katsakioris, "The Lumumba University in Moscow: Higher Education for a Soviet-Third World Alliance, 1960–1991," *Journal of Global History* 14, no. 2 (2019): 281–300.

26   Daniela Hannová, "'Většinu času věnují planým řečem a flirtu s děvčaty': Arabští studenti v Praze (1958–1967)," *Dějiny a Současnost* 36, no. 5 (2014): 40–43.

socialist model of higher education. It showcased scientific modernity and social rise for the working class, and was strongly highlighted in the local press.[27]

Universities in Warsaw and Kraków had more experience, having organized interwar summer schools for Polish language studies. In either case, the institutionalization of SJPdC was not easy, due to the lack of teaching resources. Until the 1980s, the institution was considered by key stakeholders to be more of an experimental lab than a well-established academic center.

Foreign students, unlike their Polish comrades, didn't have to take university entrance exams. As early as 1951, a preparatory course was set up in Łódź: this became the nucleus at the origin of SJPdC, which was then officially institutionalized in 1957 by decision of the Ministry of Higher Education. Exams in core disciplines were already being organized in Polish embassies abroad. The creation of SJPdC coincided with the government's takeover of academic exchanges, which had previously been managed mainly by Party-affiliated organizations.[28]

Polish was taught at SJPdC, as was nomenclature for different subjects, along with an introduction to Polish culture through lectures and domestic travel. International students could live in situ, although ads in local papers show that many preferred separate housing. In Łódź, the SJPdC building was commonly called the Tower of Babel, indicating distance between local residents and what was seen as a strange place. That strangeness was reinforced by a perceived promiscuity among the students and by their housing difficulties. While building designs accommodated 250 students, there were over 400 during the 1970s.[29]

Looking at the course syllabus, one may be surprised at the lack of political or ideological education. Accounts certainly

---

27   Agata Zysiak et al., *From Cotton and Smoke: Łódź—Industrial City and Discourses of Asynchronous Modernity 1897–1994* (Łódź: Wydawnictwo Uniwersytetu Łódzkiego, 2018), 184–92.
28   Ryszard Stemplowski, *Zrzeszenie Studentów Polskich w socjalizmie państwowym 1950–1973* (Warsaw: Wydawnictwo Naukowe Scholar, 2018), 142.
29   Report by the Rector's Office, "Informacja dotycząca problemów Studium Języka Polskiego dla Cudzoziemców w UŁ" [Memo on problems at SJPdC at the University of Łódź], November 6, 1978, BR-343, Archives of the University of Łódź (UŁ), Łódź, Poland.

show strong mobilization among students in the context of participating in socialist commemorations—which is indeed one form of political education.[30] However, language was central in the school's teaching, followed by introductory courses in various disciplines. SJPdC aimed to develop new pedagogical knowledge on Polish as a foreign language, on the presentation of Poland to foreigners, and on psychological supervision of students. As Witold Śmiech, SJPdC's director of the Department of Modern Polish Language, recalled with regret, this training had to be developed intuitively, with limited financial means and a shortage of personnel.[31]

Among the foreign students were those on Polish government scholarship, on scholarship from political organizations (the Polish United Workers' Party and the Polish Students' Association), and students who came on their own.

At the end of the 1960s, about half the government's scholarships to foreign students were distributed to students from developing countries.[32] If hospitality was part of the cooperative aid, its counterparts in controls on the foreign students, both police and medical (with thorough medical exams on entering the country), were in fact a form of governmentality. All cooperative aid can be considered as a "knowledge-power regime."[33] As a concept already used in studying student mobility,[34] governmentality expresses the double dimension of power exercised over a student body, along with new knowledge of government and control (police, administrative, medical).[35]

In Poland, knowledge of the Global South has long been book-based. For example, Joanna Mantel-Niećko (1933–2009), professor of Ethiopian Studies at the University of Warsaw's Department

30   Nowicki, "Representations of Africans," 266.
31   Witold Śmiech to Rector Romuald Skowroński, June 10, 1977, BR-343, Archives of the University of Łódź (UŁ), Łódź, Poland.
32   Błażej Brzostek, "Życie społeczne Uniwersytetu 1945–1989," in *Dzieje Uniwersytetu Warszawskiego po 1945*, ed. Piotr M. Majewski (Warsaw: Wydawnictwa Uniwersytetu Warszawskiego, 2016), 15–372.
33   Frederick Cooper and Randall Packard, "Introduction," in *International Development and the Social Sciences: Essays on the History and Politics of Knowledge* (Berkeley, Los Angeles: University of California Press, 1997), 1–41.
34   Parvati Raghuram, "Theorising the Spaces of Student Migration," *Population, Space and Place* 19, no. 2 (2013): 138–54.
35   Michel Foucault, *Dits et Écrits*, vol. 3 (Paris: Gallimard, 1994).

of African Languages and Cultures, a specialist since the 1950s in linguistics and land law in Ethiopia, only made her first trip there in 1984. However, since the late 1950s, Polish scholarly expertise on the Third World has increased,[36] as has the number of research institutions, including the Research Institute for Developing Countries at the Central School of Planning and Statistics in Warsaw (SGPiS). The African Institute was founded at the University of Warsaw in 1963, with the aim of contributing to the work of "reconstruction and social and cultural development" of postcolonial countries. According to its review's editorial in the first issue, this knowledge was able to develop in Poland thanks to global socialism, which strengthened the will to educate new professionals who could then export this expertise.

This control was legitimized by a discourse in the SJPdC administration, insisting that difficulties were due to harsh winters, new food, and cultural differences.[37] After the preparatory year in Łódź, once a student had embarked on their course of study, academic institutions were very prescriptive in their choice of study location.[38] That control can also be explained by the financial dividends. Annually in the 1980s, SJPdC generated nearly $800,000, which all went to the Ministry of Higher Education.[39]

Students were widely used in espionage, both within Poland and abroad. In the Institute of National Remembrance's archives, there are hundreds of files on student collaboration, whether in sporadic or regular contact with Ministry of Internal Affairs officers. According to reports on different students who had greater or lesser collaborations with the security services, objectives were multiple: monitoring various groups of fellow students by nationality; observing embassy activities; utilizing their mobility abroad, particularly in Germany, to spy on Poles in exile. For one local officer, Citizens' Militia Chief Henryk Bilski, SJPdC was a strategic place where in addition

36   Mazurek, "Polish Economists in Nehru's India," 588–610.
37   See for example the report by the Rector's Office, "Informacja dotycząca
       problemów," November 6, 1978, BR-343.
38   Kochanowski, *Warszawiacy nie z tej ziemi*, 108.
39   Barski, "Łódzka 'Wieża Babel,'" 3.

FIG. 2
THREE CONTINENTS CLUB, WARSAW, NOVEMBER 1969, © PAP

to language instruction, political education should be added to per-
suade students of the legitimacy of international politics in
socialist countries.[40]
        In public space, Third World students were recognized
largely in relation to demonstrations of loyalty to socialism and displays of belonging to the Eastern bloc. As they appeared in the local
press or participated in public festivities as socialist brothers and
sisters, they were viewed as coming from "backward" countries—a
typical development perspective. Their presence was thus utilized by
the communist authorities as a political and international legitimation. The SJPdC building, especially its hall, became a nexus for staging Poland's position in the global-socialist world. Members of Party
organizations, diplomats from sister countries, and student groups
met there to formulate resolutions on international solidarity.[41]
        Perception of these foreigners among the authorities,
however, was not uniform. Extant police reports provide information about some activities in places outside SJPdC. Important hot
spots of encounters and meetings included clubs that no longer
exist: next to the National Opera in Warsaw, the Klub Trzy Kontynenty
(Three Continents Club), which closed in 1974,[42] and in Łódź on
Zachodnia Street, the Klub Nowa Afryka (New Africa Club). The latter
attracted African students speaking English, reputedly further from
communist networks than French speakers.[43] These police descriptions of daily student life reveal a colonialist view of students who
are often presented, not as socialist brothers and sisters, but as personally profiting sexually and in various other pleasures.
        Linked to the communist regime, their presence
became a political issue. For those in the opposition, Third World
students were often generalized into an undefined whole participating in the government's public demonstration of power. The journal-

40   Report by Citizens' Militia Chief Henryk Bilski, December 21, 1968, AIPN,
            Ld, PF/10/829, Archive of the Institute of National Remembrance,
            Warsaw, Poland.
41   See for example the foreign student resolution on Vietnam and
            Venezuela from 1965. Dziennik Łódzki, December 11, 1965, 2.
42   Przemysław Gasztold-Seń, "Arabscy studenci w Warszawie po 1956 r.," in
            Cudzoziemcy w Warszawie 1945–1989: Studia i materiały, ed. Patryk Pleskot
            (Warsaw: IPN, 2012), 58–59.
43   Report by [X.] Chruśliński, January 3, 1967, AIPN, Ld, PF/10/829, Institute
            of National Remembrance, Warsaw, Poland.

ist Alina Grabowska noted in the émigré journal *Kultura* in 1968 that African and Vietnamese students marched on Piotrkowska Street in Łódź with anti-Zionist slogans, unlike their Polish comrades who organized anti-regime demonstrations.[44] It seems to have been more complicated than that. From the 1960s on, tensions were high among those foreign students. While the Vietnam War unified opinion, China's influence on the Third World and relations with Israel created many disagreements.

Chinese propaganda penetrated the foreign-student community in Poland not only from the Chinese Embassy but also, paradoxically, from the West. Among Third World students, questions of loyalty—China or the USSR—generated important tensions. In West Berlin, there seem to have been a significant concentration of Iraqi students who were pro-Chinese. On trips to West Berlin, records show that several students returned with material from Beijing.[45] The Party tightly controlled Chinese propaganda until 1970—especially First Secretary Władysław Gomułka, who saw it as a threat to Soviet-Polish relations.[46]

Meanwhile, Jordanian students were accused by their Syrian and Algerian peers of being too close to Israel,[47] and in Łódź and Warsaw, large demonstrations in support of Arab countries took place during the Mid-East wars in 1967 and 1973.[48]

Descriptions of such conflicts are found in security-service archives. They may not reflect the reality of interactions within the SJPdC contact zone. However, they do reveal political heterogeneity in this foreign community. Furthermore, the reports display the highly geopolitical reading taken by the security officers in their understanding of how those groups functioned. The Arab student group in particular was generally seen as fickle, subject to the vicissitudes of international politics.

44   Alina Grabowska, "Łódzki Marzec," *Kultura*, 5, 1969, 69–79.
45   Report by Citizens' Militia Chief of Łódź, undated, AIPN, Ld, PF/10/829, Institute of National Remembrance, Warsaw, Poland.
46   Gnoinska, "Poland and the Cold War in East and Southeast Asia."
47   Secret Report by Citizens' Militia, November 15, 1969, AIPN, Ld, PF/10/829, Institute of National Remembrance, Warsaw, Poland.
48   Gasztold-Seń, "Arabscy studenci w Warszawie," 58.

Local Interactions with Foreign Students: Daily Life in Łódź in the 1960s

Practically, these scholarship students were the government's guests and part of its propaganda panoply, as has been described above. Residents' relations with them were linked not only to widely shared racial stereotypes but to citizens' relations to the communist authorities. The construction of alterity under communist rule was also influenced by the political context. This combination of cultural stereotypes and a political regime promoting those students' presence seems characteristic of the framework in which the overall cohabitation took place.

SJPdC remains a relevant observation point from which to discern how the interaction between foreign students and local Poles played out. The concentration of foreign students in attendance there focused the attention of contemporaries, especially the media. In addition to that extensive documentation, archives of former Łódź Film School students highlight that, beyond the propagandist stagings, those students had immersed themselves deeply in the PRL's daily social reality.

Admittedly, media content does not correspond to general attitudes, which are naturally complex and diverse. It does give an idea about new representations of these students, and of the evolution of those representations. And the local press was indeed changing its views. Through the 1960s, foreign students appeared as ambassadors from sister countries, in accordance with official discourse. Yet a striking discrepancy exists between discourse and reality. For example, Kenyan students didn't participate in the 1966 May Day parade and Ghanaian students publicly expressed their opposition to the USSR.[49] Meanwhile, the press consistently featured the procession's foreign-student delegation. Yet exoticism is a term that often comes up. In Łódź, dubbed the Polish Manchester in its industrial heyday around 1900, the students were "exotic" or came from "exotic countries." Political proximity is often articulated with cultural distance.

49   Przemysław Gasztold, "'Szkoła przetrwania': Studenci afrykańscy w
        komunistycznej Polsce," in *Środowisko studenckie w krajach bloku sowieckiego
        1945–1990*, ed. Kamil Dworaczek and Krzysztof Łagojda (Warsaw: IPN, 2020),
        545–70, 550.

However, an independence of view can be observed in the press from the 1980s on. The question of racism was notably evoked—in the Eastern bloc, racism was almost exclusively identified with the US.[50] In the weekly paper *Odgłosy*, Joanna Sławińska innovated by giving voice directly to the overseas students. They expressed different stereotypes they heard from Łódź inhabitants. Sławińska's article also considered them publicly—not secretly, like the security services—as particularly mobile people, able to offer information about their feelings during stays in the West. "'When I was in France and Germany,' Jean said, 'the students invited me to a party. Never in Poland.'" [51]

Conclusion

In some ways, teaching disciplines, supervision, and education aims for Third World international students were not different on either side of the Iron Curtain. The number of scholarships for the training of cadres from decolonized countries took off at the start of the 1960s, both in the East and in the West. The former imperial powers may have been a bit ahead in the game.

The difference lay more in the impact of this foreign presence in Polish urban spaces. Politically, the tag of international "friendship" has long accompanied these students, who were partly instruments of propaganda yet also participated in the daily life of state socialism. Their presence was largely determined by Poland's geopolitical situation and instrumentalized for propaganda aims. Also, socialist and colonial pasts overlap. The oblivion of this (post) colonial presence can therefore also be explained, perhaps, by the difficulty of reflecting on the broad communist legacy and its influence on Polish society today.

However, the study of these circulations allows us to understand, at least in part, the path taken by Poland toward globalization. The presence of non-European students is indeed a reflection of the expanding socialist bloc after the decolonization in

50   Law and Zakharov, "Race and Racism in Eastern Europe," 113–39.
51   Joanna Sławińska, "Obcy wśród Polaków," *Odgłosy*, October 27, 1984, 6.

the 1950s.[52] In this space, Poland took a specific path with hosting foreign students—a limited number in comparison with the USSR and Czechoslovakia, but those contacts with the postcolonial world clearly contributed to its societal internationalization. A development that was then obscured in its post-1989 narrative of the Western path to globalization.

52   James Mark, Artemy M. Kalinovsky, and Steffi Marung, eds., *Alternative Globalizations: Eastern Europe and the Postcolonial World* (Bloomington: Indiana University Press, 2020), 1–4.

Monika Bobako is an associate professor at Adam Mickiewicz University in Poznań. She holds a PhD and post-doctoral degree in philosophy and an MA in Gender Studies (from the Central European University in Budapest). She is the author of two books in Polish, *Islamophobia as a Technology of Power: A Study in Political Anthropology* (2017) and *Democracy and Difference: Multiculturalism and Feminism in the Perspective of the Politics of Recognition* (2010). She edited the special issues "The Theologies of Emancipation" (*Praktyka Teoretyczna*, 2013) and "Islamophobia: Contexts" (*Praktyka Teoretyczna*, 2017). Bobako specializes in political anthropology, critical-race theory, and postcolonial theory (with special focuses on Islam and gender). She is particularly interested in the question of racialization and the forms it takes in peripheral societies, especially in Central and Eastern Europe. In 2018, *Islamophobia as a Technology of Power: A Study in Political Anthropology* received the Jan Długosz Prize and was nominated for the Tadeusz Kotarbiński Prize, major academic awards in Poland. Her current research project, "Genealogies of Peripheral Whiteness: Polish Identities in the Perspective of Racialization Theories," is funded by the National Centre of Science in Poland.

THE JEW, THE ARAB, THE POLE: MARCH 1968 IN POLAND AND THE HISTORY OF AN ALLIANCE BETWEEN THE SECOND AND THIRD WORLDS

In Gil Anidjar's book *The Jew, the Arab: A History of the Enemy*, the professor of religion and comparative literature proposes that the way Europe defined itself over the course of history has been closely bound with how it defined its Jewish and Muslim others—in particular, the Arab. According to Anidjar, Europe constructed and reconstructed its identity by simultaneously producing and erasing differences between these groups and by creating and eliminating distance with each of them (and among them, too). In this context, he also notes that the concept of the enemy, crucial to the European philosophical and political imagination, is structured by the figures of the Arab and the Jew, connected and ultimately polarized—or, more precisely, "by the relation of Europe to *both* Arab *and* Jew."[1]

I mention these reflections because they imply a theoretical postulate according to which the European should always be analyzed *together* with the Jew and the Arab. At first glance, this postulate has only a limited application to Polish history; Jews and

---

1   Gil Anidjar, *The Jew, the Arab: A History of the Enemy* (Stanford: Stanford University Press, 2003), xi. See Monika Bobako, "Żyd i Arab/muzułmanin w europejskich geometriach tożsamości i różnicy," *Teksty Drugie*, no. 2 (2017): 255–79.

Arabs have played very different and incomparable roles in it. In the Polish case, therefore, the tripolar structure outlined by Anidjar is markedly asymmetrical and discontinuous. In this essay, I will endeavor to demonstrate that in one period, the second half of the twentieth century, it is possible to observe this structure at play, particularly in the stormy sequence of events from 1967 to 1968, considered by researchers to be among the decisive turning points in postwar Polish history. It includes reactions to the Israeli-Arab Six-Day War between Israel and its Arab neighbors on one hand, and on the other, the anti-Semitic purge instigated less than a year later as part of what historians term "March '68."

Taking cues from Anidjar, I present these events and the political processes that led up to them as a sort of symbolic encounter, or confrontation, between three identity figures that carry strong connotations in Polish culture and political discourses: those of the Jew, the Arab, and the Pole. As I will seek to show, this confrontation was particularly significant as it led up to a profound reorganization of the dominant vision of the Polish political community, and, consequently, redefined the place available in it to different categories of others: Jews on one hand, Arabs on the other (and by extension, other representatives of the non-European world).

The Pole and the Jew: Postwar Contradictions
The events of March '68 seem impossible to understand without taking into account the instability that marked the position of Jews in postwar Poland under communist rule. As the historian August Grabski writes, by rejecting the prewar period's anti-Semitic legacy, the Polish People's Republic (PRL) "removed from the Polish Jews and Jewish Poles the stigma of second-class citizens. Jews were no longer restricted from entering public service, legal work, teaching, or from university studies. Poles of Jewish descent participated in politics to an extent unimaginable in pre-1939 Poland or in that state entity that was its formal continuation, the London government-in-exile [established first in France, after Poland's

defeat]."[2] Meanwhile, communist policy toward the remaining Jewish minority of Holocaust survivors was hostage to the fact that the communists were striving to legitimize their government before a society that was still strongly anti-Semitic.[3] As a result, Jews in high-profile government jobs were urged to adopt Polish-sounding names, and the general tendency in public discourse was to not highlight Jewish issues.[4] Consequently, the Jewish community's historical and contemporaneous achievements, problems, and experiences—including the extreme distinctness of its Holocaust experience—were passed over in silence, while the problem of Polish anti-Semitism, both past and present, remained taboo.

Postwar anti-Semitism found its most violent expression in a series of pogroms in Rzeszów (June 1945), Kraków (August 1945), and Kielce (July 1946), and in a wave of murders that claimed an unknown number of victims (at least eight hundred). As Grabski points out, motivations behind those crimes were manifold: racist, religious, political, criminal, or "related to the 'defense' of Jewish property the perpetrators had previously appropriated."[5] Political motivation was usually based on a sense that Jews, in their roles in the communist system, had seized power to subjugate Polish society. This was purportedly confirmed by their "overrepresentation" in the infamously brutal intelligence and secret services, and probably by their "blatant" public visibility, differing from the prewar period as Jews were functioning on an equal footing socially with

2   August Grabski, "Żydzi a polskie życie polityczne (1944–1949)," in *Następstwa zagłady Żydów: Polska 1944–2010*, ed. Feliks Tych and Monika Adamczyk-Garbowska (Lublin: Wydawnictwo UMCS; Warsaw: Żydowski Instytut Historyczny, 2011), 157–88, 169.

3   The Nazi-engineered Holocaust didn't eliminate anti-Semitism within resistance organizations that vied during and immediately after the Second World War for influence over the Polish populace, opposing the Soviet-backed communists. Anti-communist organizations, including those connected with the Polish government-in-exile in London, murdered Jews suspected of communist sympathies. This led Jewish communities, including those that were conservative and religious, to almost comprehensively support the communists' takeover of power, even if most members of those communities would then emigrate from Poland within a few years of the war's end. See Grabski, "Żydzi a polskie życie polityczne," 162–69.

4   Grzegorz Berendt, "Wpływ liberalizacji politycznej roku 1956 na sytuację Żydów," in Tych and Adamczyk-Garbowska, *Następstwa zagłady Żydów*, 359–84, 359.

5   Grabski, "Żydzi a polskie życie polityczne," 177.

Poles. The association of Jewish alterity with the alterity of the enforced communist regime generated the "Judeo-Communism" stereotype, which in postwar sociopolitical conflicts became among the intractable topoi fusing anti-Semitism and anti-communism.[6] Paradoxically, this stereotype was also employed within communist power structures, in a zone of conflict between political factions. That phenomenon would play an important role in March '68, but can be recognized earlier, for example during the post-Stalinist period of political thaw around 1956, as criticism of the status quo mounted and led to an outpouring of anti-Semitic attitudes. At that juncture, the situation had been brought under control, through official condemnation of nationalist and chauvinist views as "anti-socialist and revisionist." As the historian Grzegorz Berendt observes, anti-Semitic rhetoric was then effectively banned from public space until 1967.[7]

In Jan T. Gross's book *Fear: Anti-Semitism in Poland after Auschwitz*, the Princeton historian sums up the situation, writing that "in an ideal world, with communists safely in power, there wouldn't be any anti-Semitism. But in the ideal world envisaged by communism there wouldn't be any Jews, either."[8] Here, it is worth noting that such a vision may have stemmed as much from communist ideology's universalist component, which would view individuals as equal citizens, with their ethnic or national diversity a factor that could be politically neutralized through assimilation, as from nationalist phantasms of an ethnically pure society.

The course of events, however, proved the second interpretation to be closer to reality.

The Pole and the Arab: An Ideology of Anti-Imperialist Fraternity

Polish relations with Arabs during the Cold War, unlike with Jews, were an effect of political will rather than of centuries spent cohabitating on the same lands. These relations were spurred

6   Anna Zawadzka, "Żydokomuna: Szkic do socjologicznej analizy źródeł historycznych," *Societas / Communitas*, no. 2 (2009): 199–243.
7   Berendt, "Wpływ liberalizacji politycznej roku 1956," 375.
8   Jan T. Gross, *Fear: Anti-Semitism in Poland after Auschwitz; An Essay in Historical Interpretation* (New York: Random House, 2006), 222–23.

and regulated in a top-down manner, in large part; their chronology relied on how political dynamics were being shaped at a given juncture with the non-European world.[9] What Polish-Jewish problematics shared with the issue of Polish-Arab relations, as well as relations with other Third World countries' representatives, was the fact that in both cases social reality and political practice weren't always consistent with the authorities' official narrative.

One of Poland's three pillars of postwar foreign policy was "solidarity with liberation and emancipation efforts of nations freeing themselves from colonial domination."[10] The most important institution at which this doctrine of solidarity was declared was the United Nations, founded in 1945.[11] At the UN Forum, Poland condemned Western military interventions in Third World countries, including Algeria, Korea, Vietnam, and the Democratic Republic of the Congo.[12] Poland also protested the rise of South Africa's apartheid system very early on,[13] comparing it to Germany's Nazi regime, and participated in UN initiatives to legally declare it criminal.[14]

The second foreign-policy pillar proclaimed "proletarian internationalism and unity in relations with other socialist countries."[15] What was striking in the ideological discourse surrounding Poland's postwar foreign policy was how closely it connected internationalist and anti-colonial ideas with Polish traditions to reclaim independence through the nineteenth century (and beyond), embodied in the motto "for our freedom and yours." The Polish experience of having been partitioned through that period, and of German occupation through the Second World War, was

9   For this reason, Poland only maintained ties with Arab countries that
           weren't Western allies (as Saudi Arabia and others were).
10   Adam Rapacki, "Trzy zasady polskiej polityki zagranicznej," *Sprawy
           Międzynarodowe*, no. 7–8 (1960): 4.
11   Andrzej Abraszewski, *Polska w Organizacji Narodów Zjednoczonych (1945–1975)*
           (Warsaw: Wydawnictwo Interpress, 1975).
12   James Mark et al., "'We Are with You, Vietnam': Transnational Solidarities
           in Socialist Hungary, Poland and Yugoslavia," *Journal of Contemporary History*
           50, no. 3 (2015): 439–64.
13   Paul Betts et al., "Race, Socialism and Solidarity: Anti-Apartheid in
           Eastern Europe," in *A Global History of Anti-Apartheid: "Forward to Freedom" in
           South Africa*, ed. Anna Konieczna and Rob Skinner (London: Palgrave
           Macmillan, 2019), 151–200.
14   Betts et al., "Race, Socialism and Solidarity," 163–64.
15   Rapacki, "Trzy zasady polskiej polityki zagranicznej," 4.

presented as a source of "natural sympathy" for colonized peoples and their anti-imperialist political mobilizations, and for newly independent nations.

The ideological frameworks of postwar Poland's policies, both domestic and foreign, were explicated in propaganda publications issued by the ruling Polish United Workers' Party (PZPR). Strong emphasis was laid on connecting "true patriotism" with internationalism, and the former was sharply distinguished from nationalism, which in its turn was condemned as a harmful, anti-national, and anti-patriotic tendency that isolated one nation from another, benefitting the wealthy bourgeois classes.[16] The nationalism of anticolonial movements, meanwhile, was contrasted with the nationalism of colonial nations, after Lenin. Communist policy supported the former, which had an emancipatory role to play, unlike the latter, which was to be firmly opposed. This had consequences for domestic policy as well: according to the official discourse, prejudice against or oppression of ethnic minorities was unacceptable, as was any racial hatred or discrimination. As stated in a propaganda brochure published in 1961, "a conciliatory attitude toward nationalism in the Party ranks is intolerable and cannot be reconciled with Party membership."[17] The agenda was meant to further Marxist-humanist ideas, which blended "universal and class aspects," urged the "undoing of capitalist relations by means of class struggle," and promised the "victory of all-human solidarity and universal fraternity."[18]

The policy's third pillar was a "constructive struggle for peaceful coexistence in relations with non-socialist countries."[19] The importance attached to the question of world peace was a result of the still-fresh trauma of the Second World War, a burgeoning fear of nuclear war, and anxiety over the stability of Poland's new western border, which West Germany would not officially recognize until 1990. Peace initiatives, including plans to stop the arms race, were a permanent feature of Poland's activity at the UN Forum. These also

16   Emilia Żyro, *Aktualne problemy internacjonalizmu proletariackiego* (Poznań: Komitet Wojewódzki PZRR, Wojewódzki Ośrodek Propagandy Partyjnej, 1961), 6.
17   Żyro, *Aktualne problemy internacjonalizmu proletariackiego*, 17.
18   Żyro, *Aktualne problemy internacjonalizmu proletariackiego*, 18.
19   Rapacki, "Trzy zasady polskiej polityki zagranicznej," 4.

became an inspiration for projects of major ideological significance, including the World Festival of Youth and Students, held in Warsaw in 1955,[20] an event that proved an important if momentary experience of cultural opening for many Poles. With the participation of 140,000 Polish youth and 26,600 guests from 114 countries, the festival's key slogan, along with those opposing nuclear weapons and West Germany's remilitarization, was "Peace for all, work for all, happiness for all!"[21] The capital went into a frenzy, with press reports showing the Polish public to be particularly impressed with the presence of nearly a thousand guests from Africa and the Middle East.

The context of Polish-Arab relations was a special one. In 1947, Poland voted in favor of the UN's resolution on the partitioning of Palestine. While unequivocally supporting Palestinians' right to statehood, the resolution prioritized relations with the nascent Israeli state, which it was assumed would be a socialist country, therefore an Eastern-bloc ally. The situation changed in the early 1950s when Israel reoriented its policy toward the West, joining the "imperialist bloc," which Poland deemed hostile. Mounting conflict between Israel and neighboring Arab states, which had gradually freed themselves from colonial rule, meant that Poland, like other Soviet satellite states, became involved in providing political and military support to those countries (mainly Egypt, but also Syria, Libya, and Iraq, then Palestine as well). An additional effect were closer contacts, which saw Poland funding university scholarships for students from the Middle East and other postcolonial regions, and transferring expertise, primarily in engineering, to developing countries.

The first students from Arab countries arrived in Poland in the late 1950s, then their number grew steadily, although it must be emphasized that it remained low in comparison with other "popular democracies" in the bloc. Recruited primarily from pro-

20   Andrzej Krzywicki, "Cudzoziemcy i Polacy na V Światowym Festiwalu
        Młodzieży i Studentów o Pokój i Przyjaźń—Warszawa, 1955 r.," in
        Cudzoziemcy w Warszawie 1945–1989: Studia i materiały, ed. Patryk Pleskot
        (Warsaw: IPN, 2012), 27–40.
21   Paulina Codogni, "Rok 1955: Festiwalowe spotkanie z Afryką," in Afryka w
        Warszawie: Dzieje afrykańskiej diaspory nad Wisłą, ed. Paweł Średziński and
        Mamadou Diouf (Warsaw: Fundacja Afryka Inaczej, 2010), 131–52, 135.

communist circles in countries with which Poland established bilateral relations, these students often had previous political experience, and were war veterans, in some cases. Their community in Poland replicated the same divides that were in place in the milieus from which they came. Usually monitored by both the Polish secret services and intelligence operatives from their own countries,[22] they mainly studied in fields including medicine, applied sciences, life sciences, or exact sciences, with far fewer being humanities students. Most, though not all, were men.[23] As graduates, some remained in Poland and started families with Polish women; others returned home, including some who took their Polish wives with them. To this day in Poland, former scholarship holders and their descendants form the core of the Arab communities, while in the Arab world, Polish women who married Arab men make up the majority of the Polish diaspora communities. This gender asymmetry was due to cultural circumstances that did not encourage women to immigrate and the fact that women in the partner Arab countries were only beginning to enjoy access to educational facilities, including higher education. In turn, prejudices persisting in Polish society meant that women socializing with Arab or African students were often ostracized and stigmatized for having "loose morals."

Political declarations of "fraternity" did not always translate into actual experience for these Third World students, who often complained about social isolation and racism.[24] This was due both to ignorance and widespread stereotypes in Poland's culturally homogeneous society of the period, and to resentment caused by a sense that scholarship students enjoyed privileges including financial support from the state and less demanding treatment from their instructors. In the longer term, Polish institutions failed to sustain and strengthen contacts established through the scholarship programs, in effect wasting important opportunities; neither school nor

22   Przemysław Gasztold-Seń, "Arabscy studenci w Warszawie po 1956 roku," in Pleskot, *Cudzoziemcy w Warszawie*, 41–72.
23   The few women were usually wives of scholarship holders, who then also studied in Poland.
24   Błażej Popławski and Patryk Pleskot, "Z dziejów pewnego Towarzystwa: O początkach działalności Towarzystwa Przyjaźni Polsko-Afrykańskiej w Warszawie," in Pleskot, *Cudzoziemcy w Warszawie*, 189–202.

state officials followed up on the graduates' careers, though many
of the latter rose to eminent positions in their respective countries
in academia, government, and business.

Another form of cooperation was the transfer of expertise from Poland to Third World countries. Polish scholars, doctors,
and engineers would be contracted to longer or shorter working
stints in these countries, employed at universities and hospitals, or
on infrastructure projects. From the late 1960s on, thousands of Polish professionals were overseas each year on such contracts, which
were lucrative both for employees and for the companies and institutions delegating them. As architecture historian Łukasz Stanek
demonstrates, this cooperation left a lasting legacy in the Middle
East and Africa, from urban plans and architectural solutions to high-
ways, bridges, and factories.[25] However, first-hand accounts from
these contracted specialists show that their periods abroad were
seldom a model of building "proletarian internationalism." The Polish professionals usually functioned in their respective host countries on a level comparable to that of colonial-era elites, enjoying relatively luxurious lifestyles behind the walls of guarded communities,
separated from local people. Conflicts over laws and local customs
were not infrequent, including those restricting the consumption of
alcoholic beverages.[26] As the experts' role situated them in the dominant position of providers of advanced knowledge to developing
countries, relations were less of an anti-colonial, internationalist
partnership and more of a "Comintern version of Eurocentrism."[27]

Besides the ideological aspect, Polish-Arab relations
also carried a pragmatic one, linked with Poland's efforts to secure
its international interests, such as mustering the broadest possible
support for its western border with the Germans. Fundamentally,

25   Łukasz Stanek, *Architecture in Global Socialism: Eastern Europe, West Africa, and
the Middle East in the Cold War* (Princeton: Princeton University Press, 2020).
26   Przemysław Gasztold-Seń, "Libia Muammara Kaddafiego i PRL:
Zapomniani sojusznicy okresu zimnej wojny," in *Bezpieczeństwo narodowe
i międzynarodowe w regionie Bliskiego Wschodu i Północnej Afryki (MENA) u progu XXI
wieku*, ed. Radosław Bania and Krzysztof Zdulski (Łódź: Katedra Bliskiego
Wschodu i Północnej Afryki Uniwersytetu Łódzkiego, 2012), 312–330, 319.
27   Max Cegielski, "Polacy w Azji 1945–89: 'Kominternowski europocentryzm'
czy wschodnie okno na świat?" in *Polska & Azja: Od Rzeczpospolitej Szlacheckiej
do Nangar Khel; Przewodnik interdyscyplinarny*, ed. Max Cegielski (Poznań:
Fundacja Malta, 2013), 87.

however, these relations were of secondary importance to Poland's foreign-policy goals, nor did they translate in any significant way into the everyday experience of the Polish public. As the sociologist Mustafa Switat writes, "until the late 1960s the 'Arab issue' was neither on the agenda, nor on the radar of sociologists."[28] The historian of ideas Jerzy Szacki's 1966 survey of Poles' attitudes toward other races and nations, in which Arabs were not even mentioned, serves as a case in point.

The Jew, the Arab, the Pole: the Ideological Field's Topography

To recount: it may be said that while Polish relations to Jews concerned first and foremost matters of domestic policy and were closely bound up in a deep, shared history, relations with Arabs, along with other Third World nationals, were a strategic instrument through which Poland sought to establish itself within the global Cold War–era political and economic order.[29] Examining these two types of relations—between Poles and Jews and between Poles and Arabs—through the prism of Gil Anidjar's concept of European identity and Jews and Arabs outlined at the beginning of this essay, allows one to grasp the way they were linked together within the ideological field established during the era of real socialism (often termed "actually existing socialism"). Before 1967, the figure of the Jew—semantically among the most freighted elements of the Polish political-cultural imagination—constituted a kind of test for the progressive vision of socialist Polishness as it was officially iterated. The figure of the Arab, in turn, which for most Poles was but a vague idea of "brotherly peoples" from distant countries, served as a means of universalizing this new vision—that is, of framing it within the global project of emancipatory social progress.

---

28   Mustafa Switat, "Polsko-arabskie podróże—stracone szanse i profity," *Przegląd Orientalistyczny*, nos. 1/2 (265–66) (2018): 115–26, 123.
29   It was actually an order of "alternative globalizations" constituted by a web of relations between the Second and Third Worlds. See James Mark, Artemy M. Kalinovsky, and Steffi Marung, eds., *Alternative Globalizations: Eastern Europe and the Postcolonial World* (Bloomington: Indiana University Press, 2020).

That construction, however, was set on weak ideological foundations. The period in which it collapsed would be between 1967 and 1968.

March '68

March 1968 in Poland was a complex concatenation of tumultuous events through which several parallel crises manifested themselves. They unfolded in various spheres of social life, encompassing the state apparatus, military and Party structures, cultural milieus, universities, youth groups, notably students, and workplaces, as well as the streets of Polish cities and towns. The sociologist Zygmunt Bauman, who was forced out of his job as department chair at the University of Warsaw and into exile in the wake of these events, described the situation in Poland then:

> The working class, silent but mysterious and having reasons enough to be unhappy, an explosively charged young generation, embittered intellectuals, and a frustrated new middle class, the core of the "popular" regime, and, over that, the Party leadership, frightened and uncertain of everything and of everyone— this, then, was a situation that by all tenets of Leninist analysis must be defined as revolutionary.[30]

It was a situation joined by international tensions that included a political crisis in neighboring Czechoslovakia—today known as the Prague Spring, and soon to be terminated by Warsaw Pact forces— an intensification of the Vietnam War, mounting tensions in Soviet-Chinese relations, China's production of a hydrogen bomb, the escalating arms race between the Soviet Union and the United States, and fears of Israeli efforts to produce nuclear weapons.

Social tensions in Poland were fueled mainly by economic issues along with the gradual curtailing of civil liberties that had been wrestled from the regime since the political thaw of the mid 1950s. The event that catalyzed March 1968 was the banning of a National Theater production of *Forefathers' Eve*, a symbolic nineteenth-century play by the national poet, Adam Mickiewicz. The ban,

30   Quoted in Jerzy Eisler, *Marzec 1968: Geneza, przebieg, konsekwencje* (Warsaw: Państwowe Wydawnictwo Naukowe, 1991), 139.

provoked by the adaptation's anti-Soviet undertones and by audiences using the performances for public displays of political dissent, then led to a wave of protests, including student demonstrations dispersed by the police, and to a Polish Writers' Union resolution demanding that censorship be abolished and artistic freedom restored.

A climax came on March 8 when Warsaw University students held a campus rally, despite the school administration's warnings that it would be illegal. The authorities reacted by sending in riot police and working-class "volunteers" who brutally assaulted the rally, using rubber truncheons and arresting both students and instructors. Protests took place in other Polish cities as well, some of them resulting in clashes with the police. The regime's response was to organize hundreds of mass rallies at workplaces across the country, where activists and workers "spontaneously" declared support for the Party line and condemned "troublemakers." Over three hundred students were expelled or suspended from universities, and more than eighty protesters were jailed.

The direction of subsequent events was set by decision-making circles within the Ministry of Internal Affairs, led by Mieczysław Moczar, which put forth an officially sanctioned interpretation of the events through subservient mass media. Identifying enemies and their alleged goals became a signal for launching a cruel political witch hunt. According to the mainstream interpretation, the number-one enemy were "Zionists" acting on orders of the Israeli–West German alliance; their objective was to brand Poles as unrepentant anti-Semites and blame them for the Holocaust.[31] These "Zionists" were portrayed as traitors collaborating with the imperialist West and seeking to ruin the achievements of socialist Poland. The implication was that often they had been members of the Stalinist-era political elite (in which Jews featured prominently), now dissatisfied with changes ushered in by the de-Stalinization process. In turn, the official narrative contended, their children inspired the student protests—socially privileged and well off, unlike hard-working "ordinary" Poles.

31   Piotr Osęka, *Syjoniści, inspiratorzy, wichrzyciele: Obraz wroga w propagandzie marca 1968* (Warsaw: Żydowski Instytut Historyczny, 1999).

In the March '68 propaganda, attacks against "Zionists" were coupled with the vilification of "revisionists," a term applied to intellectuals, writers, and artists who contested orthodox Marxism-Leninism, thus promoting "ideological subversion" and "Western decay." The propaganda, in seeking to mobilize the public against "enemies of the people" and induce self-righteous citizens to join the witch hunt, provided a channel for articulating social frustration—but also for settling personal scores. Its ultimate meaning was anti-Semitic, first and foremost: "Zionist" was an euphemism for Jew, even if many of those under attack for their alleged "Zionist" sympathies had little to do with Jewishness.[32] The second target of the smear campaign was the intelligentsia.

This massive anti-Semitic media campaign ended on June 24, when First Secretary Władysław Gomułka forbade the press from using the term "Zionism." But the campaign's effects were far reaching, and would prove long lasting. Among Polish Jews and Poles of Jewish descent, it would continue to evoke recollections of historic pogroms and of genocidal experiences from the Second World War. It struck at the foundations of personal and material security, costing people jobs and careers and stripping them of their rights to function normally and raise the next generations in Polish society. March '68 resulted in an exodus of Jews—as many as fifteen thousand, around half the remaining Jewish population of Poland, who departed on one-way passports, forced in effect to renounce their citizenships—that practically ended the centuries-long history of the Jewish minority in the country. Jan T. Gross (who had been among the student activists as well as those emigrating from Poland, in 1969 to the US) summed up the situation: "Poland's communist rulers fulfilled the dream of Polish nationalists by bringing into existence an ethnically pure state."[33]

32   Dariusz Stola, *Kampania antysyjonistyczna w Polsce 1967–1968* (Warsaw: Instytut Studiów Politycznych Polskiej Akademii Nauk, 2000).
33   Gross, *Fear*, 243.

The Six-Day War, "Anti-Zionism," and the Ideological Field's Implosion

To grasp the meaning of the symbolic confrontation between the figures of the Jew, the Arab, and the Pole, which occurred in March '68 and is the focus of this essay, it is necessary to go back in time and focus on the consequences that the Six-Day War in 1967 had for Polish sociopolitical reality. The war is typically indicated within Polish contexts as a catalyst in domestic processes that led up to March 1968, and as a contributing factor in the abrupt popularity of "Zionist" as a proxy term for Jew during the 1968 witch hunt. While dominant interpretations of these events pay only marginal attention to the Arab thread, I assert that untangling the Polish-Jewish drama that culminated in March '68 requires attributing to that thread a more fundamental role. First, it is necessary to explain the significance that the Six-Day War and March events, including their anti-Jewish component, held in Polish-Arab relations, then to explicate more general ideological and political transformations related to it that occurred in Polish society.

The Six-Day War, which broke out on June 5, 1967, was fought between Israel and the combined forces of Jordan, Syria, and Egypt; its outbreak had been preceded by years of tensions between the Jewish state and its Arab neighbors. When Egypt announced the Straits of Tiran closed to Israeli vessels—a key shipping channel for Israel's Red Sea port, Eilat—the confrontation quickly escalated. Israel chose to launch a pre-emptive strike, taking the opposing armies completely by surprise. In a matter of days, it had neutralized those forces, destroying much of the Egyptian air force and inflicting heavy losses on Arab troops. Israel seized the Gaza Strip, the Sinai Peninsula, the Golan Heights, and East Jerusalem, effecting an occupation that continues to this day and that is illegal by international law. The Jewish military's rapid and resounding victory was not only a humiliation for Arab leaders, especially the Egyptian president, Gamal Abdel Nasser, but also for that country's main political and military ally, the Soviet Union.

In the Eastern bloc, the war's outcome provoked nervous reactions. The conflict was widely perceived as a proxy war between the Soviet Union and the United States, with fears that it could spill over to Europe. At a hurriedly convened conference in Moscow, Warsaw Pact leaders (except Romania) decided to sever diplomatic ties with Israel; in Poland, the break was announced on June 12 and people began to hoard food. The war exposed the lack of military preparedness among the Soviets' Arab allies, which cast doubts over Eastern European countries' security, as their Soviet-built defense systems were similar to those Egypt had imported. In Polish military ranks, those whose support for the Arab side wasn't voiced loudly enough were accused of favoring the Israelis and demoted. Similar situations were soon spreading in other sectors as well.

On June 19, 1967, Gomułka gave a speech now regarded as the fuse that ignited the anti-Semitic purge that would reach its apogee in March '68. The Party leader referred to the conflict in the Middle East and the reactions it was eliciting across Poland, pinpointing those who were being inconsistent with the official Party line: "those who in the face of a threat to world peace, and therefore to Poland's security and the peaceful work of our nation, opt for the aggressors, the peace-breakers, and for imperialism."[34] This, Gomułka stated, applied to the "Zionist milieus of Polish Jews,"[35] indicating that they should consider emigrating to Israel. The position of the authorities, he stressed, was that "every Polish citizen should have only one homeland—People's Poland."[36] He also spoke of a "fifth column"—a term that was left out of the transcript published in newspapers the next day. Gomułka's speech had not been vetted among the Party leadership, and was criticized by some members; others took it as a signal for an anti-Jewish campaign.

This June 1967 speech jump-started a discourse that may be described as a new space of symbolic confrontation between the figures of the Pole, the Jew, and the Arab. In this discourse, an ideologically established solidarity between the Pole and the Arab served as a polarization motif between the Jew and the Pole—in

34   Władysław Gomułka, "Przemówienie na VI Kongresie Związków
Zawodowych 19 czerwca 1967," in *Przemówienia: 1967* (Warsaw: Książka i
Wiedza, 1968), 202.
35   Gomułka, "Przemówienie," 201.
36   Gomułka, "Przemówienie," 201.

effect, a lever for what was about to take place in the anti-Semitic purge of 1968. Using the term "Zionist" made it possible to both condemn anti-Semitism and attack Jews, while defining as Jews—meaning strangers/traitors—those Poles (Polish Jews, Jewish Poles) who weren't demonstrating the required political solidarity with the Arabs.[37] It can be said, therefore, that under the circumstances of the Cold War balance of power and in the wake of the Six-Day War, the figure of the Arab became the trigger resulting in a final rupture of the tense symbolic bond between the Pole and the Jew. That said, the rupture did not apply solely to the centuries-long relations between the ethnic majority in Poland and the Jewish minority, but was also an operation that would be effected at the level of individual identities, with people forced to choose between their Polishness and their Jewishness—or, most often, having the latter forced on them.

This interrelation between the Pole, the Jew, and the Arab had something paradoxical about it: a germ of self-destruction that from 1967 to 1968 already heralded an implosion of the ideological field in which the PRL would officially function until 1989. That is, precisely as an anti-imperialist alliance with the Arab world was most radically affirmed in the name of progress and internationalism, with "Zionists" pilloried for the sake of that alliance, a nationalist mobilization underlying the "anti-Zionist"—in fact, anti-Semitic—campaign subverted the logic of this field. However, at the same time this was also being subverted by the grassroots, anti-systemic opposition exemplified in the popular slogan "*our* Jews have defeated *their* Arabs." The slogan held little sympathy for Jews and much antipathy for Poland's communist regime, which, in tandem with the USSR, had made solidarity with "brotherly" Arab nations into a matter of political dogma.

The Six-Day War was an event that violently and permanently transformed the balance of power in the Middle East and redefined Israeli-Arab relations, subordinating them to the logic of the

---

37   Symptomatically, Antoni Słonimski, the renowned Polish poet of Jewish descent, when commenting on Gomułka's June 19 speech, asked rhetorically: "I understand I am supposed to have one homeland, but why does it have to be Egypt?"

Cold War. One consequence was a strengthening of Israel's international standing, thanks chiefly to a closer alliance with the US. These changes also impacted how both Polish-Jewish and Polish-Arab relations were transformed during March '68. The several thousand Jews remaining in post-March Poland began to be comparable in number to the Third World citizens studying in Polish universities. The break in diplomatic ties with Israel was accompanied by a boom in contacts with Arab countries: Syria and Iraq opened embassies in Warsaw in 1968, and Poland began staunchly supporting the Palestinians in their conflict with Israel, which led to the Palestine Liberation Organization (PLO) opening a mission in Warsaw and to Poland adhering to a pro-Palestinian agenda in the UN Forum.[38] Playing a special role in this regard would be the Committee of Solidarity with the Nations of Asia and Africa, which promoted the Palestinian cause and in 1970, as part of the Social Solidarity Fund, organized a campaign called "A Plane Full of Milk for Arab Kids."[39] From the late 1960s on, there was also a steady rise in the knowledge transfer to Arab countries and in the provision of university scholarships for Arab students, as detailed above.

The Jew, the Arab, the Pole: Reconfiguring Relations after March '68

It may seem that the events of 1967 to 1968, which led to the emigration of Jews from Poland and the severing of diplomatic relations with the Israeli state—labeled reactionary and imperialist—paved the way for closer relations between Poles and Arabs along with other Third World nations, as part of a policy of internationalism and progress. However, adopting the perspective outlined above leads to more complex conclusions.

38   This included supporting the UN resolutions granting observer status to
the PLO in the UN General Assembly (1974), determining Zionism to be
a form of racism and racial discrimination (1975), and rejecting the
declaration by Israel that Jerusalem was its capital (1980). See Jarosław
Jarząbek and Marcin Szydzisz, "Beyond 'Recognition': The Polish
Perspectives on Israeli and Palestinian National Identities: Preliminary
Assumptions of Research," Polish Political Science Yearbook, no. 2 (47) (2018),
319–30, 324.
39   Jerzy Piotrowski, Stosunki Polski z krajami arabskimi (Warsaw: Polski Instytut
Spraw Międzynarodowych, 1989), 54.

The implosion of the ideological field in which Poland's policy was embedded was due to an ominous new rise in nationalist tendencies within the country, notwithstanding its alleged progressiveness and internationalism. It is not without reason that some researchers, in describing the process, refer to "national communism."[40] This ideological shift is notable in propaganda publications from the period immediately after March '68, where phraseology became markedly different from the discourse such periodicals had previously promoted. What's striking in the new phraseology is the strong affirmation of national values, the revision of previous historical valuations, and the critique of a "dogmatic-sectarian" (or even "far left") fetishization of internationalism, which could reputedly degenerate into harmful "cosmopolitism" and "national nihilism."[41] This change of rhetorical emphasis points clearly to a crisis in the regime's legitimation strategy and to an exhaustion of the revolutionary language that had previously been utilized.

March '68 can thus be interpreted as a moment when an intensifying atrophy becomes evident in an ideological framework that made it possible not only to suppress the expression of anti-Jewish xenophobia but to inspire and justify the building of official relations between Poland and Third World countries. This is consistent with the diagnosis that Jerzy Szacki would formulate twenty years later: "March marks the 'end of the ideological age' in the Polish communist movement. At least of ideology taken seriously, treated in a non-instrumental manner."[42] Paradoxically, the above assertion is also confirmed by a change in post-March thinking, described by the philosopher Michał Siermiński, among left-leaning opposition activists who, as "revisionists" before March, had called for systemic reform in the name of Marxist principles. Arrested during March events then released from jail, they decided that their previous

40   Marcin Zaremba, *Komunizm, legitymizacja, nacjonalizm: Nacjonalistyczna legitymizacja władzy w komunistycznej Polsce* (Warsaw: Wydawnictwo TRIO; Instytut Studiów Politycznych PAN, 2001). It should be noted that nationalism, according to Zaremba, had accompanied the installation of communism in Poland from the very beginning.
41   Wojciech Pomykało, ed., *Patriotyzm, ideologia, wychowanie* (Warsaw: Wydawnictwo Ministerstwa Obrony Narodowej, 1968), 19, 23.
42   Jerzy Szacki, "8 marca 1988 roku," *Krytyka: Kwartalnik Polityczny-Warszawa*, nos. 28/29 (1988): 21–23.

reflective categories were inadequate and, rejecting notions of progress, reaction, or historical necessity, began searching for a new political language capable of encompassing issues of national identity, including its religious aspects.[43]

After March events led to the exodus of Polish Jews, the only "others" whose presence could attest to Poland's internationalism, progressivism, and "universal solidarity" were from the Third World: in large part Arabs, Africans, Vietnamese. At work under the surface of that declarative internationalism, though, were tendencies that made Polish politics increasingly "socialist in form and national in content." As literary critic Przemysław Czapliński demonstrates, this trend also manifested itself in cultural production, where the start of the 1970s saw a revival of Sarmatian motifs (for example, in hugely popular film adaptations of the Henryk Sienkiewicz novels *Colonel Wołodyjowski* in 1969 and *The Deluge* in 1974). Approval of these motifs seemed to be the regime's ideological concession, because they brought issues of nobility, class difference, war, and religion into play, while the officially proclaimed values were of equality, work, and religious indifference. In reality, as Czapliński notes, this approval was meant to build imaginary community in place of an identity void that communist ideology failed to fill.[44]

Symptoms of the communist project's ideological disintegration can be found in political and cultural processes within Polish society, and also in the sphere of economic relations between the Second and Third Worlds. As historians James Mark and Quinn Slobodian indicate, the project of an alternative anti-imperialist economic system to that of Western capitalism proved unfeasible, and ideas of shared progress for these regions soon gave way to prac-

43   Michał Siermiński, *Dekada przełomu: Polska lewica opozycyjna 1968–1980*
(Warsaw: Instytut Wydawniczy Książka i Prasa, 2016).
44   Przemysław Czapliński, "Plebejski, populistyczny, posthistoryczny:
Formy polityczności sarmatyzmu masowego," *Teksty Drugie*, no. 1 (151)
(2015): 21–45, 24.

tices of building quasi-imperial relations between them. As a result, the paradigm of the First, Second, and Third Worlds was replaced by a division between the Global South and the Global North.[45]

That rearrangement was a harbinger of a new geopolitical order that would be firmly established in 1989 with the Cold War's end, the ultimate collapse of socialist internationalism, and the reorientation to the West of countries including Poland. One consequence was an official rejection of a pro-Arab orientation in foreign policy and the adoption of a pro-Israeli stance (in 1990, diplomatic relations were reestablished between Poland and Israel). This meant a new chapter in the relations between the Jew, the Arab, and the Pole. As the decades that followed would show, it was not to be free from the xenophobic hostility that found earlier expression in March '68.

Translated from the Polish by Marcin Wawrzyńczak.

45   James Mark and Quinn Slobodian, "Eastern Europe in the Global History of Decolonization" in *The Oxford Handbook of the Ends of Empire*, ed. Martin Thomas and Andrew S. Thompson (Oxford: Oxford University Press, 2018), 1–28, 10.

Beata Kowalska, a feminist sociologist and professor at the Jagiellonian University in Kraków, has focused in her research on Muslim feminism and the situation of women in Middle Eastern countries for many years. This topic has permitted her to combine academic fascinations with experience working on programs for gender equality in Poland and abroad. Her research is reflected in courses she teaches in development studies and in gender studies. She is interested in gender dimensions of citizenship and in processes of grassroots struggles for social recognition. Recent books in Polish: *Women's Development of Citizenship in the Hashemite Kingdom of Jordan* (2013); *Women's Rebellion: Black Protests and Women's Strikes* (2019); *Nowa Huta 1988: Snapshots from Utopia* (2020).

Prof. Kowalska has received the Pro Arte Docendi award, a top teaching prize. Major scholarships and lectures abroad include at the University of Cambridge, the Institute for Human Sciences in Vienna, the American Center for Oriental Research in Amman, the New School for Social Research in New York City, Rutgers University, and the University at Buffalo.

Inga Hajdarowicz is a PhD student at the Jagiellonian University in Kraków. In her research and activities, she raises issues of participatory democracy, grassroots mobilization, migration, and feminist movements. She is currently working on her dissertation on a feminist, grassroots approach to supporting Syrian women living as refugees in Lebanon.

BEATA KOWALSKA
INGA HAJDAROWICZ

UNWANTED LEGACY, AS TOLD BY ITS WITNESSES: ARAB STUDENTS IN PEOPLE'S POLAND

The social sciences make a distinction between history and collective memory. Remembering is an active, political choice, like forgetting. In researching this essay, we experienced this many times, seeking out and speaking with seven of some thousands of students from developing countries who made a key stop in Poland on their educational journeys, which then became their passports to a better life, along with three of their spouses. In the present, the memory of curiosity and openness toward students arriving on scholarship comes up against racist prejudices. Quite independently of the facts, what we have here is a dispute about memory. By the same token, each conflict is in part a struggle for the history that is told, for who will tell it, and for who will be heard.

The turning point in 1989 that began Poland's economic and political transformation[1] divided recent history along simple dualistic lines. Everything from before became bad, purportedly

---

1   The fall of the Iron Curtain, that European symbol dividing Western and Soviet spheres of influence, brought political and economic transformation to Central and Eastern Europe. The transition from centrally planned economies to capitalism was based on financial rules dictated by institutions including the International Monetary Fund and the World Bank. Those Structural Adjustment Program pillars were deep budget cuts, privatization, and market liberalization.

because only then, at the threshold of the 1990s, had our society landed on the right side of history. As we uncovered stories about a country devastated by war that had nonetheless invited young people from Third World countries—now referred to as the Global South—to its universities, our research resembled contemporary archaeology. Shards of personal memory reveal the first Arabic words learned a half-century ago by one of the present authors for welcoming Arab guests to a working-class elementary school in Kraków; the rector of the University of Basrah who came from Iraq to Poland to do his first degree, returning home after earning his doctorate, speaking fluent Polish; and Ali Chafour, also from Iraq, a Kurdish communist who remained to direct the observatory in Olsztyn for decades.

The Lebanese and Palestinian interviewees who spoke for this essay, who had studied in Poland in the 1970s and 1980s, then returned to their countries, are now in the professional elite. It is their voices we sought to hear,[2] to help draw open the curtain of forgetting in Poland and to help break through a strange social bashfulness, of not knowing what to do with this still-recent page of our history. From the point of view of today's discourse, when this page

2   The empirical part of this essay is based on in-depth interviews carried out by Inga Hajdarowicz in Lebanon in late 2018 and the first quarter of 2019 in association with Prof. Beata Kowalska. The research was one component of the East European—North African—Middle East Forum, a part of the 2019 Biennale Warszawa concerning Polish relations with Middle Eastern and North African countries, both from the historical perspective of several decades ago and from a contemporary point of view. The project included planning mechanisms for inter-regional cooperation to be utilized in the present day. See "East European—North African—Middle East Forum," *Biennale Warszawa*, accessed January 1, 2021, https://biennalewarszawa.pl/en/wschodnioeuropejsko-polnocnoafrykansko-bliskowschodnie-forum/.
Hajdarowicz collected the stories of two Palestinians and five Lebanese who lived, studied, and worked in Poland, traveling there between 1975 and 1989 then completing language courses in Opole or Łódź and studying physiotherapy, stomatology, archeology, civic engineering, and energy and aeronautical engineering in Opole, Wrocław, Warsaw, and Łódź. All returned to Lebanon after the end of the civil war, mostly in the early 1990s. The research also included three interviews with Polish women married to interviewees. Contacts to the interviewees were obtained through the Polish diaspora, the Palestinian community in Poland, and personal contacts with architects in Lebanon. The interview signature that accompanies the quotes used in this essay refers to the nationality of an interviewee and the date the meeting took place. Names used here are pseudonyms, as the participants were assured of anonymity before the interviews.

is acknowledged at all, it is seen as an embarrassment, as the prevailing attitude about refugees from the Middle East has polarized the Polish political scene and the whole of society, with vilification from politicians resulting in street violence against people with darker skin in Polish towns.[3]

The Polish Development School

This practice of social archaeology, though it is unsettling from the point of view of today's dominant discourse, is full of astonishing moments. One of these came in 1999 when British bookshops stocked Amartya Sens' new book, *Development as Freedom*. The future Nobel laureate's biographical note featured Warsaw seminars he had participated in. Again, in Poland today, that chapter of intellectual history remains largely forgotten. Yet under the aegis of the UN, the Polish capital had hosted an annual Advanced Course in Planning for Economists from Developing Countries, bringing together young scholars from Africa, Asia, and South America. Lecturers were stars of development economics at the time, including Maurice Dobb, Sen's intellectual mentor and a British Marxist, and Jane Robinson, a central figure in post-Keynesian economics, as well as Paul Rosenstein-Rodan, born in Kraków, who originated the Big Push Model postulating the accelerated industrialization of developing countries attained through large foreign-investment programs.

It thus became possible for us to identify the lively, inspiring community of economists and sociologists active in the 1960s in and around the Warsaw Center of Research on Underdeveloped Economies. One key publication reflecting the optimism of postwar thinking about development was Walt Whitman Rostow's 1960 book, *The Stages of Economic Growth*.[4] Rostow presents a linear theory of development by which each nation has to follow the same path, from a largely subsistence-agricultural economy to a mature

3   In Poland during the European migrant crisis in 2015, the main political
         dispute concerned its EU quota for admitting several thousand refugees.
         The political strategy that was unleashed of inciting fear and contempt
         against migrants was a deciding factor in the party Law and Justice (PiS)
         taking power, whose campaign relied on xenophobic slogans and whose
         government continues to do so.
4   W. W. Rostow, *The Stages of Economic Growth: A Non-Communist Manifesto*
         (Cambridge: Cambridge University Press, 1960).

industrial society based on up-to-date technology and mass consumption. Underdevelopment can be overcome and each society has the opportunity to progress on the basis of its own resources. What is needed is political will and an essential organizational foundation from the state.[5]

Many posited solutions implementing a single decisive factor to counter inhibited development—whatever that particular factor may have been, what was widely seen was the possibility of breaking deadlocks, and of underdeveloped countries advancing. Rosenstein-Rodan formulated his views in a similar way, believing that industrialization, preferably based on light industry, was the best approach to job creation and to increasing income and spending power. The stimulus for this would be state investment, creating infrastructure while educating the workforce.

Rosenstein-Rodan was among the Polish economists who, during the Second World War, had worked in Britain on modernization plans for nations then termed "backward." These economists' intellectual appeal and academic positions derived from two somewhat paradoxical features: their thorough knowledge of Western economic thinking, having graduated from Western universities, and their empirical knowledge of reality in those "backward" countries, having come up in one.[6] Eastern European countries were ideal for testing proposed economic models, which could then be implemented in other parts of the developing world. The advantage those countries had over postcolonial states was their possession of modern statistical mechanisms with which population and other data could be collected and shared with international organizations.

In the mid-1950s some from this group of outstanding specialists returned to Poland. They had gained experience working as development advisors in international organizations and

5   See John McKay, "Reassessing Development Theory," in *International Development: Issues and Challenges*, ed. Damien Kingsbury et al. (New York: Palgrave Macmillan, 2008).
6   Małgorzata Mazurek at Columbia University has drawn attention to the inspiring research of Polish economists into poverty and underdevelopment in the Galicia region. Małgorzata Mazurek interviewed by Michał Sutowski, "Co się stało z polską szkołą (rozwoju)?" *Krytyka Polityczna*, January 22, 2016, https://krytykapolityczna.pl/kultura/historia/mazurek-co-sie-stalo-z-polska-szkola-rozwoju/.

for governments of developing countries. The sources of their decisions to return were political and of a two-fold nature: internal and external. In Poland then, the time of political thaw after Stalin's death had brought enormous hope for greater freedom, including in the sphere of research. In the US, meanwhile, the rise of McCarthyism and the associated political purges had resulted in many experts with leftist inclinations losing positions, including at the UN in New York City. The economists and sociologists who then created the Polish Development School (PDS) were interested in issues of transforming traditional societies, growth barriers, conceptualizing cultural development and underdevelopment, functions of mixed economies, planning, and also issues of economic and cultural hegemonies. Participating actively in international exchanges of knowledge and experiences, their input into the worldwide study of development was in part a result of their sensitivity to sociocultural contexts, the effects of colonial legacies, and the significances of ethnic diversity.

The viewpoints of PDS specialists, at once cosmopolitan and extensive, permitted local problems to be situated and examined in a detailed global perspective. This made it possible to create diagnostic tools for challenges that had rendered previous theories ineffective. "Polish economists in the 1960s," as the historian Małgorzata Mazurek has written, "used the tools of world scholarship to diagnose problems that the West did not even have terms for."[7] Analyses and policies they proposed left behind the schematic thinking present in mainstream political-economy textbooks, including those espousing the official Marxist line. This in turn meant that in Poland, although the communist authorities tolerated their employment as advisors or theoreticians, their influence on real changes was kept well in check.

For over a decade, leading PDS representatives, including Michał Kalecki, Oskar Lange, Czesław Bobrowski, Jan Halpern, and Zofia Dobrska, made crucial contributions in defining the

7   Sutowski, "Co się stało z polską szkołą (rozwoju)?"

direction of policies in developing countries.[8] Some successes were spectacular, including a report on the prospects of change in global work distribution for the first UN Conference on Trade and Development. Nevertheless, with the onset of the government's "anti-Zionist" campaign and as student protests inadvertently provided cover for removing dozens of academics from their universities,[9] the Polish Development School community was broken up. Leading members in many cases then found work at universities abroad or in UN agencies.[10]

In the context of this essay, it is worth noting the connections from this group of specialists in linking development with knowledge and education. It was the rule that, except for strictly economic questions, proposed programs focused attention on the importance of cooperation among the cultural, artistic, and scientific disciplines, and on the struggle against discrimination on economic or cultural grounds, and to opposing racism. Emphases were laid on recruiting local staff and investing in education and culture,[11] while the effectiveness of policies introduced largely by experts from outside, as was then being done by the International Monetary Fund (IMF) and others, was questioned.

Pupils, Students, Scholars

Working in the Global South provided Polish academics more freedom than at home. In Ghana, the Economics Department

8   Titles from Michał Kalecki's reports and articles, to provide one example, indicate the great scope of this work: "Report on Main Current Economic Problems in Israel"; "Hypothetical Outline of the Five-Year Plan 1961–1965 for the Cuban Economy"; "Problems of Financing Economic Development in a Mixed Economy"; "Unemployment in Underdeveloped Countries."

9   Poland was struck in 1968 by overlapping and conflicting social phenomena: the anti-Semitic campaign led by the communist authorities that has been described above, which forced some thirteen thousand Jewish Poles or more to emigrate on one-way passports, while an anti-censorship protest organized by left-wing intellectuals and students revolted against it.

10   Ignacy Sachs worked in Paris at the School for Advanced Studies in the Social Sciences (EHESS); Jerzy Tepicht, an authority on peasant economies, also worked in France; Stefan Strelcyn, leading expert in African affairs, taught in London at the School of Oriental and African Studies; Włodzimierz Brus taught at Oxford; and Kazimierz Łaski at Austrian research institutes and universities in Vienna and Linz.

11   See Błażej Popławski, "Polska Szkoła Rozwoju—zapomniany paradygmat studiów nad transformacją Globalnego Południa," *Kultura współczesna* 3, no. 72 (2012): 184–96.

in Accra comprised academics grouped around Michał Kalecki, the leading light in the PDS. President Kwame Nkrumah, a key initiator of the Organization of African Unity, believed that Eastern bloc development planners were particularly capable of understanding situations in postcolonial countries. The question arises today, from the perspective of postcolonial or subaltern studies, of the extent to which it may have been possible to take local conditions into account in order to avoid mistakes in imposing development visions while conducting what had been regarded as civilizing missions. This requires further research.

Along with academics, there was at this time an influx into the Global South of architects, engineers, and various other specialists from the Eastern bloc. By the end of the 1970s there were over five thousand Polish specialists working in Libya, around 12 percent of all overseas personnel, and by the early 1980s this number had doubled.[12] Polish professors lectured in Sudan at the University of Khartoum, and were helping establish medical-study programs in Morocco, Algeria, and Libya. Academic and technical contacts with developing countries resulted in agreements being signed for young people to study in Poland. The few publications on this topic barely touch on the scale of the exchange—even accurate numbers of participants are as yet unclear—and painting a clear picture of this cooperation will require thorough archival research, in addition to gathering information about the experiences of the individuals involved.

Annually from the 1960s to the end of the 1980s, from several dozen to several hundred overseas students were studying in Poland. For example, in 1973, 216 citizens of African countries completed their educations in Poland, with 39 graduating from high school, 94 from university, 46 completing postgraduate studies, and 37 concluding professional training. Earlier, such training had been more accessible: from Egypt alone, up to 130 people had been coming per year. By the early 1980s, the number of Arab students had reached several thousand in total.[13] They tended to study technical subjects: economics or medicine. At times, as several professors at

12   Jacek Knopek, "Stosunki Polski z Afryką Arabską po II wojnie światowej"
            Forum Politologiczne, vol. 3 (2003): 154.
13   Knopek, "Stosunki Polski z Afryką Arabską," 149.

Kraków University of Technology recall, they made up almost half a class. The scale of this educational program is confirmed indirectly by one of the more intriguing cultural-exchange initiatives of the era. In Tunisia in 1965, the first Polish Radio Listeners' Club started, expanding in the 1970s to several more in that country, to thirty-four in Algerian towns and a few others in Morocco.

One aim of that initiative had been to maintain contact with those graduates of Polish schools in their local communities.[14] It is some of their voices that we now turn to.

Memories versus Absence
After the end of the Second World War, Poland accepted the foreign-policy priorities shared by the socialist countries, supporting colonial societies as they pursued independence. Over about the next four decades, for example, Palestinian students on scholarships were a sizeable group at Polish universities, in symbolic solidarity with and support of their right to self-determination.

Student recruitment was usually arranged through left-wing Arab political parties. In the case of the Lebanese who were interview subjects in the present research, it had been local socialist and communist parties, while the Palestinians students were sent to Poland by the Palestine Liberation Organization (PLO).

While having political parties and organizations as intermediaries might indicate ideological motives in the scholarship program, our interviews indicate that their main reason was limited access to education at home. In Lebanon, higher education was private and very expensive and remains so, accessible only to the very rich. For less well-to-do families and those with more children, even if middle-class, a scholarship to an Eastern bloc country was often the only way of continuing their education. Ongoing war in Lebanon from the mid 1970s was another factor that made studying at home impossible. Khalil (pseudonyms are used; see footnote 2), a Lebanese who left for the Warsaw University of Technology, summed up the reasons:

> Due to the war there was no way to find a spot [in university] in Lebanon. I have a cousin who was working

14   Knopek, "Stosunki Polski z Afryką Arabską," 166.

> closely with some party then, and he suggested I go
> abroad, but not particularly to Poland. I applied, took
> the exam, then they made me choose between the
> Soviet Union, Romania, or Poland. So I chose Poland.
> (LIBAN25.01.2019)

Before they were accepted, there was an exam covering basic subjects, as with the *matura* exam taken as Poles and Europeans finish high school. For some, brochures they found at the embassy upon taking this exam were their initial information about the country they would study in. Other interviewees had heard about socialist countries from friends who had been on scholarships earlier.

While decades have passed since those first trips, every interviewee had vivid memories of their arrivals in Poland. They laughed telling stories of difficulties getting to the language school where they were to spend nine months, and about challenges of the first days in a new country.

> So I arrived. The plane landed and I took a taxi to the
> Central Station. Nobody was waiting for us [at Warsaw's
> airport], as there was supposed to be. But they hadn't
> turned up. Well, never mind. So I went with another
> student to Central Station.

> At home, to get from Beirut to the mountains where I
> live, there's one bus a day. So I thought there'd be one
> train a day to Łódź. So when I missed one, I didn't know
> there'd be another. I went to look for a taxi. There was
> this guy in an old Warszawa[15] and he asks "Where to?"
> I say "Lodz." He says "Lodz?" So I show him the map. He
> says "Łódź, not Lodz" [pronounced like "woodge" in Pol-
> ish]. Okay, right. "How much do you want?" "Twenty" [in
> English]. "Excuse me?" "Twenty dollars." Okay, off we go.

> This was the very beginning of the war in Lebanon and
> people there were being kidnapped. And this guy's
> driving along, and the first impression is that roads
> have no bends in Poland, while here in Lebanon there

15   Then a common Polish car.

are a hell of a lot of bends. By Sochaczew, I was scared that he was kidnapping us. Then in Poland safety was a hundred percent certain, there wasn't any risk. But I say "Stop." I was saying it with my hands, but I was saying it. He got it, because of course he didn't know any foreign language.

He stopped. I say "Where are you taking us?" All with hand gestures. He says "Łódź." We had the little map we got at the embassy. On that little map, it looked like a short distance to this Łódź, and not a hundred and twenty kilometers. "Where are you headed? Where are we now?" In the end, he drove on a bit, and in a hundred meters, there was a Sochaczew sign, and he shows us Sochaczew on the map. I say "Good, I'm not being kidnapped," and we drive on. And then we got there. (LIBAN13.02.2019)

And we arrived. The first of October, I remember that at one in the afternoon we were in Warsaw. We phoned the embassy, but the embassy was already closed and nobody answered. We had some juice, there were five of us, two girls and three guys. When we took a taxi to Central Station, just by chance we saw someone who looked kind of Arab. "Are you an Arab?" "Yes. Where are you from?" We said Lebanon. He was Palestinian. He found a phone box, this was before mobile phones, he phoned his friends, they came. They invited us to a restaurant. By then it was five o'clock and they bought us tickets to Łódź. One guy had been there the year before, and he went with us. (PALEST23.11.2018)

In Poland, there were three main language schools for students from abroad, the first established in Łódź, the others later in Kielce and Opole. These were where scholarship students spent their first nine months, preparing to study in Polish. The first three months were to gain general knowledge of the language, the rest to learn specialist

vocabulary according to the subject to be studied. The class participants were from the Middle East and from numerous other
developing countries.

> They told us we come from sixty-nine countries. In my
> group there was one Palestinian, three of us Lebanese,
> and five from Latin America, from different countries,
> but most from Ecuador. There was a Cypriot and two
> Nigerians. That was the whole group. (LIBAN25.01.2019)

The language school in Łódź had a residence hall, rooms, classrooms,
a small cafeteria, a little shop—students had all their basic needs
catered for in situ. Though this might have made it unnecessary for
them to go out, our protagonists were keen to get to know the envi-
rons of their new homes. It was a chance to discover their foreign
surroundings and to practice Polish, which they had less than a year
to master at university level.

> I liked Łódź. I know Łódź like my own home. For the first
> month, obviously we didn't know which way was which.
> So I'd always buy some tickets and climb on [a local
> bus] in any direction, then go three or four stops look-
> ing at the buildings so I'd know how to get back. I'd walk
> around a bit then go back in the same direction. That
> was how I got to know Łódź. (LIBAN25.01.2019)

Before they'd come to Poland, our interviewees often didn't know
exactly what they would be studying. Their futures depended on several factors: exam results (taken at their Polish embassies), places
available for particular courses and fields, and the Polish language
exam concluding their initial phase of study. Some got in to study
medicine as they had dreamed of, while others found themselves at
a technical university instead. Sometimes the subject they finally
studied was a complete surprise, like the story of Maheer who,
instead of learning to be a dentist, became an archaeologist.

> I took the entrance exam for dentistry. They told me I
> got in, but because of the limited number of places, I'd
> have to choose something else. Well, I wanted to
> escape from Lebanon. I agreed to do political econom-
> ics, but with the thought that once I was in Poland I'd
> change that.

> And that's what happened. I got the scholarship and left Lebanon for Poland, left on September 14, 1975. As a scholarship student, of course I did the language course in Łódź for nine months. It was a preparatory language course, a little Polish history of course, and something from the field I was supposed to study. So there, while on the language course, I changed to Mediterranean archaeology. After all, what chance would I have with an MA in economics from a socialist country in a country like Lebanon, which has a free-market economy? I was always good at history at school, so that's how it went. Warsaw University, Mediterranean archaeology. (LIBAN22.01.2019)

After finishing language studies, while some students began their degree courses in the same city, others moved to a new place when necessary for their subject. Final decisions depended to a large extent on the kinds of scholarship and the places available in particular departments. Beginning their course work was rather challenging for most, mainly because of the language. Having studied in Polish only since arrival, they usually needed more time to absorb the material. Not knowing casual ways of speech created some distance between them and the other students in their year at first, but all the interviewees quickly bridged that gap and entered smoothly into academic and student life.

In the interviews, there were frequent stories about close relations with Polish women and men, whether at university or at work or in the local community. They described Poles as open and hospitable—but full of preconceptions, more from lack of experience or knowledge than prejudice. Postwar Poland had abruptly become almost entirely ethnically homogenous (the prewar population had been one-third ethnic minorities).

> "Arabs have camels"—where'd they get that from? Just imagine, the first time I ever saw a camel in my life was in the Wrocław Zoo. Honest. Ever seen a camel in Lebanon? (PALEST15.11.2018)

They were nice, there really wasn't any problem that we were Arabs. But sometimes they'd ask weird questions. Out of curiosity. They asked "Do you have potatoes in Lebanon? Do you drink milk?" Polish people weren't closed—they just didn't have any contact with other nations. They didn't know us, so sometimes those questions were weird. (PALEST23.11.2018)

Once I was at a tram stop with a friend from Nigeria. These people, a guy and his wife in their sixties, came up to him and rubbed him: they thought he had on body paint. Well you know Poland was never a colonial country, unlike Western Europe countries. That's why there was such limited contact with the outside world. They had their explorers who went places, and their scholars fascinated with the exotic.

But at that time, there were real limits to moving around. Just getting a passport was an undertaking, wasn't it? The average Pole who'd never left the country and had seen at most someone [Black] on TV, suddenly catches sight of somebody like that, right next to him, traipsing around town, riding trams, another human being, in no way different from him except for the color of his skin. Hence his reaction. (LIBAN22.01.2019)

No interviewees had memories of blatant unfriendliness—though as they said themselves, given their looks as Lebanese and Palestinians, they could have been taken for Greeks, Spaniards, or Italians. What comes across from Polish women who had gone out with Lebanese students is that the latter brought in some variety:

He had sneakers and frayed trousers of course. Not that that was the fashion, he just didn't have any others. So he went around in those trousers until they were worn through. His sweatshirt was pink. In those days, pink for a boy...? First time I'd ever seen anyone

> with a pink sweatshirt. And a coat, quite long, and elegant. And his curly hair, well...! (POL20.11.2018)

> All the boys and girls accepted him. There wasn't a problem with acceptance. Back then, it wasn't like now. We'd come back at night from the theater, the opera, a restaurant, or a dance. We'd come home on the night bus and nobody was afraid. It wasn't like now: "Arab, is that a Paki?" Everyone was happy the Arabs were coming, it meant restaurants were opening, dollars were on the black market, and business was taking off. (POL13.02.2019)

Although the interviewees had no complaints about how they were treated, from today's perspective some incidents recalled as awkward would now be termed racist:

> You know, Polish people used to call our building "the Zoo."
> Interviewer: Where did that name come from?
> I don't know. Well, because people living in it all came from outside Europe. Africa, Asia, Latin America. (LIBAN22.01.2019)

All interviewees were very active in organizations for overseas students. Extensive cultural activity took place, from concerts to discos and shows, providing opportunities for social contacts with others from home and including students from other places and Polish classmates. Khalil remembered the legendary Lebanon Days:

> There was a musical section. We asked our Latin American friends to do a dance or play a song, do something on guitar. From Palestine there was the *dabke*, it's a dance. Before that there'd been an official section, but very short. In a special room, a well-laid table. Music, dance, a film about Lebanon. (LIBAN25.01.2019)

Sometimes there was a joint action to support one country of origin. When Israel invaded Lebanon in 1982, one interviewee, with help from the Party's Central Committee, organized a plane for volunteers to fly to Lebanon to fight. An international group including Palestinians

and Tibetans took this Polish flight to Damascus. Another example
was of actions organized by student clubs in support of the Palestinian independence struggle.

During their stays they witnessed important events:
the rise of Solidarity, the imposition of martial law, public demonstrations that were brutally quashed. Though not involved directly,
they experienced some political and economic consequences:

> Martial law was an awful surprise for everyone. Not
> knowing what to do with yourself, sitting at home, mar-
> tial law, curfew, universities strikes. Our school had
> the longest one, thirty-one or twenty-seven days. And
> difficulties organizing necessities, food. We went to the
> dean and he said "I can't do anything for you. Stay at
> home, you'll get your money, your scholarships. Look
> for food, do some studying."
>
> And so it went. [...] We felt incarcerated, we went only
> where we had to in the daytime. Six o'clock and home.
> But there were moments—getting out under the trees,
> taking photos. Taking photos was outlawed. I took a lot.
> And I watched protests, but from a safe remove. Get-
> ting close was prohibited. (LIBAN25.01.2019)

Thanks to regular scholarship money, financial situations among the
foreign students were comparatively stable. Looking back, they
pointed out that this was better than for some Poles:

> I'm standing in line, people just about nothing to
> spend. If he's buying one tomato, I can't buy more. My
> morals won't let me, you know. I live here, and my
> scholarship is from this taxpayer. He's paying for my
> studies. (LIBAN22.01.2019)

Unlike Poles, if faced with accidents or extra costs, they couldn't rely
on family help. Some came from poor families who couldn't manage
any support for their children overseas. In addition, contact with
families in Lebanon could be very restricted during the war there:

> There was no way my parents could help. For starters,
> they had no money, and next there was zero contact.

> For a time in 1980, when there was war here in Leba-
> non, terrible war, the Israeli invasion, I communicated
> with them through the Red Cross. You were allowed to
> write one sentence, but no more. (LIBAN25.01.2019)

Lebanese and Palestinian students were aware of official state propaganda. They knew Poles were having a hard time, they could see
shortages, surveillance, and censorship. They also knew they were
in Poland to study, not for political activism. University was their one
opportunity to improve their situations—and by extension, the situation at home. Taha, a Palestinian who graduated in physiotherapy
and remains a practitioner, summed it up:

> Learning is your weapon for fighting poverty. It's the
> best weapon. And that's why I wanted to really study.
> (PALEST15.11.2018)

Those who finished studies in the 1980s remained to try their hands
on the local job market. Doctors were being sent to practice in
smaller places, while engineers stayed in university towns. Kareem,
a Palestinian dentist, got a job in the provinces, where he was joined
by his wife, also Palestinian, and recalls:

> I was well known about town. Once, I was at the mar-
> ket to get tomatoes or parsley, and this woman from
> out in the countryside said "Don't buy it, your wife's
> already been in and got it then." We were that well
> known. (PALEST23.11.2019)

Only one interviewee decided on a prompt return home, as finishing
his course coincided with the political and economic transformation in Poland and its attendant unemployment—fewer job offers for
Poles, let alone foreigners. The end of Lebanon's civil war shortly
thereafter then opened the way for returns. Interviewees arrived in
the war-ravished country after years of studying, working, and living
in Poland—in some cases, well over a decade.

For Palestinians, the decision to return was particularly
hard: as refugees in Lebanon, they had limited rights, and attain-
ments in higher education were no guarantee they could find legal
ways into the job market. Some today, even after more than half a century in Lebanon, must still live with many restrictions on property

ownership and employment. These have limited their access to professions including engineering and medicine, often forcing them to
work on the black market or in Palestinian camps or districts.[16]
        Most interviewees met their wives in Poland, who later
joined them in moving to Lebanon. Those who'd started families in
Poland wanted their children to learn other languages; Lebanon,
where French and English are norms, provided such an opportunity.
For the children, a new country and languages at school posed big
challenges, and fathers recalled their involvement being supportive
at the start. In all the interviews, an element of homesickness for
Poland and the years spent there arose, as did the difficulty of any
unequivocal assessment of having returned to Lebanon. In one discussion, Daniel and Alicja, his wife, who accompanied him in the
interview, said:

> Daniel: I was sure then that we'd be heading back, but
> it was probably the wrong decision.
> Alicja: Then again, what guarantee is there that we'd
> have done better in Poland? We just don't know.
> Daniel: I know, every place is okay except where we are,
> right?
> Alicja: The grass is always greener on the other side of
> the fence. (LIBAN13.01.2019)

Over their adult lives, due to their knowledge and abilities, all interviewees found appropriate work and built their lives in Lebanon. They
miss little things, people, regular aspects of public transportation,
the discipline and punctuality. They know Poland has also gone
through constant changes and isn't the country they spent youthful
years in. Khalil, who in the 1990s, after over a decade, returned home
with his wife and children, put things this way:

> I'm different, I'm not at home here. I'm not at home any-
> where. Really. Maybe in Poland, a little. I'm not at home

16   Jad Chaaban et al., *Survey on the Socioeconomic Status of Palestine Refugees in
Lebanon 2015* (Beirut: American University of Beirut; United Nations Relief
and Works Agency for Palestine Refugees in the Near East, 2016); Simon
Haddad, "The Palestinian Predicament in Lebanon," *Middle East Quarterly* 7,
no. 3 (2000): 29–40; Mariam Salim Hammoud, "Educational Obstacles
Faced by Palestinian Refugees in Lebanon," *Contemporary Review of the
Middle East* 4, no. 2 (2017): 127–48.

there either, because I'm not native in that sense, true. But here, I'm not at home. (LIBAN25.11.2018)

Interviewees took part in the activities of the Polish community in Lebanon, and continue to take part. They've contributed to renovating Beirut's Polish cemetery, supported Polish firms as intermediaries in importing Polish products (from car tires to matches), have maintained good relations with the Polish embassy, and regularly invite Poles to their homes. A graduate in mechanics, energy production, and aviation in Warsaw, with a rare talent for business, spoke of Lebanese-Polish trade relations:

> At one point, I was buying matches from Universal. I'd buy a couple of containers. My friend helped me, I'd buy these matches and then we'd print logos for different companies and I'd sell them. Then the chairman of this Universal says to my friend "When Daniel's here, come to my office." So I went and he greeted us nicely. He says "I really like it, that you've been buying these matches—but now you have to buy forty containers." I say "Professor"—he was a guy from some university— "we have three million people in Lebanon and everyone carries matches all the time. But there's no way we can sell that amount." (LIBAN13.02.2019)

Interviewees have supported their wives' active involvement in the Polish community, as they've organized meetings and festivals, compiled histories of Polish students in Beirut, and taught Polish. Those who have started families with Poles speak Polish at home. All visit Poland regularly; when money is limited, the priority is for the wives and children to travel. Those who have no family ties there have cultivated their language knowledge, reading books, keeping old magazines and dictionaries. Children of most interviewees have also studied in Poland.

Infrequent but regular visits there have enabled them to see changes occurring, including changes in attitudes to difference and diversity. One noteworthy story was from Magda, about escaping via Cyprus to Poland with her children in 2006, when Israel assaulted Lebanon. The journey was difficult: having lived with her husband and children in a Palestinian camp, she was not registered

in the Polish embassy's evacuation plan organized with Polish UN soldiers. Her only route had been an overcrowded boat to Cyprus; only
from there had they been able to reach Poland.

Her hometown, expected to be a safe haven for her
and her children, instead was the scene of more rough experiences,
as they were met with hostility in shops and the streets. Racist acts
directed against her children led her to decide to return to Lebanon
once Israel withdrew its military.

> Because they'd been playing in the sandbox and, being
> kids, maybe they'd been yelling and screaming with the
> other kids. And some man came to the sandbox, starts
> swearing and hit him in the face. I mean, first he [the
> man] said something to them, but they didn't under-
> stand because they couldn't speak colloquial Polish.
> And it was so upsetting for him: "Why did this stranger
> hit me?" It wasn't as hard for the younger one, maybe
> because those kids were younger and didn't know he
> was different. (POL20.11.2018)

In like fashion, Poland isn't always keen to embrace its former students. The situation is particularly complicated for Palestinians. The
Polish embassy requires extensive documentation with visa-appli-
cation forms. Proof of employment is one example. Often, as Palestinians are blocked from the formal job market at home, they can't
meet those requirements. In such situations, it becomes all the more
trying to face feelings of missing the country in which one spent one's
student years.

> Poland? I'm always homesick for Poland.
> (PALEST23.11.2018)

Remembering: A Challenge in the Present

Remembering means creating one's own version of a
lived history. Part of our aim in the present research is for memory
to work as a challenge to the xenophobic present. Research by sociologist Ziad Abou Saleh among students at Wrocław's institutions of
higher education shows but four students out of over two thousand
know any Arab living in Poland. In anonymous responses, only 17 percent showed a positive attitude toward helping Arab immigrants, or to

their presence in Poland. As many as 61 percent don't want Poland to allow them in. "The reason is poor education," Saleh said, "but also the utterly one-sided message coming from the media and politicians, who reinforce stereotypes and prejudices."[17]

Reminding Poles that Arab students have been part of student life at their institutions of higher education swims against the current of the dominant discourse today. It is important to recall the largely mutual curiosity that prevailed in that period, and the appreciation for abilities and distinctions those students brought to local communities. One interviewee was a footballer; another brought tae kwon do to Poland. The interviewees included an engineer on Metro construction in Warsaw, and a sound engineer who'd worked with the Film Production Studios in Łódź.

> I played football in Poland. I couldn't speak Polish yet but I played. From time to time, I'd get money or a crate of vodka. Really. (PALEST15.11.2018)

> I'd done martial arts in Lebanon. I was good, and I was first to bring tae kwon do to Poland. I introduced the discipline in Widzew. (LIBAN13.02.2019)

As regards the subjects of this essay, no matter how atrophying the process of societal amnesia has been to date, reality manages to continue eluding those exclusionary social and political patterns.

> I translate from Polish. Into Arabic. When I was little, I was very good at Arabic. Daddy was a poet and wrote verse. I've got his genes. There was a web page created about Adam Mickiewicz.[18] A proposal came that I translate the first book of *Pan Tadeusz* into Arabic.

---

17   Natalia Sawka, "Studenci z Wrocławia widzą w Arabach terrorystów: Zaskakujące wyniki badań," *Gazeta Wyborcza*, February 2, 2016, https://wroclaw.wyborcza.pl/wroclaw/1,35771,19567985,studenci-z-wroclawia-widza-w-arabach-terrorystow-zaskakujace.html.

18   Polish Romantic-era poet, one of the three national bards, omnipresent in the nation's culture and education.

They sent it to a professor of Oriental Studies from
Kraków. I got a letter from him saying "Keep going with
the translation—you have a feel for this Mickiewicz fellow." (LIBAN22.01.2019)

Translated from the Polish by Jolanta Scicińska.

Bolaji Balogun is a Leverhulme Trust Early Career Fellow in the Department of Geography at the University of Sheffield. He received his PhD in Sociology and Social Policy from the University of Leeds and has been a lecturer at the Department of European Studies, Kraków University of Economics. Balogun's research interests include blackness, race, and racialization in Central and Eastern Europe; his academic publications have appeared in journals including *Ethnic and Racial Studies* and *The Sociological Review*. He is currently working on the first book-length monograph examining race and racism in Poland, commissioned by Routledge and with the support of the Leverhulme Trust.

COLD WAR INTERNATIONALISM: THE MYTH OF RACE-BLIND EASTERN EUROPE

U S-Soviet relations remain a subject of intense debate in global-history scholarship and diplomacy. While partnering to defeat Nazi Germany in 1945, their alliance also contained "the single most contentious diplomatic issue of the war and the issue destined to remain at the heart of the Cold War," which then brought about the sharp division that followed between the two.[1] Over the years, this division deepened and was further intensified by diplomatic offensives. While no direct warfare pitted the United States (Western bloc) against the Soviet Union (Eastern bloc), the period termed the Cold War era was largely about ideological and geopolitical differences as both blocs sought to extend their influences globally.[2] Many of those influences were directly or indirectly manifested through psychological warfare, subtle (and unsubtle) surveillance, and global sports competitions, exacerbated by trade embargoes, propaganda campaigns, and technological rivalries.[3]

---

1   Robert J. McMahon, *The Cold War: A Very Short Introduction* (Oxford: Oxford University Press, 2003), 23.
2   Francis P. Sempa, *Geopolitics: From the Cold War to the 21st Century* (London: Routledge, 2017).
3   McMahon, *Cold War*, 75.

During the Cold War, the Western bloc, often pre-
sented as liberal-democratic, was tied to a network of its former colonies in Africa, Asia, the Caribbean, and South America. The Eastern
bloc, championed by the Soviet Union and its Communist Party, provided both physical and financial supports for many former Western
bloc colonies. This facilitated independence movements and, importantly, decolonizing projects that emerged in most African, Asian,
and Latin American countries after the Second World War.[4] This was
the point where the so-called "Third World nations" became a key
battleground. It was also a crucial point at which issues of race and
racism became Achilles' heels for both the Western and Eastern
blocs. Undoing the effects of race and racism would be an enormous
task. The reason for the magnitude of difficulty lies outside the limits of both blocs. Since long before the Cold War, race had been an
ideology embedded in the European imaginaries. With this unavoidable fact in mind, I will examine the origins of race and racism as concepts emerging in Europe, before offering a critical analysis of racism in the Soviet Union and across its satellite states.

Race and racism are not the same, yet are interde-
pendent concepts. Race is often accepted as a categorical distinction based on shared physiognomic characteristics. Racism, meanwhile, is commonly understood to be a belief in the existence of
different racial types and a superiority one race holds over another.
That superiority relies on physiognomy (skin color, hair color and
texture, facial and bodily features) as the assumption that biology
plays a decisive role in human categorization.

Race and racism are complex ideas, and they continue
to draw attention. For many scholars of race, a realistic starting point
for the understanding of race and racism requires a historical

4   Maxim Matusevich, "Soviet Anti-Racism and Its Discontents: The Cold
       War Years," in *Alternative Globalizations: Eastern Europe and the Postcolonial
       World*, ed. James Mark, Artemy M. Kalinovsky, and Steffi Marung
       (Bloomington: Indiana University Press, 2020), 229–50.

account of each idea's development, showing that the two concepts are neither natural nor biological.[5] The principal meaning of "race" has become white-black differentiation.[6]

Race historians have a great deal to say about this differentiation and its development in Europe. Although some forms of prejudice existed before the modern era,[7] race and its terminology entered Western languages in the mid-sixteenth century and had acquired its modern meaning by the late eighteenth century.[8] As a historical product, race then became a social phenomenon using a system of European categorization that emerged by the early nineteenth century.[9] By the start of that century, throughout the European orbit, race had taken up a sense of naturalness, a marking off of social arrangements, and was more or less taken for granted in ascribing superiority and inferiority, sameness and difference.[10] Through categorization processes, whiteness and blackness were invented and set in opposition to each other. European anthropologists played central roles in all this in a peculiar way.

In addition, anthropologists provided ordinary people with tools for assessing people's behavioral and mental aspects—in many circumstances, these assessments emerged in hasty judgments.[11] At the same time, it is noteworthy that these European Enlightenment ideas that gave birth to the knowledge of race science remain common today: from Carl Linnaeus's taxonomy of human races in *Systema naturae* to François Bernier, along with so-called nat-

5   Paul Gilroy, "Race Ends Here," *Ethnic & Racial Studies* 21, no. 5 (1998): 838–47; Ashley Mantagu, *Man's Most Dangerous Myth: Fallacy of Race*, 6th ed. (Walnut Creek, California: Altamira Press, 1997); Robert Bernasconi, "Who Invented the Concept of Race? Kant's Role in the Enlightenment Construction of Race," in *Race*, ed. Robert Bernasconi (Oxford: Blackwell, 2001), 11–39; George M. Fredrickson, *Racism: A Short History* (Princeton: Princeton University Press, 2002).

6   William W. Howells, "The Meaning of Race," *Journal of Ethnic and Migration Studies* 3, nos. 1/2 (1974): 26–30.

7   Dante A. Puzzo, "Racism and the Western Tradition," *Journal of the History of Ideas* 25, no. 4 (1964): 579–86, 579.

8   Ivan Hannaford, *Race: The History of an Idea in the West* (Baltimore: Johns Hopkins Press, 1996), 5.

9   Thomas F. Gossett, *Race: The History of an Idea in America* (Oxford: Oxford University Press, 1963), 3.

10   David Theo Goldberg, "The End(s) of Race," *Postcolonial Studies* 7, no. 2 (2004): 211–30, 212.

11   Howells, "Meaning of Race," 29.

uralists including Georges Cuvier, James Cowles Prichard, Louis Agassiz, and Johann Friedrich Blumenbach, all of whom propagated the concept of race.[12]

It is in Charles Davenport's *Heredity in Relation to Eugenics* as well, a source relevant not least to Russian and Soviet histories of deeply racial thinking and racial politics.[13] That book took up a translation and reproduction process that transformed the understanding of eugenics in Russia and Soviet Union. All this leads the critical-race theorist David Theo Goldberg to suggest that:

> Science and literature, scripture and law, culture and political rhetoric all worked in subtle and blunt ways to establish the presumption of white supremacy, to naturalize the status of white entitlement and black disenfranchisement, of European belonging wherever the claim might be staked, and of non-European servitude and servility.[14]

All of which cleared the path for race science's emergence across Central and Eastern Europe, including Poland, in the twentieth century.[15] In this view, the sociologist Dušan I. Bjelić reminds us that race is "a type of 'white solidarity' *vis-à-vis* the rest of the world." It is predicated on "a *type* of civilizational *unity* inside Europe as sovereign nationhood of ethno-racial hierarchies."[16] Therefore, the expansion of whiteness in the early twentieth century drew Southern, Central, and Eastern Europeans together in transforming themselves from "lesser Whites" to simply "Whites."[17] All of this was geared toward the

12   Bernasconi, "Who Invented the Concept of Race?" 11–39.
13   Eric D. Weitz, "Russia, Germany, and the Problem of Race," in *Ideologies of Race: Imperial Russia and the Soviet Union in Global Context*, ed. David Rainbow (Montreal: McGill-Queen's University Press, 1979), 160–76; Nikolay Zakharov, *Race and Racism in Russia* (New York: Palgrave Macmillan, 2015).
14   Goldberg, "End(s) of Race," 212.
15   Marius Turda, ed., *The History of Eugenics in East-Central Europe, 1900–1945* (London: Bloomsbury Academic, 2015); Bolaji Balogun, "Race and Racism in Poland: Theorising and Contextualising 'Polish Centrism,'" *The Sociological Review* 68, no. 6 (2020): 1196–1211.
16   Dušan I. Bjelić, "Abolition of a National Paradigm: The Case Against Benedict Anderson and Maria Todorova's Raceless Imaginaries," *Interventions*, January 25, 2021, 1–24, 4.
17   Theodore W. Allen, *Racial Oppression and Social Control*, vol. 1, *The Invention of the White Race* (New York: Verso, 1994); David Roediger, *The Wages of Whiteness: Race and the Making of the American Working Class* (London: Verso, 1991).

establishment of racial hierarchies within which blackness is linked to inferiority, while whiteness is associated with superiority—and not simply in moral terms. As the sociologist Abby L. Ferber argues: "To be white is to have greater access to rewards and valued resources,"[18] which implies that whiteness as a privilege has economic value attached to it.

The latter part of the twentieth century transformed racial trends, but it must be pointed out that its system and most especially the subordination of Black people that emerged over three centuries remains with us. Today, the same system indicates racial formation with its "central and most recalcitrant assumption [...] that Negroes are [...] inferior to whites in mental capacity."[19] As I will show in the case of the Soviet bloc, "Race feeds, fuels and funnels violence, property, profit and power, but can also be their modes of expression, the forms in which they manifest."[20]

This abbreviated account of race and racism in Europe helps to explore the "official uncoupling" of race and racism in the Soviet Union. In countering that view, an alternative account that places the region in globalized historical and political contexts needs to be proposed. This would bring into view a better understanding of race and racism as global circulation, and their local manifestations in the Soviet Union. As the historians Kent Fedorowich and Andrew S. Thompson contend, globalization is essential in showing how different parts of the world are connected, as part of "the new conceptual forces at work that are indeed providing a more integrated approach to migration."[21] It required a colossal movement of populations, as one way through which Europeans established global hegemony.[22] For example, there were voluntary

18   Abby L. Ferber, "Whiteness Studies and the Erasure of Gender," *Sociology Compass* 1, no. 1 (2007): 265–82, 267.
19   Howells, "Meaning of Race," 28.
20   Goldberg, "End(s) of Race," 214.
21   Kent Fedorowich and Andrew S. Thompson, "Mapping the Contours of the British World: Empire, Migration and Identity," in *Empire, Migration and Identity in the British World*, ed. Kent Fedorowich and Andrew S. Thompson (Manchester: Manchester University Press 2013), 1–41, 16.
22   Gurminder K. Bhambra, "On European 'Civilization': Colonialism, Land, Lebensraum," in *Living with Ghosts: Legacies of Colonialism and Fascism*, ed. Nick Aikens, Jyoti Mistry, and Corina Oprea, *L'Internationale Online*, 2019, https://d2tv32fgpo1xal.cloudfront.net/files/internationaleonline-livingwithghosts-2019.pdf, 19–20.

and involuntary movements of Europeans, and the largely involuntary movement of non-Europeans by Europeans—upwards of twelve million Africans abducted to the Americas, most notably by Spain and Portugal followed by Britain, France, the Netherlands, and Germany.[23] Then through the nineteenth century, some sixty million Europeans left their countries of origin to lands inhabited by other peoples, eliminating indigenous populations and appropriating their resources.[24] In addition, millions of British people established white-settler colonies across the globe; at least seven million Germans migrated to settler colonies in the lands that would become the US, Brazil, and Argentina.[25]

Furthermore, populations from across the continent including Scandinavia and Eastern Europe also migrated—populations which to this day are not considered colonizers or part of colonial endeavors.[26] It is important to remember the large-scale Polish immigration underway after the Franco-Prussian War. By the outset of the twentieth century, some two million Polish laborers and two million subjects of Austria-Hungary had migrated to the Americas.[27] Indeed, "Globalization is everywhere"[28]—it was responsible for the collapse of the Bretton Woods System that lasted until the early 1970s; for accelerating cross-border flow of capital within and outside Europe; and for the collapse of socialist states that led to their integration into the world market.[29]

By reading race and the above population movement through globalization, we are better placed to dispel the notion of any East European racial exceptionalism spreading "the idea that Southeast Europe belonged outside the history of coloniality that had produced 'race' and racism in Western Europe, North America,

23   Bhambra, "On European 'Civilization,'" 19–20.
24   Bhambra, "On European 'Civilization,'" 21–22.
25   Annemarie Steidl, *On Many Routes: Internal, European, and Transatlantic Migration in the Late Habsburg Empire* (West Lafayette: Purdue University Press, 2021).
26   Bhambra, "On European 'Civilization,'" 19–20.
27   Jerzy Zubrzycki, "Emigration from Poland in the Nineteenth and Twentieth Centuries," *Population Studies* 6, no. 3 (1953): 248–72; Tara Zahra, *The Great Departure: Mass Migration from Eastern Europe and the Making of the Free World* (New York: W.W. Norton & Company, 2016); Steidl, *On Many Routes*, 5.
28   Mark, Kalinovsky, and Marung, *Alternative Globalizations*, 1.
29   Mark, Kalinovsky, and Marung, *Alternative Globalizations*, 1.

and apartheid South Africa."[30] Yet the notion that Eastern Europe was unaware of or had little contact with the global race context is commonly assumed across the region. As is the assumption that in Cold War political divisions, the Eastern bloc had little contact with the rest of the world. While histories of that period tended to neglect the region's global connectedness, scholars including Neil MacMaster, Theodora Dragostinova, and Malgorzata Fidelis have demonstrated the ways in which Eastern bloc nations were engaging in trans-border contacts with the West through travel and tourism, popular culture, scholarly exchange, and consumer options.[31]

Globalizing the Soviet Union
To demonstrate the connectedness of Eastern Europe to the rest of the world, a good start could be exchanges and interactions between the Soviet Union and countries outside Europe, especially in Africa, Asia, and Latin America. Conversely, James Mark and Quinn Slobodian offer a fresh, compelling assessment of relations between communism and colonialism. In their analysis, Mark and Slobodian draw attention to how Eastern Europe's economic predicament foreshadowed the availability of raw materials and agricultural resources from Africa and Asia both in the 1920s and after 1945. While the "leaders of the one million-strong Polish Maritime and Colonial League argued that the attainment of colonies was an integral part of their country becoming a proper European nation,"[32] acquiring colonies became an attribute that could prove the "Europeanness" of some countries in Eastern Europe including Czechoslovakia.[33]

30   Catherine Baker, "Postcoloniality Without Race? Racial Exceptionalism and Southeast European Cultural Studies," Interventions 20, no. 6 (2018): 759–84, 775.
31   Neil MacMaster, Racism In Europe 1870–2000 (Houndmills: Palgrave, 2001); Theodora Dragostinova and Malgorzata Fidelis, "Beyond the Iron Curtain: Eastern Europe and the Global Cold War," Slavic Review 77, no. 3 (2018): 577–87, 577.
32   James Mark and Quinn Slobodian, "Eastern Europe in the Global History of Decolonization," in The Oxford Handbook of the Ends of Empire, ed. Martin Thomas and Andrew S. Thompson (Oxford: Oxford University Press, 2018), 1–28, 4; See also Bolaji Balogun, "Polish Lebensraum: The Colonial Ambition to Expand on Racial Terms," Ethnic and Racial Studies 41, no. 14 (2018): 2561–79.
33   Sarah Lemmen, "The 'Return to Europe': Intellectual Debates on the Global Place of Czechoslovakia in the Interwar Period," European Review of History: Revue européenne d'histoire 23, no. 4 (2016): 610–22, 614.

As Eastern European nations sought independence from Soviet Russia, China was one alternative engagement. Albania found a new patron in Mao there, while Yugoslavia developed its strongest cultural and economic ties in Africa and Asia.[34] This, with the support of Jawaharlal Nehru's India, Sukarno's Indonesia, Gamal Abdel Nasser's Egypt, and Kwame Nkrumah's Ghana, eventually led to establishing the Non-Aligned Movement—an organization said to transcend race.[35] The Federation of South African Trade Unions looked to Solidarity in Poland for support.[36] And Romania in the 1970s created flexible political formations with Latin America by declaring itself one of them, a move informed by race or shared history.[37] Theodora Dragostinova has demonstrated how Bulgaria, attempting to establish global influence between 1977 and 1981, staged colossal cultural events across the developing nations: 15,413 events in Asia, 3,442 in Arabian countries, 2,973 in Latin America, 1,170 in Africa.[38] Along with the opening of the Bulgarian Cultural Center in New Delhi were proposals for similar centers in Mexico City, Lagos, and Algiers.

The emergence of academic institutions in the 1960s, focused on joint activity between Eastern European scholars and decolonizing African nations, is one testimony to the Eastern bloc's global outreach.[39] The establishment of the Institute for African Studies in 1960 at Karl Marx University in Leipzig has been pointed to as a precedent by Maxim Matusevich, Daniela Hannova, and Young-sun

34   Tvrtko Jakovina, *Treća strana Hladnog rata* (Zagreb: Fraktura, 2011); Dragostinova and Fidelis, "Beyond the Iron Curtain," 586.
35   Itty Abraham, "Prolegomena to Non-Alignment: Race and the International System," in *The Non-Aligned Movement and the Cold War: Delhi, Bandung, Belgrade*, ed. Nataša Mišković, Harald Fischer-Tiné, and Nada Boškovska (New York: Routledge, 2014), 76–94, 77; David C. Engerman, "Learning from the East: Soviet Experts and India in the Era of Competitive Coexistence," *Comparative Studies of South Asia, Africa and the Middle East* 33, no. 2 (2013): 227–35.
36   Monica Popescu, *South African Literature Beyond the Cold War* (New York: Palgrave, 2010), 12.
37   Mark and Slobodian, "Eastern Europe in the Global History of Decolonization," 6.
38   Theodora Dragostinova, "The 'Natural Ally' of the 'Developing World': Bulgarian Culture in India and Mexico," *Slavic Review* 77, no. 3 (2018): 661–84.
39   Jeremy Friedman, "Soviet Policy in the Developing World and the Chinese Challenge in the 1960s," *Cold War History* 10, no. 2 (2010): 253–54.

Hong.[40] Others include the Peoples' Friendship University in Moscow and November 17 University in Prague in 1961, which led to the Center of Research on Underdeveloped Economies in Poland, founded in 1962, and the Afro-Asia Research Centers in Yugoslavia and Hungary in 1963, where students from decolonized countries received training.[41]

In non-academic contexts, accounts relate intimacies between Soviet citizens and their student visitors, including this excerpt from the political scientist Pavel Barša:

> I spent the first half of my life in communist Czecho-slovakia, where we only rarely encountered non-Euro-peans. In a university city—such as my home, Brno—these were mostly university students from "friendly states" in the Third World. Black men were popular in the pubs we used to frequent as students in the early 1980s. There were rumors—and some of these men claimed so themselves—that they had no problem establishing relations with Czech girls. They were few in number, so ordinary Czechs probably saw them as providing variety rather than as posing a threat.
>
> Those who started families and settled [here] never-theless complained about racism: their exotic origins and skin color—often seen positively in nonproblem-atic situations—could become the butt of jokes or worse at the first sign of conflict.[42]

Eastern European experts and intellectuals were active in Africa, Asia, and Latin America, from economists, scientists, engineers, and physicians to journalists, writers, and artists. As Dragostinova and

40   Maxim Matusevich, "Testing the Limits of Soviet Internationalism: African Students in the Soviet Union," in Race, Ethnicity, and the Cold War, ed. Phillip E. Muehlenbeck (Nashville: Vanderbilt University Press, 2012), 155–59; Daniela Hannova, "Arab Students Inside the Soviet Bloc: A Case Study on Czechoslovakia During the 1950s and 60s," European Scientific Journal, no. 2 (2014): 371–79; Young-sun Hong, Cold War Germany, the Third World, and the Global Humanitarian Regime (New York: Cambridge University Press, 2015).
41   James Mark and Yakov Feygin, "The Soviet Union, Eastern Europe and Alternative Visions of a Global Economy, 1950s–1980s," in Mark, Kalinovsky, and Marung, Alternative Globalizations, 35–58.
42   Pavel Barša, "The Zero Degree of Decolonisation," trans. Ian Mikyska and Alfred LeMaitre, Artalk Revue 4 (2020): 1–4, 1, https://artalk.cz/wp-content/uploads/2020/01/AR-4-EN-162045.pdf.

Fidelis have observed, these specialists were "shaping the economic, technological, and cultural landscape of the postcolonial states."[43] Architects from the Eastern bloc oversaw projects in various cities in postcolonial Africa. According to the anthropologist Christina Schwenkel, the "traveling architecture" of the Soviet bloc literally helped cement a shared global imaginary.[44] These histories, however, are often decoupled from representations of Eastern Europe, as the architecture historian Łukasz Stanek points out in an interview about globalizing socialism:

> When I give a talk in Accra, Lagos, or Beirut about the work of Eastern Europeans in these cities, there is always somebody in the audience who had a Czech, Bulgarian, Hungarian, Polish, or Yugoslav colleague, teacher, or collaborator. It is very different when I lecture about this research in Western Europe or in North America, where this history is seen as entirely new. In Eastern Europe, the histories of these relationships are present in different ways. Only now are they beginning to enter histories of architecture […].[45]

These under-recognized histories aren't only in architectural exchanges. Using emerging memoirs and interviews from Czech archives, Tom Lodge and Milan Oralek show connections between South African communists and Czechoslovakia shaped Eastern European support "especially at a time when the South African Communist Party (SACP) was becoming embedded in its alliance with African nationalism."[46] Using newly declassified archival materials in Prague, both Natalia Telepneva and Jan Koura shed light on Czechoslovakian intelligence and secret-service cooperation with Communist

43   Dragostinova and Fidelis, "Beyond the Iron Curtain," 277.
44   Christina Schwenkel, "Traveling Architecture: East German Urban Designs Abroad," *International Journal for History, Culture and Modernity* 2, no. 2 (2014): 155–74.
45   See Zoltán Ginelli, "Looking Elsewhere: Weak Actors and Architecture on the Move in Global Socialism," an interview with Łukasz Stanek, *LeftEast*, November 11, 2020, http://www.criticatac.ro/lefteast/global-socialism-lukasz-stanek-middle-east-europe/.
46   Tom Lodge and Milan Oralek, "Fraternal Friends: South African Communists and Czechoslovak, 1945–89," *The Journal of African History* 61, no. 2 (2020): 219–39, 220.

parties in Morocco and the Republic of Guinea in the 1960s.[47] Czechoslovakian weapons, military intelligence, and training went to Egyptian forces as early as 1955,[48] then Warsaw Pact military aid provided arms to Syria after the Arab–Israeli War—it's quite a list, including essential Soviet military aid to Nigeria's General Yakubu Gowon during the Nigerian–Biafran Civil War.[49]

Eastern Europe played other significant roles in global developments and conflicts in the second half of the twentieth century. Mark and Feygin demonstrate how such involvements influenced UN free-trade initiatives in the 1960s, through the UN Conference on Trade and Development (UNCTAD).[50] Other involvements included the New International Economic Order in the 1970s, and the expansion of the Council for Mutual Economic Assistance (Comecon)—an extra-European Warsaw Pact. Through UNCTAD and other UN initiatives, Poland in particular became a destination for economists from Africa and Latin America working on development issues.[51] In the 1960s, states from the Soviet republics joined UN members from the Caribbean and Africa in drafting the International Convention on the Elimination of All Forms of Racial Discrimination (ICERD). ICERD condemned and criminalized "any distinction, exclusion, restriction or preference based on race, color, descent, or national or ethnic origin."

Race and Racism in Cold War-era Eastern Europe

In the Soviet Union, race and racism were manifested in various ways. Yet the common idea was that race and racism were fixed in Western history. In other words, what was generally taken for "real racism" was believed to reside in the US, the UK, and other global-imperialist colonial powers. Propaganda denounced "the evils

47   Natalia Telepneva, "'Code Name SEKRETÁŘ': Amílcar Cabral, Czechoslovakia and the Role of Human Intelligence during the Cold War," *The International History Review* 42, no. 6 (2020): 1257–73; Jan Koura, "A Prominent Spy: Mehdi Ben Barka, Czechoslovak Intelligence, and Eastern Bloc Espionage in the Third World during the Cold War," *Intelligence and National Security* 36, no. 3 (2021): 318–39.
48   Hannova, "Arab Students Inside the Soviet Bloc," 371–79.
49   Maxim Matusevich, "Expanding the Boundaries of the Black Atlantic: African Students as Soviet Moderns," *Ab Imperio*, no. 2 (2012): 325–50, 346.
50   Mark and Feygin, "Soviet Union," 36.
51   Mark and Feygin, "Soviet Union," 41.

of Western racism and colonial oppression"[52]—though the same forms of oppression were widespread across the Soviet states. This reality was quickly discovered by Everest Mulekezi, a student from East Africa, in 1959:

> On our arrival in Moscow we were puzzled to find that we were segregated from the main student body. A thousand of us foreigners—Africans, Asians, and Latin Americans—were housed a mile from the university in five-story buildings [...]. Through the first weeks, government propagandists haunted the dormitories, asking for tape-recorded statements, which they broadcast back to our countries. "Why don't you tell how all this is so different from the colonialism of Western countries?" one interviewer suggested.[53]

This was complicated by the Soviets' recognition of civil-rights struggles in the US, especially open support for Martin Luther King Jr.'s nonviolent political activism and the appeal of Black activists, intellectuals, and card-carrying communists including Harry Haywood, Angela Davis, Claude McKay, Langston Hughes, and the famed stage-screen performer Paul Robeson, much adored in the Soviet Union and enormously contentious at home.[54] Soviet propaganda clouded ways in which race and racism floated free from wider contexts through which they are best understood. In that logic, the apparatuses of the state played a determinative role in facilitating race and racism, as Soviet state propaganda reassigned them to the past "through a temporal logic of white dislocation."[55] In doing so, Black Africans were branded "ungrateful" former colonial subjects, the descendants of enslaved people, and the still-colonized indigenous peoples of settler states.[56]

52   Matusevich, "Soviet Anti-Racism," 229.
53   Everest Mulekezi, "I Was a Student at Moscow State," *Readers Digest* 79, no. 471 (1961): 99–104.
54   Joy Gleason Carew, "Black in the USSR: African Diasporan Pilgrims, Expatriates and Students in Russia, from the 1920s to the First Decade of the Twenty-First Century," *African and Black Diaspora: An International Journal* 8, no. 2 (2015): 202–15.
55   Alana Lentin, *Why Race Still Matters* (Cambridge: Polity Press, 2020).
56   George Yancy, *Black Bodies, White Gazes: The Continuing Significance of Race* (Lanham: Rowman and Littlefield, 2008), 236.

155 EASTERN EUROPE   COLD WAR INTERNATIONALISM: THE MYTH OF RACE-BLIND

As I intend to demonstrate, such relocated racism was embedded in Soviet social aims. Racism in the Soviet Union is significant because even with the admission that it persists in society, acknowledged by individuals and institutions, as the critical-race scholar Alana Lentin argues, "there is a reticence to name it because of the dominance of the idea that 'real racism' is either over or extremely marginal."[57]

Manifestations of racism were evident in the inflammatory slogans displayed during a Red Square protest in 1963: "Moscow—Center of Discrimination," "Stop Killing Africans!" and "Moscow, a Second Alabama."[58] That protest, organized and attended by African students, was triggered by the death of a Ghanaian medical student, Edmund Assare-Addo, whose body was found in a remote, barren area of Moscow. Assare-Addo's death also led to a sit-down strike by dozens of African students at a Baku train station, and to solidarity protests by African communities in Leningrad and Minsk.[59] The killing provoked some of the largest student protests against racism in the Soviet Union.[60] Medical investigations had found no sign of physical assault except a small neck scar, concluding that Assare-Addo's death was related to "an effect of cold in a state of alcohol-induced stupor."[61] Soviet authorities concurred, dismissing allegations of race-related murder.

Despite that proclamation, many believed that Assare-Addo died in a racially motivated attack.[62] While forensic details from the death were lacking, what rang clear was the protests by which African students in Moscow and other places registered dissatisfaction both with their fellow student's sudden death and the authorities' denial of issues of race and racism. Today, it's evidence that there was no shortage of "race-blindness" during the Cold War.

Across the Soviet Union, race and racism were made manifest in cultural misunderstandings between visiting Black stu-

57   Lentin, *Why Race Still Matters*, 65.
58   Julie Hessler, "Death of an African Student in Moscow: Race, Politics, and the Cold War," *Cahiers du Monde russe* 47, nos. 1/2 (2006): 33–64, 33.
59   Matusevich, "Expanding the Boundaries of the Black Atlantic," 325–50.
60   Carew, "Black in the USSR," 204.
61   Hessler, "Death of an African Student in Moscow," 34; Carew, "Black in the USSR," 204.
62   Hessler, "Death of an African Student in Moscow," 33–34.

dents and their predominantly white host country. This was exacerbated by "rising pressures of socio-economic and political decay of
the last decades of the Soviet-era," which, as Joy Gleason Carew has
identified, pushed the fact that "African and other dark-skinned students were easy to recognize as 'outsiders'" in danger zones.[63] Rely-
ing on long-standing views of race as a biological reality, statuses of
superiority and inferiority between Blacks and whites were sustained, as Everest Mulekezi had detailed:

> There were catalogues of unpleasant incidents. Michel
> Ayih of Togo was prevented from leaving the lift at his
> floor in the university building. When he protested, a
> Russian shouted at him: "What right do you have to
> speak? You're a black monkey, not a human being."
> Once when I was walking in the heart of Moscow a gang
> followed, taunting, pushing, trying to provoke a fight
> in which I would have been mobbed. One night Benja-
> min Omburo from Kenya was mauled by Soviet police
> when they found him talking to a Russian girl at a bus
> stop. At a party, Omar Khalif of Somalia, provoked into
> an argument with a communist student, was beaten
> unconscious and spent two weeks in hospital.[64]

Romantic relations between Black men and Russian women was a
common situation where cultural misunderstandings emerged
emphatically. "Rivalry over girls," Matusevich observes, "tended
to express itself in 'racial terms.'"[65] Both locals and Soviet authorities frequently disapproved of an interracial marriage.[66] Reactions
against sexual relations, particularly within self-proclaimed socialist
internationalism, was draconian. This had been evident since 1947,
with the Supreme Soviet law prohibiting marriage between Soviet
citizens and foreigners of any nationality. Foreign students, as part
of their conditions of residency, had to pledge to abide by

63   Carew, "Black in the USSR," 213.
64   Mulekezi, "I Was a Student at Moscow State," 29.
65   Matusevich, "Expanding the Boundaries of the Black Atlantic," 341.
66   Hessler, "Death of an African Student in Moscow," 36.

that law.[67] As the historian Rachel Applebaum argues, the 1947 law should be "understood as part of a broader effort by European governments to regulate transgressive transnational and interracial sexual relations."[68]

In contrast to the official Soviet line of a race-free reality, race-related complaints were common. Evidence runs the gamut from racial slurs to threats of "lynching" African students in romantic relationships with Russian women, and includes racial profiling and unwarranted stop-and-searches by Soviet police, as Julie Hessler points out:

> Some of these merely involved intimidation and harassment, such as an alleged episode on the Moscow subway in which students were accosted by a couple of drunken Russians, who demanded that they give up their seats: "In your own country you aren't even allowed to be in the same subway car as whites, whereas here you are sitting down while white people stand."[69]

In such instances, some locals could draw a connection between reprehensible behavior in Soviet society and the Jim Crow decades in the US when Blacks couldn't share public facilities, and when lynching had been an ominous way by which whites' affected anger against their Black neighbors. Even given that connection, and even though such transgressions were rare, Soviet authorities were quick to turn a blind eye on those threats and violent acts.

Other studies have clarified how mundane situations in the Soviet Union would reinforce and endorse race-blind ideology. Matusevich reads this through Soviet "efforts to occupy the moral high ground in the ongoing Cold War context"[70]—that is, as a critique of Western racism but with no steadfast anti-racist stance. Matusevich also draws attention to the restrictive nature of Black Africans' lives in Soviet Russia in the 1960s, which led to the expulsion of four

67   M. M. Wolff, "Some Aspects of Marriage and Divorce Laws in Soviet Russia," *Modern Law Review* 12, no. 3 (1949): 290–96; Rachel Applebaum, *Empire of Friends: Soviet Power and Socialist Internationalism in Cold War Czechoslovakia* (Ithaca: Cornell University Press, 2019).
68   Applebaum, *Empire of Friends*, 60.
69   Hessler, "Death of an African Student in Moscow," 37.
70   Matusevich, "Soviet Anti-Racism," 234.

students from Moscow State University.[71] They had been involved in forming the Black Africans' Student Union and circulated restricted "books and jazz records."[72] According to them, while the Soviets' projected an image of a union championing Africans, many Blacks were being oppressed in the Soviet Union and its satellite states.

In reaction, Soviet authorities declared that the students were "Pentagon men bought by American dollars" and "inspired by [their] overseas masters."[73] Again, they were being seen through the larger, ever-pressing picture of US-Soviet colonial and racial rivalry. This is evident in Soviet media coverage of Soviet-African relations. In Charles Quist-Adade's analysis, the sociologist has pointed out how Soviet politicians' and journalists' paternalistic undertone about African nations intensified racism against Black Africans living in Russia at the time. As Quist-Adade explains: "Soviet television was saturated with images of homeless, unemployed blacks lining up at soup kitchens or dole offices in London or Washington [DC]. Meanwhile, numerous cases went unreported of racially motivated attacks and murders of Africans in the Soviet Union."[74]

Within this political atmosphere, created in part by the propagation of a raceless society, continuing arrivals of Global South students settling in the Soviet Union and in satellite states kept both the propaganda and race-related issues alive. When Constantin Katsakioris focused on a group of students from Angola, Mozambique, Guinea-Bissau, and Cape Verde who studied in Bulgaria, Czechoslovakia, East Germany, Hungary, Poland, Romania, and Ukraine between 1960 and 1974, the scholar showed how the Soviet sphere was no safe haven of anti-imperialism and internationalist solidarity.[75] Meanwhile, intra-elite social and political struggles were accessorized by racializing Black African students. Alena K. Alamgir has shown racial roles through Czechoslovakia in its perceptions of Romani, Vietnamese, and Cubans living in the country—despite overt

71   Matusevich, "Expanding the Boundaries of the Black Atlantic," 339.
72   Matusevich, "Expanding the Boundaries of the Black Atlantic," 339; W. N. Appleton, *Friendship University Moscow: The Student Trap* (Stuttgart: Pro Libertate, 1965).
73   Matusevich, "Expanding the Boundaries of the Black Atlantic," 340.
74   Charles Quist-Adade, "From Paternalism to Ethnocentrism: Images of Africa in Gorbachev's Russia," *Race & Class* 46, no. 4 (2005): 79–89, 81.
75   Constantin Katsakioris, "Students from Portuguese Africa in the Soviet Union, 1960–74: Anti-Colonialism, Education, and the Socialist Alliance," *Journal of Contemporary History*, 56, no. 1 (2021): 142–165, 164.

efforts to act as a race-blind society. Before socialism, Czechoslovak anthropologists had already identified what appeared to be "racial" or "biological" particularities of the Romani, responsible for their "Gypsy character."[76] This later influenced the racialization of the group, who were perceived as an obstacle to nation formation in Czechoslovakia: state norms required the Romani community to adopt living "conditions considered 'normal' enough to pass as 'Czech' or 'Slovak.'"[77]

Vietnamese and Cuban populations were racialized through the State-Sponsored Labor Migration in East-Central Europe. This labor-migration scheme was deployed across Eastern Europe, providing labor training for those from Third World countries so they could return home and help their countries develop.[78] Alamgir provides an estimate of at least sixty thousand Vietnamese and over twenty-three thousand Cubans accepted by the Czechoslovak Labor Ministries between 1967 and 1989[79]—a dense presence of non-white, non-Europeans in a predominantly white society, making an environment primed for racially motivated incidents. Some of these situations became evident in, for instance, Czechoslovak concerns about Cubans' "expressive temperaments." As foreign workers, Cubans were expected to deliver "honest socialist work" yet were perceived as unable to maintain an Eastern European work ethic and standards. As Alamgir explains:

> The Vietnamese were most frequently compared with Cubans, and only occasionally with other foreign workers, such as Poles. In this way, the supposed division of humankind into three distinct races, which Czechoslovak citizens were taught in biology classes throughout elementary and high school, was articulated in that both the Vietnamese and the Cubans were perceived

76   Alena K. Alamgir, "Race Is Elsewhere: State-Socialist Ideology and the Racialization of Vietnamese Workers in Czechoslovakia," *Race & Class* 54, no. 4 (2013): 67–85, 74.
77   Vera Sokolova, "A Matter of Speaking: Racism, Gender and Social Deviance in the Politics of the 'Gypsy Question' in Communist Czechoslovakia, 1945–1989" (PhD diss., University of Washington, 2002).
78   Alena K. Alamgir and Christina Schwenkel, "From Socialist Assistance to National Self-Interest: Vietnamese Labor Migration into CMEA Countries," in Mark, Kalinovsky, and Marung, *Alternative Globalizations*, 100–24.
79   Alamgir and Schwenkel, "From Socialist Assistance to National Self-Interest," 101.

as racially different from the Czechs and Slovaks, and hence comparable to each other, whereas the Poles were perceived as fundamentally similar to the local population and not so easily comparable with the overseas workers. Hence, racial criteria trumped mere foreignness, which suggests that the "othering" of Vietnamese and Cubans was not "just" xenophobia, but, in fact, had racist roots.[80]

The Soviet principles of "proletarian internationalism" and the much-vaunted "solidarity with peoples fighting for their spiritual, political, and economic liberation"[81] reached Poland, as a satellite state with Black students arriving from Africa and Latin America. Many of those students assimilated into Polish society and spoke Polish, often as a third language, appearing in the Polish press, which represented Blacks in Poland as friends, revolutionists, and comrades in liberation struggles.[82] As with other Eastern bloc states, however, the comradeship being touted didn't shield Blacks from being subjected to race issues and racism. Bartosz Nowicki has focused in an essay on images and representations of Blacks in Poland of the period, as they were published in The Polish Review. In communist-era Poland, the experience of being out of space was all too familiar for many Black students.[83] This aspect of Soviet-style racism was discussed in my conversation with the educator and former Polish radio and TV journalist Brian Scott, from Guyana.[84]

80   Alamgir, "Race Is Elsewhere," 81.
81   Quist-Adade, "From Paternalism to Ethnocentrism," 79.
82   See Bartosz Nowicki, "Representing Africans in The Polish Review: A Projection of the PRL as Racism-Free," in this book.
83   Sara Ahmed, Strange Encounters: Embodied Others in Post-Coloniality (New York: Psychology Press, 2000); Nirmal Puwar, "Fish In or Out of Water: A Theoretical Framework for Race and the Space of Academia," in Institutional Racism in Higher Education, ed. Ian Law, Deborah Phillips, and Laura Turney (Stoke on Trent: Trentham Books, 2004), 49–58.
84   Brian Scott is Poland's first Black journalist, known for his radio work as an RMF FM presenter in the 1990s and for the TV documentary Etniczne klimaty (Ethnic Climates) on the TVP3 channel of Polish public television. Scott is currently an educator working with primary and junior high schools in Kraków and with Polish universities. For more details on Scott, see his bio entry at RMF FM, accessed October 12, 2021, https:// 30lat.rmf.fm/tiki-index.php?page=Brian+Scott.

I had arranged to meet Scott in 2018 at a Kraków café, having requested an hour's conversation about his experiences upon first arriving in Poland in 1985. Little did I know the magnitude of the treat I was in for, with the location he chose and the fact that the conversation lasted for over six hours. Our topics ranged from Scott's personal experiences of the Iron Curtain era, the fall of Berlin Wall, the nearly democratic elections in Poland that effectively ended communist rule, Solidarity, then Poland entering NATO and later the EU, and its present sociopolitical conflicts with the EU.

Scott, following the Guyanese writer Jan Carew's footsteps, who had been the first South American student to receive a scholarship to an Eastern bloc university,[85] was funded by the UN for mechanical-engineering studies in Eastern Europe. He began our discussion by speaking of his decision to study journalism at the Jagiellonian University in Kraków, and explained why he chose Poland among the Eastern bloc countries. As a young political activist in Guyana, Scott knew of Poland's political struggles and of Solidarity, and had a good understanding of the roles of Pope John Paul II and Lech Wałęsa in those struggles—"so these people, especially Lech Wałęsa, influenced my decision of choosing Poland," as he stated. He also arrived fully aware of racial differentiation in Poland and other communist and socialist countries:

> I remember one incident as a student, I was going to do an exam and I was on a tram with one of my Polish female friends. I noticed someone tapped my shoulder and it turned out to be an old Polish man who asked me to give up my seat in order for him to sit down. Rather than giving up my seat, I asked "Why me and why not other people?" And the old man replied "You know, in Africa, you don't sit, and white people stand." I said "Maybe in South Africa during apartheid, and this is Poland, not Africa." I told him I'm tired and needed to sit down and he should ask one of the younger white kids to give up their seats.

> Then the old man started telling me about the superior-
> ity of white men [...] during this situation, the only per-
> son who stood by my side was my friend, as everyone on
> the tram either ignored me or was against me [...].

This sense of Polish self-conception, the nation's whiteness marking out Scott's body, had subjected him to the racialized experience he recounted. In the Polish psyche, an essence of being different is clearly captured in his experience of being singled out to give up his seat. This not only displaced a racialized body, but subjected it to "a process of 'confiscation,'"[86] with what is termed the "white gaze" elid-ing responsibility for taking a Black's body captive. That perception is inherited through toxic assumptions and the bodily perceptual practices of the white gaze, which perceived Scott's body through the lens of biological differentiation.

In that instance, a racialized gaze/white gaze was oper-ative from beneath the Soviet race-blind veil, but still manifested as a burden—a frustration many Black students had to endure in Soviet-era Eastern Europe. What is particularly interesting in Scott's case is the centrality of processes of racism, which, as Magdalena Nowicka explains, do "not significantly differ from the ones that emerged in the west of Europe, but they were perceived, transformed, and repro-duced with a certain delay."[87]

The Soviet Union and its satellite states were and are often presented as a unique race-free region where contemporary understandings of race—of civilizational and cultural racism and of the concept of white supremacy—had been completely rejected. In that sense, race was often and continues to be misread.

Communist elites in Eastern Europe were fully aware of racial differentiation and its global operations. The Soviet focus was not specifically on race, but on equality among differing peoples,

86   George Yancy, "Elevators, Social Spaces and Racism: A Philosophical
      Analysis," *Philosophy & Social Criticism*, 34, no. 8 (2008): 843–76, 843.
87   Magdalena Nowicka, "'I don't mean to sound racist but ...': Transforming
      Racism in Transnational Europe," *Ethnic and Racial Studies* 41, no. 5 (2018):
      824–41, 827; Woodford McClellan, "Africans and Black Americans in the
      Comintern Schools, 1925–1934," *The International Journal of African Historical
      Studies* 26, no. 2 (1993): 371–90; Mark and Slobodian, "Eastern Europe in the
      Global History of Decolonization"; Ian Law, *Red Racisms: Racism in Communist
      and Post-Communist Contexts* (New York: Palgrave Macmillan, 2012).

yet they still recognizing racial differentiation.[88] The equality being proclaimed didn't really permeate through to everyone; racism was still experienced at the interpersonal level, as indicated by the Czechoslovak and Polish cases above.[89] And forms of racism would leave Black visitors—having fled North American racialized realities—disillusioned about the professed race-blind utopia in the Soviet sphere.[90]

Notwithstanding such elite-level proclamations by Eastern bloc states, interpersonal racisms and unmarked discrimination were common to the region—and in many ways similar to racial stereotyping and racial hierarchies then too easily found in the West (and rampant in the US). For many Black people living in or visiting Eastern Europe, the region proves to be another white space, that is not too different from the US of the Jim Crow era, Nazi Germany, and apartheid South Africa.

88   Quinn Slobodian, "Socialist Chromatism: Race, Racism and the Racial Rainbow in East Germany," in *Comrades of Color: East Germany in the Cold War World*, ed. Quinn Slobodian (New York: Berghahn, 2015), 23–39.
89   Allison Blakely, *Russia and the Negro: Blacks in Russian History and Thought* (Washington, D.C.: Howard University Press, 1986).
90   Maxim Matusevich, "Probing the Limits of Internationalism: African Students Confront Soviet Ritual," *Anthropology of East Europe Review* 27, no. 2 (2009): 28–30.

Bartosz Nowicki is a photographer, storyteller, curator, and researcher based in Wales. He has been a trustee and curator of the Third Floor Gallery in Cardiff. He received his PhD from Ulster University in Belfast. Representations of race and race relations in Poland is his main area of expertise, which he explores through his photography ("The Wall of Silence"), research ("Afro PRL"), and writing (*Iron Man*, a short comic book, explores the life of Sam Sandi, for which he and artist Łukasz Pawlak received the 2019 Grand Prix at the International Festival of Comics and Games in Łódź).

REPRESENTING AFRICANS IN *THE POLISH REVIEW*: A PROJECTION OF THE PRL AS RACISM-FREE

The tendency in Poland has been to explore domestic attitudes toward Africa and Africans separately from the wider European context.[1] This approach, based on the idea of a "clean conscience," presents the nation's lacking any colony as sufficient argument for distancing itself from Western colonial experiences. Proponents of this opinion, including the reportage writer Ryszard Kapuściński,[2] seemed to skip the fact that a historical lack of a colony wasn't due to an absence of interest in them, but to differing political conditions, which kept "Poland's dream of colonies" just a dream.[3] Failed attempts to claim foreign lands had been bolstered by the widely accepted Western ideology of race and the unequal status of Black and white people within it. That ideology, as the Harvard critical theorist Homi K. Bhabha puts it, aimed "to construe the colonized as a

[1]   Maciej Ząbek, *Biali i Czarni: Postawy Polaków wobec Afryki i Afrykanów* (Warsaw: Instytut Etnologii i Antropologii Kulturowej Uniwersytetu Warszawskiego; Wydawnictwo DiG, 2007).

[2]   "Busz po polsku" (The Bush, Polish-style), a story printed in his book of that title, is one example promoting this view. Ryszard Kapuściński, *Busz po polsku* (Warsaw: Czytelnik, 2007), 125–31.

[3]   Marek Arpad-Kowalski's book *Kolonie Rzeczypospolitej* (Colonies of the Republic) (Warsaw: Dom Wydawniczy Bellona, 2014) is an introduction to this subject (though the book fails to reference source materials).

population of degenerate types on the basis of racial origin, in order to justify conquest and to establish systems of administration and instruction."[4] Among the most efficient mechanisms for producing "evidence" to support that ideology was photography.[5]

An affirmation of such practices, following Western standards of representation of Africa(ns), can be found in various Polish cultural products from the late nineteenth and early twentieth centuries. The novel *In Desert and Wilderness* (1911) by Nobel laureate Henryk Sienkiewicz is one example; another is a photo series taken in East Africa around 1910 by Stanisław Wilhelm August Lilpop, an aristocrat and amateur photographer who imitated visual anthropology.[6]

Another representational direction began after the Second World War, under newly imposed Soviet domination. The introduction of internationalism in the new PRL and its support for decolonization resulted in an influx of students from African nations, and stimulated a gradual emergence of photographs of them in Poland. By the 1960s, these students were no longer being portrayed as curiosities from far away. They lived next door, they spoke Polish, and photos in the daily press maintained a representation of the African as friend, revolutionist, freedom fighter, comrade, and

4   Homi K. Bhabha, "The Other Question: The Stereotype and Colonial Discourse," in *Visual Culture: The Reader*, ed. Jessica Evans and Stuart Hall (London: Sage, 1999), 370–78, 371.

5   See James R. Ryan, *Picturing Empire: Photography and the Visualization of the British Empire* (London: Reaktion Books, 1997); Eleanor M. Hight and Gary D. Sampson, "Introduction: Photography, 'Race' and Post-Colonial Theory," in *Colonialist Photography Imag(in)ing Race and Place* (London: Routledge, 2002), 1–19.

6   Lilpop's photos were published in *Portret dżentelmena* (Portrait of a Gentleman) (Warsaw: "Twój Styl," 1998), written by his granddaughter Maria Iwaszkiewicz. The photos illustrate the author's memories of her grandfather and are left unanalyzed. Original plates can be studied at the Museum of Anna and Jarosław Iwaszkiewicz in Stawisko, near Warsaw. Lilpop's African photographs were exhibited at the History Meeting House in Warsaw in 2013. The exhibition catalog includes images showcasing Polish travelers in Africa as part of the wider European presence in the continent. See the image "Doctor Zaborowski at the head of the caravan" in Małgorzata Zawadzka, *I Will Be Capturing it in Colour: The Beginning of the 20th Century in Stanisław Wilhelm Lilpop's Three-Dimensional Photographs* (Warsaw: Dom Spotkań z Historią, 2013), 109.

intellectual.[7] Such official images touching on race projected the
PRL as progressive and non-racist, contra to reports of institutionalized racism in the West.

However, in this thoroughly political imagery intended
for the overwhelmingly white Polish audience, there was no space for
representing an African as a citizen or family member. That side of
Africans' lives in the PRL was hidden under a thick layer of propaganda, intending to serve communist ideological interests and little concerned with the realities of actual domestic race relations.
Yet one PRL-era journal potentially undermines that
statement. *Miesięcznik Polski*, also published as *The Polish Review* (*TPR*)
and in French as *La Review Pologne*, from our perspective today, may
be seen as a chronicler of the African diaspora in Poland. Its issues
didn't shy away from publishing photos from different spheres of
life in the PRL, including private lives in the African community.
In this essay, by analyzing two such features that ran
in *TPR*, along with a contact sheet with unpublished material by one
TPR photographer, and the documentary film *Black and White*, along
with supporting material from the discourse, I aim to display how
the magazine projected a vision of the country with its racism-free
society, and to uncover unwanted truths about Polish society's
race relations.

Miesięcznik Polski / The Polish Review / La Review Pologne

Miesięcznik Polski was a propaganda magazine promoting the PRL in newly independent countries of Africa and Asia. It was
published from 1961 to 1972. Initially, the English-language version,
The Polish Review, was designated for Asia and the French version, *La
Review Pologne*, for Africa, but from 1962 the African version was also
printed in English.[8] It was one of a family of titles published by the
Polonia Publishing House,[9] of which the most popular was *Polska*

7   See my PhD dissertation, "Representations of Africans in Polish Press
Photography: 1955–1989" (PhD diss., Ulster University, 2020), https://
pure.ulster.ac.uk/en/studentTheses/representations-of-africans-in-
polish-press-photography-1955-1989.
8   The research presented in this essay is based on the English-language
version.
9   From 1967 it was published by the Polish Interpress Agency.

(*Poland*), which was printed in eleven language versions and had a monthly circulation of 212,000 copies.[10] By comparison, the circulation of the three versions of *TPR* peaked at 15,000 copies.[11] *TPR* was distributed through Polish embassies in the countries that were its intended focal points. It was also posted free of charge to anyone in Asia and Africa who wrote the editorial office and requested it.[12]

Propaganda in *The Polish Review*

Tadeusz Rolke, one of Poland's greatest photojournalists, described *Polska* as "a colorful credential of power"[13]—words Rolke might have used about *TPR.* The propaganda publication promoted the PRL as a country thriving due to the utilization of socialist principles in various aspects of life. Each of the titles Polonia published had an editorial office, including staff photographers, and produced their own material, as the propaganda content depended

10   Renata Piasecka, "Polska Agencja 'Interpress' 1967–1980: Zarys problematyki badawczej," *Rocznik Historii Prasy Polskiej* 7, no. 1 (13) (2004): 85–111, 88. During the four decades of *Polska*'s run, main editions were published in Russian, Spanish (two versions), Hungarian, German (two versions), Czech, Polish, English, French, and Swedish. The magazine was distributed on both sides of the Iron Curtain to promote Poland as a modern country swiftly rebuilding from wartime devastation. Adam Krzemiński observes, however, that *Polska* quickly became a monthly culture journal in which economy and politics were kept to a minimum. "The magazine's success in the 1960s," he writes, "was determined not only by its great team and the post-thaw directory of Polish culture but also by a specific fashion for Poland in the West. [...] Especially in East Germany, where after the construction of the Berlin Wall, Poland was viewed as a taste of 'freedom and diversity.'" Quoted in Marta Przybyło, "Oddziaływanie przez fotografię: Miesięcznik 'Polska' w latach 1954–1968," in *Początek przyszłości: Fotografia w miesięczniku "Polska" w latach 1954–1968,* ed. Marta Przybyło and Karolina Puchała-Rojek (Warsaw: Zachęta—Narodowa Galeria Sztuki, 2019), 23–31, 36.
11   See Marta Przybyło-Ibadullajev's research on the subject of distribution. References in this essay are to the Polish-language version of an unpublished article by Przybyło-Ibadullajev, "Fotografia przemysłowa w *Miesięczniku Polskim* w świetle archiwów Tadeusza Sumińskiego i Jana Jastrzębskiego," from 2017, which I obtained from the author. It was later published in German as "Die Industriefotografie in der Zeitschrift *Miesięcznik Polski* im Lichte der Archive von Tadeusz Sumiński und Jan Jastrzębski," in *Erweiterung des Horizonts: Fotoreportage in Polen im 20: Jahrhundert,* ed. Iwona Kurz et al. (Göttingen: Wallstein Verlag, 2018), 271–90. Renata Piasecka, however, reports that the circulation totaled 16,000. See their "Polska Agencja 'Interpress," 88.
12   Jan Morek, interview by Bartosz Nowicki, 2018.
13   Rolke quoted in Łukasz Modelski, *Fotobiografia PRL: Opowieści reporterów* (Kraków: Wydawnictwo Znak, 2013), 280.

on the recipient's geographical location.[14] *TPR* staff photographer Jan Morek bluntly described the periodical's profile from a more recent perspective: "we, in our edition, had been photographing rough things: industry, some politics. Industrializing Poland was to be a model for 'backward' Africa."[15]

TPR as Chronicler of the PRL's African Diaspora

As Morek remembers, and as the researcher Marta Przybyło-Ibadullajev observes, *TPR* focused mainly on subjects of industrialization and trade (in the African context). But *TPR* is much more than that. It is an important source for mapping out postwar Africans' experience in Poland. Almost every issue of the journal included a photo, article, or feature (often all at once) showing one such person living in or visiting Poland. These images and the articles they accompany form a decade-long visual chronicle of the PRL's diaspora from the continent.

Photos of the domestic sphere were the most significant addition to representing the diaspora in *TPR*, in comparison to other periodicals and press publications. The questions that arise are: Why were they only made available for overseas readers? Why were such images absent in papers circulated for Polish readership? The *TPR* photographer Morek addressed the issue:

> This is obvious to me. The primary purpose for the editors of this magazine was to get the readers inspired to come and study in Poland where they could be indoctrinated into communism. It was also a way to advertise Poland.[16]

While Morek's point may seem to simplify the editors' aims, it also inspires another question: How was this done? How were these images used to promote the country as a viable destination for potential students?

This was achieved through diversifying the range of published information according to markets, and the intentionality with which that information was presented. Three main themes

14   For more details, see Przybyło, "Oddziaływanie przez fotografię," 23–31.
15   Morek, quoted in Modelski, *Fotobiografia PRL*, 66.
16   Morek, interview, 2018.

emerge from the pages of *TPR*, corresponding with different spheres of diaspora life in Poland: professional endeavors, leisure, and personal time. Each is an important component of the overall view, but in this essay I will focus on the last one.

"Wedding Bells"

Numerous photos show close interactions between Africans and Poles, which could have suggested to *TPR's* overseas readers the prospect of romantic relationships upon their arrival.[17] The "Wedding Bells" feature from the first issue (77) in 1968 solidifies that possibility as the prospect of marriage. As the single feature of this kind that I have found from that period, it is remarkably revealing.[18]

"Wedding Bells" is a spread on facing pages, with seven photos of the wedding between Gregoire Noe Baylon and Aleksandra Dworczak: both law students at Adam Mickiewicz University in Poznań, with the former on scholarship from "faraway Congo"—a couple of "mixed race." *TPR's* graphic designers divided the feature horizontally, placing a white strip between the reportage text (title, article, and captions). The two largest photos sit heavily on the top, with five smaller images below, seeming to bear that weight like bricks. The top and the bottom are divided thematically. The two large photos depict the couple's marriage ceremonies, with civil at left and religious at right. The five images below are photos showcasing moments just after those ceremonies ended.

In the top-left photo, the couple sit on a pair of tall chairs at the marriage office. They are the photo's main subjects, so they are at the center of the frame, neatly dressed according to the occasion. They look at once content and confident. On each side of

17   See Nowicki, "Representations of Africans."
18   During PhD research on which this essay is based, I examined all available issues (in the 1955–89 time frame) of *Trybuna Ludu*, the official Party paper; *Sztandar Młodych*, the Polish Socialist Youth Union paper; *Zielony Sztandar*, the paper of an agrarian Party satellite, the United People's Party (ZSL); *Świat Młodych*, a paper for children and Scouts; two major local papers, *Życie Warszawy* from the capital and *Dziennik Łódzki* from Łódź; the weekly travel magazine *Dookoła Świata*; and, of course, *TPR*.

the young couple sit their witnesses: beside Gregoire, a Black man, with a white woman next to Aleksandra, and the front row they form looks polarized.

But there's more. Since a union between an African man and a Polish woman was seen as an outcome of internationalism, it occasioned further "mixing" of other people, as this photo showcases. Behind the four principal actors, a crowd forms the supporting cast. One may assume they're close family and friends, as civil ceremonies are usually much smaller than religious ones, where uninvited participants appear. Eleven adults are in the photo and two kids can be seen, one almost invisible in the top-right corner. Two Black men smile, but the white crowd seems mostly unmoved. Except, possibly, for two women, who show at least a desire to smile.

In the crowd at the back is a man whose body language and facial expression may expose his discontent. His hands crossed on his chest, his face in a grimace of dissatisfaction, he glances at a man to his left as if to say, What can we do about it? The other man isn't looking back and seems less concerned, or his concern is expressed differently. He seems saddened. Who are those two men? Brothers, cousins, or close friends? We'll likely never know, as with what they and the others were thinking then.

One way or another, the contrast between Blacks and Poles attending the ceremony makes me question this image. What's the reason for it? Is it just related to the wedding, or maybe also to the fact that a regime representative is photographing them?

The text certainly does everything possible to push such a reading far away. It recalls a fairy tale, but with one difference: there's no tragedy or difficult situation that the couple found themselves in before living happily ever after. On *TPR*'s pages their love story seems perfect:

> The groom, Gregoire Noe Baylon from faraway Congo, came to Poland three years ago to study law at Adam Mickiewicz University in Poznań. Back then it never crossed his mind that he would choose one of the girls he met in Poland as his soulmate. But in the way these things happen a young Poznań miss stole his heart and

the Congolese student popped the question. When the answer was "yes" there was nothing left but to ask her parents formally for their daughter's hand. Of course there could be no difficulties: though seeking parental consent is an old tradition in Poland, today, after coming of age, the girl decides for herself. In any case the girl's parents immediately took to the prospective lawyer and welcomed him into the family. The engaged couple quickly settled the necessary formalities in the Registry Office and the marriage took place as announced. Afterwards the bride's parents gave a slap-up party at which everyone celebrated away until the small hours. Among the guests was a photographer from our magazine who recorded the whole occasion on film. The staff of *The Polish Review* sent Mr. and Mrs. Gregoire Noe Baylon their best wishes for many years of happiness together.[19]

Images and text skillfully execute the editorial intention to promote Poland. Gregoire, the Congolese law student is marrying Aleksandra, his Polish fiancé, three years after coming to the PRL. While an old Polish tradition sets the rules of how a couple should proceed, her parents' possible refusal to give Aleksandra away is the only potential difficulty Gregoire would find on his way to marrying their daughter. Lest a reader grow concerned, however, the possibility is quickly dismissed by the insertion that "the girl decides for herself." Of course, in our particular example, her parents embrace Gregoire as their son-in-law with open arms. With "Wedding Bells" being evidently the only feature of its type an overseas reader might pick up, that reader is left reassured that marrying a Polish girl wouldn't be unduly complicated.

I will return to this theme later when I discuss *Black and White*, a documentary film exploring love relationships of mixed couples in Czechoslovakia. First, however, I will analyze another somewhat dubious photo from "Wedding Bells" that, as I will detail below, reveals PRL propaganda's lack of scruples, its subjectivity and incon-

sistency—reliant on who is being addressed—and contradictions
with that propaganda that was at the same time being presented to
a domestic audience.

In the photo at the top right, the church's large interior is packed with onlookers. It's difficult to say if it was actually
filled to the last pew, but in the photo, those standing seem squeezed
enough to indicate no more seats (or much standing room, to be
exact). It's hard to imagine so many participants who were just family and friends. Their presence seems likely related to the groom's
skin color, and fascination with exoticism. A Black person was a sen-
sation in Poland throughout the era of communism—and beyond.[20]
However, this likely reason for the turnout is well hidden in the feature, with readers directed to see it as social and religious approval
of this "mixed-race" marriage.

The Party, being in perpetual conflict with the Catho-
lic Church, worked ceaselessly to reduce the latter's influence in
society.[21] So the presence of a photo showing a packed church wedding in any organ of the official press might seem a surprise. But it
isn't. This image was never intended for domestic distribution. It
would, however, fit neatly with other images and texts helping gen-
erate an outside view of Poland as a viable study destination. A coun-

20   During the Fifth World Festival of Youth and Students in Warsaw in 1955,
such fascination was widespread, with some 26,000 foreign delegates
from 114 countries. More than 900 African delegates came, mostly from
areas still subordinate to European countries—making it Poles' first
large-scale opportunity to interact with African people. Images in the
Central Photography Archive and Military Photography Archive (both at
the National Digital Archive in Warsaw) show the stares and Poles'
"curious strokes" of a delegate's hair and skin. A major task for the press
was to inform their publics about contemporary African people,
consistent with the Eastern bloc manner: seeing delegates as people
who love life and smiling friends, not just as representatives of societies
"freeing themselves from the bondage of colonialism." Yet editors and
journalists had to learn themselves to represent things "correctly."
In 2009, I traveled to Poland with my Guinean partner (now my wife) and
witnessed similar responses to the sight of a Black person walking the
streets of my town (pop. circa 5,000). People stared, pointed, slowed
their cars to take a closer look. I'd never considered such awe from the
perspective of the person on the receiving end, and this spurred my early
research into the subject.

21   Jan Żaryn, "Kościół katolicki w PRL: Wybrane zagadnienia, hipotezy,
prowokacje," *Pamięć i Sprawiedliwość* 7, no. 1 (2005): 11–34, 13.

try in which freedom of faith is cherished—*TPR* published images of Muslims, as well.[22] And where there was no bad blood between the Party and the Church.

There are two more images from this reportage I'd like to give attention, at the bottom of the feature's second page. The first shows the couple kissing, and is the one photo of a "mixed-race" couple kissing I have found in the press archives to date, thus evidently the first published trace there of their intimacies. The second is in the bottom-right corner, and it's a perfect image with which to close a happy story. In a room full of family and friends, we see Gregoire held aloft by two men: at the right of the frame (the groom's left), a Black man, and on the left (his right) a white man, in the mutual effort of tossing him into the air. Around them the mostly white crowd, with a third Black man in the foreground, though we see only the back of his head. In this image, we see people for whom "race" as a divisive factor has left the building. These are among the most personal photographs *TPR* had then published, but wouldn't be the only ones.

"Studies, Happiness, Family"

The reportage "Studies, Happiness, Family," published a year later, focused on the family lives of other students in the PRL. There are ten photos in the feature, taken by Jan Morek, who doesn't recall this assignment very well.[23] The reader first sees an image of another "mixed-race" couple on a walk with a little child. It seems to be cold but not freezing, and they are well dressed and smiling—a happy family photo of Mr. and Mrs. Milen Mongo and their child.

When one's sight moves clockwise toward the title of the feature, it lands on the page's smaller picture. This depicts the couple, this time without the child, side by side at a desk strewn with books. Morek probably photographed them at their place, in the safety of home.

At first, it looks like they weren't focused on studying but on themselves. What we see is a moment of rest, when the subjects have taken a breather to share an intimate, loving moment.

22   See "Solidarity of Youth," *The Polish Review* 10 (50) (1965).
23   Morek, interview, 2018.

Their bodies touch, their hands meet, he appears to be saying something affectionate, she's not focused on books but on her partner's words. Looking again at the image, a different reading becomes apparent. With his left hand on the book she was reading, in his right hand a pen or a pencil, he appears to be explaining something to her. One thing that doesn't change in these readings is the affection on her face. The photo is a message seeking to emphasize that two aspects of life, studying and love, don't interfere with each other—as the feature's title states, there's space for "Studies, Happiness, Family."

My eyes move right and I begin the article. The man, Milen Mongo, is Congolese, and the woman, introduced as Mrs. Mongo, is Polish. It follows the couple's life from their meeting in Łódź, when Milen was studying Polish at the School of Polish for Foreign Students, to Warsaw in the present day, where they live with their son, Alain Richard Mongo, as Milen studies at Warsaw University of Technology (aviation is his passion). It describes fantastic relations Milen had with his fiancée's parents—to the extent, she says, that "I was at a loss at first whether Milen was coming to see my father or me."[24]

The approval from Mrs. Mongo's parents and others in their life—the couple's landlady and a neighbor, Magda, are always willing to babysit little Alain when the couple go out on a date—suggests that Africans in Poland are treated equally to the rest of Polish society. In this tolerant country, life and studies are facilitated by good health care, to boot. Alain was born a month early, but modern Polish medicine has enabled him to develop into a healthy boy, as readers see for themselves in the pictures.

Milen and his wife are no exception—it's not known exactly how many "mixed" marriages there are, for "no one has been keeping track of this in Poland."[25] But since a director at the Three Continents Club has danced at twenty such weddings in Warsaw

24   "Studies, Happiness, Family," *The Polish Review* 10 (98) (1969), 13.
25   "Studies, Happiness, Family," 14.

alone, there must be plenty more all over the nation.[26] Photos seem to confirm this prospect, with four of another "mixed" couple. They're friends of the Mongos: Nicolas Bakenda (also Congolese), Alina, his Polish wife, and Nicolas Jr., their child. Readers learn that Poland has institutions providing childcare for parents who work and study, and that Mrs. Mongo's decision to put her education on hold was a choice, not a necessity, as Alina Bakenda has continued her studies. But although the article dovetails neatly with the photos for the most part, we don't see photos of the Mongos and the Bakendas together.[27]

In reading "Studies, Happiness, Family," one could believe Poland to be that dream of a racism-free European state, where ample support is provided to students and young parents, making possible the fulfillment of their responsibilities. The single hint against this reading is in the quote below:

> Little Alain is learning his first words in the Polish language, too.
> "Polish will doubtless be useful to him in the future," Mrs. Mongo told us. "A Congolese with a knowledge of that language will be needed in Kinshasa, for contacts with Polish experts, businessmen and scientists are becoming more and more numerous."
> It is the privilege of every mother to dream about a most wonderful future for her son, but neither does Mrs. Mongo forget about her own future. In Kinshasa, where she will sometime go, she wants to be a working woman, active and useful. Next year she intends to start studies at a post-school certificate course. Perhaps for laboratory assistants?[28]

Something troubling about Polish society lurks in those words. Everybody around the Mongos loves little Alain. They want to babysit him, even, like his self-proclaimed "auntie" Magda, begging for an opportunity! Doctors and nurses adore him so much he becomes

26   I have yet to come across precise statistics confirming the number of marriages between foreigners and Poles during the discussed period.
27   Jan Morek stated that usually the article was done to accompany the photos, not the other way around.
28   "Studies, Happiness, Family," 14.

their "pet baby," with Alain seen in the photos being held, hugged, and smiled upon. There's no doubt that the boy is surrounded by love: born in Poland, to a Polish mother. Yet he's spoken of as a foreigner, with the writer using his mother's words in support of such an idea. His skin tone and that of his father let society perceive him that way.

Another tendency in *TPR* that is suggested here was a slant toward students returning home upon completing their studies.[29] We see the happy Mongo family, yet are told they won't be staying indefinitely. The anthropologist Maciej Ząbek details the issue of scholarship students staying in Poland or leaving:

> After their graduation, the administrative authorities usually forced them back to their countries of origin. Some of them married Polish citizens and could stay in Poland, but usually, they also went. There were also those who managed to get a doctoral degree or, in the case of medics, take a professional internship and then extended their stay even by a dozen or so years. Generally, however, until the nineties, only a few Africans remained in Poland permanently. Poland's economic unattractiveness, formal difficulties in the event of staying, lack of a wider African environment in our country effectively discouraged such a decision.[30]

29   The theme of return in *TPR* features may be divided into two main types. The first concentrates on individual students: along with photos of graduation, celebrating success with friends, etc., a photo of the student's diploma was run, as in "Goes Back the Physician" (*TPR* 12 (100) 1969). In "Hagos Keleta: An Excellent Student" (*TPR* 11 (111) 1970), we read: "'We watched Hagos with great pleasure, his earnestness, enthusiasm and self-denial,' said during the ceremony Dr. Kaczorowska [...] 'But the pleasure will be even greater when our experience transferred by the young scientist to his country brings that country benefits.'" The second type, usually a variation on the Farewell to Graduates column, typically consists of photos of African or Asian students at an official event. Politicians make speeches, shake hands with students, raise toasts, congratulate them on fulfilling their scholarship missions. The photos showcase a joyful win for both sides: taken in a student club in "Farewell to Postgraduates" (*TPR* 11 (51) 1965), and in the opulent interiors of Marshal Marian Spychalski's residence, the president of the Council of State, and at the Polish-African Friendship Society in Warsaw's Palace of Culture and Science in "Farewell to Graduates" (*TPR* 2 (90) 1969) and in "Farewell to Students" (*TPR* 7 (107) 1970).

30   Ząbek, *Biali i Czarni*, 40–41.

Such formal difficulties, "forced" returns, or the PRL's lack of a wider African diaspora environment are far from what *TPR* aimed to impart about Poland. And an overseas reader probably wouldn't be concerned by those eventualities before their arrivals in the PRL. Ultimately, most scholarship students never viewed remaining in Poland as an option.[31] Their responsibilities, their opportunities, were to acquire skills at a professional level then apply those in their own countries to help the societies from which they came, wither along socialist lines or not.

But if a visiting student about whom *TPR* wrote had wanted to remain, despite the difficulties? Would the editors slip in such information, given the era's stringent censorship? It appears nowhere in the magazine's photo reportages, though a feature about the graduation of Gregoire Noe Baylon (whom we've met above, in "Wedding Bells") may hint at how it was dealt with.

That feature consists of two photos and the accompanying report. The photos show him at the ceremony and in the office of his supervisor, Dr. Józef Górski. He has accomplished his goal of studying to become a lawyer. "A Graduate from Congo" lets us in on changes in his personal life as well. We learn that he's now a father. Interestingly, no mention is made of his future—atypical for this type of article. With no mention of this, maybe he's decided to stay— maybe he's an example of a student who chose not to return? If so, *TPR* may have not promoted remaining in Poland simply by not mentioning the possibility.

Of course, it could also be suggested that the above is speculation. But it should be acknowledged as a possibility, especially given the omnipresent topic of students' returning home throughout *TPR*'s issues (see footnote 29), and in light of research conducted by Marta Przybyło-Ibadullajev.

Przybyło-Ibadullajev's interest is in *TPR*'s industrial photography. Her investigation is based on editorial-office documentation, and the archives of two *TPR* photographers, Tadeusz

31   In the case of Abdel Harbim, a Sudanese scholarship student whose family photos I researched during PhD studies, his daughter Nadia said the family never considered staying in Poland: "He always meant to go back to Sudan." Nadia Harbim-Grabowska, interview by Bartosz Nowicki, 2019.

Sumiński and Jan Jastrzębski. Przybyło-Ibadullajev has traced changes made to photos before fitting them in layouts for printing, and to detail how those changes modified an image's "original" meaning to one better suiting *TPR*'s editorial interests. Her analysis of a feature about a Gdynia harborside facility ("Dry Dock," *TPR*, 1963, no. 3 (19)) is especially relevant. She refers to three of the four Jan Jastrzębski photos published with the feature:

> While the manipulation in the last picture, showing people at work, seems to be a rather aesthetic correction of the composition [...], the changes in the first two photos are more significant. In the picture on the title page of the article, presented in the form of a vertical rectangle, the proportions of the original frame have been radically changed, and the final frame is less than half of the original frame. On the negative, there is not only a characteristic palisade structure but also a wider perspective of the dock during construction. The deletion of the lateral parts of the image obliterates the awareness of space behind the construction and emphasizes the graphic qualities of the photograph with the geometric arrangement of shadows in the central part. In combination with the characteristic increase in contrast associated with the printing technique, this procedure prompts the viewer to concentrate on the artistic qualities of the photo. The same was done for the second picture, where while the space in the background is better seen, the crane in the background is significantly cut and is not clearly readable.[32]

Przybyło-Ibadullajev analyzes the photo images in the context of the feature, which reports on the completion of a "miracle" construction to expand the main Baltic port at Gdynia. The report and photos work with each other to great effect, as with *TPR*'s family-life stories discussed above. However, setting the "Dry Dock" pages against Jastrzębski prints and negatives, she highlights the editorial sleight-

32   Przybyło-Ibadullajev, "Fotografia przemysłowa."

of-hand, pointing out that the uncropped images capture a dock that's far from finished, while in the article the project seems completed. Such disparity could be related to *TPR*'s publication process (six months' lag from an issue's completion to publication, followed by overseas distribution), as Przybyło-Ibadullajev acknowledges— but then points out that "even a reader who is not familiar with construction can see that the work is still far from complete."[33] She concludes that "graphic form and aesthetic solutions legitimize the meaning of the text and distract attention from the inconvenient truth about the state of work on the investment."[34]

This is a pointed example of how truth was veiled from an overseas reader in favor of an altered presentation in the form of a "perfect" feature. "Studies, Happiness, Family," about the Mongo family and their friends, counts among such perfected features, in which a similar one-sidedness is apparent. What's being hidden? What aren't we seeing? What was cropped from the original photos, and which were left out in portraying an evidently tolerant and supportive society? Unfortunately, we'll never have answers about that feature article's specific example. A comparative analysis of the Morek photos is impossible—as he told me, the box with those negatives was damaged in a cellar flooding and disposed of.

I can offer an analysis of a contact sheet from *TPR* photographer Tadeusz Sumiński (shot in Warsaw, June 1963). No images I will discuss were printed in *TPR*; what I will do is point out several images similar to photos in the "Studies, Happiness, Family" feature, then compare these with others on the contact sheet that seem unsuitable for such a feature, at least as uncropped originals—as they'd disrupt the projection then being generated of the PRL's open-minded, racism-free society.

The contact sheet comes from negative number 913 in the Tadeusz Sumiński archive at the Archeology of Photography Foundation in Warsaw [FIGS. 1–2]. It contains a dozen images, of which seven depict a coffee shop/bar scene, on which I will concentrate below.

33   Przybyło-Ibadullajev, "Fotografia przemysłowa."
34   Przybyło-Ibadullajev, "Fotografia przemysłowa."

FIG. 1
TADEUSZ SUMIŃSKI, NEGATIVE NUMBER 913, JUNE 1963,
© TADEUSZ SUMIŃSKI, ARCHEOLOGY OF PHOTOGRAPHY FOUNDATION

In the foreground of the first, we see three people at a café table. At the left, a Black man holds a cigarette; he looks across at a blonde woman on the other side. (He is Mamadou Diakite, a Malian about whom *TPR* ran another feature with photos by Leonard Dudley.) Her attention is on something outside the frame, looking curiously (and joyfully) to her left. Between them is a woman who is noticeably older. Perhaps she's the younger woman's mother? It's difficult to deduce if the first two are a couple, but the image would certainly suit a feature about family life and intimate relationships between Black students and Polish women. It could represent a loving couple spending time with her caring, smiling mother who publicly accepts their relationship. In the café interior, others sit, minding their own business—the man's presence seems nothing out of the ordinary.

That vision, however, is disrupted by three images of this scene taken from a wider perspective. A close-up illusion of normality pales when we consider curious stares of passersby on the sidewalk that the man would've had to endure.

These images would surely have been cropped so the curious gazes wouldn't ruffle overseas readers. They provide considerable information regarding the setting: we glean that the café is open to the sidewalk, and customers and pedestrians could exchange looks and comments. Bizarrely, no customers at the three other tables have beverages. They might be waiting for their orders—the customer line now visible in the frame shows the café was quite busy as the shutter released.

Of the customers in the interior, a lone man is at the table to the left of the three subjects, and doesn't change his position much in these images. He faces the three, and stares. This may have lasted a few seconds, during which Sumiński took the images. Maybe he glances at the group because they're seated in front of him.

But four pedestrians quickly alter this impression of normality. Each turns their head to look at the Black man: an elderly woman stops to take a better look, a girl and a man in another image stare as well, as does a girl in the third image, while no one in these frames looks at anyone or anything else.

FIG. 2
TADEUSZ SUMIŃSKI, NEGATIVE NUMBER 913, JUNE 1963,
© TADEUSZ SUMIŃSKI, ARCHEOLOGY OF PHOTOGRAPHY FOUNDATION

It's impossible to know Sumiński's intentions today. Did he release the shutter only when a passerby gazed at the man? How many passed without looking at him? How many did, who Sumiński didn't photograph? He was surely aware that such images "won't run," so why waste film taking them?[35]

But when they are scrutinized in the context of Poles' fascination with Black delegates during Warsaw's 1955 Festival of Youth, or when we bear in mind that today this blatant curiosity remains unmistakable and unavoidable (see footnote 20), dismissing the racial dimension of those stares is but admission through denial.

Racism: The Great Unseen

"I feel terribly awkward when people look at me as if I were some spook, just because I am Black"—*Black and White*, 1968

The above quote could caption the long-range images discussed above. It comes from the documentary film *Black and White*, written and directed by Krishna Vishwanath, an Indian student studying at FAMU in Prague. Vishwanath's film is a fascinating account of race relations in Czechoslovakia in the late 1960s, openly discussing racism there, a taboo subject in the CSSR, according to FAMU lecturer Tereza Stejskalová.[36]

Racism was among the critical high points raised against capitalism by the authorities in the Eastern bloc; Poles, for example were steadily exposed to that through public media, reading about its prevalence in the UK, South Africa, and the US, and as a key component of colonialism. Yet all but no word was delivered about racial abuse happening then in Poland.

Black and White, therefore, is an astonishing source of information about racial relations in an Eastern bloc society. As with

---

35   As Marta Przybyło-Ibadullajev observes, when film rolls were issued by the *TPR* editorial office, while "black and white materials weren't stinted on, expensive materials for color photography were issued with more care." Przybyło, "Oddziaływanie przez fotografię," 28.

36   Tereza Stejskalová, "Students from the Third World in Czechoslovakia: The Paradox of Racism in Communist Society and Its Reflection in Film," in *Filmmakers of the World, Unite! Forgotten Internationalism, Czechoslovak Film and the Third World* (Prague: Tranzit.cz, 2017), 51–63, 52.

TPR's "Studies, Happiness, Family" feature, it concentrates on a "mixed-race" couple, narrating a love story from their meeting to their wedding to their baby's birth.

Black and White also bears visual similarities with *TPR*: stills from the film could easily have fit into the magazine's feature articles. The visual narrative Vishwanath creates, however, shapes a different reading of that visual material. Local women dating Black men are harshly judged, insulted as gold diggers and sluts. One mother won't accept her daughter's boyfriend, beating her and kicking her out of the house for dating a Black man.[37]

Czechoslovaks are envious of possibilities that foreigners' status provide in their country:

> I think Czech lads are envious of them colored ones, they smoke good cigarettes, they frequent posh bars, so they look well-off, and it's pure envy that registers some of these things. They tend to exaggerate. I think Czech students are jealous. It's because they think either these foreigners have more money, or that these black guys score with hotter chicks than they'll ever get.[38]

This quote recalls the opening photo in "Wedding Bells," the *TPR* feature from the same year, and the two men in its top-right corner. Could the one there whose arms are crossed be jealous, too? Another man whose voice-over we hear in *Black and White* admits that when it comes to local women dating Black men, "in this respect, I guess I'm kinda racist."

In several scenes, *Black and White* follows a Black man and a white woman walking busy streets in Prague. It seems like a simple ploy by Vishwanath to get this footage. The couple could just be actors, the director's friends, and might have been told how to behave (he plays with her hair in public).

What's obvious, however, is that the passersby weren't actors. They were everyday people in their streets, involved in their transient concerns. Their reactions to accidentally meeting this cou-

37   Stills that follow from *Black and White* and their subtitles provide quotes in the main text.
38   *Black and White*, 1968, 10:16.

ple, therefore, are natural and honest. We see them stare, shake their heads in disapproval, comment to one another about what they're seeing—and about how it makes them feel Before shooting these scenes, Vishwanath surely knew what revealing footage was likely to be caught on camera. We might not hear what the passersby say, but voice-overs make the scenes crystal clear:

> When I'm in the city on my own, troubles are scarce and random. But when I'm in the city with Hana it's catastrophic. Every now and then someone shouts at us. They scream Hana's a whore. And when I ask them why they tell me off. We're a source of unrest to the people.[39]

As Tereza Stejskalová observes: "the voice-over constantly confronts the opinion society has of itself as tolerant, modern and progressive with a reality that remains taboo because it does not fit the accepted image."[40] By this period, the connection is evident between criticism of racism issued by socialist societies and crises underway in the Party apparatuses that those societies were being run by. Stejskalová states that making *Black and White* was possible because the Czechoslovak system was in crisis, and that it can be appreciated as part of the Prague Spring.[41]

In Poland, the sole open criticism I know of society's attitude to foreigners—especially those who differed superficially from the population at large—was in a "Foreigner in Warsaw" article in *Sztandar Młodych*, the Polish Socialist Youth Union's paper, in 1984.[42] Illustrated with a photograph of an African man wearing a

39   *Black and White*, 1968, 09:45. After this quote, the voice-over excerpt
      starting with "I think Czech lads are envious" begins.
40   Stejskalová, "Students from the Third World," 52. Similar criticism of the
      societies' approach to race is found in the student short *Adopcja* (*The
      Adoption*) by Mostafa Derkaoui. For more on this film, see the essays by
      Monika Talarczyk, "WE WANT THE SUN! Short Films by Łódź Students from
      the Global South, Compared with Models from Polish Art Cinema," and
      Katarzyna Mąka-Malatyńska, "The Familiar, the Strange: Works by
      Students from the Global South in the Context of the Polish School of
      Documentary Film," in this book.
41   Stejskalová, "Students from the Third World," 56.
42   "Cudzoziemiec w Warszawie," *Sztandar Młodych,* May 23, 1984.

dashiki and writing on a blackboard in Polish, the article tells of
scholarship students describing incidents of appalling behavior
they'd endured.[43]

"Foreigner in Warsaw" is inseparable from the political situation, published when the country was in intractable economic crisis, after martial law ended, with Solidarity firmly established as the second power. It is a rare but telling statement on the
hypocrisy of PRL-era communism.

It's clear from these overseas students' voices, marginal as they may be, that Eastern bloc societies were rife with racism—at which point efforts to fight Western racism lose much of
their impact. Not just because a society suffers from its racism, but
because its leaders, in failing to tackle the issue, flouted an idealism out of self-interest rather than to act toward the public good.
In the end result:

> Racism in socialism is unthinkable [...]. If it begins to
> appear in any socialist country, it is indicative of cer-
> tain practices that take place and of the fact that
> something is wrong with the socialism in the country
> in question.[44]

PRL-era authorities, busy fighting for wider influence
in international politics, couldn't permit this to be seen openly, even
when they were fully aware of it.

43   Brian Scott arrived from Guyana to study in 1985; the journalist and radio
       presenter remembers his fellow students' racist behavior. "How much
       can you stand? If you have: 'Poland for Poles' or 'Negro to Africa' sprayed
       on the door of your room in the dorm, would you feel good? [...] And it was
       done by people who are the supposed future of Poland. Students!" Scott
       considered dropping out of university and leaving Poland. Brian Scott
       and Maria Mazurek, *Pierwszy Murzyn RP: Brian Scott o Polsce, mediach i polityce*
       (Kraków: Wydawnictwo WAM, 2016), 90.
44   Prohaska quoted in Stejskalová, "Students from the Third World," 52.

189　　　　　　　　　　　　　PART III

Gabrielle Chomentowski, a historian, is a research fellow at Centre d'histoire sociale des mondes contemporains (CNRS—Université Paris 1 Panthéon Sorbonne). Her major research field is social and cultural histories of cinema from a transnational perspective, focusing on Soviet, French, and African case studies. Her work addresses, specifically, film school history, film festival history, and film cooperation and competition during the Cold War. Her initial research work considered national policy in Soviet cinema during the 1920s and the 1930s. She teaches social history at Université Paris 1 and transnational perspectives on film history at Université Paris 8 Vincennes-Saint-Denis. Recent published work includes: "Filmmakers from Africa and Middle East at VGIK during the Cold War," *Studies in Russian and Soviet Cinema* (June 2019); *Filmer l'Orient: Politique des nationalités et cinéma en Union soviétique 1917–1938* (2016). With colleagues from Italy, Germany, and France, Chomentowski coordinates a European project on the history of the film schools in a transnational perspective, namely foreign students and teachers. She further coordinates, with La Fémis and École nationale des chartes, a research project about the history of film pedagogy in French art schools.

THE TRAINING OF THIRD-WORLD FILMMAKERS IN EASTERN BLOC SCHOOLS BEFORE 1991

Both a feeling of joy and of sadness engulfs the student presenting his graduation film, soon to leave VGIK [...]. Sadness, for [...] it is time to say farewell to those who have taught me to speak Russian and to understand the Russian language, who have taught me to understand the art of film, to those with whom I have shared a crust of bread, smoked a cigarette, shared tea in one and the same glass, with whom I have slept in the same room. [...] I am overcome by the feeling of joy too, for I am going home to my country, back to my people, whom I must serve. During my years in Moscow, at VGIK, I have changed. I have received a training [...], been enriched morally; I have prepared to become a professional filmmaker.[1]— Touré Mandiou

1   Excerpted from the graduate-film report by Touré Mandiou of the Republic of Guinea in the VGIK directing department, 1967, f. 2900/op. 4/del. 546, Russian State of Archive of Literature and Arts (RGALI). Translations of this and subsequent materials from Russian archives are by the author (Russian to French) and Melissa Thakway (French to English).

T his testimony, written by a graduating student at the Moscow All-Union State Institute of Cinematography (VGIK) in the 1960s from Guinea, sheds light on the under-recognized history of scholarship students from Asian and African countries, the Middle East, and Latin America who, after the Second World War and up to 1991, received scholarships from communist countries of Europe to train in the filmmaking professions. On returning to their countries, they then contributed to the development of state film structures, worked for local television, or shot their own independent films, making their artistic mark on their national cinemas. Such was the case, to provide several examples, for Nabil Maleh of Syria, who studied in Prague, Ahmed Lallem of Algeria, who studied in Łódź, and Sjuman Djaya of Indonesia and Abderrahmane Sissako of Mauritania, who both studied in Moscow.

Estimated at almost six hundred who came to the Soviet Union alone,[2] these men and women's paths constitute a field of study rich in numerous respects, within the histories of cinema and of political, cultural, and artistic circulations. Their paths are part of overlapping historical contexts. First is that of the Cold War, which saw the two major blocs compete to influence states, hearts, and minds.[3] These filmmakers' lives must also be situated within the historical context of independence movements and campaigns against neocolonialism, while also taking into account the singular history of relations between each of these African, Asian, Middle Eastern and South American countries—then collectively referred

2   This estimate is for the number I have drawn from VGIK files in Russian archives; to be combined with estimates of social-science researchers working on other Eastern bloc film schools.

3   The term "bloc" is used here for convenience's sake. Recent work in the social sciences demonstrates that this notion presumes a homogeneity between groups of countries that poorly reflects either the actual political and social diversity within both the Communist bloc, which included the Soviet Union, its satellites, and the People's Democracies of China and Cuba, and the Capitalist bloc, or the many internal conflicts.

to as the Third World[4]—and the various countries of the Communist bloc. Finally, the postwar period saw the emergence of a passion for cinema's creative potential among young people, who sought to express themselves through this medium. This movement coincided with an institutionalization of filmmaking studies on either side of the Iron Curtain as the authorities moved to satisfy that desire and to consolidate national pools of professionals in this burgeoning field.

This essay aims to provide pointers in understanding the trajectory of this group of Third World film students receiving training in Eastern bloc countries across this period. What did they have in common? Were they card-carrying communists, or were circumstances more nuanced? Did they have a clear idea of the profession they were training to pursue? Was their experience as satisfactory and fulfilling as Touré Mandiou's statement that opens this essay would suggest? What has become of them? Answers to these questions and other issues will be attempted by situating the context enabling these students' circulation, thereby enriching what has long remained a blind spot of the cultural history of cinema—namely, the history of its professional schools.

Third World Students' Reception

Student mobility increased significantly after 1945, as the local elites moved to improve the lives of their colonial charges in return for their contributions to the war effort. In France, for example, the government's awareness of the colonies' dearth of access to higher education led to reforms including the establishment in mainland France of specific institutions for students from the broader French Union,[5] and of universities in the overseas territories—that is, its colonies. Initially limited to those arriving from the colonies to

4   Also used here for convenience is the term "Third World," first used by
         Alfred Sauvy in 1952 and renounced by him twenty years later, which will
         be used rather than repeating "the African, Asian, Middle Eastern, and
         South American countries" and similar formulations. In this essay, Third
         World designates countries that, having endured colonialization and
         obtained independence, sought a third way that was distinct from the
         First (capitalist) and Second Worlds (communist) in the hierarchy that
         Sauvy posited.
5   The postwar years saw the French Empire transformed into the French
         Union (Union française), with the new constitution of the Fourth Republic
         and with subsequent reorganization of France's overseas territories.

the mainland, this new student mobility evolved in the 1950s to include the US and Eastern Europe. The Soviet Union, meanwhile, which in the 1920s had already begun receiving political activists from Indochina, Persia, the Middle East, and African countries,[6] opened its doors to foreign students in the late 1940s, notably from Asia (Mongolia, Korea, and Vietnam), then from Eastern Europe.[7] In the early 1950s, political militants from Nigeria and Ghana found refuge as students in East Germany, Hungary, and Czechoslovakia.[8] This movement grew as postcolonial independence expanded, along with the departure of experts from among the colonial elite. Those roles needed to be filled in the new states—and the rival powers made competing efforts to attract these new nations' future elites, and to extend their influence and spread their ideological models.

Most of these countries in Asia, the Middle East, then Africa, having been granted or winning independence after the Second World War, chose to diversify their political and economic partners to break out of binary, often exclusive foreign relations that had bound them to the former colonial centers. The new governments, depending on their ideological position and pragmatic needs, signed cooperation agreements with countries of the Western bloc and/or the Eastern one. The US and the USSR, since the Bandung Conference in 1955 brought together Asian and African states, with the

6   Masha Kirasirova, "The 'East' as a Category of Bolshevik Ideology and Comintern Administration: The Arab Section of the Communist University of the Toilers of the East," *Kritika* 18, no. 1 (2017): 7–34. For further information on African students, see Irina Filatova, "Indoctrination or Scholarship? Education of Africans at the Communist University of the Toilers of the East in the Soviet Union, 1923–1937," *Paedagogica Historica* 35, no. 1 (1999): 41–66.

7   In late 1947, the Soviet Union signed agreements with Bulgaria to take its students, and then with Albania. See data collected at the Ministry of Foreign Affairs of the Russian Federation, accessed July 20, 2021, https://www.mid.ru/foreign_policy/international_contracts/2_contract.

8   Sara Pugach, "Eleven Nigerian Students in Cold War East Germany: Visions of Science, Modernity, and Decolonization," *Journal of Contemporary History* 54, no. 3 (2019): 551–72; Philip Muehlenbeck, *Czechoslovakia in Africa, 1945–1968* (Basingstoke: Palgrave Macmillan, 2016).

adoption of nonaligned status[9] in response to the dichotomy between the two major blocs, had been assertively persuading those countries to join their respective camps. Less than a year after Bandung, during the Twentieth Party Congress in Moscow, its first secretary, Nikita Khrushchev, officially stated the Soviet Union's desire to embrace the "developing countries,"[10] to develop a policy of "peaceful coexistence," and to back the new states' economic development.[11] The European communist countries also embarked on this assistance to the decolonizing nations.

The chronology of official state recognition and cooperation agreements being signed differed between Eastern bloc countries. It is noteworthy that the Soviet Union finalized agreements with North Vietnam in the early 1950s, with Indonesia and Tunisia in 1956, and Egypt in 1957, then with Ghana, Guinea, and Cuba in 1959.[12] Other treaties followed and then were extended or not, depending on political events specific to each country: relations with Iraq, for example, were broken off in 1963 following the overthrow and execution of General Qāsim and the banning of the Communist Party, before relations were restored in 1972 with the new Ba'athist regime.

Cooperation policies and higher-education assistance clearly comprised the cornerstone of Soviet bloc–Third World relations and embodied the international solidarity being advocated by communist countries. While universities built to host Third World students including the new Peoples' Friendship University in Moscow and November 17 University in Prague have long garnered focus

9   At the Bandung Conference, President Sukarno of Indonesia declared that it was "not a meeting of Malayans, nor one of Arabs, nor one of Indo-Aryan stock. It is not an exclusive club either, not a bloc which seeks to oppose any other bloc." For his full speech, see *CVCE*, accessed July 30, 2021, https://www.cvce.eu/education/unit-content/-/unit/dd10d6bf-e14d-40b5-9ee6-37f978c87a01/c28105d8-8f82-4f57-b077-7e87dfbc7205/Resources#88d3f71c-c9f9-415a-b397-b27b8581a4f5_en&overlay.
10   On pre-1950s relations between the Soviet Union and African countries, see Maxim Matusevich, *Africa in Russia, Russia in Africa: Three Centuries of Encounters* (Trenton: Africa World Press, 2007).
11   The Soviet Union, as a UNESCO member since 1954, was already engaged in a process of economic, educational, and technical assistance to Third World countries.
12   All agreements signed between the Soviet Union and African countries in different fields of cooperation, specifying dates of and changes in these agreements: Leongard Gončarov et al., eds., *Sovetsko-afrikanskie otnošeniâ: Spravočnik* (Moscow: Akademiâ nauk SSSR, Institut Afriki, 1982).

in public opinion and among researchers, they represented a small proportion of student circulations.[13] From the late 1950s to 1991, almost 130,000 students from sub-Saharan Africa, Arab countries, and Cuba came on scholarships to study in the Soviet sphere. Most studied medicine, engineering, defense and strategics, and the sciences, along with painting and cinema, in an array of institutions of higher education.[14]

The Institutionalization of Film Training

Are studies at a film school essential to becoming a director, screenwriter, or cinematographer? In cinema's early years in the interwar period, people learned to use equipment and run film productions by way of the theater or by working directly in film studios, often at the bottom of the ladder. Yet by 1919, the world's first national film school was established in Moscow as the State College of Cinematography (GTK), which became the State Institute of Cinematography in 1930, then in 1934 was renamed the Higher State Institute of Cinematography (VGIK). At the outset, in the civil strife of the 1920s, the teachers and students, lacking adequate equipment in sufficient quantities, instead trained without film stock, watched for-

13   Constantin Katsakioris, "The Soviet Union, Eastern Europe, and Africa in the Cold War: The Educational Ties," *Working Paper Series des SFB 1199 an der Universität Leipzig*, no. 16, accessed October 14, 2021, https://research. uni-leipzig.de/~sfb1199/app/uploads/2019/04/wp16_katsakioris-et-al_ web_190419.pdf; Constantin Katsakioris, "The Lumumba University in Moscow: Higher Education for a Soviet Third-World Alliance, 1961–1991," *Journal of Global History* 14, no. 2 (2019): 281–300; Monique de Saint Martin, Grazia Scarfo Ghellab, Kamal Mellakh, eds., *Étudier à l'Est: Expériences de diplômés africains* (Paris: Karthala, 2015); Michèle Leclerc-Olive, "Éditorial," *Revue européenne des migrations internationales* 32, no. 2 (2016): 4.

14   In December 1991, 43,562 students from sub-Saharan Africa and 60,000 from Arab countries had graduated from institutions of higher education in the USSR. See Monique de Saint Martin and Patrice Yengo, "Quelles contributions des élites 'rouges' au façonnement des États postcoloniaux?" *Cahiers d'études africaines*, no. 226 (2017): 231–57, 234. Despite the lack of official data, Rafael Pedemonte has stated that nearly 22,000 students from Cuba were trained in the USSR. See Rafael Pedemonte, "The First Generation of Cuban Students in the Soviet Union: Shaping a Revolutionary 'Culture of Militancy' (1960s)," http://www.iheal.univ-paris3.fr/sites/www.iheal.univ-paris3.fr/files/The First Generation of Cuban Students in the Soviet Union.pdf. Unfortunately, I have no serious estimate regarding students from the rest of Latin America.

eign films, discussed montage, acting, and lighting, and danced and
painted, while debating society's upheavals and the diverse political
measures being taken by the Party's Central Committee.[15]
        This interdisciplinarity and the combination of theo-
retical and practical studies became the new school's trademarks,
and would influence pedagogical models when the Centro Sperimentale di Cinematografia in Rome and the Institut des hautes études
cinématographiques (IDHEC) in Paris were founded over the next two
decades.[16] In most countries, where there were no schools, learning
accrued by practice; by starting at the bottom and making one's way
up in the industry, people became screenwriters, cinematographers,
and directors.
        But what was the situation in countries where there
were no production infrastructures and where it was impossible to
start at the bottom of the ladder? "We were familiar with film screenings, we saw films in our African towns, but there was no connection
to any known vocational path,"[17] recalls Timité Bassori, a Paris-
trained filmmaker from the Ivory Coast. Indeed, while French, British, Belgian, and Portuguese colonial regimes had built movie theaters to entertain their own nationals and educate local populations,[18]
this at the same time had stymied vocational opportunities in filmmaking. A fear of colonized populations using cinema as a subversive weapon led Pierre Laval, minister of colonies in 1934, to imple-
ment an arsenal of administrative authorizations to control filming
and sound recording in France's African colonies. By the late 1940s,
British imperial authorities, as with the Belgian authorities in Congo,

15   Juri Martinenko, M. Garkushenko, VGIK, Shkola kinoiskusstva (Moscow: Sojuz
          kinematografistov SSSR, Vsesojuznoe bjuro propagandy kinoiskusstva,
          1982); Jamie Miller, "Educating the Filmmakers: The State Institute of
          Cinematography in the 1930s," Slavonic and Eastern European Review 85, no. 3
          (2007): 462–90; Masha Salazkina, "(V)GIK and the History of Film
          Education in the Soviet Union 1920–1930," in A Companion to Russian Cinema,
          ed. Birgit Beumers (Chichester, West Sussex: Wiley Blackwell, 2016),
          4–65.
16   See Duncan Petrie, "Theory, Practice and Significance of Film Schools,"
          Scandia 76, no. 2, (2010): 31–46. IDHEC was renamed La Fémis (École
          nationale supérieure des métiers de l'image et du son) in 1986.
17   Timité Bassori, "Soumanou Paulin Vieyra, un pionnier: Cinéaste et
          critique," Présence africaine 2, no. 170 (2004): 35–40.
18   See Odile Goerg, Tropical Dream Palaces: Cinema in Colonial West Africa, trans.
          Melissa Thackway (London: Hurst Publishers, 2020).

had also made access to film careers extremely difficult. In French Indochina, the situation was a little different, leading to the emergence of film productions by local entrepreneurs.[19]

The postwar period, meanwhile, featured the widespread institutionalization of film training. The IDHEC admissions brochure in 1945 stated: "Cinema is not just an art, it is also a profession, a difficult and thrilling one. In addition to a broad, vivacious general cultural [grasp], its practice requires wide-ranging and varied technical knowledge," proposing to "replace chance by method" in order to "avoid the fits and starts of intermittent apprenticeships" and "bitter experiences."[20] Aware of cinema's importance as a means of communication, governments in both the East and the West invested in training film professionals.

National film schools gradually opened on the Iron Curtain's opposing sides: the Film and Television School of the Academy of Performing Arts (FAMU) in Prague in 1946; the Łódź Film School, Poland, in 1948; the Babelsberg and Munich schools in the two Germanies in 1954. In the English-speaking world, university programs were offered mainly in Los Angeles and New York City; in the UK, training was offered at the London School of Film Technique. In the 1940s, citizens of imperial colonies were granted access to this latter training. Training sessions were held in London for a handful of Ghanaians, Sudanese, and Nigerians to meet the need for Colonial Film Unit staffs in those three British colonies.[21] IDHEC, like all French higher-education institutions, was open to the entire *Communauté française*, which made study available to those who were able to come to Paris. But until independence, glass ceilings limited film-school graduates' freedom of expression: technicians in local Colo-

19   See Philippe Dumont, "Les débuts du cinéma vietnamien," *La Revue des Ressources*, February 4, 2011, https://www.larevuedesressources.org/les-debuts-du-cinema-vietnamien,1839.html.

20   Institut des hautes études cinématographiques, *Carrières auxquelles prépare l'Institut des hautes études cinématographiques: Conditions d'admission pour 1945* (Paris: Librairie Vuibert, 1945), 3.

21   In the late 1940s, the Colonial Film Unit, set up in 1939, established local units producing educational films and documentaries. The Sudan Film Unit, the Nigerian Film Unit, and the Gold Coast Film Unit were significant among these. In the 1950s, five Sudanese students trained in London then returned to work in the Sudan Film Unit as camera operators, sound engineers, screenwriters, and editors. Others also trained in Cyprus to meet the needs of other units.

nial Film Units could only be assistants, not directors, and IDHEC
graduates from Francophone Africa were forbidden from shooting
films in their own countries.
      Yet for many intellectuals and artists in colonized
nations, it was vital to show their countries as they saw them, not as
the colonial authorities deigned to represent them. This notion grew
even more urgent after independence. In making their own films,
local artists sought to challenge caricatural representations of their
histories, values, and contemporary political situations. Urbain Dia
Moukouri, a Cameroonian filmmaker, expressed it this way: "African
filmmakers must look at their continent as if it had not been scrutinized by anyone before. They must look at Africa in a new light."[22]
There was, however, a pervasive lack of film equipment and, above
all, of people with filmmaking experience. Apart from the Cairo
Higher Institute of Cinema, set up in 1954, no other film schools were
operating on the African continent in the early 1950s. In Asia, training that developed in North Vietnam and in China was more technical than artistic. In India, with its long tradition of film both as entertainment and in terms of production, training wasn't introduced at
the Film Institute of India until the 1960s.

Choosing a Film School: East or West?
      In general, a correlation is evident between the train-
ing followed by filmmakers—those who went into higher education,
that is[23]—and ties between former colonies and their recent ruling
lands for reasons related first to language, then to personal networks, and finally to film-sector agreements now in place between
the two countries. In an interview, Ateyyat El Abnoudy, an Egyptian
filmmaker, explained how after several years of Cairo Film School
studies, she chose London over other potential destinations: "It was
easy at that time to go to the Soviet Union or to Poland but I didn't

22   Urbain Dia Moukouri cited by Semyon Čertok, in "Kino černoj Afriki:
      problemy i naděždy," in *Mify i realnost': Zarubežnoe kino sevodnâ* (Moscow:
      Iskusstvo, 1972).
23   Roy Armes has noted that about half of African filmmakers took degree
      courses in universities or film schools. See Roy Armes, *African
      Filmmaking: North and South of the Sahara* (Bloomington: Indiana University
      Press, 2006), 61.

want to waste my time learning a new language and I knew English well so I preferred to go to the National Film School in London for three years."[24]

African students from former British colonies went to train in London or in the US, for example at the UCLA School of Theater, Film and Television. From 1946, when IDHEC admitted its first student who was not a French national, to 1988, 566 foreign nationals were among the 1,439 graduates, with many from Francophone countries or countries where French was common among the cultural elite: 131 African students (mainly from Algeria, Egypt, Tunisia, and Morocco), 109 from Northern Europe, 67 from South America, 64 from Southern Europe, 60 from North America, 50 from the Middle East, 47 from Eastern Europe, 35 from East Asia, and 3 from Oceania.[25] As noted above, speaking the language used by the particular school was not these students' sole criteria.

From 1948 to 1989, Third World students came to VGIK to study, as well as to the Leningrad Institute of Motion Picture Engineers (LIKI), the Theater, Cinema and Television University in Kiev, FAMU in Prague, and the Łódź Film School. At VGIK, which received the most Third World students, over a hundred Vietnamese students attended, along with some thirty Algerian students, about a dozen Colombians, and around sixty Syrians—these comprise the largest national cohorts, not all of whom graduated.[26]

FAMU admitted the first of the Syrian and Algerian students. Nabil Maleh, who was encouraged in Damascus by a Czech diplomat to go to Prague, arrived to study nuclear physics, which he rapidly dropped in favor of cinema. Maleh later become a founder of Syrian cinema.[27] Similarly, well before Algerian independence, Bou-

24   Rebecca Hillauer, *Encyclopedia of Arab Women Filmmakers* (Cairo: American University in Cairo Press, 2005), 46.
25   *Annuaire des anciens élèves de l'IDHEC*, Institut de Formation et d'Enseignement pour les métiers de l'Image et du Son, FEMIS, 1994, 9. These figures exclude young professionals who arrived from abroad for courses of four to six months run by IDHEC, who were admitted at the request of the Ministry of Foreign Affairs, the Ministry of Cooperation or the Ministry of Economic Affairs, or at the behest of their governments.
26   These figures are from the list of foreign students recently drawn up by VGIK, provided by Rossen Djagalov, whom I heartily thank.
27   Kay Dickinson, *Arab Cinema Travels: Transnational Syria, Palestine, Dubai and Beyond*, (London: Palgrave, 2016), 47.

baker Adjali, then a member of the National Liberation Front (FLN), was wounded during an FLN operation in Paris, found refuge in Prague in 1957 and entered FAMU. He was joined two years later by Mohammed Lakhdar-Hamina, another FLN militant, renowned today for *The Winds of the Aures* (1966) and *Chronicle of the Years of Fire* which received the Palme d'Or in 1975 at the Cannes Film Festival.[28] At FAMU from 1950 to 1989, nearly one hundred Third World students learned the ropes of their craft.[29] Other students were from Korea, Iran, Cyprus, Indonesia, Benin, Tunisia, and Lebanon; some then played essential roles in developing their national cinemas, while others dropped off the radars of the film and audiovisual networks.

In Łódź, where the PRL's leading film school operated, out of 170 foreign students studying there during the Cold War, sixty-three came from Third World countries: one from the Caribbean, five from Asia, six from the Middle East, nine from sub-Saharan Africa, nineteen from North Africa, twenty-three from Latin America. Only two were women.[30] These circulations appear to have been most numerous in the 1960s and 1980s, but with an especially African presence in the 1970s. Some didn't graduate, while several went on to work in television or cinema, including Ahmed Lallem in Algeria, the Moroccan directors and DOPs Mostafa and Abdelkrim Derkaoui, and Abdelkader Lagtaa.[31] Some went into film production, including the Congolese directors Gilbert-Ndunga Nsangata and Hyacinthe Mienandi. Finally, to mention other Eastern bloc film schools, Third World students—albeit fewer—trained at the Potsdam-Babelsberg film school, or completed internships at the film studios in Belgrade, Bucharest, and Budapest.

28   On the experience of these two filmmakers in Prague, see Olivier
            Hadouchi, "Mohammed Lakhdar-Hamina and Boubaker Adjali: The
            Careers of Two Algerian Film-makers who Attended FAMU," in *Filmmakers of
            the World, Unite! Forgotten Internationalism, Czechoslovak Film and the Third World*,
            ed. Tereza Stejskalová (Prague: Tranzit.cz, 2017), 123–35.
29   Stejskalová, *Filmmakers of the World, Unite!*
30   I warmly thank Prof. Monika Talarczyk at the Łódź Film School—and
            co-editor of the present volume—for these details from the school's
            archives.
31   For more on Moroccan students studying at the Łódź Film School, see
            Marie Pierre-Bouthier, *"Podróż* to Poland: In Search of a Potential
            Moroccan Cinema," in this book.

Many students from Third World countries were led to choose film schools in the Soviet sphere by the prospect of studying for free and having a scholarship covering living expenses, as well as by political persuasion and the attractions of a renowned film school. Choosing a country with no colonial past—though largely a false perception, it was one that was encouraged by communist countries—held appeal for students in favor of the anti-imperialist struggles of the era. Filmmaker Piyasiri Gunaratna, at the time a member of a Sri Lankan youth organization, learned from a Czech correspondent that he might obtain a scholarship to study cinema in Prague. Gunaratna went to Czechoslovakia in the late 1950s and studied at FAMU from 1960 to 1965.[32]

Some students, though, knew nothing about cinema or film schools in their host countries' before arriving, or even intended cinema to become their field. Attracted by the potential of a free education, chosen by their governments for a scholarship, they'd left without knowing which field of study they'd eventually opt for. Once there, during their first year spent learning the language, they chose cinema. The Moroccan filmmaker Mohammed Abouelouakar, when he was nineteen, obtained a study scholarship for the USSR; when asked "What field did you choose?" Abouelouakar answered "the visual arts" without elaborating.[33] His preparatory-year teachers at the Moscow Automobile Institute recognized his artistic abilities—he'd been involved in theater and painting since he was fifteen. They advised him to take the VGIK entrance exam. The modalities of the exam were the same required of all candidates: an application detailing the candidate's previous path and motivations, followed by general culture questions, and finally an improvised acting or directing exercise.

Others, however, were sent by their governments to receive training in cinema and on their returns then worked for local cultural institutions. Michel Papatakis—now considered one of the key figures in Ethiopian cinema—went to the USSR in early 1961[34]

32   Interview with the filmmaker and translator Piyasiri Gunaratna by Tereza
            Stejskalová, in Stejskalová, *Filmmakers of the World, Unite!*, 203–7.
33   VGIK Archives, d. 260, Mohamed Abouelouakar, 12.
34   VGIK Archives, d. 2172, Michel Papatakis, 20.

under these expectations, and "in conformity with the agreements signed between the Soviet Embassy in Addis Ababa and the Ethiopian Ministry of Information."[35] His compatriots Getachew Terreken and Tafesse Jara, who went at that same time, and others who arrived in 1966 and 1967, including Desta Tadesse and Tefferi Busuaechu, later occupied roles at the Ministry of Information as the Derg regime's official cameramen.[36]

Daily Life in Łódź, Moscow, and Prague

Whether in Poland, the Soviet Union, or Czechoslovakia, scholarship students arriving to study had to spend up to twelve months in intensive language study—that is, forty hours a week. All foreign students transited into their stays in the PRL via Łódź and its School of Polish for Foreign Students, opened in 1952 and in operation until the late 1970s. Contrary to VGIK, where students had a room in the residence halls, film students in Łódź lived with scholarship holders in other disciplines in a building known as the Tower of Babel, in a district named Lumumbowo after Patrice Lumumba. It was similar in Prague: the university residence housed Third World students and Czech experts headed for stints in technical cooperation with these countries. As in the USSR, if they were not already bound to train in a particular field by specific agreements between their home and host countries, the students could choose their focus and institution of higher education before or after this first year.

In the Soviet Union, students who chose their specialization during their year of language studies could also take various arts classes to prepare for the VGIK entrance exam. If students passed the exam, they were admitted to the school's five-year pro-

35   VGIK Archives, d. 2172, Michel Papatakis, 26.
36   Tefferi Busuaechu, Desta Tadesse, and Tafesse Jara worked together on the film *3002: Wondimu's Memories*, commissioned by the Ethiopian authorities and screened at the Second World Black and African Festival of Arts and Culture (FESTAC) in Lagos in 1977. Under threat during the Derg regime, Tefferi Busuaechu took refuge in Britain after Desta Tadesse was assassinated during political repressions—the latter had been appointed to head the Film Development Department and as Head of Censorship at the ministry. See Dennis Austin, *Politics in Africa* (Hannover: University Press of New England, 1978), 154; Aboneh Ashagrie Zieyesus, "Ethiopian Cinema in the Era of Barrack Socialism (1974–1991)," *Cultural and Religious Studies* 8, no. 1 (2020): 14–27.

gram. Some failed the first time, as Abbas Al Shalah did, who came from Iraq in 1960 and who took classes for two consecutive years to prepare for the exam before passing in 1963 and entering the directing department. The Prague and Łódź entrance exams were no easier. Jerzy Toeplitz, head of the Polish film school, stated in 1963 that "on average, one in fifteen candidates [was accepted]," making it "not a school for the masses, but a school with a strictly limited number of students."[37]

VGIK's courses were organized into seven departments: cinematography, directing, acting, screenwriting, set design, film production, and film criticism. In their first year in the directing department, students had to shoot a 16-mm silent film; in their third year, complete a production-studio internship and make a 35-mm film; and, in their fifth year, make their final degree film. Courses varied from one instructor to another. Filmmaker Jean-Pierre Lledo, who'd come from Algeria, recalls that in the early 1970s, the director Mikhail Romm asked his student group whether they wanted him to tell his memories from the 1920s and 1930s or teach them directing. The students initially chose the former. Only later did Romm initiate them into directing with a 16-mm camera. Each student then presented their work to the class, who debated the film's qualities and weaknesses.[38]

Courses were intensive. Added to classes in their field (mise-en-scène, image, etc.) were classes in Russian and foreign literature, Russian history, economics, and politics, all of which were directly related to the ideology advocated by the Soviet authorities. Free time was devoted to things including going to the capital's theaters and cinemas. Many screenings were also organized at VGIK, including film projects by the instructor-filmmakers, which they previewed to their students, and Soviet and foreign films not distributed in local cinemas.[39]

37   *Sputnik kinofestivalia* (festival edition of *Sputnik*), 1963.
38   Interview with filmmaker Jean-Pierre Lledo in December 2016, who studied directing at VGIK from 1970 to 1976.
39   Two types of screening venue existed in the USSR: commercial cinemas and non-commercial installations, including screening rooms in factories, clubs, unions, and cultural institutions.

Discussions and debates about the films, and disagreements that could arise between instructors and students at work on their degree films, often contrasted sharply with the image of this renowned Soviet institution held by certain Third World governments, and of other schools, as well. On returning home, fledgling filmmakers could find themselves confronting official rigor both in their treatment of subjects addressed in their films and about technical and artistic issues—and even with aggressive political repression. Costa Diagne from Guinea, who received an award at the 1966 Dakar World Festival of Black Arts for *Les Hommes de la danse* (*Men of the Dance*), which was shot in Moscow, was arrested in 1970 and sentenced to ten years in a prison camp. Jean-Pierre Lledo, on returning to Algeria, failed to find the same innovation among local cameramen he'd experienced at VGIK. The films of Mostafa Derkaoui, who'd trained in Łódź, were censored and banned in Morocco. As for Piyasiri Gunaratna, like many other filmmakers trained in these Eastern bloc schools, he was treated with suspicion on his return and was ignored by the profession in Sri Lanka for several years.[40]

Conclusion

While it is possible to retrace in broad strokes circulations among these scholarship film students in terms of a history of international relations, a more in-depth social history is needed to present the complexities of their lives. And though the Eastern bloc initially welcomed students who had overt political motivations, the situation evolved as time went on. Opportunities the host countries were offering with their scholarships, as well as what were often highly advantageous student-living conditions, became additional criteria when it came to political persuasion. The opportunities for advanced studies and the film schools' international reputations influenced some people's choices.

A singularity among the film students also needs to be considered. Their passion for cinema, their study conditions (small groups) and living conditions (in a separate residence at VGIK, for example) unquestionably resulted in specific experiences. A photo

40   See the interview with Gunaratna in Stejskalová, *Filmmakers of the World,
        Unite!*, 207.

on the cover of the main journal of the Moscow Festival, the *Sputnik kinofestivalia* edition dated July 15, 1983, shows about thirty foreign students gathered at the VGIK main entrance. The caption reads: It was too much of a squeeze in the rector's office. The Moscow Festival's guests and participants were quite moved. How could they not be! Most of them had spent memorable student years here [...]. "The VGIK students are lucky," American filmmaker Godfrey Reggio told us. "Here they have what professionals don't have in other countries." The nostalgia that VGIK students appear to have felt, however, must include other nuances: the many negative experiences of students who encountered racism, or had difficulties in their course work—even a certain disillusionment on discovering real existing socialism and hardships of daily life within it. Not to be overlooked, also, was ostracism many faced on their returns home, whether from VGIK, FAMU, or Łódź. Nonetheless, the testimonies gathered to date tend to confirm Godfrey Reggio's comment from the photo caption: all received a high-quality, extremely rigorous education, which opened a world of possibilities to these students—at least in terms of imagination and creation. Films by numerous of these students, which merit close analysis, testify both to their makers' hopes and, at the same time, to frustrations they encountered in these communist host countries and on returning to their own.

Monika Talarczyk is a film scholar and associate professor at the Łódź Film School. She is the author of *Wanda Jakubowska: Revisited* (forthcoming in 2022), *Biały mazur: Kino kobiet w polskiej kinematografii* (2013, The White Mazur: Polish Women's Cinema), *Wszystko o Ewie: Filmy Barbary Sass a kino kobiet w drugiej połowie XX wieku* (2013, All about Eve: Barbara Sass's Film and Women's Cinema in the Later 20th Century) and publications about women film directors including the *Pantoptikum* issue "Women in Cinema" (2022, no. 23), and the collection *(Nie)widzialne kobiety kina* (2018, *(Non) visible Women in Film*), edited with Małgorzata Radkiewicz. Talarczyk's major research field is Minor Cinema (women's cinema, minorities in film culture). In 2014, she received the Polish Film Institute Award. A member of the European Women's Audiovisual Network (EWA), the Polish Women of Film society, and FIPRESCI (the International Federation of Film Critics). Currently developing the research project about Jerzy Toeplitz's activity in the international network of film schools and film archives in the twentieth century.

WE WANT THE SUN! SHORT FILMS BY ŁÓDŹ STUDENTS FROM THE GLOBAL SOUTH, COMPARED WITH MODELS FROM POLISH ART CINEMA

The flow of students from the Global South to the Łódź Film School began at the end of the 1950s. The school was then run by educators from the START generation (1930–35), art-film enthusiasts from that prewar cohort of committed cinephiles: Jerzy Toeplitz, the founding rector, Eugeniusz Cękalski, Wanda Jakubowska, Stanisław Wohl, and Jerzy Bossak. Cinephilia may be more commonly associated with the French New Wave and with postwar film-club networks, yet film historians have taken the lead in applying the term retroactively to such groups of enthusiasts in the 1930s whose fascination with cinema didn't leave them blind to social problems of the era.[1] Cinema, for START and like-minded factions, was to be the means of casting light on those problems, heightening public sensitivity to them, and calling for change. The appropriate forms for "useful" films—an idée fixe for START—would be realistic feature films and politically engaged documentaries on social themes.

1   Łukasz Biskupski, *Kinofilia zaangażowana: Stowarzyszenie Miłośników Filmu Artystycznego "Start" i upowszechnianie kultury filmowej w latach 30* (Łódź: Wydawnictwo Przypis, 2017); Malte Hagener, *Moving Forward, Looking Back: The European Avant-Garde and the Invention of Film Culture 1919–1939* (Amsterdam: Amsterdam University Press, 2007).

Unsurprising, then, that after the START veterans took control of postwar Polish cinema this model of social realism became the cornerstone of the Łódź Film School's aesthetic. Reinforced and simplified by socialist-realist propaganda, by the mid-1950s the aesthetic then underwent revision and in some instances rejection by pupils who were fashioning the Polish School, including Andrzej Wajda, Andrzej Munk, and Kazimierz Kutz, and by students of what was termed the film "preschool" in Kraków[2]—Wojciech Has, Jerzy Kawalerowicz, and others. These directors were filtering the perception of reality through their characters' subjectivities, endowing it with intriguing visual forms, and using the symbolism in objects and scenes to encode what couldn't be overtly declared at the time. Some, including Has and Kawalerowicz, joined the teaching staff in Łódź and were academic advisers on short student-film projects.

This essay will examine models of Polish art cinema that had the strongest influence on the school's students from the Global South, how they then adapted those models to their own sensitivities and experiences, and, finally, whether they enriched the models with elements from outside Polish film culture. Short films give students the chance to practice their abilities while passing successive stages in their studies; they can also be an art form in their own right. For this essay, this latter criterion of quality, in addition to a filmmaker's national origin, was the deciding factor in the choice among their existing short films.

Student shorts are a very particular form: while limited by their length and budget, they're also sometimes made under very strong influence from the adviser's creative personality. Yet the phenomenon of "anxiety of influence," defined by the literary critic Harold Bloom in relation to poetry's generational inheritance,[3] isn't applicable here. In Łódź, there was none of that intergenerational tension between artists from the same culture. Quite the opposite: foreign

2   The Film Institute in Kraków, set up at the Polish Army Film Studios, was derived from the Youth Film Workshop held in 1945. Renamed the Kraków Branch of the Łódź Film Institute, it is located at 16 Józefitów Street, and currently houses the Museum of Photography. In 1945–46, the new institute had run a one-year film training course.

3   Harold Bloom, *The Anxiety of Influence: A Theory of Poetry* (New York: Oxford University Press, 1973).

scholarship students soaked up their host nation's cultural models,
then sought to adapt them to their own circumstances. Above all,
the field of documentary film inspired them—it could be used to
shape the identity of a postcolonial nation. When it came to feature
films, before beginning their course of study, students for the most
part could identify Andrzej Wajda and his seminal works from the
Polish School canon: *Pokolenie* (*A Generation*, 1955), *Kanał* (1956), and
Popiół i diament (*Ashes and Diamonds*, 1958). Close contact with Polish
directors serving as their artistic advisers led to the direct influence
of those filmmakers.

Hasówki: Directing Oneiric Cinema

The particular influence of Wojciech Has is clear from
statements of these former students. Has, director of the iconic *Ręko-
pis znaleziony w Saragossie* (*The Saragossa Manuscript*, 1964), taught directing in Łódź from 1974 for nearly thirty years.[4] Under his tutelage, an
exceptional number of the short films by overseas students were
made—a total of twenty. Their value and distinctiveness in the
school's archive is expressed collectively in the colloquial term
hasówki, used for them and for more than two hundred other shorts
made under his tutelage (the term works as a diminutive of the director's name: "Has-skis"). Longer pieces of ten to twenty minutes are
based on literary texts though, as in Has's œuvre, the students treat
those as raw material for generating films, resulting in very sparse
use of dialogue.

Most Has films were adaptations, but all of that material was then subordinated to his imagination. Thus even a classic
novel, *The Doll* (1890) by Bolesław Prus—a masterpiece of the realistic
form—found in Has's 1968 adaptation a highly original articulation.
While he was working on *The Doll*, his student José María Sánchez Ariza
paid tribute to him in the documentary short *History of a Shot* (1968).
Has's filmmaking—oneiric, visional, and atmospheric—became a

4   These particular mentions of Has are due in part to the fact that most
        graduates who could be contacted made their shorts in the 1980s, when
        Has was particularly active as an instructor and adviser. After 1990, his
        influence on students continued, but as rector of the Łódź Film School.
        Has's likeness in relief adorns an outer wall of the rector's building—the
        only such commemorative relief that's been placed there.

FIG. 1
WOJCIECH HAS ON THE SET OF *THE HOURGLASS SANATORIUM*, **1973,**
COURTESY FINA/WFDIF

model for student shorts revolving round the subject of death, with
protagonists meeting their younger incarnations, brooding over lost
time, drifting between past and future, waking and sleeping.
A typical *hasówki* protagonist is the dignified old man in
Shadows (1982), in Beverly Joan Marcus's short for her directing
diploma, based on "Regret," the de Maupassant story, and codirected
with Eduardo Coronado Quiroga. In the twilit privacy of his elegant
flat, their protagonist recalls his unrequited love and occasionally
speaks to her. Old clocks tick and chime, light picks out paintings on
the walls, the old man gazes at his reflection in the mirror. In his
mind's eye, he sees himself in a boyhood setting, as the old professor does in *An Uneventful Story*, made that year by Has.

Another nostalgic story of old age, but with elements
of horror, is *Miriam* (1984), the directing-diploma short by Djamel
Benkhaled, based on a Truman Capote short story of that name. A
chic elderly woman meets a little girl at the cinema, they share the
same name and, without explanation, the girl moves into her home.
The luminous little figure from Capote is at once a symbol of child-
hood and a harbinger of death. Marcus, along with *Shadows*, also
delved into Sylvia Plath's poetry, biography, and mounting dread in
the short *Top Floor* (1980), with cinematography by Rolando Loewenstein. Suicide's temptation is omnipresent among Has protagonists;
irrespective of gender and age, they struggle with it, and when left
in one place for any length of time, feel the noose tighten around
them, as in Has's acclaimed debut, *Pętla* (*The Noose*, 1958). Marcus, in
Top Floor, tracks a poet in a psychiatric hospital experiencing her environment as increasingly oppressive, even as she nears recovery.
Double-mirror reflections link her dissociation with that of various
Has doppelgängers.

The moment of passage between life and death,
rehearsed in Has's work as if on a balance beam suspended between
waking and sleeping, also appears in original student shorts not
based on any literary inspirations. In *Aleksander* (1987) by José Morales
Perez, with cinematography by Jolanta Dylewska and Katarzyna
Remin, an old woman rubs an amber pendant, calling up in her memory an image of her beloved, naked on a beach. Seeing a nurse who

resembles her dead husband, she first gets a surge of energy, then ultimately dies in his arms. Under Has's influence (not his tutelage), Jakub Barua made *The Rider* (1990), which was the diploma work for cinematographer Stan Barua. The camera lets us share the subjective viewpoint as a young man is wheeled to the operating table. He'll leave the hospital ward independently, half-naked on horseback, riding straight onto an open field.

Among the *hasówki*, particularly the short ones, death isn't always taken seriously. Quite the opposite: it can be treated with gallows humor or a surrealistic joke. In *The Best Customer* (1975) by Gilbert Nsangata, with cinematography by Hyacinthe Mienandi, an old man buys up all the funeral wreaths designed for men; at least after death, this lonely man wants to be surrounded by fond memorial tokens from nonexistent loved ones. In Saer Mussa's *Hibernatus* (1983), the Syrian student shows a middle-aged man who feels hemmed in by others. His misanthropy pushes him to get into...the fridge. The hero of *The Source* (1983) by Abdesselam Mezerreg is equally irritated by his surroundings and all the sounds there. He tapes over Mona Lisa's mouth from da Vinci's painting, then the tape falls off and a woman's voice is again heard, clearly singing.

Most original and interesting in terms of the present book's focus are the shorts based on original screenplays, with non-European actors, which bring issues to Polish cinema that were practically absent before. One is the poetic *Born in Chains* (1983) by JAM Karanja, in which a director wrestles with the double shackles of discrimination on grounds of race and a disability. The view of a white Polish winter is accompanied by the sound of prison doors clanging shut. Figures move independently of each other across an open, snowbound space in a park. A woman sits with a bag of wool on a bench—to which she turns out to be chained. A man on another bench eats an apple; his wrists are also cuffed. All these figures are whites, including a child whose mother is offering milk. A noise like the clamor of war heralds the appearance of a Black woman (B. Khaemba, whose first name is not used; not all actors will be named in this essay). The child, observed by an elderly man, runs forward and discovers chains coiled beneath the snow. In this visual metaphor, Karanja transfers into the world of whiteness a sense of imprisonment, which has been the condition of his compatriots and forebears for centuries, grown almost innate as with the laws of nature. In *Born in Chains*, color is both the subject and a visual value, while in Has films it had been a way to diversify the backdrop references, like the Napoleonic soldiers who are Black in *Sanatorium pod Klepsydrą (The Hourglass Sanatorium)*. Similarly, when an Arab theme appears, in *Aureliano* (1989) by Chaouki Mejeri, assisted by Fayçal Hassaïri, cinematography by Stan Barua, its function isn't to add exoticism and some fascination about the literary Orient. When the old woman in the film deals tarot cards, the threat to the life of her son (Bahjet Sulaiman) is real. We see an army unit crossing the desert. An unnamed Arab country has just had a rebellion, which is about to be violently quashed. Instead of an Oriental tale, what breaks through into the Polish viewer's awareness today is an echo from or prediction of political violence in the contemporary Arab world.

Surrealism in Polish cinema was not limited to Has, of course. Janusz Majewski revealed a strong liking for surrealistic elements in his early work, demonstrated in his student film *Rondo* (*Roundabout*, 1958), with playwright Sławomir Mrożek in a leading role, and in the comedy *Sublokator* (*The Lodger*, 1966). The short films created under Majewski's tutelage can hardly be classified as stories—their continuity comes instead from associations and the poetry of song. The hero of *About-Face* (1970), the directing-diploma work of Raul Saucedo Zermeño, performs the eponymous maneuver at the altar, leaving a dumbstruck bride-to-be, parents, priest, teachers, and Scouts (the wedding guests are an assemblage of all the groups exerting social pressure). The hero takes aim at them from a roof onto which he has climbed. Societal pressure squeezes up images of parental drudgeries, forced labor like in a concentration camp, a lashing from the rector. Conveyed in a particularly drastic shot is the tense atmosphere of that day in institutions of higher education, after government repressions struck in 1968: in it, the rector sinks his teeth into the student's skull and sucks out his brain. What finally kills him, though, is a brick thrown by one of the wedding guests.

Idriss Karim, completing his directing diploma work under Majewski's tutelage, realized a musical short, *Song for the Deaths of the Young* (1973), with cinematography by Tatiana Dębska. Its heroes are restaurant guests seen—or seen through, rather, right to their hidden longings—by a visitor from another world who can read people's subconscious minds. Expressive visual images are accompanied by a protest song by Janusz Kusza, sung by a women's chorus from the music academy in Łódź. X-raying the subconscious reveals desires resulting from hunger, sexual tension, or voyeurism. Between the lines in Kusza's hymn, meanwhile, it's possible to read derision of intelligence agencies spying on both citizens and foreign guests (overseas students were under constant supervision by the secret services). The singers use the form of a religious hymn to jeer at the cult of the political leader.

The figures emerge outside and form a column of young, diverse protestors with a banner that reads WE WANT THE SUN! in several languages. Cuts between the young protestors and footage of brutal clashes between police and strikers in different parts of the world leave the viewer in no doubt that their demands are not connected to the climate, but with the May 1968 slogan in Paris, "Under the paving stones, the beach!" In accordance with Kusza's intention, the title song expressed a posthumous tribute to victims of student strikes, including Jan Palach, who self-immolated after the 1968 Warsaw Pact invasion of Czechoslovakia. Along with the hymn, Karim's film features Joan Baez's recording of "Jackaroe." Baez had long been a symbol of politically engaged music from the US, and a few years later she also became a voice of Solidarity with her rendition of "Piosenka dla córki" ("Song for a Daughter").

(Third) Political Cinema

While the *hasówki* enjoy special attention from archivists, and while fascination with Wojciech Has continues unabated among students and researchers (and audiences), a second group of student shorts is also worth highlighting. Little interest in them has been generated to date, despite the enrichment they provide in the way of international themes, including those connected with student revolts of the 1960s. This group comprises short films by students from the Global South made under Wanda Jakubowska's tutelage. Another veteran of the START group, Jakubowska directed *The Last Stage* (1947), the first non-documentary film made about the Auschwitz-Birkenau camps. As an enthusiast of the Communist International, she was eager to work with students from socialist countries and with those engaged with socialism. Of those from the START generation, she worked longest at the Łódź Film School, from its founding through 1973. Her colleagues Jerzy Toeplitz, Aleksander Ford, Stanisław Wohl, and Jerzy Bossak were dismissed by the ministry in 1968, when the PRL leadership fomented an anti-Semitic campaign targeting the Jewish-Polish intelligentsia.

But Still, It's a Pity... (1971), a short by Roland Paret made under Jakubowska's tutelage, presents the disappearance of publicly visible people intriguingly, with its reference to the Bulat Okudzhava song with the lyric "every age has its order and form," sung here by Edmund Fetting. The hero of Paret's film is a journalist who wrote a piece about Pushkin's death in a duel, and whose own death, complete with a hoax funeral, is then simulated by the editor-in-chief of the Party newspaper *Głos Robotniczy* (*Workers' Voice*). In essence, *But Still, It's a Pity...* tells the story of a journalistic career cut short by one article. A few days after his mock funeral, the journalist demands his life back, but is declared mentally ill. In a park, he meets his article's hero, Pushkin, and together they walk into the distance.

Notable among the shorts made with Jakubowska as adviser are those by José Luis di Zeo, as are those Latin American students made with other advisers, including Henryk Kluba. These endeavored to transplant elements into a Polish production from Third Cinema as that movement spread in the 1960s and 1970s, reacting to both Hollywood and the Second Cinema of European art film, with its bent for artistic freedom. Third Cinema's demands and its name were consolidated in the manifesto "Toward a Third Cinema," written by the independent Argentine filmmakers Fernando

Solanas and Octavio Cetino.[5] Those from Argentina who studied in Łódź, including di Zeo, kept an eye on events at home, and made use of the student-short form to join in the movement.

Even when a short adapted a Pole's writing, elements would be introduced to backdrop the main action, transporting the viewer across the Atlantic. An example is *The Meeting* (1968) by di Zeo, based on a story by Kazimierz Orłoś. A boy from a broken home is walking through the city to meet his father. He passes a group of men: a policeman and two security-service agents leading someone who looks like a student. On the radio, a song can be heard, half in Spanish, half in Polish, followed by an advert for the sports lottery. The lottery, in conjunction with the Polish Olympic Committee, offers as a prize a ticket to the Olympic Games in Mexico. The Mexico City Olympics in 1968 were brutally politicized. Ten days before the opening ceremony, a student demonstration protested against state funding for such a large-scale event, given their country's poverty levels. When they clashed with the army, perhaps 250 protesters died in the fighting and over a thousand were taken to hospital. The events have gone down in history as the Tlatelolco Massacre. In *The Meeting*, di Zeo doesn't develop the topic, leaving a seemingly neutral allusion to the events in the soundtrack instead.

In di Zeo's silent miniature *Wake* (1965), he uses the camera to paint a picture of an Argentine partisan's body being washed by a woman close to him. In Spanish, the title, *Wake*, signifies a vigil for the dead. The atmosphere and the costumes and framing of the protagonists reveal inspiration from religious iconography. Here one can discern the influence of Jakubowska, who tended to dignify scenes from the lives of political warriors using conventions recognizable from religious painting. Di Zeo's later short about Che Cuevara, *Che* (1968), is no longer extant. In *Guerrilla* (1966), the starting point is an intimate scene similar to that in *Wake*. A man in uniform sleeps in an abandoned building while a woman (María Rosa Hernández) keeps watch. When she is certain he's asleep, she gives

5   The filmmakers coined the term in their October 1969 manifesto, "Hacia un tercer cine," and it was popularized in *Militant Cinema: An Internal Category of Third Cinema* (1971). See Mariano Mestman, "Third Cinema / Militant Cinema: At the Origins of the Argentinian Experience (1968–1971)," *Third Text* 25, no. 1 (2011): 29–40.

a signal and a trio of armed village partisans enters. They tie up the soldier, take him outside, and bury him up to the neck in the ground. They put a noose around his neck and tie the rope to a horse, then leave. It's unclear with which guerrilla faction the trio should be identified, although clearly what's being shown is a micro-scale example of resistance to Argentina's military regime of the period.

A similar convention of small-scale drama, in which men fall victim to deadly political violence and women to sexual violence, is employed in shorts made by two Moroccans: *Amghar* (1968) by Mostafa Derkaoui and *Shadow among Others* (1969) by Abdelkader Lagtaa. In *Amghar*, the director recreates the capture of Moha Ou Hamou Zayani (1863–21), the Berber tribal leader waging guerrilla war on the French colonial army from 1914 to 1921. Derkaoui's modest short was the first and for a long time the only celluloid trace of this episode in Moroccan history. *Shadow among Others*, meanwhile, takes a contemporary stance, showing scores being settled among international Marxist revolutionaries, with allusions to the 1965 abduction of the exiled politician Mehdi Ben Barka. Derkaoui plays the role of the left-wing Ben Barka, victim of the Brigade for Eliminating Political Enemies.[6] In Polish cinema, analogous films would be the war films of Ewa Petelska and Czesław Petelski, with charismatic, politically engaged heroines who are spies and scenes of guerrilla war with elements of savagery, such as *Ogniomistrz Kaleń* (*Burning Mountains*, 1961).

Returning to South American student films, another of note is by Raul Saucedo Zermeño—director of *About-Face*, discussed above, and an actor in di Zeo's *Guerrilla*. With Antoni Bohdziewicz as adviser, he made *Without Requiem* (1969), a short that makes explicit reference to South American revolutionary efforts. In the prologue, a student pastes a Che Guevara poster on a wall. The slogan reads: THE BULLET'S PATH IS THE LIBERATION PATH FOR ALL THE AMERICAS, TO TRUE SOCIALISM. Secret police tear down the poster, but the young man is already painting the next slogan: SOCIALISMOS. They get to him as he paints HAND OVER THE KILLERS OF FREE SPEECH!

6   For more about films by Moroccans and their context, see the essays by Marie Pierre-Bouthier, "*Podróż* to Poland: In Search of a Potential Moroccan Cinema," and Léa Morin, "*Lesson 41*: Going to Poland to Become a Moroccan Filmmaker," in this book.

Their pursuit of the student is accompanied by bright, rhythmic music. Once captured by the police in a park, he is beaten to death. The officers take the body to the station, apply makeup to suggest the young man was victim of a gay-related crime, then throw the made-up corpse in a ditch. The next day, headlines declare a crime in the homosexual community. One of the policemen reads the paper at home, having breakfast in bed with his wife and daughter in an idyllic family setting.

The entire film is a mosaic of scenes in contrasting moods. From the policeman's home, we move to the room of another student to the sound of "We Shall Overcome" sung by Pete Seeger, a song with a long tradition in American protest culture, which was sung in Spanish as well, and widely adopted during the Cold War by politically engaged milieus. On his wall is a Che Guevara poster. Prompted by what he reads in the paper, that young man goes outside and paints an anti-government slogan on a wall: THE SERVILE POLICE KILL AND BRING INFAMY. *VENCEREMOS!*, which ties in with the slogan in the prologue.

This is how walls of the Łódź Film School on Targowa Street came to bear militant Third Cinema slogans—but unfortunately not for long. That story is a clear-cut example of the spirit of those times, as well as of feedback the Latin American students got from Poles, which is to say completely ignoring both their language identity and their political goals. The school received a call from the Party's local committee, saying that workmen passing the school then complained about "Zionist"[7] slogans, and that a squad car had been sent over. As a result, the students had to remove their graffiti.[8] In the school's official version, the incident remains a funny anecdote, with neither commentary nor awareness of what was happening in Third Cinema at the time.

7   The term "Zionist" had a negative connotation around the time of the Six-Day War, and was frequently repeated in anti-Semitic speeches by First Secretary Władysław Gomułka, which led to the forced emigration of around half of the generation of Polish Jews who were Holocaust survivors and their children. See Monika Bobako, "The Jew, the Arab, the Pole: March 1968 in Poland and the History of an Alliance Between the Second and Third Worlds," in this book.

8   Krzysztof Krubski et al., *Filmówka: Powieść o łódzkiej Szkole Filmowej* (Warsaw: Prószyński i S-ka, 1998), 192.

Another student short set in the Americas is *The Cat
Died of Hunger* (1968) by José María Sánchez Ariza. It shows an episode
in the life of a rural family of three and their cat. They suffer from
hunger, apparently living isolated in a deserted area. When the
woman sets their last tortillas on the table, the man has the idea of
killing the cat for their next meal. After that's been done, the child
looks for the cat, to share some scraps with it. Intercutting shots of
this quiet drama are panels written in Polish and French—for example, a quotation from the Larousse encyclopedia about how mental
states can influence the perception of hunger, delaying, diminish-
ing, or magnifying it. Though the drama takes place in a small family, it's intended to show a part of the big picture of "mass hunger
during social disasters," as one panel states.

The Cat Died of Hunger precisely fits with "The Aesthetics
of Hunger" (1965), a cinema manifesto by the director Glauber Rocha,
in which he rejects the European reception of primitivism in the
cinema novo movement. Rocha states: "[hunger] is the essence of our
society. Herein lies the tragic originality of *cinema novo* in relation to
world cinema. Our originality is our hunger and our greatest misery
is that this hunger is felt but not intellectually understood."[9] Sánchez
Ariza's short film proves *cinema novo* can belong to anyone, just as
Rocha argues: it is not the exclusive property of Brazilian cinema.

As has been discussed, the contexts of shorts made
with Wanda Jakubowska as academic adviser went far beyond the
spheres of interest of Polish cinema. It was also thanks to Jakubowska's determination that the only feature-length diploma film by a
scholarship student from the Global South was shot—about the Vietnam War.

Kaweh Pur Rahnama, a political refugee from Iran studying directing, requested a longer form for his subject. The opportunity to shoot a feature-length diploma film under the auspices of
the state film-production company, however, was available only to
Polish students at the school, as has been mentioned above.
Rahnama had made two very successful shorts: the documentary

9   Glauber Rocha, "The Aesthetics of Hunger," trans. Burnes Hollyman and
Randal Johnson, in *Twenty-Five Years of the New Latin American Cinema*, ed.
Michael Chanan (London: BFI, 1983), 13–14.

Evening-Class Test (1966) under Kazimierz Karabasz, about Łódź textile workers attending evening classes; and the fictional *The Wallet* (1966) under Jakubowska, about a pickpocket who falls in love with his mark. He was known for his considerable literary form. Evidence of this includes the screenplay he next submitted for production, *No Way Back, Johnny*, a small-scale dramatic story of the Vietnam War, which plays out between the eponymous Johnny, a GI with the US forces, and Hue, a farmer he suspects of being with the Viet Cong. The heroes, handcuffed to each other, are looking for an American unit in the jungle. As they wander, the frustrated GI realizes that he, too, is a prisoner of the handcuffs he's used to chain his captive to himself. In the finale, their roles reverse. In Rahnama's explication, which became the dissertation for his master's degree, he wrote:

> I therefore wanted to show all the things that can divide people, as well as those that bring them together despite everything, and make them alike. Finally, I wanted to show two points of view on the same subject, the savagery of modern warfare. [...] Both are in a situation that makes conflict unavoidable. They are soldiers in opposing armies and, despite the chain that binds their wrists and condemns them to a certain kind of fellowship, they have contradictory goals and are in constant rivalry, the stake in the game always being one of their lives.
>
> In spite of this, there's something that's common to both, that rises above them, above their situation. I'd call this the human condition. It's a condition they share as, even given all their hostility, they're both human. It's the presence of this element surpassing the individual that's decisive in giving the film its anti-war edge, helping to indict pointless, barbarous war. It lends the film a humanitarian significance.[10]

10   Kaweh Pur Rahnama, "Analiza zagadnień warsztatowych w filmie *Nie ma powrotu, Johnny*" (MA diss., Directing Department of the National Film, Television and Theater School in Lodz, supervised by Wanda Jakubowska, 1971). Archive of the Leon Schiller National Film, Television and Theater School in Łódź.

FIG. 2
KAWEH PUR RAHNAMA ON THE SET OF *NO WAY BACK, JOHNNY*, 1969,
COURTESY FINA/WFDIF

These elements of thriller and psychological drama, along with a consistency along Cold War divides in Rahnama's film, led screenwriter and director Antoni Bohdziewicz to compare the script's standard of storytelling to the work of Wojciech Żukrowski, who wrote the screenplays for Wajda's *Lotna* (1959), Jerzy Hoffman's *Potop* (*The Deluge*, 1974), and Jerzy Passendorfer's *Barwy walki* (*Battle Colors*, 1964). Films Bohdziewicz used in comparisons were even more prestigious: "In our homegrown repertoire, we have nothing on this subject, and even when it comes to foreign films, we've not before seen the like of those by [Joris] Ivens or the French compilation *Loin du Vietnam*."[11] Bohdziewicz refers to *Le 17e parallèle: La guerre du peuple* (*17th Parallel: Vietnam in War*, dir. Joris Ivens, 1968), and *Loin du Vietnam* (*Far from Vietnam*, dir. Joris Ivens, William Klein, Claude Lelouch, Chris Marker, Alain Resnais, Agnès Varda, Jean-Luc Godard, 1967).

Rahnama's film was made in 1971, after permission was granted by the deputy minister of culture and art. The production was mounted, not at the film school, but at the Vector Film Unit, because Jakubowska's START Film Unit had been disbanded—another casualty of March 1968's purges. Rahnama made full use of striking Baltic-coastline locations, with filming pinioned to a concept of mood fluctuations (the now-renowned cinematographer Sławomir Idziak was one DOP), and with skillfully sequenced sound effects compounding the sense of menace. The part of the GI was played by German actor Jack Recknitz, with the role of Hue taken by non-actor Nguyen Van Quynh.

Despite the success of his debut feature, Rahnama did not continue into a film career, instead taking up an academic teaching position at the University of Warsaw, and writing several Farsi-language textbooks, as well as novels in Polish. From *Dziesięciu Irańczyków i trup w Warszawie* (*Ten Iranians and a Corpse in Warsaw*, 2006), a reader may make inferences about the conditions of Rahnama's life in the PRL's capital, and discover the attitude of Iranians there to "real existing socialism." "Political refugees here keep their eyes

---

11   Antoni Bohdziewicz, Opinion about the screenplay *No Way Back, Johnny*, May 30, 1968, Kaweh Pur Rahnama's personal file. Łódź Film School archive.

open and their mouths shut,"[12] as Rahnama wrote in the novel. In it,
his protagonists suffer from refugee sickness, which makes you
"learn to live in a world without paradise, without this idea of a better world."[13]

Iranians who'd benefitted from higher education in the
PRL had been impressed by the education system's freedom, its lack
of fees, and the openness to people from abroad. And by state spon-
sorship of culture, sport, and recreation, and by the free universal-
health service. Their disillusionments concerned the political practice of "real existing socialism," and the shallowness of any idealism:
"Socialism here is deceptive; you feel like a fish in snow—it might be
wet, but you can't swim," as Rahnama writes in *Ten Iranians*. He continues: "how to create a full narrative of our lives. The lives of inhabitants of a puddle that's already drying out."[14]

Conclusion

The period of intense attendance of scholarship students from the Global South at the Łódź Film School ended with the
democratic breakthrough of 1989 in Poland, the end of the Cold War,
and the Soviet Union's collapse and dissolution in 1991. It was around
this time that the Barua brothers, Jakub (b. 1967) and Stanisław (b.
1965), were studying film. One could say that they were children of
the scholarship program: their parents met in the 1960s when both
were medical students, their father from Kenya and their mother
from Łódź—in the midst of that golden age of the scholarship program. The films directed by Jakub Barua, with cinematography by
Stanisław, bring together the two models of art cinema discussed
above, the oneiric and the political, and fuse them into an original
whole. The link joining the two models came from a reflective perspective on postcolonialism.

While remaining under the influence of Wojciech Has,
his mentor, and employing a poetic idiom, Jakub Barua produced
shorts utilizing the language of filmic symbols to analyze colonial

12   Kaweh Pur Rahnama, *Dziesięciu Irańczyków i trup w Warszawie* (Warsaw:
          Wydawnictwo Dialog, 2006), 101.
13   Rahnama, *Dziesięciu Irańczyków*, 155.
14   Rahnama, *Dziesięciu Irańczyków*, 103.

relations: the presence of whites on the African continent and the counterflow relations of Africans in Poland. In *Sabou* (1990),[15] Barua staged a series of typical situations in overtly arbitrary settings to show what motivates whites in Africa—rapacious tourism, field studies, recreation—along with the story of the witness to these situations, a young local man, in reaction to them. An important element of the set is a school chalkboard on which is written *Amandla!* This means "Power!" in Nguni—the South African equivalent of "Power to the People" was used by apartheid opponents and, over time, human-rights and worker-rights activists. The young man, frustrated by colonialism, is being interrogated by an indigneous official. He takes a sheet of paper he has been given, folds it into an airplane and, with a smile, lofts it in the direction of a washerwoman.

Barua, mediating between the European North and the Global South, evading unequivocal moral judgements, opens his perspective to the viewer, a viewpoint that is unique due to his family background and his education (University of Warwick; Łódź Film School). In a short film that straddles documentary and fiction, *The Welcome* (1990), he shows a young man (Patrick Ondire) in a wide-angle shot of the inner courtyard of a typical Łódź apartment house: high, scruffy walls, parked car, a tall metal frame for beating rugs. The protagonist takes an African folk outfit from his rucksack. On the rug-beating frame, he hangs ribbons with little mirrors, creating the effect of a swaying mosaic of the reflected surroundings. As accompaniment, a Kenyan song of welcome plays on the soundtrack. The children playing nearby pay no attention to him, evidently used to "Southerners'" presence in Łódź. Cutaways during this ritual show us photos of the Barua brothers. A quotation from Joseph Conrad's *Heart of Darkness* is delivered as a voice-over in translation, serving an autobiographical function:

> Now when I was a little chap I had a passion for maps. I would look for hours at South America, or Africa, or Australia and lose myself in all the glories of exploration. At that time there were many blank spaces on the earth and when I saw one that looked particularly invit-

---

The title is a phonetic transcription of the Swahili word *sabau* ("reason").

ing on a map (but they all look that) I would put my finger on it and say: "When I grow up I will go there."[16] In the Kenyan song, the singer weaves in the Polish greeting *dzień dobry*. Yes, the photos are on fire, but a jigsaw of Africa has been completed. By Kenyan custom, a voice-over explains, the last rite you perform for a lost loved one is to destroy all images of them and free their spirit. The protagonist leaves the courtyard, just as the Barua brothers left Łódź to pursue their international careers.

On the basis of what has been shown above, a conclusion may be drawn that the shorts made by students from the Global South in Łódź, like those by the film school's other students, show the dual influences of their academic advisers and of models of Polish art cinema—from social realism to poetic oneirism, from original scripts to literary adaptations, from films by Wojciech Has and Wanda Jakubowska to those of Henryk Kluba[17] and other instructors. The set of *hasówki* provide evidence of students' abilities to work in a poetic idiom, create mood, and adapt literature for cinematic purposes.

Simultaneously, those students created a transnational variant of Third Cinema, within the parameters both of Eastern bloc cinema and that of developing countries. Their works brought elements into Polish cinema that were new and unexpected: non-Slavic protagonists, echoes of student protests in Paris in 1968 and of Latin American student revolts, and a youthful non-European socialist idealism. In those short films with a social or political message, students could imprint their identities as citizens of Global South nations while those nations were liberating themselves from colonialism, to a much greater extent than on their more European shorts based on literary classics and engaging Polish actors.

They took the shallowly exotic, traditionally anachronistic orientalism present in both highbrow and popular Polish culture and empowered it with a new legitimacy. On getting acquainted

16   Joseph Conrad, *Heart of Darkness* (New York: W. W. Norton, 1988), 11.
      Conrad (1857–1924), while he wrote in English, was born Józef Konrad
      Korzeniowski in partitioned Poland.
17   Henryk Kluba (1931–2005), film director, dean of the directing
      department (1978–81; 1993–96) and rector of the Łódź Film School
      (1982–90; 1996–2002), academic adviser for the narrative shorts *Sabou,
      Wake, To Serve Twice, Imaginaria*.

with their student output, it's impossible not to appreciate the potential the scholarship program activated and its enlivening effect on higher education in Łódź. It's also distinctly possible to trace paths along which a broader perspective than the confined range of the Eastern bloc was then penetrating into the newly monoethnic PRL.

Translated from the Polish by Jolanta Scicińska.

Katarzyna Mąka-Malatyńska is associate professor in the Film and TV Direction Department of the Łódź Film School, author of articles on documentary film and Polish cinema published in the journals *Images, Kwartalnik Filmowy*, and *Studia Filmoznawcze*, and in *Krall i filmowcy* (Poznań 2006; *Krall and the Filmmakers*), *Europa Europa* (Poznań 2007; *Holland's "Europa Europa,"* trans. Daniel Polsby, Poznań 2007), *Ludzie polskiego kina: Agnieszka Holland* (Warsaw 2009), *Widok z tej strony: Przedstawienia Holocaustu w polskim filmie* (Poznań 2012; *A View from This Side: Presentations of the Holocaust in Polish Cinema*); coeditor of volumes on nonfiction film (*Zobaczyć siebie: Polski film dokumentalny przełomu wieków*, Poznań 2011; *Pogranicza dokumentu*, Poznań 2012; *[Nie]zapomniani dokumentaliści*, Łódź 2020), and editor of *Od obserwacji do animacji: Autorzy o filmie dokumentalnym* (Łódź 2017) and *Theory of Practice* (Łódź 2019). Editorial-board member for the Filmoteka site filmpolski.pl.

KATARZYNA MĄKA-MALATYŃSKA

THE FAMILIAR, THE STRANGE: WORKS BY STUDENTS FROM THE GLOBAL SOUTH IN THE CONTEXT OF THE POLISH SCHOOL OF DOCUMENTARY FILM

Familiarity and strangeness, similarity and difference, are key categories in describing contemporary European societies in countries far removed from self-containment. The migration researcher Ewa Nowicka writes that relations of closeness "are associated with acceptance, commitment to services, and a sense of naturalness. As far as beliefs are concerned, most important are a belief in similarity, comprehensibility, meaningfulness. Strangeness, therefore, is related to the lack of these values."[1] In works of culture created by foreigners at work in a given social milieu, those categories appear at structural levels that differ from those deployed by artists from that same milieu.

Student films made by foreigners at the Łódź Film School—Poland's sole film school until 1978—can be considered an interesting extension within this field. These films provide an opportunity to reevaluate certain issues and symbols that are constantly present in Polish cinema, and to deconstruct the stereotype of its being a purely national cinema. Within this group of films, a special subset is documentaries, usually closely related to the Polish com-

1   Ewa Nowicka, "Swojskość i obcość jako kategorie socjologicznej analizy," in Swoi i obcy, ed. Ewa Nowicka (Warsaw: Uniwersytet Warszawski, 1990), 6.

plex by the principle of referentiality, through which new generations of Poles can see themselves through other people's eyes, and sense how foreigners find places in Poland. As film theoretician Filip Nowak has stated, inspiration is to be found in "unveiling the transnational nature of selected phenomena from the past, even if they were not perceived as such at the time."[2] It probably won't lead to deconstructing the centrality of mainstream film production and historical and film narrative, and the peripherality of minority and independent cinema or student films. However, it can certainly heighten interest within that periphery, furthering possibilities to exhibit its distinctions from mainstream production, given its remove from the accepted canon.

I propose that in including these works by student filmmakers from the Global South in the recognized currents of Polish film, we look at them through the lens of similarity and dissimilarity: what's familiar in them and what's unfamiliar to common perceptions of the nation's cinema and, through the latter, to Polish society.

From an Educational Film to a Documentary Portrait
The group of films in question, made at the school from the early 1960s to around 1990, range across almost all genres, methods, and topics appearing concurrently in films by its Polish students.

More surprising than the shared presence of certain themes is what is missing from or appears only sporadically in the latter works, including the issue of ethnic identity. In the group by foreign students, several recurring motifs are also found in their peers' documentaries: Polish art and its creators, cities (mainly Łódź) and their architecture, sport, the fate of people living on the margins (orphans, the elderly, single mothers, ex-prisoners, addicts).

This last topic was taken up especially often in the 1970s and 1980s, as Polish documentary cinema produced works categorized within the New Change—films showing the real situation of workers for the first time in the postwar period, after decades of

2   Filip Nowak, "Problemy z transnarodowością," in *Kino polskie jako kino transnarodowe*, ed. Sebastian Jagielski and Magdalena Podsiadło (Kraków: Towarzystwo Autorów i Wydawców Prac Naukowych Universitas, 2017), 256–57.

propaganda had so distorted their image. Major examples include *Z miasta Łodzi* (*From the City of Łódź*, 1969) by Krzysztof Kieślowski; *24 godziny Jadwigi L.* (*24 Hours in the Life of Jadwiga L.*, 1967) and *Nasze znajome z Łodzi* (*Our Friends from Łódź*, 1971) by Krystyna Gryczełowska; *Robotnicy 71: Nic o nas bez nas* (*Workers '71: Nothing About Us Without Us*, 1972) by Kieślowski and Tomasz Zygadło.

In most student films that dealt with workers' issues, Łódź was the scene of the human drama. Whether this was a result of a trend among young filmmakers or perhaps an expression of social sensitivity and understanding cultural needs, it's difficult to notice differences between domestic and foreign student works. One surviving film contradicts this: Eduardo Coronado Quiroga's *The Prologue* (1979), in which footage of palaces and gray courtyards is juxtaposed with voice-over statements by people from overseas studying in Łódź. In *The Prologue*, the filmmakers' attitude to the city is at once personal and noticeably ambivalent—as one character says, Łódź seems like a film shot from a tram's windows.

Idriss Karim, in *Marta* (1969), presented a portrait of a woman who has worked in a Łódź textile mill since she was sixteen. As the wife of an alcoholic and a mother of three, Marta also struggles with the difficulties of daily life. In her duty-bound existence, there's no time for even a moment's rest. *Marta* opens with shots in the mill, which will reappear throughout the film. The drone of industrial looms reflects the monotony of the protagonist's work and existence. Then long minutes in line at the grocery shop, and finally returning home: a neglected tenement building where work awaits for her, preparing a meal for the children, washing clothes, and constantly in doubt if she'll find her husband sober and in charge of the children—or if he's sold off some household item for vodka. This very depressing depiction of women's fate is part of the era's wave of documentaries about female workers, which includes works by Gryczełowska and Irena Kamieńska.

Both *Marta* and *Elżbieta K.* (1973), a subsequent student film by Karim, were created under the supervision of Kazimierz Karabasz, who in 1967 had made *Rok Franka W.* (*Year in the Life of Franek W.*), a pioneering in-depth psychological portrait in documentary form.

The structure of Karim's two films is largely derived from Karabasz's masterful method at the time: based on patient, long-term observation, enhanced by the persistence of the hero's voice, individual, even intimate (off-screen monologue; a diary being read). Utilizing similar poetics, Syed Ali Haider Rizvi made *Marek* (1978) under the supervision of Andrzej Brzozowski, another great authority in documentary film. The durability of this observational method of storytelling is also demonstrated in Saer Mussa's *Buy a Newspaper*, made in the first half of the 1980s, which varies the formula developed by Karabasz. Łódź remains the scene. Mussa shows a teenage boy from a poor family who makes extra money selling papers in the Centrum Hotel lobby. The director uses the protagonist's off-screen narration, characteristic of Karabasz films, and follows him patiently, although some shots are obviously staged. Most importantly, the filmmakers introduce a creative element, using black-and-white stock in the teenager's house and color for shots inside the Centrum. This simple procedure corresponds exactly with the teenager's statements about viewing these two realities as completely separate.

While Hamid Bensaïd's *Pensioners' House* (1969) and Laredj Khader's *The Family* (1982) are also films depicting poor, lonely, and rejected people, and remain based on observation, their poetics operate somewhat differently. They are less intent on the individual hero than on the community and on social phenomena revealed through it. *Pensioners' House* shows the facility in the title. Unfortunately, the print in the school's archives has no sound. Given the year it was made, it is assumed to have had diegetic sound, as with Andrzej Titkow's *Home* (1967) made two years earlier, with off-screen narration by selected characters.

In *The Family*, a sequence of brief, extremely expressive shots captures the terrible situation of its members: drunk parents, dirt, mess, drinking in front of the children. The narrative is then built in a more traditional way: a series of longer shots showing their lives, day-in, day-out, accompanied by off-screen narration by the eldest son. He takes up mothering his younger siblings: he washes, irons, darns, applies for custody of the youngest kid who'd been taken to the orphanage—though he also has a dark past, with ten of his thirty-three years spent in prisons and correctional facilities. The makers of both films diagnose crucial social phenomena, with an accusatory tone characteristic of student productions of their day. Among these films oscillating around loneliness and rejection is an excellent short by Bensaïd, *Zofia and Ludmiła* (1971). It records daily life for two Roma girls, Zofia and Ludmiła. They aren't liked by schoolmates or accepted by teachers. They go to school merely out of duty, and spend their free time in their own company. The construction of Bensaïd's film is based on a principle of contrast. Scenes of the title characters' family life are juxtaposed with shots from school. In the former, the sound layer is dominated by music, with a song sung by girls and with the traditional Romani melody "Doina de jale" played on a pan flute. In the latter setting, the word is predominant—that is, statements by the teacher and pupils.

The former scenes show the girls' joy and vitality. In two school scenes, children sit upright at their desks, listening to the teacher, who is out of the frame but influences class responses completely. Pupils willingly repeat negative opinions the adult states, stigmatizing Zofia and Ludmiła. All the while, the two girls remain largely silent. They answer questions and accusations briefly and with a sense of shame. The camera focuses on them—on their faces that hardly differ from those of other children. Yet their origins and the environment they're growing up in entirely determine how others perceive them. They're strangers in the classroom, although they speak Polish and in their home, like most other Polish homes, the walls are decorated with religious pictures.

The topic of life among the country's Roma had appeared in documentary films by the 1960s. The poetic, observational *Zanim opadną liście* (*Before the Leaves Fall*, 1964) by Władysław Ślesicki, is an example, with Ślesicki returning to the subject of camp communities after his student film *Jedzie tabor* (*Gypsy Camp*, 1955). *Zofia and Ludmiła* provides a similar take on Roma issues, and Bensaïd made it under the supervision of Karabasz, who had worked with Ślesicki at the beginning of his career.

What's completely different, however, is Bensaïd's documentary language. While in *Before the Leaves Fall*, Ślesicki uses the method of long-term, patient observation, *Zofia and Ludmiła* utilizes the aesthetics of the New Change documentary. Classroom scenes recall a film by Tomasz Zygadło, *Szkoła podstawowa* (*Primary School*, 1971). For Zygadło, school was a model of society; for Ben Said, schoolmates' attitudes to the two girls seem to reflect the dominant not-one-of-us relations—which may be assumed to have been a determinant element in his life while at film school. In the 1980s, the issue of minorities in Poland returned in this group of student films. At mid-decade, Samir Zedan made *Land* (1986), then at its end, Chaouki Mejeri directed *Scent of Islam* (1989)—both about Polish Tatars and their religious- and cultural-minority status.

In the World of Culture

The number of student films dealing with topics of domestic culture and art demonstrates the curiosity and at times fascination with Polish culture and the people who have created it. Among these films are valuable records of theater and cabaret performances, including in *Chronica anonyma* (dir. Eduardo Coronado Quiroga, 1980), which in part documents a staging in Piwnica pod Baranami, the renowned cellar club in Kraków. The film's prologue is built from observational shots around the city's Old Town, accompanied by the "Hejnał mariacki" bugle melody (blown hourly from a steeple of St. Mary's Basilica) and a recurring visual motif: the bugler's shadow, cast on one steeple's wall. The camera moves inside the church and its crypt, the bugle call turns into choral singing in Latin then into dissonant contemporary music. A parade passes through the streets of Kraków. In closer shots, the popular actor Daniel Olbrychski becomes visible dressed as Prince Józef Poniatowski, accompanied by Anna Szałapak and Anna Dymna, the leading ladies of Piwnica pod Baranami. Finally, the club's MC, Piotr Skrzynecki, appears. We watch silent shots of the theater ball that took place on June 14, 1980.

The structure of *Chronica anonyma* is built by disturbing and mysterious music that doesn't belong to the world represented.

It's a film that differs significantly from *Gdańsk*, made two years earlier (dir. Rolando Loewenstein, 1978)—which was colorful, with music by Georg Philipp Telemann, showing monuments, tourist spots, the streets and cafés full of people. Loewenstein's work is closer to a typical, efficiently made sightseeing film than to an impression revealing the spirit of a city.

Polish religiosity also aroused interest among filmmaking students from the Global South, especially monastery life (*Mea culpa*, dir. Raul Saucedo Zermeño, 1968) and the theatrical dimension of religious ceremonies. This theme is constantly present in postwar Polish documentary-making. An early depiction is *Pamiątka z Kalwarii* (*A Souvenir from Calvary*, dir. Jerzy Hoffman, Edward Skórzewski, 1958). It appears in student films including *Nowicjat* (*Novitiate*, 1978) by Tomasz Przestępski and, above all, in one of the most acclaimed fiction films from the Łódź Film School, Krzysztof Zanussi's *Śmierć prowincjała* (*The Death of a Provincial*, 1965). Juan Caicedo, director of *In claro monti* (1987), chose the famed Polish monastery at Jasna Góra. Caicedo didn't shoot monks' daily lives; he focused on rituals related to Holy Thursday (washing the feet), the process of revealing and covering the Miraculous Image, a celebration related to the arrival of crowds of pilgrims. The roving camera shows the dynamic presence of the faithful (from joy just after entering the gates to solemn prayer), contrasted by detail shots around the interior of the temple, especially the figure of Christ crucified.

Works by Mostafa Derkaoui, especially *Cellar People* (1969) and *Somewhere, Someday* (1971), certainly stand out against these city-portrait films and those featuring religiosity and culture. They aren't only testimonies to interest in Polish culture, to its external overall perception; they enter into it and influence it from inside. In each film, Derkaoui is primarily interested in meetings as moments when thoughts are openly exchanged and doubts are raised, and of intellectual quest. The musical performances are important but serve as accompaniments.

Cellar People begins with a scene in which the characters listen to a speech: delivered in Paris in the aftermath of 1968's transformations by Jean Charvein, representing the États généraux du cinéma (Estates General of French Cinema), and recorded by Derkaoui. The action takes place in the Kurylewicz Arts Club, founded in the mid 1960s in Warsaw, hosted by the composer and jazz bandleader Andrzej Kurylewicz and vocalist Wanda Warska, his wife. The actors Barbara Brylska and Stanisław Tym are among the guests. In the smoke-filled club, relaxed conversations cover contemporary times, art, and philosophy. The artists joke, poke fun at each other, and discuss appearances in the media and on stage. Live jazz resounds. For the finale, the music completely fills the soundtrack.

Cellar People surprises with its form, devoid of classical dramaturgy and, to a large extent, of an informational layer. Scenes seem fragmented and dialogues incomplete. The filmmaking team wanted above all to convey the club's atmosphere and for this purpose they used a narrative structure resembling jazz improvisation. The camera ranges among those who've assembled, zooming in and panning. It leaves one clique to return to them moments later. The result is a film based on leitmotifs and repetitions. Two years later, Derkaoui again took up the subject of the artistic community for his graduation film, Somewhere, Someday (1971). Some performers appear again, including actor-writer Stanisław Tym. However, Somewhere, Someday has a much more compact structure, pivoting around preparations for presenting the Régis Debray text "Notes on Gramsci."

Rapprochement through History

Other films in this group approach aspects of Polish history, with several focused on themes of the Holocaust and Jewish cemeteries. These topics also appear in films by Polish students—but that wave of increased interest didn't rise until the 1980s, and was undertaken mainly in those students' fiction films.

The earliest documentary made by foreigners and referring to Auschwitz is Letter to the Children (1964) by José Luis di Zeo. Its visual layer is composed of photographs of children among ruins: a boy with a bird cage, a sad little boy in a sideways hat, and photos of the Warsaw ghetto from SS commander Jürgen Stroop's Report on its liquidation. These include the infamous image of a boy with arms raised, later the subject of a Cannes award-winning student film: Z

podniesionymi rękami (*With Raised Hands*, 1985), by Mitko Panov, also a
Łódź alum. In the last section of *Letter to the Children*, photos appear
that are among the iconic images of the Holocaust: people driven
into cattle cars, screened-off ventilation gaps on a freight train, children in inmate stripes behind barbed-wire fencing, women on bunks,
emaciated faces, naked mothers with children in their arms, an
empty trolley, gas-chamber interiors, mounds of shoes. Documentation and photos came from CAF Archives and the collections of the
Main Commission for the Investigation of Nazi Crimes in Poland, the
Auschwitz-Birkenau Memorial and Museum, and the Jewish Historical Institute in Warsaw. The film's soundtrack has not been preserved. However, a title card—"This is the last letter of Rudolf Höss,
Commandant of the Auschwitz concentration camp, written on May
11, 1947, to his children"—indicates that a significant component of
the sound layer may have been the words of Höss, which he addressed
to his five children. That letter was sent from the Wadowice prison
in April, after the trial in which he was sentenced to death and as he
tried to reconcile with God.[3]

      Di Zeo's film was close to Polish documentary tradi-
tion of the day for two reasons. The 1960s in its nonfiction cinema
was a period of increased interest in the use of still photographs in
film.[4] An artistic supervisor for di Zeo's film was Kazimierz Karabasz,
who was then using more and more photographs in his productions.
A year after di Zeo made *Letter to the Children*, Karabasz directed the
self-referential *Na progu* (*On the Threshold*, 1965), showing advantages
and disadvantages of three documentary methods in portraying
characters: observation, on-camera interviews, and, last but not
least, a photo film with commentary derived from letters. As Karabasz described:

      The longer I observe the use of photographs (photo-
      grams, not freeze-frames) in a documentary, the more

3   Rudolf Höss, *Wyznania spod szubienicy: Autobiografia Rudolfa Hössa, komendanta
            KL Auschwitz spisana w krakowskim więzieniu na Montelupich* (Warsaw: Oficyna
            Wydawnicza Mireki, 2016). For letters to his family: 135–40. The first
            edition of Höss's memoirs was published in Poland in 1956.
4   For more on the subject, see Mikołaj Jazdon, "Fotografie w roli głównej:
            O polskim filmie ikonograficznym ze zdjęć," *Kartalnik Filmowy*, nos. 54/55
            (2006): 212–30.

I see the charms of this procedure. Two things fasci-
nate me: the possibility of contemplating the moment
when a person and their surroundings are present only
for a fraction of a second; a possibility to see the "material substance" of what is in the photo (landscape,
sculpture, people's clothes, the shape of furniture).[5]
The function of photos in a documentary, then, was a topic being discussed vigorously by filmmakers. The second element bringing di
Zeo's Letter to the Children closer to professional productions of the
1960s was its subject matter. The Holocaust was taken up in about a
dozen documentaries between 1956 and 1968—then the topic almost
disappeared from Polish cinemas for years. These include two excellent documentaries from photographs: Album Fleischera (The Fleischer
Album, 1962) by Janusz Majewski, and Powszedni dzień gestapowca Schmidta
(Gestapo-man Schmidt, 1963) by Jerzy Ziarnik.

Juan Caicedo, in his De profundis Psalm 88 (1984), also
shows traces of the past. He focuses his documentary impression
on the Jewish cemetery in Łódź.[6] Its wall and gate are visible in the
first frames. Then in long, majestic shots, the camera films tombs
and matzevot. Some are covered with snow, tilted and forgotten.
Symbolic ornaments become visible in close-ups. The cemetery in
Caicedo's film is a quiet, forgotten place. The paths are not walked,
nobody comes to set pebbles on the matzevot anymore.

De profundis is part of the group of works that represent
Jewish and the Holocaust themes through the material traces of their
presence in contemporary times. The cemetery is a recurrent motif
in the Polish cinema of the Holocaust, both in the documentary
(Cmentarz Remu [Remu Cemetery], dir. Edward Etler, 1961) and feature
film (Sanatorium pod Klepsydrą [The Hourglass Sanatorium], dir. Wojciech
Has, 1973).

Although students from Morocco, the Republic of the
Congo, Sudan, and Algeria formed the first significant group that
came to the Łódź Film School from the Global South, there are no

5   Kazimierz Karabasz, Cierpliwe oko (Warsaw: Wydawnictwa Artystyczne
i Filmowe, 1979), 6.
6   The Łódź cemetery, with its imposing Poznański-family tomb, appears in
Ekos (1990) by Sergio Vega.

traces of cultural distinctiveness in most of the dozens of films they made that survive in the school's archives. Certainly this was due to the influence of their artistic supervisors and of lecturers at the school, and the nature of tasks delegated to students. The student short wasn't always a film form in which an artistic "I" was to be expressed. In this context, similarities between films they made and those of their Polish colleagues isn't surprising.

In 1979, Beverly Joan Marcus presented *Patrik*, a reportage less than five minutes long, about a visit by Patrik Mabinda to Poland. Mabinda, an African National Congress activist, is shown in an almost minute-long sequence during his time at Auschwitz-Birkenau. It is preceded by a scene in which Mabinda is welcomed: the camera films a choir of black women, their song accompanying the first shots. The Auschwitz scenes, shot in close-up, are built around details: barbed-wire spikes, a mouth, an ear, a finger tearing a metal ring out of a wall, Mabinda's face. Camp barracks and fences remain in the background while clearly defining the site. The few shots of camp space seem to reflect Mabinda's gaze—Auschwitz is shown in a symbolic abridgement.

At one point, he looks up and then, in a sequence of moving images, a photograph appears of Mabinda during protests in South Africa. Heard off-screen are his laconic thoughts about overwhelming fear and the need for constant mobilization to fight for freedom. *Patrik* ends with an excerpt from his speech to supporters of the African National Congress. Black participants shout the slogan of liberation: *Amandla*, which in Nguni means power. Auschwitz-Birkenau, filmed in such a surprising way and placed in this particular context, isn't for Mabinda among the must-see points in Poland. His time there becomes a strong, intimate experience. Its symbolic meaning has expanded. Mabinda's presence in the former camp, the nature of his voice-over monologue, and references in the first and last sequences to the persecution of South African Blacks make it a symbol of violence against any otherness that's being deprived of rights and voice.

In all likelihood, *Patrik* is the only Polish-made film in which the omnipresent subject of Auschwitz is so closely entwined with apartheid policy. Marcus's short changes the perspective of looking at other documentaries made by Global South students in which they portrayed excluded and persecuted people, whether the Jewish children from *Letter to the Children* or the Roma protagonists of *Zofia and Ludmiła*.

Global South Students in the PRL

By pointing to similarities and tracing differences among films by Łódź students from the Global South, a sub-group can be distinguished featuring variations from domestic cinema. Its basic determinant is subject matter: the issue of foreigners—most often judged by their skin tones in the abruptly all-but monoethnic social paradigm of postwar Poland—presented in line with aesthetic conventions over the decades of Polish documentary-making. It's present almost constantly in films discussed since the early 1960s. Especially from the 1980s, the theme has been undertaken with greater intensity and greater openness. A specific introduction is provided in *Anthropology* (1982) by Djamel Benkhaled.

Anthropology is a record of race research based on physical characteristics among participants in a study. However, it's not a typical scientific film. It opens with a series of close-ups of body parts and descriptions: hair, bellies, navels, skin, noses, foreheads. A Nigerian asks scientists about their research purposes, and receives the answer: "to describe differences between people and investigate their causes." The shot sequence parceling human bodies is supplemented by shots of people performing mundane activities outside the lab in their social environments. Only such depictions, empowering the study's participants, seem complete.

In Abdul Khalik's *Foreign Students in Łódź* (1961), shot at the School of Polish for Foreigners, the scholarship students appear as a cheerful, multiethnic group painstakingly but successfully learning Polish, singing and dancing in attire from home. "If it weren't for the opening credits," writes film scholar Monika Talarczyk, "we wouldn't guess that the author of the script and the film's

director came from overseas."[7].While other students hadn't taken
up this topic, *Foreign Students in Łódź* doesn't reveal the filmmaking
team's ethnic diversity, as the documentary's authorial "I" remains
deeply hidden.

It's not revealed in an observational documentary on
the hardships of learning Polish, *Lesson 41* (dir. Abdellah Drissi, 1966),
either. Clusters of rustling sounds, complex rules of Polish declen-
sion, the meanings of specific words and whole phrases are just the
start of the path to enter culture through language. The first shots
show lips of characters with different skin colors pronouncing syllables and words with difficulty. Gradually, more and more insert shots
appear—portraits of students. Finally, the camera shows the entire
room, declination tables, and the teacher. Starting from details, the
filmmakers slowly widen the field of view—they reveal a group of
scholarship students learning Polish. The gradation also applies to
a deeper layer of meanings: from single sounds, the characters move
on to an excerpt from the national epic, *Pan Tadeusz*: from the need
or necessity to communicate in a foreign language to approaching a
culture through its literature. Using close-ups, the filmmakers
emphasize the learners' effort, discomfort, and confusion—and language learning is but one of the many adaptation obstacles these
characters are encountering.

An entirely different tone is adopted by the team
behind *Reserved for Foreigners* (dir. Fayçal Hassaïri, 1988). They depict
the isolation in which scholarship students lived, in a separate dormitory to which guests cannot be invited. Young people from all over
the world eagerly await letters from relatives, and hang photos from
home on their walls. They suffer from loneliness and monotony.
Learning Polish is limited to classes—otherwise, the characters seek
understanding in their own languages and close themselves within
ethnic groups. *Reserved for Foreigners* is critical of living conditions for

7   Monika Talarczyk, "Filmy z Wieży Babel: Edukacja polonistyczna jako
temat etiud studentów z globalnego Południa w Szkole Filmowej w Łodzi,"
Pleograf: Kwartalnik Akademii Polskiego Filmu, no. 1 (2020), https://
akademiapolskiegofilmu.pl/pl/historia-polskiego-filmu/pleograf/
edukacja/21/filmy-z-wiezy-babel-edukacja-polonistyczna-jako-temat-
etiud-studentow-z-globalnego-poludnia-w-szkole-filmowej-w-lodzi/708.

the scholarship students, but that's not the only way it differs from previous productions: characters comment in voice-over, the first time we hear their statements.

A subtle, veiled critique of relations between the students and Poles appeared much earlier in *The Adoption* (dir. Mostafa Derkaoui, 1968). The camera films children in an orphanage. Toddlers play, cry, babble, utter their first words. Offscreen, a conversation engages a married couple who want to adopt and an orphanage employee showing them around and presenting the children—first boys, then girls when it turns out that the woman would prefer a daughter. The couple consider children as if they were in a store: some are unsuitable for legal reasons, others are disabled, and still others don't suit them for various reasons. Finally, the employee shows the couple Agnieszka, the daughter of a Polish woman and a Kenyan, whom her mother gave up after she married a Pole. With the shot of the sleeping girl in a freeze-frame, the couple gently refuses, withdraws, stating that they will wait and stay in touch. "It wouldn't be the right arrangement," says the man. Unaware of this, Agnieszka is rejected for the same reason for the second time in her very short life.

I, Foreigner as Protagonist

At the beginning of the 1980s, films began to appear in which the subject of relations between Poles and non-Poles was taken up more boldly and, at the same time, in more intimate ways. The decade brought increased interest from documentary filmmakers in the performative model. According to critic and theoretician Bill Nichols, it was a moment in which "the referential quality of a documentary that attests to its function as a window onto the world yields to an expressive quality that affirms the highly situated, embodied, and vividly personal perspective of specific subjects, including the filmmaker."[8] It should be noted, however, that the direct presence of filmmakers in a narrative structure, in the frame or through voice-over, remained rare in Polish documentaries at that time, and doesn't happen in student films. Young filmmakers adopted

8   Bill Nichols, *Introduction to Documentary* (Bloomington: Indiana University Press, 2001), 132.

a solution halfway between distanced observation and autobiography[9]: they reached for other people's stories, but now it was those which were familiar to them.

Of course, changes then taking place in the poetics of documentary cinema were only one of the factors that determined the shape of student shorts. An equally significant impact came from the sociopolitical situation in Poland—the gradual easing of censorship and pressure from the authorities, both on the school's instructors and on student filmmakers. During this period, due to social movements, the ways of perceiving issues around the familiar and the strange were also transforming.

A recurring theme in the period's student films is a relationship or a marriage between a Global South scholarship holder and a Pole. In Ewa Nowicka's analysis:

> When [sociologist] Emory S. Bogardus created the distance scale, he adopted an accepting attitude toward a marriage with a person of a different ethnicity as an indicator of the lowest level of distance between ethnic groups. Until now, this indicator is still used in research and is rarely criticized. There is no closer, more intimate, and at the same time socially important contact between people than the permanent physical (sexual), emotional and familial relationship [...] of marriage.[10]

In *Wait, Wait* (1980) Beverly Joan Marcus portrays a young couple with a small child living in a cramped, cluttered dormitory room. He studies, and works as a gardener to support his family. In the evenings, he gets involved in household chores. She feels overwhelmed and tired from the constant bustle, work, childcare—but most of all by loneliness. Their intermittent conversations express tension, a smoldering conflict that can break out under any pretext, yet at the

9   I wrote about this phenomenon in "Autoportret na progu: Autobiografizm
        w etiudach szkolnych na tle tradycji polskiego kina dokumentalnego," in
        Polski film dokumentalny XXI wieku, ed. Tadeusz Szczepański and Małgorzata
        Kozubek (Łódź: Wydawnictwo Biblioteki PWSFTviT, 2016), 49–62.
10   Ewa Nowicka, "Wprowadzenie: Problemy do badania i problemy badane,
        czyli o cudzoziemcach w Polsce raz jeszcze," in *Blaski i cienie imigracji:
        Problemy cudzoziemców w Polsce*, ed. Ewa Nowicka (Warsaw: Wydawnictwa
        Uniwersytetu Warszawskiego, 2011), 19–20.

same time, they share strong bonds. *Wait, Wait* is actually about the lack of communication between two people fixed in their social roles. Does their inability to communicate also result from cultural differences? It's not indicated. The protagonists' situation is quite similar to that acutely presented by the director Piotr Szulkin in his short *Życie codzienne* (*Everyday Life*, 1976). There, in film historian Mirosław Przylipiak's description, Szulkin "exaggerates some effects in the soundtrack enormously, choses low-contrast filmstock, films the protagonists in shots not showing their heads to render an effect of their lives being gutted by work."[11] Both Marcus and Szulkin share a tendency to experiment with form. Interior shots have been staged, while the element of improvisation has certainly been preserved. In *Wait, Wait*'s apartment scenes, the camera is almost static, the sound layer is diegetic, while scenes of gardening work are accompanied by disturbing, uniform music, and the shots grow more dynamic.

The theme of difficulties in building mutual relations by mixed-ethnicity couples was raised several other times in the 1980s. Young filmmakers would express their own concerns, but most often they gave the floor to protagonists' Polish relatives. In *What Next* (dir. Abdesselam Mezerreg, 1982), the expectant mother speaks of her fears of childbirth, feeling lonely, and her husband's remaining distant. He spends his time at work, his free time at the table over the newspaper or in front of the TV. The frustrations felt by the young woman, however, are shared by many other women expecting a baby, regardless of their partners' ethnic background. Yet this difference was exposed by Mezerreg through photos hanging on the apartment walls, shots of the silent protagonist, a black rag doll.

The picture that emerges from these films of Poles' attitudes to ethnic and racial diversity is far from the propaganda message in the Eastern bloc of the early 1960s. As Mezerreg had done in *What Next*, Fayçal Hassaïri in *North-South* (1990) shows what happens in a mixed marriage when mutual infatuation and love have given way to everyday life. However, Hassaïri focuses not on what such part-

11   Mirosław Przylipiak, *Poetyka kina dokumentalnego* (Gdańsk: Wydawnictwo Uniwersytetu Gdańskiego, 2004), 5.

ners may have in common, but on what their differences bring out. Cultural and religious differences, fears and underlying mutual dislike all emerge with full force in *North-South*. The protagonist's mother would prefer her daughter did not leave Poland, worried that something might happen to her "there." Both her parents are skeptical about their son-in-law: "He should never have married anyone." Neither the young woman nor her parents—that is, the children's grandparents—want them to be brought up as Muslims. So the children pray with their grandparents in the apartment full of images of the Virgin Mary and they go to church with them. Grandma is convinced that past the age of thirty-five, Muslims become fanatics. In her opinion, "Poles are a completely different nation from the rest. One way or another, it's the Slavs who are the best breed." The final credits read: "Three days before filming began, the main character of the film, Kinga M., a nurse by profession, left with the Polish Red Cross for Kuwait." The story gets an ironic punch line.

Perhaps the most emotionally charged of these set of family films is *Beloved Father* (1983). Made by Laredj Khader, it is about a boy who remained in Poland with his mother when his father, Hamini, a graduate of the Łódź University of Technology, left for Algeria for work as an engineer. In the visual layer are photos of father and son. Letters and photos are the threads that connect the two. However, they live in different worlds, with these consistently presented in opposing ways: a gray, cloudy autumn in Poland, while in Algeria it's warm and sunny. A mood of sadness weighs on the boy, who sends his father letters, telling him about advancing to third grade, about notebooks he's kept for his dad to see, about his tonsils being removed. He asks for toy cars to be sent, then sends thanks for the toy. He dreams of visiting his father, but what he wants most is that he come to Poland. There's no place in *Beloved Father* for social engagement in criticizing and altering relations between Poles and non-Poles—Khader's film is too personal for that. Yet the director manages to grasp the problems of difference and remoteness.

By that period, students from the Global South were frequently returning to their home countries with a camera.[12] In previous decades, that had been rare for practical reasons, as well as complex requirements for crossing borders. An early result is Leonardo Palleja's *The Passage* (1990), made entirely on the Buenos Aires streets. More wide-ranging interests are in evidence in Marcus's *Patrik*. Many years earlier, in cooperation with the production company WFO (Wytwórnia Filmów Oświatowych), Rupen Vosgimorukian's *Report: September 1969* (1970) was made.

Footage for *Report: September 1969* was shot at the Palestinian refugee camp set up outside of Amman after the Six-Day War. Statements by Palestinians and volunteers are illustrated by a documentary record of daily camp life. Living conditions in Baqa'a are frightful. One person shouts directly at the camera: "Film this! Show the world that the Palestinian people have been turned into beggars." Volunteers and medical staff speak of helplessness, of suffering they're ill-equipped to alleviate. *Report: September 1969* ends with shots of abandoned houses, broken dishes, ruined toys, and bodies of the dead and wounded. It is obviously a student film, with enormous emotional impact, made with great commitment and empathy. The political context of its creation and WFO's involvement prove how important this topic was then for decision-makers.

Leonardo Palleja's *Traces* (1989) has an entirely different dimension—a more personal one. The director chose a Nicaraguan student as the protagonist, who talks about relations with his father and the trauma of his death, along with the former's involvement in guerrilla warfare with the National Liberation Front, which in 1979 had overthrown the Somoza regime. The filmmaking team focused on this moving family story of an individual—a monologue by the protagonist, shot in close-ups; his mother's letter read aloud—dominated by big-picture history illustrated by archival footage. *Traces* seems to simply give viewers the chance to familiarize themselves with problems in distant Nicaragua—even if ultimately it didn't reach too many viewers.

12   For more about student films made by scholarship students at the Łódź Film School, see my text "Między kulturami: Transnarodowy charakter etiud z łódzkiej Szkoły Filmowej," in Jagielski and Podsiadło, *Kino polskie*, 91–104.

The specificity of films made in Poland by Global South students is born of sustained tension between the categories of similarity and difference. Today, we may look at the group of their films as manifesting a transnational character within the country's national cinema—the appearance of young filmmakers from far-ranging parts of the world providing an opportunity to enrich a monoethnic domestic culture.

However, that way of thinking bears the trap of Eurocentrism. These students' presence in Poland and in other Eastern bloc countries carrying out similar scholarship programs was largely the result of Soviet policy with its vested interests and clear aims at geopolitical influence. At the same time, the processes of their educations and adaptations to local life, not always intentional, completely bypassed cultural and moral separateness. Traces of this are found in their 1980s films critical of Polish society, and in films that testify to absorptive adaptation—in some cases episodic—by Poles and their culture.

Studying documentary films by international students today allows us to point out similarities and differences and, in a diachronic perspective, to outline the sinusoid of approaching and moving away from works by Polish filmmakers. Documentaries by student filmmakers from the Global South are but a concise part of the broader cultural presence of scholarship students in the PRL. With that said, the metamorphoses of Polish society remains reflected more strongly in them than in the fictional counterparts those students made, more focused on creation and on artistic expression. As the eminent sociologist Georg Simmel notes, in the dichotomous "one of us–stranger" division, we're actually dealing with complementation, and creating a model image of social reality. All relations contain both a closeness and a distance factor. The strangeness category, as a key component of mutual interaction, wields a positive connotation.[13]

Translated from the Polish by Jolanta Axworthy.

13   See Georg Simmel, *Sociology: Inquiries into the Construction of Social Forms,
Volumes 1 and 2*, ed. and trans. Anthony J. Blasi, Anton K. Jacobs, and
Mathew Kanjirathinkal (Boston: Brill, 2009).

Marie Pierre-Bouthier is an associate professor in film history at Jules Verne University in Amiens. Her Phd dissertation (Paris 1 University, 2018) focused on resistance-documentary cinema and relations between filmmakers and politics in Morocco since the 1960s. Her research now deals with the decolonization of film's gaze, its forms and production, and with building new national/community cinema(s). She has been investigating the student years of Moroccan and Tunisian filmmakers, and careers of neglected pioneers and film activists. She has published in French journals (*Trafic*, *Revue d'Etudes des Mondes Musulmans et Méditerranéens*, *1895*) and in international journals including the *Journal of North-African Studies*. Pierre-Bouthier is a film curator for le Maghreb des films (http://www.maghrebdesfilms.fr) and is involved in projects of valorizing and preserving film-related archives, such as les Archives Bouanani (https://archivesbouanani.wordpress.com).

PODRÓŻ TO POLAND: IN SEARCH OF A POTENTIAL MOROCCAN CINEMA

After Morocco's independence in 1956, it was soon apparent to everyone from high schoolers to state officials that their new country should build a national cinema to relate its history, culture, and society through the eyes and lenses of its own filmmakers. But even though the French colonial regime had bequeathed independent Morocco a more or less structured administration, film industry, school and basic college systems, it was unavoidable that those who aspired to become filmmakers and create this national film art with its new Moroccan viewpoint would need to leave home and go study their craft in Europe.

Until 1968, most of these young Moroccans went to IDHEC, the film school in Paris, supported by Coopération française et technique scholarships, the French agency helping former colonies build their state agents and infrastructures. Yet most were disappointed with IDHEC, where training was just two years and where most students from former colonies along with female students were discouraged from enrolling in the film-direction class. They were more enthusiastic about the French capital's multinational political and cultural life.

Along with those Moroccans attending IDHEC, several others had gone to Belgium, the USSR, Czechoslovakia, or to the US for their film training. Then by the mid-1960s, Łódź in the Poland of the PRL-era, with its national film school, quickly became the second key destination for Moroccan filmmakers-to-be. Seven Moroccans were in attendance there in the 1960s and early 1970s, studying film direction, for the most part. Mohamed Ben Soude had arrived in 1961, with Abdellah Drissi arriving in 1964, then Mostafa Derkaoui and his brother Abdelkrim (who studied cinematography) in 1965, Abdelkader Lagtaa the next year, along with Idriss Karim and Hamid Bensaïd in 1967.[1] In contrast to IDHEC's policy, foreign students in Łódź spent six to ten years studying and training—which made the stay for each of them a genuinely life-changing podróż, or voyage.[2]

My purpose in this essay is thus to identify the specificity and richness of this Polish experience. And more specifically: In what way may it have informed and influenced the potential national cinema they imagined for their newly independent country, and then experimented toward as students?

My essay will argue that in these intense Polish experiences, and in each of the four "studies," or student films, that the directing students made, one can glimpse traces of a sort of agenda toward a Moroccan cinema-to-be—which was then left undernourished, for the most part. The prospects they laid out in Łódź were later prevented from being carried out at home by official or covert censorship, revealing a Moroccan state that preferred thoroughly controlled, submissive, frustrated filmmakers over a free, creative, openly communicative cinema. Within that framework, the essay establishes a premise that to write the history of early postcolonial cinemas, the imaginary, that which was aspired toward, the sketched cinema, along with student films and film projects, must be taken into account.

Thus this essay, after briefly expounding conditions of their arrival, living, and staying in Poland, will follow and show various

1   Years listed here indicate their arrivals in Łódź, not their entrances to
         the film school.
2   Podróż (Voyage, 1975) is Abdelkader Lagtaa's final student film.

aesthetic and political ways toward a potential Moroccan cinema that were then being explored by these student filmmakers—the Polish ways of a Moroccan cinema-to-be.

The data conveyed here stems from testimonies, personal archives, and student films collected and considered between 2015 and 2020, in the framework of a curatorial and research project developed jointly with the independent curator Léa Morin. What follows makes very little use of the voluminous paper archives at the Łódź Film School, as their inventory and translation projects remain a huge, ongoing endeavor.

Arriving, Living, and Staying in Poland

Unlike Lagtaa, the Derkaoui brothers, Karim, Bensaïd, and Drissi had all started university after their baccalaureates: theater schools in France for Bensaïd and Karim, a sociology diploma in Morocco for Drissi, and so forth. Coming from modest origins, and being very well educated, they were also politicized and committed—most had a strong will to study in the communist world, though not necessarily in Poland. Most of their testimonies agree that meeting such exceptional willingness among the country's embassy staff prompted their choice of Poland over the USSR, Czechoslovakia, or China. This may be a reason leading to the concentration of Moroccans at the Łódź Film School by the 1960s, more so than any agreements between the states or between that state and opposition parties at home.

Arrival was tough and disappointing. Lagtaa recalls Łódź looking so grey, industrial, and poor, with shop windows devoid of anything colorful and attractive...that he thought of leaving right away.[3] Derkaoui's wife, Khadija, hated the cold.[4] Nonetheless, Lagtaa and Derkaoui agree in retrospect that what lay before them then may have been their most beautiful years.

3   Abdelkader Lagtaa, interview by Léa Morin and Marie Pierre-Bouthier, March 28, 2019. All interviews conducted in French and translated by Marie Pierre-Bouthier.
4   Mostafa Derkaoui, interview by Léa Morin and Marie Pierre-Bouthier, September 22–October 3, 2016.

The stay in Poland began with a year of Polish language studies, in a building they lovingly called the Tower of Babel. There, they met people from all over the world: in class, in the dorms, during holiday trips offered by the student union, and during various events organized by the different foreign communities. Lagtaa remembers that he spent his first March 8 celebration with Vietnamese girls, before delivering his first speech in Polish[5] [FIG. 1]. The film school was also utterly multinational. From the Derkaouis' class, their close collaborators were Lebanese (Rupen Vosgimorukian), French (Gilles Moizon), Haitian (Roland Paret), and Norwegian (Haakon Sandøy). Other foreign students were met at marches (against the Vietnam War; May 1); in political conferences and meetings (in particular, in the framework of the foreign-student union); at the student's club; and in university dorms (some shared the film-school dorms with fine-arts students, others were scattered across other university lodgings, such as that of medicine students).

From these encounters arose long-lasting friendships. The Moroccans were in constant discussion, in particular with friends from the Arab world (the Algerian Djamel Bourtel), sharing university dorms, meeting at Mostafa and Khadija Derkaoui's apartment—which according to Lagtaa was an "open house," and where they freely drank vodka and talked at length.[6] They would later keep in contact, and even work together.[7] The Derkaouis also had strong ties with students from the Third World: the Costa-Rican sociology student Miguel Sobrado, who features in Abdellah Drissi's Lesson 41 (1966), a documentary about the Polish language class, and in Derkaoui's last student film. They also built very strong ties with Poles: Juliusz Janicki, an older student working at the school and helping out younger friends, pops up in the credits of various student films made by the Derkaouis' cohort. The great actor Stanisław Tym and the movie star Barbara Brylska participated in Mostafa's last two student films.

5   Abdelkader Lagtaa, interview by Léa Morin and Marie Pierre-Bouthier,
           May 29, 2019.
6   Lagtaa, interview, May 2019. Mostafa and Khadija, married with a child,
           lived in their own apartment.
7   Abdelkader Lagtaa, interview by Marie Pierre-Bouthier, October 23, 2015;
           Mostafa Derkaoui, interview, September–October 2016.

FIG. 1
ABDELKADER LAGTAA [SECOND FROM RIGHT], MARCH 8 FESTIVITIES, 1967,
COURTESY ABDELKADER LAGTAA

Except for Mostafa Derkaoui,[8] most would marry Poles: Lagtaa and a young chemist, Bożena, who met during a conference on the Palestinian issue; Bensaïd and a director of photography, Ewa Strzałka, with whom he collaborated artistically at school[9] then in Morocco (she took the name Nadia Bensaïd); and Drissi to the Polish actor Tomira Kowalik, who recalls him dearly, though she chose to resume her acting career in Poland after he was sent back to Morocco.[10]

The Aborted Careers of Politicized Filmmakers
As has been noted, most of the seven moved to Poland in part because of their political convictions.[11] Such was not the case for all Moroccans studying in Poland—or other foreigners, for that matter—who did not feel very concerned about politics nor any great reluctance to accept grant funding from the Moroccan regime.[12] Lagtaa, the Derkaouis, and Karim knew their commitments exposed them to political surveillance and embassy threats. From exchanges with comrades in Morocco—in particular, with Abdellatif Laâbi, editor of the vanguard journal *Souffles*, who would be arrested in 1972 and sentenced to ten years in prison in 1973[13]—they knew the danger of returning to Morocco, and were laying plans to settle elsewhere: the Derkaoui brothers in Costa Rica, Karim and Lagtaa in Iraq or even Algeria.[14] Ultimately, the latter were expelled to Algeria, in the midst of the political crisis triggered by Morocco's Green March into Western Sahara in November 1975.[15]

8   Mostafa was married to Khadija, whose nickname was Douja.
9   Ewa Strzałka was cinematographer for Bensaïd's first two student films, *Realism Does Not Pay* (1969; not preserved) and *Pensioners' House* (1969), and wrote the screenplay and dialogue for his final diploma film, *To Serve Twice* (1973).
10   Remigiusz Grzela, "Teatr jest sadomaso," February 4, 2006, *Wysokie Obcasy*, https://bit.ly/3rXAjEZ.
11   Mostafa Derkaoui, interview, September–October 2016.
12   Lagtaa, interview, May 2019.
13   He was released in 1980, after an international campaign to secure his freedom.
14   Lagtaa, interview, March 2019; Abdelkrim Derkaoui, interview by Léa Morin, 2017.
15   Abdelkrim Derkaoui, interview, 2017; Lagtaa, interview by Marie Pierre-Bouthier, 2018.

They were very probably paying for their involvement with local student unions, as well as for Karim's last two student films, which rather openly denounced Poland's conservative society and its inflexible, repressive regime. Indeed, *And Everyday Exile* (1975) should have been the fictitious portrait of a working woman destroyed by the puritanical cabal from one of the workers' leagues at her factory.[16] As for *Song for the Deaths of the Young* (1973), it is a highly metaphorical symbolic evocation of violent repressions across Poland and Czechoslovakia in the spring of 1968. According to Karim's widow, both films were banned and seized in 1975 and 1976 respectively, with only *Song for the Deaths of the Young* available today.[17] Nevertheless, letters in his personal file in the school archives lead us rather to believe that he was prevented from shooting *And Everyday Exile*.

Things did not get any better for Karim at home. While still a student, he left unfinished a documentary about unemployed young men from the Haouz region (north of Marrakech), begun there during his 1969 summer vacation: *Les enfants du Haouz* (*Children of Haouz*). The film, written and commissioned by the Moroccan sociologist Paul Pascon, met the disapproval of the interior minister, then wound up being re-edited in 1970 by an appointed producer, A. Zerouali, who then quite simply had it disappear, though its absence aroused some scandal in the pages of culture journals.[18] After his return to Morocco through Algeria, Karim moved to Paris. From there, he attempted to direct a new film in Morocco, but to no avail, though toward the end of his life he received a CCM grant (Centre cinématographique marocain) to direct a feature film. He had become more of a French television director, remaining a friend to and something of a sage for his fellow filmmakers, who highly valued his views to the day he died.

16   *And Everyday Exile* was inspired by a short news item; in it, anonymous letters had brought a young woman into disrepute. She chose to commit suicide.

17   Danielle Lavigne, interview by Léa Morin and Marie Pierre-Bouthier, February 28, 2020.

18   Noureddine Saïl, "En attendant Karim," *Cinéma* 3, no. 1 (January 1970): 57; Abdellatif Laâbi, "Les Enfants du Haouz et les Bérets verts," *Souffles* 18 (March–April 1970): 87; Paul Pascon, "Les Enfants du Haouz," *Lamalif*, no. 48 (May 1971): 32; Paul Pascon, "Mise au point à propos de l'article de Zerouali sur Les Enfants du Haouz," *Lamalif*, no. 45 (January–February 1971): 47; Abdallah Zerouali, "Quand mûrissent les cinéastes," *Lamalif*, no. 44 (December 1970): 44–45.

It also proved very difficult for Hamid Bensaïd to work in Morocco. In 1981 he directed his first feature, *L'Oiseau du paradis* (*Bird of Paradise*), as well as a documentary, again written by the sociologist Paul Pascon, whom he had most likely met during his year at the sociology institute before leaving for Poland. That film, *Le rite du ligoté* (*Binding Ritual*, 1981), was about an unorthodox religious Berber tradition. The ritual of the title consisted of collective libations, the worship of a saint, and the miraculous levitation of a bound victim—all practices sternly disapproved of by Orthodox Islam and by the supposedly enlightened modernists espousing anti-obscurantist, anti-superstition positions. *Binding Ritual* was hotly debated by its select audience of intellectuals,[19] then disappeared. Bensaïd's problems deepened after his wife, Ewa Strzałka, returned to Poland with their daughter: he abandoned a project that was in process[20] and then the film industry. Eventually, Abdellah Drissi did the same.

The first years Lagtaa spent in Morocco were also very frustrating. At CCM, as well as in Moroccan television, he felt isolated and hindered, with his projects consistently aborted. In 1984, he managed to broadcast several documentaries: about the new wave in Moroccan painting (the Casablanca Art School), and one directed with Mostafa Derkaoui about rural life and agriculture. Ultimately, from 1991 to 2014, he directed five feature films, most of them focusing on his beloved city of Casablanca, including *Un amour à Casablanca* (*Love in Casablanca*, 1991), *La Porte close* (*Shut Door*, 1995), and *Les Casablancais* (*Casablancans*, 1999).

Mostafa Derkaoui, before becoming among the most prolific of Moroccan filmmakers with nine features directed between 1982 and 2004, had to overcome many hardships. His first professional feature, *De quelques événements sans signification* (*About Some Meaningless Events*, 1974)—financed in part by painters of the Casablanca Art School, who sold paintings for the film's benefit—was judged too free and subversive by the censorship commission and was banned, and remained unseen for several decades.

19   "Cinéma, Le rite du ligoté: Un documentaire sur le Maârouf de Lalla Aziza," *Lamalif*, no. 127 (July–August 1981): 59.
20   That film was an adaptation of Claude Ollier's first novel, *La mise en scène* (*The Mise-en-Scène*, 1958). See Claude Ollier and Christian Rosset, *Ce soir à Marienbad et autres chroniques cinématographiques* (Paris: Les Impressions nouvelles, 2020).

Mostafa's brother, Abdelkrim Derkaoui, became an eminent cinematographer, working with his brother and with Lagtaa, as well as with renowned Moroccan filmmakers including Jilali Ferhati, Moumen Smihi, Saâd Chraïbi, Izza Génini, and Mohamed Abbazi. Abdelkrim also directed four features: *Le Jour du forain* (*Day of the Carnie*, 1984), *Rue le Caire* (*Cairo Street*, 1998), *Chroniques blanches* (*White Chronicles*, 2009), and *Les griffes du passé* (*Claws of the Past*, 2015).

Polish Ways for a Potential Moroccan Cinema

Whether they wound up quitting the business or maintained their efforts for a decade or more until they could get feature-film projects made, what is clear is that state control and censorship prevented these directors from realizing the ambitions they originally had in mind. Untold restrictions, frustrations, bans, self-censorship, and passing years obviously blunted and diluted their creative fire and certitude, their political and aesthetic audacity, along with technical aptitudes they had acquired in Poland.

Thus it seems all the more important to carefully study film experimentations they conducted in Łódź. There, we find some of their propositions for building a new Moroccan cinema. As such, those experiments and studies can be construed as a Moroccan cinema from Poland: a potential Moroccan cinema that was a trial run, imagined through, aspired toward, yet never fully realized and fulfilled outside the Łódź Film School's halls and screening rooms and golden days.

The pages that follow are an attempt to describe and analyze this potential cinema by discerning the various aesthetical ways, trends, and tendencies these pioneers of a Moroccan aesthetic could have introduced in their national cinema, had they managed to continue their student experiments at home. I will therefore distinguish: 1) the social-documentary trend (and, more particularly, a certain taste for documentary portraits); 2) the way of (classical) political cinema; and 3) a tendency to decompartmentalize art practices by opening to poetry, drama, and contemporary art, and a resulting way of experimental, symbolical (yet still political) cinema.

The Social-Documentary Trend

One of their mentors was the greatly admired Polish documentarian Kazimierz Karabasz. Lagtaa remembers that Karabasz's film-direction classes were atypical, being based on discussion focused on case studies and observation exercises.[21] Along with his free way of teaching, and in addition to the Moroccan students' personal interests in the Canadian[22] and French documentary schools (including Pierre Perrault, Michel Brault, and Claude Jutra in the former; and Jean Rouch, Alain Resnais, and Chris Marker in the latter), Karabasz converted them to the documentary methods and themes of his own filmmaking and of the Polish documentary school, in particular the Black Series (Czarna Seria).[23] For instance, they share with that aesthetic an interest in art and music, and in performing artists: *Wacław A.* (dir. Lagtaa, 1969[24]) is about a strange street musician, half-scholar, half-beggar, while *But Hope Is of a Different Color* (dir. Lagtaa, 1972) films Roma performers at a music hall—but has unfortunately lost its soundtrack. In a similar vein, Karabasz had made a short film about musicians (*Muzykanci* [*The Musicians*], 1960) and about circus performers (*Ludzie*

21   "With Karabasz, we were in constant dialogue. Sometimes we took the train back to Warsaw with him, because class was over and we still had things to discuss with him! [...] This is the reason why I said that teaching was not normative: students had all freedom to explore, to research." Lagtaa, interview, March 2019.

22   Lagtaa recalled that he organized a film program dedicated to documentary cinema from Quebec in a screening room at the school. There was no official programmer: teachers and students could program any film, in distribution or not, censored or not, provided that it could be sent to Poland.

23   Karolina Kosinska, "Style and Attitude: Social(ist) Realism in the Polish Black Series and British Free Cinema," *Studies in Eastern European Cinema* 2, no. 2 (2011): 193–209.

24   At that time, Wacław Antczak (of the title) was indeed part-musician, part-beggar, part-poet, living on his veteran's pension and "haunting" the school (Lagtaa, interview, May 2019.) Initially a tailor, Antczak was spotted, after appearing as an extra in the now-iconic comedy *Rejs* (*Cruise*, dir. Marek Piwowski, 1970), by members of the Workshop of the Film Form, with whose "artistic actions" he participated until his death in 1974. See the film by Ryszard Waśko, "The Journey of Wacław Antczak to the Kiosk in Główna Street," *MSN*, accessed October 14, 2021, https://artmuseum.pl/en/filmoteka/praca/wasko-ryszard-podroz-waclawa-antczaka-do-kiosku-przy-ulicy; and Józef Robakowski's "Hommage a Wacław Antczak," *MSN*, accessed October 14, 2021, https://artmuseum.pl/en/archiwum/druki-artystyczne-galerii-wymiany/2929/130184.

w drodze [*People on the Road*], 1960) in their daily lives, quite comparable to the Roma people filmed by Lagtaa, but also Bensaïd (*Zofia and
Ludmiła*, 1971).

More generally, the student filmmakers seem to have
shared a vivid interest in marginality, minorities, and exclusion, particularly the experiences of women and the elderly: in the very amateur, silent *Pensioners' House* (1969), Hamid Bensaïd's first student film,
an echo may be found of *Dom starych kobiet* (*Elderly Ladies' Home*, dir. Jan
Łomnicki, 1957). Idriss Karim seems to have specialized in portraits
of working women, with *Marta* (1969), *Elżbieta K.* (1973), and the censored short feature *And Everyday Exile*. As for *The Adoption* (dir. Mostafa
Derkaoui, 1968) and *Zofia and Ludmiła* (dir. Bensaïd, 1971), they portray
little girls, tackling the ostracism undergone by Blacks and Roma,
respectively. Bensaïd explored the latter subject together with Lagtaa (*But Hope Is of a Different Color*, 1972), after they had admired *Skupljači
perja* (*I Even Met Happy Gypsies*, dir. Aleksandar Petrović, Yugoslavia,
1967) at a screening in Łódź. Whether they knew *Zanim opadną liście*
(*Before the Leaves Fall*, 1964) by Władysław Ślesicki or not, they decided
to take an opposing view from that Polish film, which enhanced a
beautifully nomadic way of life, with its caravans, card-playing, riv-
erbank laundering, and wild dancing and music into the night. Lagtaa and Bensaïd focused instead on the gloomy forced settlement
imposed on Roma in the PRL and the virulent racism they experienced from the Poles.

Politicized, from working-class families, the Moroccans were aware of comparable poverty, exclusion, and destitution
at home, and they were aware that the tools provided by Karabasz's
tutelage and example should allow them to show care and respect
for people being rendered invisible by society, and to direct a clear
viewpoint on exposing the unjust system that was condemning them.
Lagtaa explains: "In Poland, we learned that social themes are important: you cannot disregard people's living conditions. [...] We were
mostly concerned with the social aspect of cinema. How to point a
critical gaze at Moroccan reality, through an understandable tale."[25]

25   Lagtaa, interview, March 2019.

Lagtaa, Bensaïd, and Karim did then attempt to extend this social-documentary trend in Morocco. Lagtaa and Derkaoui directed *La femme rurale* (*The Rural Woman*) in 1989, and Bensaïd went from filming the Roma minority to the Berber minority, in *Binding Ritual*—though both films were barely screened and now appear to be lost. As for documentary portraits, we have already recounted Karim's misadventures with *Children of Haouz*. In like fashion, in the 1970s Lagtaa began a portrait of a handicapped child in a neglected neighborhood, but was expelled from CCM before he could complete the editing: "You've wasted the state's money to film a futureless child," as Lagtaa recalls the indignant *"directeur"* saying.[26] That condemnation seems evidence of Polish documentary means being entirely incomprehensible to the Moroccan authorities of the day, and completely discordant with what they expected from the documentary-film genre and its practitioners.

Lagtaa, Bensaïd, Derkaoui, and Karim were allowed to utilize neither their remarkable abilities at immersing the camera into a chosen environment and generating a unison with their subjects as they were filmed, nor the talent they shared for short, warm, black-and-white close-ups. Once one discovers the beauty of their student documentaries, one can only regret the lack of an equivalent in Morocco, and the loss of *Children of Haouz*. Morocco then had plentiful material for a filmic gaze such as theirs were: beautiful, tender, and accurate in coping with its own realities. Indeed, most of these student films aim to comprehend their characters' lives in their various facets, with cross-cut sequences showing both family and public lives: *Marta* and *Elżbieta K.* show their female protagonists alternatively at work (a weaving factory; the school of fine arts) and at home with their children; *But Hope Is of a Different Color* shows the Roma family either singing on stage or waking, drinking coffee, and bickering at home; *Zofia and Ludmiła* shows the Roma girls at home and at school, baby-sitting while answering the teacher's questions.

What's more, their cinematic gazes are never intrusive or squalid. On the contrary, they feel like caresses. Admittedly, the soundtrack can contribute to this impression: images are often

26   Lagtaa, interview, October 2015.

accompanied by mundane sounds, hubbub in the classroom or the tavern (in *Wacław A.*, *Zofia and Ludmiła*, *The Adoption*, and *Lesson 41*), or voice-over interviews (*Elżbieta K.*, *Marta*). In *The Adoption*, the voice-over dialogue of a couple wanting to adopt was scripted by Mostafa Derkaoui. *Elżbieta K.* by Karim is an empathic portrait of an art-school model: images of her work, home, and little daughter are accompanied by a testimony in voice-over, obviously delivered to a female accomplice. According to Laâbi, the same technique of using interviews and testimonies as voice-over was used in *Children of Haouz*, making the voice-over sound like the characters' stream of consciousness.[27] Beyond the portrait *Elżbieta K.* renders of a woman earning a living from her nudity in spite of prevailing moral judgements, the film provides a subtle reflection on representation, self-representation, and inner representation, self-gaze and others' gazes, by including shots on inscribed frames, mirrors, pictures, and still lives like memento mori.

Where does the true self of this woman lie? In her voice, speech, tears, long hair, small home, dusty dinner table, loneliness and complaints? Or when art magnifies her and reveals the unearthly beauty of a reverse Madonna? In most of these student films, and in particular in *Elżbieta K.*, music is astutely applied, appearing in general just before the credits reel, or adding poignancy and nostalgia in the most spontaneous shots (camera forgotten, the character true to life): a Romani flute in *Zofia and Ludmiła*, the seventh movement of Pergolesi's *Stabat Mater* in *Elżbieta K.*

The Way of (Classical) Political Cinema

For the filmmakers in training, Łódź was a period during which they were exceptionally free from family and state control (despite Moroccan spies), and they took advantage of it to increase their political commitment. This political concern is visible in Lagtaa's first silent fiction film, *Shadow among Others* (1969), in which a Moroccan political opponent (inspired by their beloved Mehdi Ben Barka) is exiled, tracked, trapped, and tortured: he is played by Mostafa Derkaoui, himself a former member of the clandestine

27   Abdellatif Laâbi, "Les Enfants du Haouz et les Bérets verts," *Souffles* 18 (March–April 1970): 87.

Moroccan Communist Party. The setting is built out of their own possessions: opposition newspapers (*Granma*, the Party paper in Cuba), political posters from May 1968 in France (a closed fist, with the subtitle LE CINÉMA S'INSURGE! [Cinema uprising!]), portraits of Ben Barka, Che Guevara, Ho Chi Minh, and so forth, revealing their participation in "world youth"[28] and "word youth revolt"[29] that grew blatant after 1968. Lagtaa recalls reading the *Tricontinental* journal and marching against the Vietnam War. They felt such concern about May 1968 in France that the Derkaouis went to Paris before the school year began to record testimonies from organizers of the politicized filmmakers organization, États généraux du cinéma (the Estates General of Cinema in France): Jean Charvein, Pierre Geller, and Hélène Arnal. One excerpt from these interviews remains, at the beginning of Mostafa's student film *Cellar People* (1969).

Derkaoui's student films are evidence of this world-scale commitment: his thesis film, *Somewhere, Someday* (1971), shows students discussing a proposed conference on Third World liberation movements,[30] among them their friend Miguel Sobrado, a guerrilla fighter and theorist.[31] Actually, the entire film questions the necessity to substitute political action for theory: close by, a stage director rehearses a play about "partisans" and ends up shot by an actor, who breaks through symbolically to action, while the director's efforts to join the struggle through theory and art are symbolically cut down.

Despite this politicized 1970s atmosphere, Derkaoui's last student films are not purely political films: they are very different from portraits of political leaders he and Lagtaa had directed early on. Indeed, before Lagtaa's *Shadow among Others* (1969), Derkaoui's first silent fiction film, *Amghar* (1968), had been about Berber

28   Geneviève Dreyfus-Armand, "Les années 1968 ou la jeunesse du monde," *L'Histoire*, no. 330 (April 2008): https://www.lhistoire.fr/les-ann%C3%A9es-1968-ou-la-jeunesse-du-monde.

29   Dominique Dhombre, "Retour sur une révolte mondiale de la jeunesse," May 12, 1998, *Le Monde*. Quoted in Kristin Ross, *Mai 68 et ses vies ultérieures*, trans. Anne-Laure Vignaux (Paris: Agone; Le Monde Diplomatique, 2010): 213–14.

30   The discussed titles are: "Leninist Theory of Peaceful Coexistence and the Struggle of Peoples of the Third World for Peace and Democracy" or "Lenin's Internationalism and Support for liberation movements."

31   Sobrado was then writing "Anthropology of the Guerrilla."

leader Moha Ou Hamou Zayani's capture, having battled French forces in northern Morocco from 1914 to 1921.[32] These films, though short, amateur, and silent, are very much in the manner of a nascent political cinema (for example, Francesco Rosi had been at work since 1958, and *Z* by Costa-Gavras dates back to 1969). They are also influenced by Andrzej Wajda's gripping war films of the decade before (*A Generation* [1954], *Kanał* [1956], *Ashes and Diamonds* [1958]).

These two unique portraits of Moroccan resistance heroes are both very rare and important objects. They prove that a Moroccan political, oppositional cinema was being aspired for, though the remaining traces of it remained abroad, in their film school's archives. Indeed, Lagtaa and Derkaoui were fully aware that in Morocco, they would never be allowed to release such material: Ben Barka's face and name were taboo, while Moha Ou Hamou Zayani, as a Berber leader, was inherently suspect and assumed to represent anti-state and anti-monarchy rebellion. In fact, almost no other films were ever shot on Berber anti-colonial resistance. As for films portraying contemporaneous leftist leaders and political opponents, the first would be a work by Lagtaa, which he completed in...2015. *La Moitié du ciel* (*Half the Sky*) is Lagtaa's portrait of his close friend, the committed poet Abdellatif Laâbi.

Comparably, in Poland, tackling similar subjects taken from the Polish realm was no more conceivable. This may explain why, as the years went by, the Moroccans tried more experimental forms and symbolic meanings, drawing inspiration from the ways in which Polish cinema was diluting its political message in order to bypass censorship, and from other artistic practices, as well.

Other Arts' Inspiration: Experimental Cinema

Most of these filmmakers had in fact practiced other arts before arriving in Poland. Bensaïd and Lagtaa read and wrote poetry. The latter, through the periodical *Souffles* (which published one of his poems in November 1966), met the members of the Casa-

32 Lagtaa plays the role of a Moroccan soldier in the French army, and Derkaoui that of a Berber resistance fighter. Others roles are handled by non-Moroccan actors. Abdelkrim Derkaoui is cinematographer.

blanca Art School[33] in the summer of 1968: Mohamed Melehi, Mohamed Hamidi, Driss Khoury, Mohamed Chebâa (Melehi conceived *Souffles'* renowned monotone cover page adorned with a black sun; a Hamidi painting followed Lagtaa's "Poèmes" in issue no. 5).[34] He was impressed with how Moroccan painting was being renewed, and returned to Poland convinced that his nation's cinema should follow a similar path. These older interests in poetry and in painting's fresh perspectives may explain Lagtaa's involvement in the 1970s in conceptual art. He started as Ewa and Andrzej Partum's Polish-French translator, while they ran the small Adres gallery in Łódź and another, Bureau de la poésie, in Warsaw. Lagtaa then continued helping the Partums on some of their creations and happenings, and ended up creating his own pieces of concrete poetry—words spread in space or diverted from their original use.

Later, conceptual art would become a major stream in Eastern European art, bringing attention to the absurdities of the communist system. Lagtaa was deeply influenced by his early experience with the movement, which opened new ways of playing with words, objects, and reality, and of conveying a critical message. However, he never managed to sustain this once back in Morocco. Yet it may have inspired his final, heavily symbolical, subtly critical feature, *Podróż*, or *Journey*, which was about a man being pursued by his younger self (at least in Lagtaa's interpretation), who asks him if he has been faithful to his youthful ideals.

Others among the Moroccans had worked in theater. Derkaoui "haunted" Casablanca's drama school. Drissi had a degree from Strasbourg's National Drama Art School (École nationale d'art dramatique), and in Paris, Karim took a degree at the National School of Theatre Arts and Techniques (École nationale supérieure des arts et techniques du théâtre; ENSATT). He then worked for part of 1962 with the company Groupe de théâtre antique de la Sorbonne. A decade later, Karim assisted the director Jan Maciejowski when he staged his recent production of *Hamlet* with the Jaracz Theater in Łódź. The theater scholar Marta Cibińska describes Maciejowski's

33   *Souffles* 5 (1967): 25–27. Lagtaa, interview, March 2019.
34   He had returned to take part in an UNEM congress in Rabat. Lagtaa, interview, March 2019.

Hamlet as a "sound and fury" production, focused on the characters' passions and sexual obsessions, but with a political edge. This aspect had grown even more obvious when the director mounted his production in Łódź in 1972:

> Between the Toruń [1970] and the Łódź production the political tragedy of shooting workers in Gdańsk took place. [...] Hamlet there became a representative of his generation [...]. There is no question that the later version reflected in its bitterness and pessimism the political climate in Poland in the early seventies: after the fall of [Party leader] Gomułka, accompanied by the massacre in Gdańsk, the new order of [de facto leader Edward] Gierek was not looked upon as very promising, and general pessimism [prevailed].[35]

When Karim shot *Song for the Deaths of the Young*, in 1973, he had likely learned from working with Maciejowski how to depict political discontent through sexual metaphors and symbols.[36] His *Song* shows a succession of absurd, surrealistic situations in a restaurant. A nun unravels her habit then starts to dance half-naked. A blind man (Karim) takes photos, a barely clad starving fakir conjures up a chicken,[37] an Algerian customer orders a sewing machine.[38] There's a dog carrying a plate of bones and an old man in a wheelbarrow, along with naked waitresses (among them, the lead from *Elżbieta K.*), and so forth. These situations may represent subconscious flare-ups among this restaurant's patrons, all of whom are obviously yearning to throw off the lid heaved over them by incessant surveilling eyes. These weird visions allude also to the broader political situation in Eastern Europe, in particular events in spring of 1968 and crushing repressions in Poland and in Czechoslovakia: demonstrators before a building with a METEOROLOGY sign brandish photos of Vietnamese and African casualties and slogans including WE WANT THE SUN! These

35   Marta Gibińska, "Polish Hamlets: Shakespeare's *Hamlet* in Polish Theatres After 1945," in *Shakespeare in the New Europe*, ed. Michael Hattaway, Boika Sokolova, and Derek Roper (London: Bloomsbury Academic, 1994), 167–68.
36   Up to pace with their era, some student films of this period resort to sexuality and nakedness, as well as to very abstruse and far-fetched symbolism.
37   Played by the filmmaker Piotr Szulkin.
38   Played by Karim's friend Djamel Bourtel.

images are accompanied by Joan Baez singing "Jackaroe"[39] and by Janusz Kusza protest songs sung by Music Academy of Łódź students. In Karim's various résumés, the director always describes this film as a metaphor for the death of Jan Palach in 1969, the young Czech protestor who self-immolated, and as a call for "socialism with a human face."

As for Mostafa Derkaoui, he was particularly impressed by the Polish jazz scene. For his last two student films, he cast members of the Andrzej Kurylewicz Quintet: Wanda Warska, the vocalist, and Włodzimierz Nahorny, the sax player, pianist, and composer, who wrote the soundtracks for *Cellar People* (shot in Kurylewicz's basement arts' space in Warsaw) and for *Somewhere, Someday*, which was shot in the capital's Klub Stodoła. Nahorny also contributed to Derkaoui's debut feature, *About Some Meaningless Events*. Jazz dives, jazz cats, and jazz music was evidently inspirational to the cinema Derkaoui was envisioning in those days—and which directly impacted that first Moroccan feature.

Each of these three films surpasses literal political cinema, and each searches for a political form with which to embody social resistance and the quest for freedom and political meaning. Seen today, *Cellar People, Somewhere, Someday*, and *About Some Meaningless Events* share a viscerally jazzy improvisational device: their rhythmic montaging, and the free, dancing cinematography of Abdelkrim Derkaoui, bopping at the soundtrack's tempo from close-up to close-up, from face to face. Voices overlap, interrupt each other. Interviews are improvised, generating a possibility of liberated speech—a potential danger, from a repressive state's point of view. Besides, the films are shot in smoky underground bars where the alcohol flows, and in popular streets. The result displays both the sheer euphoria of cinema's potentially unlimited power and an underlying forlorn awareness of an ingrained powerlessness of image and camera, doubting even the mere possibility of acting politically through effective, politicized works of art. All three films tackle cinema's incapacity to fully embody reality, and its potential treachery: in *About Some Meaningless Events*, its lead is betrayed by the camera; it has indeed

39   The 1963 song tells of a young woman disguising herself to go to sea and rescue her lover, who's been impressed into the navy.

witnessed and recorded his attempt to murder his boss, which leads to his being convicted and imprisoned. All of which results in the film's explosive liberty and extraordinary disorderliness. Logically, the great potential and the unruly appeal of this singular experiment was promptly banned by Hassan II's regime. Thus were ended, sadly, these Polish dreams and trial runs of a potential and promising new Moroccan cinema.

I warmly thank Léa Morin for her precious partnership and contributions, Gabrielle Chomentowski and Peter Limbrick for fruitful discussions, and Mostafa Derkaoui, Abdelkrim Derkaoui, Abdelkader Lagtaa, and Danielle Lavigne for the priceless gift of their testimonies and for opening their personal archives. My gratitude goes also to the Łódź Film School, for the unrivaled efficiency with which Monika Talarczyk, Monika Sarwińska, and others provided access to the student films mentioned in this essay.

Olivier Hadouchi is an independent film curator and researcher. His PhD was on "Cinema and Tricontinental Struggles" (Paris Sorbonne Nouvelle, 2012), and his research is focused on Global South and Tricontinental aesthetics and internationalism. He has published in academic journals including *Third Text* (on *The Pan-African Festival of Algiers*, dir. William Klein) and *CinémAction* (on militant Latin American cinema and on Algerian and Lebanese films), in collections (on FAMU and the Third World, ed. Tereza Stejskalová), and in exhibition catalogs including *Southern Constellations: The Poetics of the Non-Aligned*, ed. Bojana Piškur, Moderna Galerija, Ljubljana. He has published a booklet for MSUM-Belgrade, *Images of Solidarity with the Algerian Revolution*, and about Yugoslav reporters in the collection *Non-Aligned Modernisms*, ed. Zoran Erić. He has curated film programs at Museum Reina Sofía ("Tricontinental—Cinema, Utopia and Internationalism," 2017), the Jeu de Paume ("Echoes of Algerian Resistances," with Zineb Sedira's 2019 exhibition), among others.

VOICES AND FACES FROM THE THIRD WORLD

O ver several Cold War decades, the Łódź Film School, founded in 1948, enrolled sixty-three students from the Global South. Those coming from African countries included the Algerians Ahmed Lallem, Abdesselam Mezerreg, Djamel Bourtel, and Djamel Benkhaled, along with the Moroccans Mostafa and Abdelkrim Derkaoui, Abdelkader Lagtaa, Idriss Karim, and Abdellah Drissi. Those from Latin America included the Argentines José Luis di Zeo and Oscar Gamardo, the Colombian Ricardo Torres Ramírez, the Mexicans José María Sánchez Ariza and Raul Saucedo Zermeño. Rupen Vosgimorukian was among the students arriving from the Middle East, and there were a plethora of students of other nationalities.

       This intake of international students gained the host country a certain prestige, as it became a point of reference and a model of education in filmmaking and film technique. The school, city, and country integrated into a broad network of international exchange among other prestigious Eastern bloc film schools, including FAMU[1] in Prague and VGIK in Moscow. Polish graduates of the Łódź Film School, to name just Andrzej Wajda and Jerzy Skolimowski, were becoming internationally renowned filmmakers whose œuvres attracted critical attention and received prizes at diverse festivals. Wajda first came to prominence in the 1950s. Skolimowski's work, over the course of the following decade, gained traction in *Cahiers du cinéma* as that journal promoted auteur cinema, and regarded Skolimowski a key director in new-cinema trends of the 1960s. Other periodicals such as *Positif* enthused about European "young cinemas" and new waves (Godard, Bertolucci, Jancsó, Skolimowski, etc.) and like movements across the globe (a new wave in Japan, Brazilian *cinema novo*, etc.), which weren't shy about shaking up conventions and portraying young characters revolting against their respective societies.

In some countries of the Global South, too—such as Algeria, which in the 1960s and 1970s had a dynamic moviegoing scene and a vibrant Cinémathèque—the Łódź Film School and contemporary Polish cinema appeared as pertinent models and points of reference. The Algerian paper *El Moudjahid* ran an article titled "One of the Best Film Schools in the World: The Łódź Film Institute in Poland"[2] in September 1965. The Cinémathèque put on a program of Polish cinema in February and March 1966,[3] with a lecture by screenwriter and director Antoni Bohdziewicz on the subject. Bohdziewicz had lived in Paris in the 1930s, spoke fluent French, and headed the Łódź Film School's directing department from 1948 until 1966.

1   See Tereza Stejskalová, ed., *Filmmakers of the World, Unite! Forgotten Internationalism, Czechoslovak Film and the Third World* (Prague: Tranzit.cz, 2017), which includes my essay "Mohammed Lakhdar-Hamina and Boubaker Adjali: The Careers of Two Algerian Filmmakers Who Attended FAMU."

2   The unsigned article was published on September 29, 1965; it may have been written by the critic Guy Hennebelle, who wrote pseudonymously for *El Moudjahid* as Halim Chergui. It is in the list of Hennebelle's articles identified by Sébastien Layerle, "Articles de presse de Guy Hennebelle (1963–1968)," in *Chroniques de la naissance du cinéma algérien: Guy Hennebelle, un critique engagé*, ed. Sébastien Layerle and Monique Martineau-Hennebelle (Condé-sur-Noireau: Éditions Charles Corlet, 2018).

3   In February and March 1966, *El Moudjahid* ran numerous unsigned articles discussing Polish cinema, films, and filmmakers. See, for example, "Pologne: un cinéma en autogestion: Originalité des films, liberté d'inspiration, autonomie des cinéastes," collected in Layerle and Martineau-Hennebelle, *Chroniques de la naissance du cinéma algérien*, 436–37.

Through the 1960s and beyond, the process of decolonization continued in the Third World, progressing from anti-colonialism to anti-imperialism, though the apartheid regime in South Africa would not be abolished until after the fall of the Berlin Wall, in the early 1990s. Even to this day, however, the PLO has not succeeded in creating a Palestinian state alongside Israel (within the 1967 borders, in the areas now called the West Bank and Gaza). Rupen Vosgimorukian's *Report: September 1969* (1970), was made by the Lebanese filmmaker of Armenian origin at the end of his studies in Łódź, and documents living conditions among Palestinian refugees in Jordan, as they subsisted in precarious conditions, reliant on international aid that neither met their needs nor quelled their desire to regain their homeland and homes, their lost country. Their resistance was hit with violent repressions by the Israeli armed forces, and *Report*, through violent images that are difficult to watch, presents their human and material losses. The film bore witness to a particular moment in the history of the Middle East, and of the Palestinians in specific. Filmed as a reportage, an indictment in images and sounds, today it remains a valuable historical document.[4]

Across the Atlantic, Cuba was being touted as the first fully liberated territory in Latin America following the victory of the revolution there in January 1959. Although Latin American nations had been formally independent for a century, they were being subjected to newer forms of domination and exploitation (marshaled in large part by the US) that greatly compromised their sovereignties. The first Tricontinental Conference, held in January 1966 in Havana, brought together the leaders of liberation movements (including PAIGC in West Africa and MPLA in Angola) within a new organization, the Organization of Solidarity with the People of Asia, Africa and Latin America (OSPAAAL), which advocated armed struggle—rural and/or urban guerrilla warfare—to free populaces from imperial, colonial, and neocolonial domination.

---

4   It may be assumed that almost two years later, many of these Palestinian refugees were injured, killed, or displaced again during Black September events, when the Jordanian regime reacted against declarations and actions of the Palestinian movements, carrying out a deadly large-scale offensive against those movements and the Palestinian camps.

Shouldn't cinema bear witness to these struggles, or even engage fully and follow them? As nations were liberating themselves from their colonial yokes, wasn't it it time to present these other viewpoints, especially among those taking on their oppressors in the countries of the Global South?

As this period was unfolding, Polish cinema was already very dynamic and held in high regard outside Poland, as noted above. And the Łódź Film School had real know-how, and could therefore offer professional training to students, including those from the Third World.

Rebirth(s) of a Nation?

Poland, over about two centuries of especially troubled history, had fought to preserve its identity against powerful expansionist neighbors closer and farther afield. Like a phoenix, it had been reborn several times. It seems likely that Polish teachers and filmmakers were sensitive to issues of national identity and culture. As with any other nation, its art, poetry, music, theater, and eventually its cinema enabled its people to acquire greater visibility and to assert themselves in producing a particular culture and language, open to the universal but with their own traits and idiosyncrasies. Lenin considered cinema "the most important of all the arts," as he famously put it, because of its popular aspect, its "mass art" side—that is, as an art that could appeal to large sections of society, and inform and mobilize them if necessary.

Many students arriving in Poland from the Global South came from countries afflicted by colonialism. Algeria had been a French settlement colony since 1830; Morocco and Tunisia were former protectorates. Following independence, artists and filmmakers sought to participate in the rebirth of their nations and the revival of their cultures—they had often been driving forces in the anti-colonial struggle,[5] striving in the face of imperial and colonial

5   Poetry played an important role in the resistance movements and independence struggles of Portuguese-speaking countries including Angola, Guinea-Bissau, Cape Verde, and Mozambique. See the anthology: Pierre Jean Oswald, ed., *La poésie africaine d'expression portugaise*, trans. Jean Todrani and André Jouclau-Ruau (Honfleur: PJO Poche, 1969).

powers to affirm their personalities, their singularities and autonomy, as those powers had denied them specificity, trying to erase it
or to confine it to a kind of silent, self-annihilating invisibility.
Thus Abdellah Drissi's *Lesson 41* (1966) opens with a succession of close-ups, mouths opening and closing with other facial
parts out of frame as Polish words are repeated. The viewer then discovers that these aren't youngsters—their voice registers didn't fit
that, anyway—but young adults: the students at the School of Polish
for Foreign Students at the University of Łódź. The teacher steadily
corrects them, having them repeat words and syllables until they
pronounce them correctly, and reminds them of particular grammar
rules. The students then recite verses from *Pan Tadeusz*, the famous
epic poem Adam Mickiewicz composed while in exile, a text emblematic of Polish Romanticism and national revival.

These foreign students, who had often experienced
and sometimes fought against the colonial system, are now representing and expressing themselves in order to help see through the
decolonization process. Their studies in art and cinematographic
technique involves first learning another language (Polish), opening
up to another culture (Slavic, European), all of which, however,
doesn't keep them from also reflecting back on themselves, on their
own history (histories). This temporary self-reflection activates a
potentially fruitful kind of dialectic between the particular and the
universal, the here and the elsewhere, the past and the present.
While at the Łódź Film School, the apprentice filmmakers would meet
students from other Third World and Eastern bloc countries, which
led to working together, to playing roles or handling technical
aspects in one another's productions (the Colombian Ricardo Torres Ramírez was cinematographer on the Tunisian Fayçal Hassaïri's
Reserved for Foreigners, 1988).

Internationalism was a positive value in the PRL-era,
as part of the overall communist project, which claimed to rise
beyond differences in origin, skin color, or religion. And many of the
foreign students felt they belonged to a larger whole than just their
home countries. A whole that was then called the Third World—not

a place but "a project," according to the historian Vijay Prashad[6]—
and which is now called the Global South. Many believed in socialism or communism, or at least sympathized with these models. The
term "Third World," after all, had been inspired by the Third Estate
of the French Revolution: unlike the nobility and the clergy, it was a
nothing on the political scene—but wanted to become something.[7]
It denotes an emergent phenomenon, a rebirth accompanied by a
surge and a large-scale movement, an emergence from the long
"colonial night," to invoke an image used by Ferhat Abbas, first Algerian President of the Constituent Assembly and FLN representative
during the war of independence, and by Frantz Fanon in *The Wretched
of the Earth*.[8] Notions of emergence, of passaging from invisibility to
visibility, of recognition and collective affirmation, are therefore very
important for everything to do with what since the 1950s was being
called the Third World.

On location or in Polish studios, films reconstruct
remote guerrilla units (remote in place and in some cases in time:
Mostafa Derkaoui's *Amghar* was set in the 1920s) in African or Latin
American settings. Uniforms are used to represent a regular army—
in Oscar Gamardo's *Imaginaria* (1967), for example—while a scarf knot-
ted around the neck of an actor wearing street clothes immediately
designates them a member of an underground unit or a revolutionary movement, as in José Luis di Zeo's *Guerrilla* (1966) and *Wake* (1965).
In *Guerrilla*, a woman has an active role in the ongoing rebellion to liberate the country. The film begins with a mysterious shot of a two

6   Vijay Prashad, *The Darker Nations: A People's History of the Third World* (New
        York: The New Press, 2007).
7   The term "Third World" was coined by Alfred Sauvy and Georges
        Balandier. Sauvy was inspired by Emmanuel-Joseph Sieyès' famous
        formula designating that which "is nothing in the political order and
        wants to become something" when he wrote that "the ignored third
        world, despised like the third estate, also wants to be something." See
        Emmanuel-Joseph Sieyès, *Qu'est-ce que le Tiers-État? (1788)* (Paris:
        Flammarion, 2009), and Alfred Sauvy, "Trois mondes, une planète,"
        L'Observateur, August 14, 1952.
8   Frantz Fanon, *Les damnés de la terre* (Paris: Maspero, 1961); *The Wretched of the
        Earth* (New York: Grove Press, 1963). Fanon's book had great influence
        with Latin America filmmakers including Glauber Rocha, Fernando
        Solanas, Octavio Getino, and Ugo Ulive—a Uruguayan-Venezuelan
        filmmaker and playwright—along with Black Panther activists in the US.
        As the publisher François Maspero recalled in *Frantz Fanon, mémoire d'asile*
        (2002), a documentary by Bachir Ridouh and Abdenour Zahzah, Che
        Guevara read it and intended to preface the Cuban edition.

people lying in an abandoned house with its roof half collapsed. A man in uniform, shirt open, is next to the woman: Is she his lover, perhaps his wife, or a woman he has just raped? In flashback, quick and incisive sequences tells us that he's an officer who ordered the execution of a partisan, signaling his men to fire on the prisoner. Taking advantage of his momentary inattention, the woman is seen hanging a towel on the end of a stick, which she hoists above the roof for nearby partisans to see. The officer is then buried alive by the partisans, his body lodged upright in the earth, with only his head sticking out and bound with a rope to a horse a few meters away. The woman, who's brought about his capture (and subsequent execution), is now in charge of giving a feed bucket to the horse to get it moving, with foreseeable consequences. Was she the spouse of the partisan who was executed in the flashback? She would then have acted in revenge for his murder, as well as out of political conviction.

In *Wake*, we attend a rather special vigil. With slow, delicate, attentive gestures, a woman washes the body of her dead husband, a bearded man with a Christ-like appearance, wearing only a loincloth around his hips, reminiscent of the corpse of Che Guevara. Hanging from the wall, one can only make out a dark suit and a white shirt. The staging and compositions are very much inspired by biblical representations and religious painting. With her long dark scarf and her luminous and even face, the woman is reminiscent of a pietà, the representation of the compassionate Virgin Mary. Generous and devoted, she readily gives the only clean shirt she has to a fleeing partisan in worn and sweaty rags, preferring to offer it to a living fighter rather than a dead one.

A fighting nation in the process of liberating itself from imperialism and neocolonialism thus accords a place to women, young people, and the excluded. Other films including *Elżbieta K.* (1973) by Idriss Karim and *Blindman's Buff* (1982) by Djamel Benkhaled depict daily lives—of a young Polish woman in the former, and of a couple of "secret lovers" in the latter. The music for *Blindman's Buff* is by Ahmed Malek,[9] sometimes called the Algerian Ennio Morricone, having composed film scores through the 1970s and 1980s, including for *Omar Gatlato* (dir. Merzak Allouache), *Les vacances de l'inspecteur Tahar* (*Inspector Tahar's Holiday*, dir. Moussa Haddad), and *Leïla et les autres* (*Leïla and the Others*, dir. Sid Ali Mazif, exploring the condition of women). Among the first shorts made in Algeria by Ahmed Lallem after his return from Łódź (his study films made in Poland have yet to be found) is simply titled *Elles* (*The Women*, 1966).[10] It gives voice to high school girls laying out their visions of the world and of Algerian society, and discussing problems they face. Some are quick to make comparisons: they invoke certain socialist countries as examples, for there women occupy jobs and positions that were previously the preserve of men, and they make precise, eager diagnoses of the world in which they're developing and seeking to thrive.

How does one manage to express oneself, to be seen and heard, when one comes from a small country with practically no film tradition or industry? Some national film industries in Latin America and Africa had great difficulty exporting themselves: their films were shown domestically but rarely circulated beyond their borders or region, with a nation's cinemas dominated by Hollywood productions[11] or B-movies (especially across Africa), to the point of blocking the emergence of a lively, pluralistic, dynamic national cinema, with the exception of highly commercial productions. Having gained recognition abroad, at festivals or among foreign critics, a Latin American or African filmmaker could sometimes enjoy an

---

9   The Museum of Modern Art in Algiers held an exhibition devoted to Ahmed Malek in 2019. A documentary short about his career, *Planet Malek* (2019), was made by Paloma Colombe, and the German label Habibi Funk released a compilation of his music.

10   Ahmed Lallem shot a sequel to *Elles* during the Dark Decade in Algeria, while in exile (some of the former high school girls also chose exile): *Algériennes, trente ans après* (1996).

11   See the writings and interventions of Tahar Cheriaa, who directed the Journées Cinématographiques de Carthage, founded in 1966, and who supported African and Arabian cinema that was willfully critical, anti-colonialist, and anti-imperialist.

uncensored release in his or her country.[12] The 1960s saw the emergence of filmmakers from the Global South whose films were able to gain greater visibility in the context of the world's "young" or new cinemas, while Hollywood cinema was in full transition. Cinema played a major role among young people, reflecting multiple aspirations and becoming a preferred medium for expressing similar desires for revolution and radical social change to those animating students at the Łódź Film School.

Internationalism and Global Youth Contestation(s)

The students' rooms in Raul Saucedo Zermeño's *Without Requiem* and in Abdelkader Lagtaa's *Shadow among Others*, both films from 1969, resemble dorms of politicized and engaged students in other countries—in Paris or Berlin, for example—during the same period. Double references to Che Guevara (assassinated in Bolivia in 1967) and Ho Chi Minh was common to myriad student protesters. Their portraits were on posters carried by demonstrators chanting both names in one breath—"Che Che Che, Ho Chi Minh!"—in *Berlin 68—Rudi Dutschke* by Jacques Kebadian and Michel Andrieu, who would go on to document conflicts and demonstrations in Paris in May and June 1968, working within their own ARC collective, one of the most active during that period.

In *Shadow among Others*, one sequence, a horizontal panorama preceding a new focus on the threatened student, twice links the opposition leader Mehdi Ben Barka with Che Guevara and Ho Chi Minh (who enter and leave the frame). One of these panning sequences is followed by a sequence that takes place elsewhere, like a flashback (or an imaginary reconstruction) of a man surrounded and presumably arrested by soldiers and police. Repetition—which allows a new notion to be understood, an idea to be transmitted—is

12   This, however, was far from guaranteed. In a filmed interview with curator Léa Morin in Sophie Delvallée's *Librement, Mostafa Derkaoui*, the Moroccan filmmaker, talks about the censorship of his film *De quelques évènements sans signification* (*About Some Meaningless Events*), shot a few years after his return from Łódź. During an affecting sequence filmed in Łódź, Derkaoui meets with Barbara Brylska, a Polish actor who'd played in one of his student films: they hug and burst into tears, very moved to find themselves there again, fifty years later. The introductory text for *Librement, Mostafa Derkaoui* states that "his journey to Poland" is one of the sources of his cinema: http://kaleo-films.com/mostafa-derkaoui.

one motor of pedagogy, and this repeated shot aims to remind us of the importance of Ben Barka in the internationalist and anti-imperialist struggles of the tricontinental constellation (Africa, Asia, Latin America). He is a figuration of the Third World in its struggle, a metonymy, in which the part stands for the whole, for Africa—Ben Barka was a leader in Morocco and recognized across the Third World—which connects him with other metonymic figures, from Asia and Ho Chi Minh to Latin America and Che Guevara.

Ben Barka[13] was president of the preparatory committee for the Tricontinental Conference being planned for Havana. In October 1965, he was kidnapped in the middle of Paris (and presumably assassinated) and eliminated from the conference he'd contributed so much to in its organization and eventual success the following year.[14]

The second sequence connecting Ben Barka, Ho Chi Minh, and Che Guevara is followed by a shot of the student's bookshelf. Among the books and magazines that are easily discernible and highlighted is the cover of *Partisans*,[15] issue 42 from May–June 1968, with its slogan "Students, Workers, One Fight!" This significant connection associates the May–June 1968 movement with the tricontinental struggles in the Third World. Transnationally, the young then had many tastes and cultural features in common: folk music, blues, and jazz, often associated with the existentialist vibe of postwar

13   On the career, ideas, and activity of Mehdi Ben Barka, see *Mehdi Ben Barka, Écrits politiques, 1957–1965* (Paris: Éditions Syllepse, 1999); René Gallissot and Jacques Kergoat, eds., *Mehdi Ben Barka: De l'indépendance marocaine à la Tricontinentale* (Paris: Karthala-Institut Maghreb Europe et Eddif, 1997); Bachir Ben Barka, ed., *Mehdi Ben Barka en heritage: De la Tricontinentale à l'altermondialisme* (Paris: Éditions Syllepse, 2007).

14   The following year, a new organization was created in Cuba, OLAS (Latin American Solidarity Organization), and Che's message to the Tricontinental was made public, exhorting Third World peoples to "Create Two, Three... Many Vietnams" and rejecting "peaceful coexistence" between the two Cold War superpowers. Che Guevara dared to criticize Soviet aid to Third World countries—which he felt was not substantial enough—in his 1965 Algiers Speech.

15   This magazine was edited by François Maspero, who published Frantz Fanon's *Les damnés de la terre* in 1961, along with numerous texts by revolutionaries (Mao, Fidel Castro, Mehdi Ben Barka, Che Guevara, General Giáp, etc.) and the French edition of the periodical *Tricontinental*. Maspero ran a bookshop in the Latin Quarter, which was a meeting place for politicized students. Chris Marker devoted a film to this important figure: *On vous parle de Paris: Maspero; les mots ont un sens (Calling from Paris: Maspero; Words Have a Meaning*, 1970).

Saint-Germain-des-Prés (embodied by Juliette Gréco, Miles Davis's lover during his stay in Paris, and the emblematic couple of philosophers Jean-Paul Sartre and Simone de Beauvoir). In wine cellars like the Caveau de la Huchette, romantic encounters mixed with live jazz music,[16] political discussions, and social critique.

That same ambiance is transposed to Poland in shorts by Mostafa Derkaoui: *Cellar People* (1969) and *Somewhere, Someday* (1971). In festive places where people came to dance and remake the world through discussion, the young characters resemble Dostoyevsky's protagonists (*Notes from Underground*) with their continual reiterations and those from Kerouac's *The Subterraneans*, set against the backdrop of a fashionable counterculture completely opposed to the (conservative) culture of their parents and elders.

In Third World countries, consequences could be far more violent and dramatic: student protestors, as with other political opponents, could be arrested, kidnapped, tortured, and murdered for their political ideals. This happens to students and oppositionists in Raul Saucedo Zermeño's *Without Requiem*, in which a political assassination is covered up, the corpse tampered with by the authorities to infer a crime involving homosexuals, and in Abdelkader Lagtaa's *Shadow among Others*. Two or three hundred students were massacred infamously in Mexico City by the army during a demonstration in October 1968. Is José Luis di Zeo referring to this dramatic event in *The Meeting* (1968), when the voice-over announces a lottery and the chance to win a ticket to the Mexico City Olympic Games? Other features common to the global youth culture then included pop (or folk) music and fashion culture (casual attire; men with long hair). *Without Requiem* is set in Venezuela, yet the film ends with the famous song "We Shall Overcome," a protest standard sung by Joan Baez and others, which breaks in as a cry of hope, a kind of international anthem of youth and protest. The torch passes on, the struggle relayed, taken up by others.

16   Years later, Paweł Pawlikowski's *Zimna wojna* (*Cold War*, 2018) reenacted this atmosphere of Paris in "black and white"—jazzy, melancholic, with languid songs sung in Polish—and received best-director commendations at Cannes.

Toward a Cinema of Liberation—a Cinema from the Insurgent Third World?

These protest and even revolutionary currents are very much present in the films of the foreign students at the Łódź Film School, who were assertive in taking a stand, in engaging with the global upheavals of 1968—notably by way of the États généraux du cinéma (Estates General of Cinema) in May–June 1968 in France[17]— and in extending a dialogue with the insurgent cinemas of Latin America. Glauber Rocha, Fernando Solanas, and Octavio Getino were making films and publishing manifestos to put that film practice into perspective. Rocha wrote "The Aesthetics of Hunger / The Aesthetics of Violence" in 1965. He associated hunger, understood as an economic obstacle and a creative driving force, with recourse to a liberating violence, something that he took from the writings of Fanon, speaking of a violence synonymous with liberation, creativity, formal and narrative upheaval, forcing the colonizer to take heed of aspirations and the genuine existences of the colonized. In their 1969 manifesto, "Toward a Third Cinema," Solanas and Getino also refer to Fanon ("We must discover, we must invent") and his invitation to invent a new world, free from colonial and imperial domination, by inventing a new cinema owing nothing to Hollywood (in their view, the anti-model par excellence), one that would go even further than auteur cinema (the Second Cinema, according to their classification).

Filmed in the widescreen CinemaScope format, José María Sánchez Ariza's *The Cat Died of Hunger* (1968) presents a couple with a child in an arid atmosphere of distress, who have only a simple cottage, its only decorative element being a portrait, a black-and-white photo of Emiliano Zapata (the Mexican Revolution leader, linked to the peasant struggle) tacked on a small wooden cross. The intense luminosity and dryness of the climate seems to accentuate

17   Rather than focusing solely on May–June 1968 in Paris, I prefer to speak of a global 1968, which can be seen to have started in 1967 and to have extended into the early 1970s, shaking up cities around the world, from Belgrade to Tokyo to Mexico City. Within the context of May 1968, French filmmakers and technicians launched the Estates General of Cinema to promote a different way of making and showing films, by bringing politics (back) to the fore, questioning societal blockages, attacking the star system, and campaigning for internationalism, solidarity, and social change.

the destitution and desolation that reigns inside and around this impoverished home. A moral dilemma arises: Will they be forced to eat the emaciated cat to survive and overcome the ordeal of hunger? An inter-title gives us the Larousse definition of hunger,[18] asserting an essayistic dimension and directly pointing to the preoccupation that drives the need to eat.

This poverty, placed in full view, is both emblematic of the state of affairs in certain regions of the Global South, with few resources and no real film industry (with the exceptions of Mexico, Argentina, and Brazil, the most dynamic Latin American countries), and of a way of presenting the problem of poverty in an ethical and political manner. Rocha, speaking of an "aesthetics of hunger" and an "aesthetics of violence" in his 1965 manifesto, positioned himself on the aesthetic and political level, while advocating the use of a double violence—visual and political—to change society and the way cinema is made, understood, and received. Thus, *The Cat Died of Hunger* is in dialogue with at least three Brazilian feature films from the 1960s, each shot in the country's parched northeast, where hunger rubs shoulders with revolt and reinforces the urge for it: *Vidas Secas* (*Barren Lives*, 1963) by Nelson Pereira dos Santos; Ruy Guerra's *Os Fuzis* (*The Guns*, 1964); and Rocha's *Deus e o Diabo na Terra do Sol* (*Black God, White Devil*, 1964).

After making their *La hora de los hornos* (*The Hour of the Furnaces*, 1968), Solanas and Getino wrote "Toward a Third Cinema"; the manifesto was published in the journal *Tricontinental* (which at the time was multilingual).[19] They advocated the use of the camera as a weapon, an instrument of liberation. This "Third Cinema" that Solanas and Getino wanted to create wasn't very clearly defined, as it was a project

18   Hunger is an important theme in Latin American cinema of the 1960s and 1970s. See a lecture I gave on this issue: Olivier Hadouchi, "De 'l'esthétique de la faim' à la dénonciation de la 'porno-misère' dans les films contestataires d'Amérique latine (1960 et 1970)," *Forum des images*, accessed October 14, 2021, https://www.forumdesimages.fr/app_beta. php/les-programmes/toutes-les-rencontres/cours-de-cinema-de-lesthetique-de-la-faim-a-la-denonciation-de-la-porno-misere-par-olivier-hadouchi.

19   For a study of the manifesto and a look back at the experience of the group Cine Liberación, see Mariano Mestman's writings or "Le groupe Cine Liberación et la décolonisation culturelle," in *Le nouveau cinéma latino-américain*, ed. Ignacio Del Valle Dávila (Rennes: PUR, 2015).

and a process that started from observation. According to them, the First Cinema (Hollywood and big Soviet productions such as those directed by Sergei Bondarchuk) is alienating, it serves imperialism and cultural colonization and must be rejected and combated. The Second Cinema is European-style auteur cinema, which in their view doesn't offer a real alternative because it doesn't propose a total break with the world system and often seems confused, insubordinate instead of revolutionary. The Third Cinema is resolutely combative, it wants to outstrip the Second Cinema, evading censorship, proposing a collective cinema of cultural decolonization, open, unfinished, and transitory, creating its own networks of production and distribution, parallel and alternative, to avoid censorship.

"Toward a Third Cinema" had broad international impact.[20] It was discussed in Europe and Japan and circulated in Third World countries—Tunisia and Morocco, where it was published in *Souffles* in 1970[21]—where audiences were taking advantage of film-club screenings to gather and discuss political issues. But it didn't circulate widely in the USSR,[22] probably because it fancied itself Guevarist, quoting Chairman Mao (China and the USSR were rivals) and prioritizing Third World struggles. It didn't align with Soviet Marxism, peaceful coexistence, or détente, so it had all the necessary features to be judged "heretical" and "sectarian." In an interview in Berlin in 2014, Mario Handler, the Uruguayan documentary filmmaker—among the inspirations for Solanas and Getino and the Third Cinema—revealed to me that in the 1960s and 1970s, the Leipzig Documentary Film Festival rejected Latin American films supporting Guevarism, anarchism, or Maoism.

However, plenty of Global South students at the Łódź Film School were aware of the manifesto. From there, Idriss Karim sent a letter[23] to *Souffles* referring directly to it (the journal published

20   See the international inquiry of Guy Hennebelle, "L'impact du troisième cinéma," *Revue Tiers-Monde*, no. 79 (1979).

21   See Octavio Getino and Fernando Solanas, "Vers un troisième cinema," *Souffles*, no. 18, March–April 1970. This issue also featured an article about Clauber Rocha's *Black God, White Devil.*

22   The scholar Gabrielle Chomentowski has explained that she found no trace in Russian film literature of debates on the Third Cinema of Solanas and Getino, both in seminars and in private discussion with me.

23   Idriss Karim's letter can be read at: https://www.lehman.edu/deanhum/langlit/french/souffles/S19/94aa_19.HTM.

his letter). He was reacting to an article criticizing his *Children of Haouz*, and said he shared some of Solanas and Getino's views, adding that he would be glad to see their manifesto accompanied by a debate on *The Hour of the Furnaces* and on Third World cinema, a cinema of combat. Those same issues are raised in *Without Requiem* and in films by Derkaoui and Lagtaa, which advocate for a committed cinema in which the intellectual, like the student, has a political role to play.[24] It should be a cinema of "counter-information," "destruction" of images of colonialism and neocolonialism, and "construction," to take up three elements common to their films and to the manifesto of Solanas and Getino. When activists are being hunted down, arrested, and sometimes murdered, when the political field is blocked because the regime and its state apparatus control and censor the press, radio, television, and cinematography—not to mention the circulation, screening, and distribution of films—then walls must become the medium for free expression (of information, demands, agitprop slogans in *Without Requiem* and *Shadow among Others*) before those slogans are effaced and the posters torn down by the security services.

Whether they belong more precisely to the Third Cinema or to the Second Cinema (auteur, but committed), a considerable number of films made in Łódź by foreign students still appear politically subversive, formally audacious, and visually excellent. *Without Requiem, Guerrilla,* and *Wake* openly advocate revolt, resistance, insubordination, and insubmissiveness. In *Imaginaria*, a young soldier rebels by turning his gun on the man who represents power and hier-

24   The philosopher Régis Debray left to join Guevara's guerrillas in Bolivia; he was arrested and imprisoned several times. One of Debray's texts (about Antonio Gramsci, the Italian Marxist keenly aware of the importance of cultural questions) is quoted in a film by Mostafa Derkaoui. See Régis Debray, "Notes on Gramsci," *New Left Review*, no. 59 (January–February 1970). On the question of intellectual engagement and the experience of *Souffles*, see Kenza Sefrioui, *La revue Souffles 1966–1973: Espoirs de révolution culturelle au Maroc*, with a preface by Abdellatif Laâbi (Casablanca: Editions du Sirocco, 2012). On the engagement of Latin American writers, see Claudia Gilman, *Entre la pluma y el fusil, Debates y dilemas del escritor revolucionario en América Latina* (Buenos Aires: Siglo XXI editores Argentina, 2003). The use of cinema during the period of the tricontinental struggles is a focus of my doctoral thesis, from 2012: Olivier Hadouchi, "Cinéma dans les luttes de liberation: Genèses, initiatives pratiques et inventions formelles autour de la Tricontinentale (1966–1975)" (PhD diss., Université de la Sorbonne Nouvelle, 2012).

archy: grabbing his weapon, he shoots the commanding officer who's been ceaselessly shouting orders in his ears. Several short films wield audacious sound (seeking expressive effect) and equally audacious narratives, telling a story that confronts multiple viewpoints: on the escape (which ends badly) of a couple in *Fan* (dir. Sergio Vega, 1985) or the viewpoint (hostile and prejudiced) of a mother about her Arab-Muslim son-in-law and about her daughter in Fayçal Hassaïri's *North-South*.

These student films still contain winds of revolt and freedom, with a critical spirit that continues to surprise, and to challenge preconceived ideas about how cinema was taught and practiced in Poland during the Cold War.

Translated from the French by Dominika Cajewska.

Rachael Diang'a holds a PhD in Film Technology and has over eighteen years' experience in film research and scholarship. Her research interests lie within African and postcolonial cinemas. She is the author of the first book on Kenyan Cinema: *African Re-creation of Western Impressions: A Focus on the Kenyan Film* (2011) and several journal articles and book chapters on filmmaking and African cinema. In practice, she has made a mark in the film industry as a filmmaker, film workshop trainer and mentor, film critic and adjudicator in several international film festivals. Diang'a has produced and/or directed several films including: *Our Strength* (2012), *The Invisible Workers* (2013), *Drugnets* (2015) *Mad Love* (2018), *Unbalanced* (2019). Her film production interests are in scriptwriting, directing, acting, and production. She currently serves as an assistant professor of film and is chair of the cinematic arts department at United States International University-Africa.

SAO GAMBA'S CREATIVE LEGACY IN KENYA

> Gamba was among the first Kenyans (and East Africans) to be trained in a film school when he got a scholarship to study film in Poland, and his dedication to art was intense.[1]—Peter Pages Bwire.

Kenya's creative community remains heavily indebted to Sao Gamba, an inventive cornerstone who straddled several artistic frontiers so readily and seamlessly that one wonders whether he was ever restrained by far-ranging differences in the genres he produced. Gamba was a visual artist, a poet, a documentarist—perhaps most crucially for this essay—and a feature filmmaker. Kenya's film industry is in fact anchored in Gamba's work, thought, and the policymaking he contributed to and played a major role in shaping. His film *Kolormask* (1986), at once his most known and acclaimed, and deliberations in the 1980s that preceded its production, forged a strong pillar on which today's Kenyan film industry established its identity.

1   Peter Pages Bwire, "Toolkit: Kenya Screen Worlds," accessed June 13, 2021, https://screenworlds.org/wp-content/uploads/SW_Lagos_Toolkit_Peter-Pages-Bwire_1.pdf.

FIG. 1
ENTRANCE EXAM [FROM L–R]: SAO GAMBA, PROF. MARIA KANIEWSKA,
PROF. ROMAN WAJDOWICZ, PROF. JERZY BOSSAK, AND PROF. JERZY TOEPLITZ,
ŁÓDŹ 1965, PHOTO BY EUGENIUSZ HANEMAN, COURTESY ŁÓDŹ FILM SCHOOL ARCHIVE

However, not much is known or at least written about Gamba's vast range of creative abilities, the breadth across which he obviously excelled. This essay will document that range of his creative works, from feature films and documentaries to painting and poetry. As a multivalent artist, Gamba embodies through his works what the creative economy in East Africa has come to be today. In the region, artists find themselves in a market of varied creatives traversing the various disciplines. There are cross-genre movements of artists from theater plays to moviemaking to poetry, spoken word, radio, and television. There is also intra-genre movement in which, for example, a scriptwriter evolves into a director, an editor doubles as a designer, a producer also directs, and so on.

First on Diverse Fronts

Gamba was among the first Kenyans to study professionally then make a feature film. He had grown interested in the film medium long before the first East African film school was set up in the newly independent nations. That first school, the Kenya Institute of Mass Communication (KIMC), which had begun as a vocational-media school in 1961, extended to film training in 1967.[2] The film-training component was initially funded by the German government, later becoming a film school sponsored by the Kenyan government.

For his early accomplishments in the field, Gamba is honored in the Kenyan film industry, which itself is a major influence in East Africa overall. He studied filmmaking at the Łódź Film School from 1965 to 1971. Over those seven years, he became an accomplished director, scriptwriter, and cinematographer. While in Łódź, Gamba was very active as a student director and cinematographer, participating in the production of numerous student films including *The Moon Children* (1970).

Along with his diverse pioneering endeavors, Gamba also stood out as a strong guide in policymaking in his work at the Kenya Film Corporation (KFC), the establishment of which he participated in after his film training in Poland. He engineered plans for Afrocentric film production and distribution. Initially, KFC had been

2   Rachael Diang'a, *Africa Re-creation of Western Impressions: A Focus on the Kenyan Film* (Saarbrücken: LAP, 2011).

established as the governmental distribution agency for foreign films in Kenya, housed strategically at the Nairobi Cinema building—where the Kenya Film Classification Board has its seat today. At that point, nothing was yet being produced locally to distribute. When the corporation expanded its initial mandate for distribution to cover production as well, Gamba's efforts began bearing fruit. He took the lead in this new responsibility, scripting, directing, and producing *Kolormask*, now widely considered Kenya's first feature film. And Gamba, having been among the first Africans to study filmmaking at the Łódź Film School, was now a pioneer feature filmmaker, and *Kolormask* was very well received domestically. His decision to study abroad had proved a unique leap of faith, through which he acquired superlative professional skills in the audiovisual medium.

In Kenya, artistic freedom was curtailed in fear of political interference. More vocal artists including Ngũgĩ wa Thiong'o, who was later detained without trial for a year, and Ngũgĩ wa Mĩriĩ, coauthors of the controversial play *I Will Marry When I Want* (1977), were seen by the authorities as inciting audiences to rise against neocolonialism and had to go under the radar in the diaspora to remain safe. Thus, *Kolormask* stayed away from politics but delved more into cultural themes. The film's production was state-funded, with a crew largely comprising state and para-state employees—again, steering clear of politicized issues was important.

Prior to Gamba's training and return from Łódź, films shot in Kenya had been mainly foreign productions, save for the Department of Film Services' documentaries. Plenty of these were safari-expedition documentaries by major Hollywood studios such as the Metro-Goldwyn-Mayer (MGM) and 20th Century Studios. Kenya was known as a Hollywood destination for location filming, not as a production ground for local creatives.[3] Gamba's documentary filmmaking is another area that has yet to be fully researched and brought to the fore. Jakub Barua, another Kenyan filmmaker who studied in Łódź, has documented this facet of Gamba's output. Gamba's first documentary, *Imaashoi El Maasai* (*People of the Red Ocher*, 1975), broke a pattern by which foreign filmmakers (in large part American

3   Rachael Diang'a, "Themes in Kenyan Cinema: Seasons & Reasons," *Cogent Arts & Humanities* 4, no. 1 (2017).

and European) had been consistently presenting the Maasai, the wide-ranging pastoralist community in East Africa, through film. The Maasai, due to their rich, largely unadulterated cultural repertoire, are among the continent's most filmed communities, to an extent bordering on cultural exploitation. Representation matters—and in *People of the Red Ocher* Gamba chose, for the first time, to approach things differently.

Championing African Culture

People of the Red Ocher would spearhead a cultural liberation within the documentary genre. Gamba took up a more realistic approach in producing the documentary. He got the local Maasai more involved and narrated his film from their perspective, thus giving a rare voice to the unheard, who had long been documented from a subjective outsiders' viewpoint. In Barua's recounting, Gamba was using film "[to] reappropriate the dignity and freedom of an African people."[4] This restatement became Gamba's defining motif, and it would cut across most of his films and paintings. It is perhaps most thoroughly explored in *Kolormask*, given the creative freedom he found in a feature film as opposed to a documentary.

Kolormask gave Gamba a podium from which to articulate pertinent social issues of the period. Through this film, as the truly committed artist Gamba was, he moves from being a critic of sociocultural misconceptions, ambiguities, and misunderstandings to championing Afrocentrism and decolonization as a master of creative and visual representation of those social themes, by means of his fine scripting, directing, and cinematographic skills, by the standards of the time. While cultural-emancipation themes had dominated sub-Saharan African films across the rest of the broader region, East Africa had lagged somewhat behind.[5] Following hot on the heels of *Arusi ya Mariamu* in Tanzania (*The Marriage of Mariamu*, dir. Nangayoma Ng'oge, Ron Mulvihill, 1985), East Africa was finally wak-

4   Jakub Barua, "The Documentary Film in East Africa: Sao Gamba's Secret Legacy," in this book.
5   Manthia Diawara, *African Film: Politics and Culture* (Bloomington: Indiana University Press, 1992).

ing up to the earlier clarion call from Francophone West Africa through the works of Paulin Soumanou Vieyra, Ousmane Sembène, Djibril Diop Mambéty, and others. Taking their cue from the ideological environment in a post-independence Africa, African filmmakers were joining other African artists and revolutionary leaders in articulating the need for cultural liberation, especially through art. Filmmakers, as I have written elsewhere, saw "cinema as a means of seeking cultural liberation and progress."[6] In an undated article, "Nyamweya et. al.," to which Sao Gamba greatly contributed, key features of what African films should look like are provided, in the Kenyan context. The article is believed to have been written based on Gamba's ideology while at KFC in the early 1980s. After the article was published, the KFC production function came alive under Gamba's leadership, with his strong advocacy for film and cultural policy. The report's main emphasis is on cultural liberation and representation through creative works, including feature films, documentary films, and painting.

Between his critical thought and the production of *Kolormask*, Gamba brought to East Africa those pan-Africanist discourses that had been activated more clearly elsewhere in the continent through film-industry concerns including the Pan-African Film and Television Festival (FESPACO), the Pan African Federation of Filmmakers (FEPACI), the Algiers Charter, and the Niamey Manifesto. Gamba's early initiative to leave and study film had ultimately brought the region to the round table alongside much of the rest of the continent.

At face value, *Kolormask* dwells largely on its two leads, Eliza and her husband, John, and their marital disputes. Further into the movie, it narrates the culture-clash experienced by the young couple soon after they migrate to Kenya from London. John, a Kenyan studying medicine in the UK, meets Eliza, a British woman; the couple fall in love and later marry. The film begins when they have relocated to Nairobi, where John runs a private clinic while Eliza is a stay-at-home mom. Due to their marital issues, both have an extramarital affair, each with a partner of their respective race. Gamba,

6   Diang'a, *Africa Re-creation*, 60.

through this pair and other well-developed supporting characters, takes us through the challenges of hardline cultural polemics: both John and Eliza hold strongly to their opinions, and things end tragically. Set in the 1970s, *Kolormask*'s depiction of Eliza as a difficult, controlling, and destructively rigid wife is understandable, given that Gamba presents John as the victim. One may be deceived in thinking their racial differences is what fuels the main conflict of the film; yet the director is careful to present an antithesis for Eliza in Agnes, a European married to a member of John's extended family.

Agnes is presented as having fully adapted to her new life with her Kenyan husband. She is flexible and has embraced village life, fetching water from the river in a clay pot, mingling freely with the locals during traditional cultural ceremonies. Agnes is too good to be true, and her characterization validates criticism the film received at FESPACO's 1987 edition. Her main function is to provide contrast with Eliza and to help the director make his point. Gamba may have had a personal story to tell and needed his characters to join in. Thus, Gamba's main constraint is the auteur's approach to filmmaking, which is visible in both *Kolormask* and *The Moon Children*. Auteur filmmakers sometimes push an agenda too hard. Yet it may also be understandable that in the 1980s there were few if any professional film people of his caliber available, and he had to be in charge of various major production requirements in order to deliver his personal vision.

Kolormask clearly flaunts indigenous cultures by ascribing significance to them that had long been stripped away by colonial cultural interactions and in the aftermath of that impact. Gamba gives value to practices that Eliza, his antagonist, wouldn't tolerate, not because she's European, but because she has a fixed attitude toward "other" cultures. She can't tolerate mourning and burial rituals and ceremonies, and refuses to shave her hair, a standard part of those mourning ceremonies. She doesn't want her son circumcised in the traditional way. She doesn't welcome the idea of extended-family members coming to her house in the city. She's so snobbish about the way of life of John's community—and that cultural intolerance is what destroys her marriage in the end. Gamba gives voice to his thesis in the film through John's thoughts: "I am not anti-white [...] the color of the skin doesn't control our brains." Yet, even as he emphasizes this statement, Gamba takes the opportunity to parade a variety of traditional cultural practices from different Kenyan ethnic communities that he brings together in the film.

In the present day, such decolonization discourses have greatly molded not just the content but also the style of African cinema. One recent product and example of these discourses and their outcomes is the Nollywood film phenomenon, currently a global force. Key figures in this new wave have anchored their works on foundations the continent's pioneering filmmakers established. Emerging in the neoliberal era,[7] Nollywood originated mainly in Nigeria[8] and is referred to by localized names in various countries: Hillywood in Rwanda, Challywood in Ghana, Kannywood in Kano in northern Nigeria, Sallywood in South Africa, Bongowood in Tanzania, Riverwood in Kenya. Stylistically, these contemporary film subcultures share similar patterns of evolution; some, including Nigerian Nollywood, are ahead of the rest. Kenya's Riverwood has also evolved from foundations laid by its largely KIMC-trained film crew, some of whom worked on *Kolormask*.

Gamba as Mentor

Gamba's impact on the film industry was felt much more directly by people who worked with him on his productions. As a ministerial employee, Gamba worked closely with colleagues in the Department of Film Services, which produces infotainment documentaries, and at KIMC. Gamba mentored fledgling filmmakers including Henry Bwoka and Ingolo wa Keya, who later became directors and influential policymakers—that is, instrumental in shaping opinions and production style in the country. Most have now retired from active production, having made impactful, well-received films in the decades following the release of *Kolormask*. Bwoka, filmmaker and now-retired KIMC film instructor, was cinematographer for *Kolor-*

7   Claudia Böhme, "Bloody Bricolages: Traces of Nollywood in Tanzanian Video Films," in *Global Nollywood: The Transnational Dimensions of an African Video Industry*, ed. Mathias Krings and Onookome Okome (Bloomington: Indiana University Press, 2013).
8   Krings and Okome, *Global Nollywood*.

mask. Ingolo wa Keya, a talented director, is best known for his adaptation of the Francis Imbuga play *The Burning of Rags*, as *The Married Bachelor* (1997).

Other familiar names in the Kenyan film industry who worked under Gamba's mentorship include Levis Ngure, Bob Muchina, and Seth Adagala, along with many KIMC film-production students including Charles Manyara, whose inspiration came from critiquing Gamba's documentaries. Gamba, unlike many artists, valued constructive criticism. He often screened his films for KIMC students for feedback before releasing them. When *Kolormask* premiered at the Nairobi Cinema, KIMC students had been invited. He mentored and inspired many whose stories have yet to be told.

Gamba's works have drawn particular interest from the scholarly community. When *Kolormask* was released in 1986, critical appraisal of films hadn't come of age in Kenya. Personally, I only learned about Gamba days after his violent death in 2004, at a period when I had been in the midst of snowballing research references that would surely have taken me to him next. It was my first painful setback in researching contacts that would later result in my book *African Re-creation of Western Impressions: A Focus on the Kenyan Film*, the first to study Kenyan film.

Scholarly work attributes great significance to Gamba's role in the birth and development of local film culture in Kenya. He's attracted critical and scholarly attention, largely focused on *Kolormask* and its role as cultural critique.[9] However, little is on record regarding Gamba's other films, except by Barua. He establishes that Gamba produced over twenty documentaries. Yet access to these works has been a challenge to many who'd love to watch and learn from them. There is urgent need to locate, digitize, and make them accessible for viewership as well as scholarly research.

9   Edwin Nyutho, "Evaluation of the Kenyan Film Industry: Historical Perspective" (PhD diss., University of Nairobi, 2015); Diang'a, "Style and Content in Selected Kenyan Message Films: 1980–2009" (PhD diss., Kenyatta University, 2013); Diang'a, "Themes in Kenyan Cinema"; Diang'a, *Africa Re-creation*.

Camba's Painted Stories

A true artist tells stories with whatever tool they find themselves holding. Camba, in a telling reflection of this, told stories while making use of any form of creative expression he could. His paintings tell stories and have a particular idiosyncrasy that sets them apart and permits them to speak to wider society in an inclusive manner. A look at some of the works in a special exhibition in 2005 reveal an interest in the community. It, rather than the individual, takes center stage in the artworks, giving an impression of a traditional African village's communal fabric, complete with assorted activities and contexts, all in one frame.

Selected paintings were shown as a tribute to Camba's broad range at the Kampala-based Amakula International Film Festival in 2005, a festival I participated in and at which I was pleased to see these artworks for the first time. Barely a year after his death, this was a gesture of honor and the exhibition was a clear signal to filmmakers and other cinema enthusiasts to connect with Camba's varied ways of creative storytelling. In the festival's catalog, published a few months afterwards, a section is dedicated to Camba, with photos of some untitled paintings and with a title heading that summarizes Camba's range in the visual arts: "Painted stories."[10]

One of the paintings showcases a beautifully balanced framing of singers in traditional costumes performing a dance. The costumes include sisal skirts, typically worn in East Africa by song-and-dance performers. Bare-chested men and the women performers' partly covered torsos can be identified in the painting. At the one side, a large drum is depicted, while some performers play an assortment of instruments. However, in the background there's what looks like a unit of warriors advancing with spears, approaching a barrier separating the two groups.

Another painting is rather heavily Freudian and also depicts a wide variety of (almost unrelated) activities in one frame.

---

10   Amakula Kampala Cultural Foundation, *Storylines* (Kampala: Amakula Cultural Foundation, 2006). This fourteen-chapter festival catalog covers topics from film synopses and directors to scholarly articles, seminar summaries, oral narratives, historic and landmark cinematic innovations, and painting exhibitions at the Amakula Kampala International Film Festival's second edition.

Most prominent in the foreground is a woman giving birth. She is stark naked, like most characters in the painting. Fishermen drift in a boat, there is a traditional African grinding stone and its mortar. Many women seemingly bathe in the open, a pot of food cooks on an open fire, set on three stones, children sit as if to follow a storytelling session, one woman seems to perform magic, and in the background are some healthy looking banana trees. The painting may seem crowded, yet each of its component images tells a story and helps create the whole village's aura: from food processing and production to transportation, procreation, economic activities blending in with the social and recreational ones. This work speaks voluminously about the community represented in a single piece of art. Feminine energy tends to dominate, with a dense presence of what have largely been constructed as female-gender roles.

A third painting presents a similar story to the first two, though with more of a masculine presence. The setting is equally busy but not congested. A manifestation of the presence of someone very important resonates in it. Two comparatively huge feet are hanging, and being attended to by one man. Furthermore, most of these men seem concerned about security and are prepared to defend and safeguard whoever it is that is to be protected. Two very distinct men guard a doorway into an inner chamber, within which there is a lot more activity, with more people going about various endeavors. There are musical instruments, there is a traditional three-legged stool, and a person lying on the floor, probably sick and being attended to through the performance of a ritual. To the left and right in the background, respectively, are three huts, indicating a community, and children playing.

Gamba's paintings, just like his feature film *Kolormask*, tend to embody and valorize local cultural activities in an intentional manner that can be interpreted as culturally revolutionary, just like the thinking that dominated the work of so many of the continent's artists in the postcolonial era.

Early Filmmaking: *The Moon Children*

One of Gamba's student films, *The Moon Children* (1970), is so artistically layered that after multiple viewings, a spectator may still draw a blank as to what the film is really about. *The Moon Children* is so experimental and rather abstract that you can readily read impressions from new avant-gardism that thrived in Europe when Gamba studied in Łódź, and evidently influenced his works.

Another way to discuss Gamba's abstract style in his short films may be linked to his visual-art training. With a Fine Arts BA and as an established painter and poet at the time he went into film school, he was compelled by artistic forms that call for deeper critical interpretation. This is reflected in his films, too, which tend to be laden with imagery and which require more penetrating inferencing and a reading of the unstated in order to decipher meanings. This holds true from his casting to cinematography as well as the scripting.

The Moon Children is as abstract as its title, with quite an unconventional plot. From the start, with a call for liberation and drastic gunshots, then several sequences of seemingly unrelated scenes, all that's clear is the film's ambiguity. However, it turns out to be centered around an unnamed inmate in a prison cell, who is so disturbed and empty, then reminisces through flashbacks of happier days. Those past images become central in the film, coming alive in the protagonist's mind. Gamba manipulates color to show life as the protagonist becomes fully immersed in his (day)dreams about the past. Whenever he wakes from his imagination, he looks dejected, desperate, and disturbed.

The director explores montage to connect an insurgency to the prison sequence. *The Moon Children* is rich in visual symbolism as a way of advancing the plot and of transitioning. Cries of desperation and destruction follow a montage sequence that depicts mass killings, which is artistically presented through shots that are both abstract and explicit. Gunshot sound effects have heightened the tense mood just before the prison scenes are introduced. This prepares the viewer for the cell in which the story is largely set. There, the protagonist is seen sipping (nothing) from a dirty, empty, rusty old mug symbolizing his state of mind and life in general. He has long been in prison and is probably going to be there even longer, hence the despair.

The film is quite poetic in its presentation. Gamba uses voice-over narration to piece together strands of the story—without that narration, as we've seen, the story seems disjointed. The narrator's words are poetically paced, however, with rhyme, articulation, and intonation that create rhythm, making them sound more like lyrics than film narration. Twice in the prison-cell scenes, the narrator recites, first just after the two-minute mark:

> Time turns twice
> Then turns again
> Kansas moon children
> Watch from their houses
> With all their windows open wide
> Wanting to be touched by everything

About three minutes later, that narrator returns during a very desperate moment for the protagonist:

> Pearl is white
> Onyx, black
> Both are smooth
> And in Kansas, feeling hands
> They come alive

To further the symbolic and poetic presentation, Gamba applies music with pointed lyrics that goes beyond the expected nondiegetic layer that can add mood and rhythm to the dialogue. In the final song, the lyrics sound like a prayer and a call for ease and hope after the destructive conflict *The Moon Children* reveals and the devastating aftermath, especially for its protagonist:

> May the longtime sun shine on you
> And love surround you
> And the pure light within you guide your crayon

Music in the protagonist's nostalgic memories plays a major role, calming him, if only temporarily, and opening his thoughts and wishes to the audience, since he doesn't speak throughout the film. His emotional expressions meld with the music to communicate his

inner feelings, some of which is in ironic denial of his current state.
About four and half minutes along, one passage goes:

> All I hear you there
> Absolutely no strife
> Living the timeless life
> I don't need a wife
> Living a timeless life
> If I need a friend, I just get a Barico
> Straight right down I may go

Conclusion

Sao Gamba is certainly a stable founding fixture in film culture in Kenya. His creativity spans poetry, painting, and documentary filmmaking, along with his short drama films and features. These endeavors broke new ground, and he stands tall above other creatives of his time as a consistent pioneer, especially regarding the country's filmmaking. His works speak to the wider society, with indigenous culture placed at the core.

Gamba's death coincided with the founding of Riverwood, a new film-production approach in Kenya with a drive and style challenging the conservative professional-filmmaking style of the 1980s and 1990s. Emerging in the early 2000s and fashioned in the same pattern as Nigeria's famous Nollywood, Riverwood ushered in a new dispensation of the current wave of more vibrant film culture in Kenya. Thus, the foundations that Gamba put in place with the first feature film telling an authentic Kenyan story set the pace for the country's thriving cinematic culture, if not its creative culture as well.[11]

The biggest challenge to the full appreciation and recognition of Sao Gamba's films remains access. Most are documentaries, and all were made on celluloid. They're currently kept in KIMC's archives on U-matic tapes. The lack of functional U-matic machines for playback leaves them inaccessible. There is a glaring need to digitize these invaluable cultural documents, as a key step in the process of documenting Kenya's cinema history.

11   Diang'a, *Africa Re-creation*, 18.

305

PART IV

"DOCUMENTARY FILM IN EASTERN AFRICA: SAO GAMBA'S SECRET LEGACY" (2009)

The filmmaker, poet, thinker, painter, village architect and sculptor Sao Gamba is East Africa's artist extraordinaire, who saw the arts holistically as a way of life. Yet during his lifetime, Gamba was shunned in his own country and relegated to oblivion, having never been accepted for taking on his own paths and for never bending to the authorities and to social pressure. Despite attempts to stifle the power of his creative force, his artistic spirit endured and has permeated the region. It can be traced in particular in the trajectory that the practice of the documentary film has taken in his part of Africa.

Gamba is considered the pioneering professional filmmaker in East Africa. In 1964, he became the first African from the sub-Saharan regions to enroll at the Łódź Film School. The narrative of his life was to become dramatically intertwined with the turbulence of regional history. On returning home after completing his studies, he was kidnapped by henchman of Idi Amin, Uganda's strongman president, who whisked him off to Kampala for the sole purpose of installing him as a captive court chronicler. What Gamba found himself chronicling through the viewfinder of a 16mm camera were the gory and by turns grotesque and comic exploits of the media-hungry dictator. In 1973, he finally made his escape from his minders and fled back to Kenya. Gamba was reluctant to speak about this harrowing chapter of his life, and always made a point of stressing that he couldn't do so freely as long as Amin was alive and comfortably in exile. He never got to go public with this story. Then he was found lifeless in 2004, battered and tied to a tree, in a long valley outside Nairobi.

Besides an amazing body of phantasmic paintings, sculptures, and village structures, he left behind twenty documentaries, among them *Imaashoi El Maasai* (*People of the Red Ocher*), a landmark achievement in the history of documentary filmmaking in East Africa. Made in 1975, *People of the Red Ocher* takes the viewer on a journey through the social fabric of the Maasai community. The Maasai have, far beyond any other communities in the region, become the most easily recognized internationally, through an almost obsessive focus on them for over a century—to the exclusion of other groups—in films, photography, and written media.

What makes Gamba's film significant and sets it apart from the profusion of exploitative renditions about the Maasai is that it was the first such study made by a filmmaker from the region, eager to give genuine voice to his subjects rather than just be another in a long procession of voyeurs. Instead, the film reappropriates the dignity and freedom of an African people, with the director recognizing his project as a political statement on behalf of the Maasai. He presents them as a civilization that is autonomous and fully self-sufficient. To achieve this, Gamba worked on the film by closely involving the community itself in his creative process.

People of the Red Ocher is also one of the first attempts to liberate the East African documentary from the strictures of a ponderous newsreel style that had stifled much creative growth, particularly in Anglophone countries in the region. The narrative of the film is both tender and poetic, drawing on the structure of the Maa language, interpolating images which liberate their own readings. The documentary contains an exquisite sequence that can only be described as trancelike, during which viewers have stated that they felt time was suspended. Gamba uses film superbly to restate the power, the philosophy, the dignity, and the sophisticated aesthetics of an African culture.

Where then has the art of documentary filmmaking in East Africa traveled since Gamba's seminal work? By looking at one example from each country in this region, we can map out his legacy.

The Avant-Garde

The experimental documentary *Lomokowang* (*The Calabash*, 2004) by Petna Ndaliko Katondolo of eastern Congo [the Democratic Republic of Congo], though only thirteen minutes long, burst on the region's scene like a rare comet. Here for the first time a filmmaker was taking pure delight in the possibilities of a cinema so totally grounded in traditional African lore, yet at the same time as modern in its outlook as it could possibly be. Petna has dispensed in this film with the unspoken fallacy that African cinema isn't capable of pushing the limits of film language and expanding its vocabulary. There is no narrative, no story, and no protagonists in the conventional understanding of those terms. Film itself is both the object and vehicle of discourse. Using symbolism taken directly from traditional settings, Petna convolutes them, in an explosion of refined poetic imagery. Countless images, such as the apparently simple and rustic calabash, are turned into most sophisticated keys to the power and endurance of age-defying yet at the same time living cultures.

Political Conscience

Walking Shadows: Undying Spirits (2004) by Ndungi Githuku from Kenya is the first explicitly politically defiant documentary from the region. Using eyewitness accounts and reenacted scenes, the film describes in great detail the persecution and torture that had been meted out to the opposition by the Moi regime. Githuku traced and then unearthed personal trauma among victims who had their lives and health shattered, and who still underwent the indignity of having to rub shoulders on the streets of Nairobi with their former persecutors, who have now taken on the guise of respectably ordinary citizens. Recurrent motifs in *Walking Shadows* are the sinister torture chambers that were operated underneath one of the capital's tallest buildings. The bare concrete walls filmed in scarcely perceptible light eerily evoke the sacrifice that so many Kenyans, often unrecognized even today, endured in their struggles for democracy. Those walls absorbed blood, tears, and cries of defiance. Githuku's film poses the unnerving and universal question of the price that an individual pays in order to assert their basic human rights and dignity.

Social Conscience

The Mgongowazi Documentary Project (literally "the bare-backed"), by any standards a unique phenomenon, was born in Tanzania. A group of young women—Safaa Ali, Yasinta Mtarasha, Sara Alex, and Anna Nabulaya—came together to form a documentary film collective. They would first search out, research, and script stories that mainly, though not exclusively, centered on issues pertinent to women. The group would then work closely with the film director Lars Johansson to give a structure to their stories. The collective has created a whole body of work that can be readily identified by its sharp wit, compassionate humor, and biting social criticism.

House Girl is a tale of poor rural girls being forced to work as urban housemaids, where they are treated like slaves. The film, however, rather than going for a clichéd tearjerker structure, uses a hilarious song to underpin the images. The effect on the viewer of this jarring superimposition is, quite intentionally, devastating. Other of the collective's titles include *Women Marrying Women* (2004) about an enclave in Musoma where widow[er]s traditionally marry younger women, and the lyrical *Love in the Time of AIDS,* on the courage of a refugee willing to publicly divulge his status in a jittery community.

Memory

The most traumatic experience for the region remains the genocide that took place in Rwanda, in 1994. Can film, can any film at all for that matter, possibly encapsulate the horror and pain of such an unfathomable scale? Eric Kabera and Kavila Matu in their Rwandese film *Through My Eyes* (2004) take a humble path, indicating that even if such encapsulation is not at all possible, then at least film should be used as one of the means to try to heal those festering scars. *Through My Eyes* keeps the actual genocide as a vast hovering backdrop, without at any point taking recourse to graphic depictions. The only picture of it is mental and spiritual, as it were, as carried around within the memories of a group of young Rwandans. These young women and men have decided to use poetry, painting, music, song, and dance to keep that memory alive—but at the same time to place that memory, not on the side of vengeance, but of understanding and healing. The mission and conviction of these youth is awe-inspiring, and even more so for their faith in the redeeming ability of the arts. What *Through My Eyes* does is commendable, as its structure is totally subservient to observing, almost in cinema verite fashion, the progress of this group. Here is indeed a quiet, self-effacing and at the same moment gripping encounter with the confluence of pain and art.

Aesthetics

Rockamilley, a Ugandan documentary directed by Caroline Kamya in 2006, is probably the most joyous and life-affirming story to have come out of the region. Taking liberties in moving away from a burden of obligation to delve into matters political or social, Kamya celebrates the pure energy of life itself. She takes up the story of Milton, popularly known in Kampala as Rockamilley, who most improbably is a conservative dentist conscientiously treating patients' teeth during the day and who, come night, transforms as with Jekyll and Hyde into a performing musician with a passionate mission to live out a fantasy as an Elvis impersonator. This perplexing lifestyle, to those looking from the outside, is further exacerbated by his prosperous family, who try to make him "see sense."

But in *Rockamilley*, even that conflict is being lovingly fought, with the only outcomes being a peaceful embrace of flamboyance or the startled contemplation of it. At the heart of Kamya's soft-hearted drama is the concept of "sense." For what indeed constitutes "sense"? The style of the film mirrors the tone of Milton's daily transmutations, by way of its prying camera and mischievous and spirited editing. Beneath the playfulness, Kamya is a director with abundant control over the story's emotional flow. What an amazing privilege it is to be in a cinema where, when the lights go up, the whole audience is beaming with such infectious inner joy elicited by this gentle gem of a documentary.

First published in 2009 for *Côté doc du Fespaco News*, Ouagadougou. The text has been lightly edited for this publication.

FIG. 1
JAKUB BARUA AND SAO GAMBA, HIPPO VALLEY, NAIROBI, KENYA,
COURTESY JAKUB BARUA

FIG. 2
DOCUMENTATION FROM THE SET OF *PEOPLE OF THE RED OCHER*,
COURTESY JAKUB BARUA

"THE CINEMA AND I (A BLACK FILMMAKER)"
(JULY 1986)

First delivered as an MA thesis, prepared under the supervision of Prof. Jerzy Bossak, Łódź Film School. The thesis was prepared in Polish ("Kino i ja: Być czarnym filmowcem") and in English. The below is an excerpt from the English-language version and has been lightly edited for clarity. Editorial remarks are provided in parenthesis when more substantive interventions are made. Footnotes have been supplemented to provide additional relevant details for the reader. —Eds.

The Third Cinema, the Third World cinema, began establishing its structural coordinates and intellectual justifications in the context of New Wave cinema and theory. The central figure who facilitated this transition toward the Third World cinema was Jean-Luc Godard. The position of Godard within the history of cinema is comparable to that of Picasso within the history of art and James Joyce within the history of the novel. It was while Godard was moving politically between Maoism and anarchism and back to Maoism that he transformed our complete understanding of the history of the cinema and reformulated the language of film.

First, those films made just before the Paris events of May 1968, and in fact in some ways anticipating those historic events, combine both the documentary-film and feature-film forms into a synthesis without parallel in the entire history of the cinema. Second, Godard influenced a whole generation of filmmakers, stretching from the Japanese filmmaker Nagisa Ōshima through Bernardo Bertolucci and Rainer [Werner] Fassbinder to Glauber Rocha, the founder of Third World cinema. Third, Godard in films such as *Le gai savior, Weekend, Wind from the East,* and *La Chinoise,* and not leaving out *Two or Three Things I Know About Her,* all made between 1967 and 19[70], interrogated film language that had been in existence since the inception of cinema, and attempted to replace it with a new language. Anarchically, because Godard vowed to destroy the whole structure of film. That Godard's cinema of those years collapsed eventually is not of central importance. That is for posterity to evaluate.

What is fundamental is that Godard's cinema showed beyond a doubt that European cinema was a historical construct reflecting the development of film within European history and cultural systems, rather than being immanent in film as a technological and cultural product. That is, Godard was not arguing this theoretically, but indicating it in the constructional form of these films, some of which are [monuments] of our time. It was this that facilitated the opening of cinema historically to the Third World. It is not accidental that Glauber Rocha in [*Wind from the East*] (1970) asked to interrupt class struggle to indicate the way toward political cinema. Though left hanging at the crossroads, seemingly unable to help out Godard, the Brazilian filmmaker went to Africa where he formulated his answer to Godard in *The Lion Has Seven Heads* (1970), on the imposition of imperial European history on national African histories with specific reference to Congo-Brazzaville [today's Republic of the Congo].

It was out of this intellectual dialogue between *cinema novo* films of Rocha and the New Wave films of Godard that a part of Third World film culture emerged. Another part of Third World cinema traces its ancestry through the films of Satyajit Ray,[1] who traces his formation through John Ford, Jean Renoir, and Akira Kurosawa. Concerning Godard, it was not accidental that, after the Mozambique Revolution ended in 1974, he assisted in setting up a film institute in Maputo. But it is not enough.

With the emergence of Third World cinema, if it is to be unique and original and not a neocolonial imitation, there should also emerge a region-by-region Third World cinema language; correspondingly, there is the [Ntongela] Masilela[2] statement: "Emergence of African national cinema should also necessitate the birth of African film language."[3] As it will be remembered, the emergence of film within European culture was in highly developed economic and industrial structures. Many Third World countries have no sufficiently developed economic structures to produce cultural capital to facilitate the growth of cinematic economic structures. Hence the differential process in the development of Third World cinema within many of the industrializing countries. [...] As 90 percent of Africans were illiterate, the colonists came to the conclusion that the use of motion pictures was one of the ways of influencing the African mind.

This opened the door for both commercial- and documentary-film companies to flood Africa with propaganda material in audiovisual form. The field was dominated by the two British production units [Crown] Film Unit, which produced three hundred

1   [Satyajit Ray (1921–92), the Indian director, scriptwriter, lyricist, illustrator, and composer, is among the great filmmakers, celebrated for works including the acclaimed Apu Trilogy of *Pather Panchali*, *Aparatjito*, and *Apur Sansar* (1955–59), *The Music Room* (1958), *The Big City* (1963), and *Charulata* (1964).]

2   [Ntongela Masilela (1948–2020) was born in South Africa; professor of English and world literatures and adjunct professor in African-American studies at the University of California. Masilela's family went into exile due to apartheid when he was a teenager, settling in Nairobi, Kenya. At UCLA, he obtained his BA, MA, and PhD degrees; his doctoral thesis was on "Theory and History in Marxist Poetics." Masilela then enrolled at the Łódź Film School in 1979 (no shorts have been preserved). Among his published papers, he also analyzed African cinema.]

3   Ntongela Masilela, "Issues and Problems in the African Cinema," in *DSE*, ed. K. Gottstein, G. Link [n.d.], 157. [Ntongela Masilela, "Issues in the South African Cinema," accessed February 12, 2021, http://pzacad.pitzer. edu/NAM/general/essays/cinemasouth.pdf.]

films.[4] Needless to add that the crew was exclusively white, with blacks doing menial jobs or serving as exotic backdrops. T. W. Koyinde Vaughan, a young Nigerian assistant film director working in England, points out how shallow these films were: "The director in his report admitted that he had no idea about the erosion of soil when he set out to shoot the film *Soil Erosion*, hoping to pick it up as he went along. He exposed 75 percent of the raw stock, because he hadn't the slightest idea of what soil erosion was all about, or that the film shoot was on the wrong track."[5]

Another important feature handicapping the European filmmaker, apart from the language barrier, was the mentality of superiority with which they came. Armed with a presupposed superior culture, they lacked the will to absorb the cultures they were operating within and shunned various taboos, and from their high pedestals were in no position whatsoever to understand the African mentality. If the African was therefore to assess himself through the eyes of colonial filmmakers, as [sociologist W.E.B.] Du Bois espouses the measuring of oneself through the eyes of others,[6] he would then gain a clearer idea of the colonial mentality than of himself. Edmund Husserl in *The Idea of Phenomenology* was right in stating that: "I cannot live, experience, think, value, and act in any world which is not in some sense in me, and derives its meaning and truth from me." And yet that is the task the colonial European filmmaker set himself.

[The historian] Henryk Zins rightly points out that most of the short stories and novels at the time were written by foreigners and tended to show only one side of colonial life—the exotic and hunters' safaris, without a sentence about Africans or even their way of life.[7] It applies also to such renowned authors as Ernest Hemingway. Zins goes further to point out that the popular Mau Mau Uprising of 1953 was viewed by British historians and Christian authors as

4   T. W. Koyinde Vaughan, "Czarna Afryka w filmie," *Kwartalnik Filmowy*, no. 2 (1957): 42–60, 48.
5   Koyinde Vaughan, "Czarna Afryka," 49.
6   [W.E.B. Du Bois, "Strivings of the Negro People," *Atlantic Monthly*, vol. 80 (August 1897), 194–98, https://www.theatlantic.com/magazine/archive/1897/08/strivings-of-the-negro-people/305446/]
7   Henryk Zins, *Historia Afryki Wschodniej* (Wrocław: Zakład Narodowy im. Ossolińskich 1986), 355.

a barbaric uprising, a product of primitive mentality against Western capitalist civilization and Christianity (the works of [anthropologist] Louis Leakey, etc.). This popular peasants' uprising, which accelerated Kenya's independence, provoked unparalleled anti-African propaganda.

[T. W. Koyinde Vaughan points out some examples in Western productions]: in the film *Mau-Mau* (1955),[8] one African stabs another for no apparent reason, except maybe instinct (sic). The first frames of *Simba* (1955),[9] produced by J. Arthur Rank, shows an African who alights from his bicycle on hearing the cries of an injured European farmer, in order to finish him off. To show the other side of the coin, after location shooting of the film, reports appeared in the British press that the film crew was using Kikuyu prisoners who were sentenced to death. They were executed three days after the last take![10]

Through the rise of black consciousness, from Kwame Nkrumah's Pan-Africanism[11] to Afro-American militarism (James Baldwin tips the scale in the opposite direction with his claim that Afro-culture is morally and aesthetically superior to white civilization), Jean Bisping points out that one critic of the concept of a black culture was the Caribbean black scholar Frantz Fanon, who believed that it perpetuated the racist assumption that all blacks were alike, since the conceptions of a common set of black values had originated from white-racist ideology.

However it would be untrue to give the impression that all European filmmakers working in Africa represented, [as the critic Jadwiga Siekierska has called it], "masked pseudohumanism within colonialism."[12] There stands out a small group of people who worked

8   [*Mau-Mau*, dir. Elwood G. Price, 1955. An exploitative documentary reconstruction of the rise of the Mau-Mau resistance movement against British rule in East Africa in the early 1950s.]
9   [*Simba*, dir. Brian Desmond Hurst, 1955. A European family in East Africa is caught up in the Mau-Mau uprising pitting local Blacks against colonists.]
10   Koyinde Vaughan, "Czarna Afryka," 47.
11   [Kwame Nkrumah (1909–72) the politician and revolutionary, was first president of Ghana, an influential advocate of Pan-Africanism, founding member of the Organization of African Unity, and recipient of the Lenin Peace Prize in 1962.]
12   [Jadwiga Siekierska, "Piśmiennictwo filmowe," in *Historia filmu polskiego*, ed. Jerzy Toeplitz, vol. 4 (Warsaw: WAiF, 1980), 328.]

in favor of Africans with sincere understanding. The film *Les statues meurent aussi* (*Statues Also Die*, 1951) directed by Alain Resnais and Chris Marker, which the French censors tried to muffle, starts off with the picture of a French girl adoring the beauty of an African statue in one of the Paris exhibitions. After this portrayal and appreciation of African art, the camera pans off to reveal French lecturers, lecturing to Africans on the craftsmanship of carving. Whenever Resnais turns the camera to America, it is with even more chilling irony. One sequence starts off with an abrupt beat of African jazz drums; edited to this are newsreel clips of police attacks, striking black Americans on a picket line. The spectacle is cut to jazz music. Resnais's film bravely spotlights the downtrodden and the systematic liquidation of their culture.[13]

Here is a clear example of a clean break from bourgeois culture. The culture of fantasy, replete with comfort, equilibrium, sweet reason, order, efficiency, and the possibility to "be someone."[14] When a colonized man accepts this situation, he becomes a good boy, no matter his age. A pauper on his own land, a beggar in his own country—no matter how intelligent, how able bodied he might be. But when he refuses to accept his fate, he becomes a dangerous animal, a savage unable to appreciate the guardianship of the all-knowing Tarzan in all his grace, thus bound to wallow in abject anarchy should he escape from white protection. "Tarzan died and in his place were born Lumumbas, Nkomos, and the Dedan Kimathis—this is something that neocolonialism cannot forgive," in the Kenyan writer Ngũgĩ wa Thiong'o's words.[15]

It cannot be overstressed that with the emergence of the African culture, if it is to be unique and original and not a neocolonial imitation, African film language has to emerge as well. This is necessitated by the fact that each national group or subgroup has its own specificity built in, within its own cultures or subculture as the case may be, its own system of coding and decoding of images;

13   Koyinde Vaughan, "Czarna Afryka," 55.
14   Fernando Solanas and Octavio Gettino, "Toward a Third Cinema," in *Movies and Methods*, ed. Bill Nichols (Berkeley: University of California Press 1976), 54.
15   Ngũgĩ wa Thiong'o, *Homecoming: Essays on African and Caribbean Literature, Culture and Politics* (London: Heinemann 1972), 42.

as will be exemplified further on. It is in this sense that African cinema can better fulfill some of the tasks that have been attempted by African novelists: Ngũgĩ wa Thiong'o, Chinua Achebe, Wole Soyinka, Es'kia Mphahlele... "What the African novelists have attempted to do is restore the African Character to his history [...] bring back to the African Character the will to act and change the scheme of things,"[16] as Thiong'o states.
[Which genre—documentary or feature—would be more useful in creating the African cinema?] It was with justification that [filmmaker and anthropologist] Jean Rouch, a year after the triumph of revolutionary struggles in Mozambique, discouraged the emerging Mozambican documentary movement from a concentration on filming party congresses, and recommended rather that it concentrate on the central problems of the day: social problems of cultural creation and political problems of national reconstruction. Jerzy Bossak and his school of filmmakers were the first to diverge from the mainstream of the Polish documentary of the day, and between 1956–59 (the highest point of the "Black Series" in documentary films) they tackled burning social issues.[17] [It seems that] the place of the documentary-film form will play a very important part in Third World film for reasons that will be made clear below.
After only a few years of filmmaking, I felt that it is such an expensive undertaking that if it is not creative enough to prove interesting to the audience, it loses usefulness and becomes a luxury that few can afford, particularly governments of developing countries. From some of the comments expressed publicly about Kenyan film and TV production so far, there is a general indication that Kenyan electronic-media (including film) directors still have to develop the creative sort of skills that can make media-finished productions to interest and hold audiences in order for them to receive

16   Thiong'o, *Homecoming*.
17   [The Black Series was a documentary-film movement that emerged early in the October Thaw period as sociopolitical restraints began relaxing in the mid 1950s, which was informed by social commitment and an ambition to portray the ordinary life of underprivileged communities neglected by official cinema (the homeless, prostitutes, hooligans, those living in Warsaw's ruins). The series included works directed by Jerzy Bossak, Jerzy Hoffman, Edward Skórzewski, Kazimierz Karabasz, Jerzy Ziarnik, and Władysław Ślesicki.]

messages oriented to cultural development. What skills Kenyan film and TV directors have now are not enough; in fact, in the long run, the process proves expensive for the government, as the cost of delivery of message per thousand grows higher. The already strained resources devoted to filmmaking thus often cannot be justified. This state of affairs will only be resolved when resources are invested to develop the manpower and creative ability in media production to justify even the small budgets that are normally allotted!

Senegal, Upper Volta, Ethiopia, Mali, and Nigeria are at the forefront in developing an African cinema, but it must be observed that this is on very fragile economic structures with very low levels of cultural capital. With this in mind, and given the limited nature and capacities of many African countries in constructing national cinemas, given the urgencies being felt in the sphere of national development, social integration, and cultural unity, it seems that the documentary is the genre most eminently possible and capable of meeting the needs and potentialities of many African countries. Documentary production is cheaper than feature-film production, and it is film formed by the dictates of its aesthetics and most amenable to being utilized for pedagogical purposes, for forging national consciousness, political ideologies, and cultural values. Education is an urgent problem across the African continent, which needs to be the priority. In this context, the documentary-film form would attempt to grasp the elements of teaching literacy; the documentary should serve as a national information reservoir of our cultural history.

The way ahead for the development of Third World cinema is not going to be easy. Given the fact that most Third World countries—or since cinema is a child of industrialization, the industrializing countries—have had a prehistory deeply embedded in colonialism, then some elements of neocolonialism have been left behind. Therefore, the filmmaker is encompassed by a double problem, especially if he has been trained without his cultural environment to fall back upon. The filmmaker trained in European modes of communication has to guard against automation. As tape recorders and movie cameras have been simplified, the cinema is going through a process of demystification. Chris Marker in France experimented with a group of workers by giving them 8 mm equipment; then with only basic operational instructions, they went out to film the world as they saw it. With the advent of video, the camera is falling into more hands, workers' hands, and opening up unheard-of possibilities. A new concept of filmmaking is at hand.

Though the documentary form has been forced on us by the dictates of our historical position within the present state encompassed in our development timescale, this does not mean the neglect of the fictional-film form. African cinema cannot fail to produce the idylls of our vanishing cultures and civilizations, the frescoes of our contrasting societies and the dialectical reportages of trials and tribulations. Indeed, it is works of Ousmane Sembène, *La noire de...* (*Black Girl*, 1966), *Xala* (*Impotence*, 1975), which have given legitimacy and respectability to African cinema.[18] Sembène, the founder of African cinema, has attempted to establish the sociological coordinates of this cinema. After all, Kazimierz Karabasz, a documentarist of the Black Series in Poland, under the tutelage of Jerzy Bossak, was moved to declare that in a fairy-tale you might find more truth than in a reportage.[19]

I will leave the conclusion to Ntongela Masilela, the renowned African scholar of great brilliance and deep insight into the varied spectrum of the problems facing the African continent:

> It seems to me that the most effective contribution the African cinema could make to modern civilization and world culture today would be to produce historical epics and historical dramas. At the center of them should be the living drama and living history of African

18   [Ousmane Sembène (1923–2007) is the Senegalese film director, writer, and producer held in regard as a father of African film. From 1962 to 1963, Sembène studied filmmaking in Moscow at the Gorky Film Studio, where his supervisor was the director Mark Donskoy; he received an Honorable Prize for his contributions to world cinema at the Eleventh International Film Festival in Moscow (1979). He produced films in his native Wolof language and attracted a worldwide audience with his films including *Mandabi* (1968), *Ceddo* (1977), *Guelwaar* (1992), and *Moolaadé* (2004). The latter received the Un Certain Regard award in Cannes; Sembène also received the Grand Prix FESPACO at the Pan-African Film Festival held in Ouagadougou, Burkina Faso.]
19   Kazimierz Karabasz, *Cierpliwe oko* (Warsaw: WAiF, 1979), 148.

civilizations and empires. These historical dramas should not merely be period pieces, nor for that matter romanticization of our history and creation of false myths about its past, but rather demystification of the grandeur of its tragic nature as was attempted by Yambo Ouologuem in his novel [Le Devoir de violence] (1968). Only in this way can we understand who we are, why we are here and where we are going.[20]

        These are challenges not beyond the grasp of the African intellect.

---

20   Masilela, Issues and Problems in the African Cinema, 157. [Yambo Ouologuem (1940–2017), the Malian writer, when awarded the Prix Renaudot for his debut novel, Le Devoir de violence, became the first African to receive a major French literary prize.]

Léa Morin is an independent curator and researcher engaged in projects of editing, exhibition, and film restoration that bring together researchers, artists, and practitioners. Her research attempts to contribute to a better knowledge of artistic and cinematic modernities that have been rendered invisible by dominant narratives. She is especially interested in the circulation of ideas, forms, aesthetics, and political and artistic struggles in the period of independence movements (1960s and 1970s) and in cultural decolonization. She is a codirector of Talitha, a nonprofit organization devoted to alternative and experimental cinematic and sound archives, preservation, and redistribution. She is cofounder of l'Observatoire (Art et Recherche) in Casablanca.

LESSON 41: GOING TO POLAND TO BECOME A MOROCCAN FILMMAKER[1]

We dreamed of several unities: Arab, African, Third World, global. A unity of peoples struggling for independence and socialism on all continents.[2]
—Abdelfettah Fakihani

DON QUIXOTE

The Cinema: To Bring Change
ABDELKADER LAGTAA I come from a working-class background. My taste for cinema and literature was born thanks to school. There were no extracurricular activities at my middle school

1   This research-staged dialogue features selected commentaries of Mostafa Derkaoui, Abdelkrim Derkaoui, and Abdelkader Lagtaa, and relates their years of study in Łódź in the 1960s and 1970s, along with added insights from their peers Ahmed Lallem and Miguel Sobrado. Like a compilation of film excerpts, these filmmakers' statements, gleaned largely from interviews between 1965 and the present day in Poland, Algeria, Morocco, Costa Rica, and France, layer into a narrative that is illustrated with a selection of previously unpublished and rare images and archival materials unearthed in the course of research.

2   Abdelfettah Fakihani, *Le couloir, bribes de vérité sur les années de plomb* (Casablanca: Tarik éditions, 2005).

in Casablanca, so we came up with the idea of creating a club: we all paid our membership dues and rented a room. To "furnish" it, we invented activities: reading, theater [...] That's how I discovered my particular interest in literature. Then I realized I had things to say. That there was a particular reality that needed to be expressed, and that I couldn't find elsewhere. I first wrote poems, articles, and short stories. And then it occurred to me that in a country with such a high illiteracy rate, perhaps it was through cinema that I could make a difference.

Paris

MOSTAFA DERKAOUI My father was a carpenter. I studied philosophy at the Lycée Lyautey and at the same time I attended the Casablanca theater conservatory. I was preparing to teach philosophy. One day, during a visit from a guidance committee, I was told about a film school in Paris that accepted Moroccan students. I got a scholarship from the Moroccan Cinema Center to study at IDHEC, but cinematography, not filmmaking. I confirmed my interest nonetheless and went there at the end of September 1962. But I had a problem. I had fallen in love, madly in love, with Douja,[3] who was in Casablanca.

Mao and Marx

ABDELKADER LACTAA My social awakening also occurred around the same time as that of my school friends. We were all sons of blue-collar workers. Especially in high school, we were really sensitive to how we differed socially from the sons of the bourgeoisie, those who got driven to school. As for us, we had bicycles.

And then there was reading too. I was in regular contact with the Chinese embassy: I read *Pékin Information*, *Chine en construction* [...] I read Liou Chao Chi's book, *How to Be a Good Communist*. I read Mao too, of course, and then I discovered Marx. I used to go to the embassy with these friends, and we were shown films. You see, despite the authoritarian, liberticidal regime in Morocco, there were opportunities to keep oneself informed and everything.

3   Khadija "Douja" Nour, whom Derkaoui married in 1965.

I wrote in Arabic. I did everything to get published. As
fate would have it, I felt complicity with the UNFP newspapers [Union
nationale des forces populaires; the left-wing National Union of Popular Forces]. So their magazine published some of my texts.

"Les 4 murs"
MOSTAFA DERKAOUI When I came back from Paris in
1964, I adapted Sean O'Casey's *Hall of Healing*. It was Brechtian theater,
I was keeping my distance. The UNEM [the National Union of Moroccan Students] asked me to look after TUM [the Moroccan University
Theater], which had to be present in Algiers. I organized the dress
rehearsal in the courtyard of the Lycée Moulay Youssef in Rabat. And
the police arrived. They were going to arrest me.

It must be said that during those years I was involved
in the resistance: I had joined the Moroccan Communist Party and I
had a project for a first feature film to be produced by CCM [the
Moroccan Cinema Center] and RTM [the Moroccan Radio and Televi-
sion]. A sort of cooperative of filmmakers, members or sympathiz-
ers of CCM had formed around this project.

"An embarrassment of riches"
ABDELKRIM DERKAOUI Mostafa only stayed in Paris for
a couple of months because he didn't like it. He felt that IDHEC was
a school that mainly trained critics, not filmmakers. And he wanted
to make films.

He taught French at the Lycée Al Azhar, he made a play
and even a film: *Les 4 murs* [*The Four Walls*], and he continued looking
for a good film school. Of course we were familiar with Russian, Polish, and Czech cinema, and Mostafa had seen some Polish films while
at IDHEC in Paris, including Andrzej Wajda's *Ashes and Diamonds*.

We were members of the Moroccan Communist Party,
active militants, we'd taken part in the demonstrations of 1965, with
Oufkir firing from his helicopter... you know the song. And so thanks
to that we had a scholarship for VGIK in Moscow, a scholarship for
FAMU in Czechoslovakia, and a scholarship for Łódź in Poland. It was

an embarrassment of riches. And as we knew the USSR was still Stalinist, that there wasn't yet much freedom of expression, whereas
Poland was more open, we went to Poland.

The Cultural Revolution and a Recommendation
ABDELKADER LAGTAA When I got my baccalaureate, I
went to the Chinese Embassy to ask if I could study cinema in China.
I rang the bell: nothing. Nobody came. The gate was ajar, I pushed it
open, and I saw a group of young Chinese in overalls working in the
garden. They looked at me. "I'd like to see Mr. So-and-so." "Gone to
China! Gone to China! Not come back!" That's how it ended. For me,
the Cultural Revolution was an extraordinary event, I couldn't
imagine [...]

So I began thinking of going to the USSR, but it was too
late. And there, on my way back to the station, I came across the
Czech Embassy. And in the same building I stumbled on the Polish
Embassy, by chance. I explained that I wanted a scholarship. You had
to have your baccalaureate and a letter of recommendation from a
"progressive" organization, something like that. That's all I needed.
Of course, they couldn't say "communist party," the PCM [Moroccan
Communist Party] was a clandestine organization at the time. I asked
for a letter of recommendation from the UNFP.

I think the important thing for the Poles was to spread
their culture. To have fellow travelers all over the world. In Poland I
met a lot of foreigners who were not left-wing at all.

Rue Mégret
MOSTAFA DERKAOUI In Rabat, I lived in a two-room
apartment on rue Mégret. By pure coincidence, I met the consul general of the Republic of Poland in the stairwell. He lived in the same
building. I told him that I was making films. And he told me about a
school in Poland, very famous, where film professionals like Wajda
teach. "I absolutely want to go where the director of *Ashes and Diamonds* teaches." "Well, if you can prove your sympathy for the Moroccan Communist Party, I could help you go there."

So I went to see Aziz Belal, an economics professor at the university who was a member of the Communist Party. I told him that I needed the backing of the party to make my case to the Polish government. He supported me. So I got a scholarship for Krimou, my brother [Abdelkrim], and for myself.

Departure
MOSTAFA DERKAOUI In 1965, Khadija and I got married. On September 11, 1965. And immediately I left Casa Port [Port of Casablanca] with Krimou, with five suitcases, three of them full of books, and two full of clothes. Casa, Tangier, Madrid, Paris, all without changing trains. I arrived in Paris with a hundred francs in my pocket. I bought *Don Quixote* from a bookseller for fifty francs. I slept for thirty-six hours. Krimou woke me up, and we got back on the train. With only fifty francs in our pockets, we didn't have enough to pay the deposit to get our suitcases back. I told Krimou, "We're leaving the suitcases behind." Finally, we were helped by a Moroccan engineer I knew who lived in Paris, who paid the deposit. In Berlin, two Poles paid for our visas. They knew what it was like.

DAILY LIFE IN EXILE

Curious Strangers
ABDELKADER LAGTAA At Łódź, the foreigners—there were nearly three thousand of us—studied Polish for a year and then were dispatched to various universities and schools in Poland.

Arriving in Poland for me was first of all the discovery of a country, a people. I was not a model student. That is to say I cut language classes, but only in order to get to know the reality of the people. I had a lot of Polish friends whom I visited, with whom I did things. I wasn't blamed for cutting class because it helped me be a better speaker.

We were a curiosity in Poland. Poles weren't used to seeing foreigners. There were Vietnamese, Mongolians, Cubans, Chileans, Algerians, Tunisians, Cameroonians, even French... At the film school, there were about thirty foreigners, a Lebanese, an Iranian, a Tunisian, an Algerian, a Brazilian, a Ugandan, a Czech, two Argentines, a Mexican... The Tunisian dropped out in second year. People dropped out along the way. We were few in number, so we were very connected.

The Tower of Babel
MIGUEL SOBRADO The 1960s were the culmination of decolonization with the Vietnam War and the agrarian wars around the world. The Soviet Union, China, and Cuba played a very important role in this. The Socialist bloc was educating students from the Third World, and that's how Mostafa Derkaoui and I ended up in Poland. The Derkaoui brothers were my Polish-language study buddies at Łódź from 1965 to 1966 at the Tower of Babel, and it was there that we developed a special friendship. I later studied sociology and they studied cinema, but we remained very close.

A Polish Education
AHMED LALLEM We had all kinds of courses in our first year: art history, literature, chemistry, physics, painting, descriptive geometry, aesthetics, film psychology, film history, film analysis, etc. I could go on and on. There were seventeen branches. It should be noted that every day, from 3 P.M. to 8 P.M., we had film screenings. There was an exam at the end of each semester. In Poland, there was no general average. You had to score the average from each teacher. If you missed two averages, you were failed.

In the second year, the system was less strict. The timetable was left more to our initiative. We had to make a silent fiction short of about ten minutes and a documentary of similar length. Naturally, we were still taking courses. This was the year when the courses began for directing actors. In third year came the making of sound films. We had to make three shorts or two medium-length films. The diploma included writing a thesis of about forty pages on a cinematographic problem or a topic even remotely related to cinema. In addition—and this was the strongest originality of the Łódź school—students finished by making a full-length movie or a medium-length experimental film.

Films

ABDELKADER LAGTAA I did some exercises in which I tried to achieve something. It was an opportunity to follow through on ideas that were perhaps insane. For example, I did an exercise where you never see the person speaking. At the time, I thought it was a way to set myself apart from realistic cinema. It was misunderstood. Maybe it was a bit radical. It made the film a little boring. It was the last one, in 1975: *Voyage*.

Shadow among Others [1969] was more political. Abdelkrim did the camera work. It was set in Morocco but it was shot in Łódź. It tells the story of a left-wing political leader who is arrested, tortured, there are demonstrations.

I also made a poem about gypsies. A documentary. *But Hope Is of a Different Color* [1972]. It's a line from a poem I wrote. About a family I got to know while location scouting. It was a sedentary family, tinkering for a living. For example, they'd go to the corner store to buy cloth then sell it as expensive imported cloth. They were forced to become sedentary, they had a separate neighborhood in Łódź. At the edge of town. And they got by, they sang. They were marginals. My idea was to offer a critical view of Polish society through them.

The Jazz Cellar

MOSTAFA DERKAOUI It was a great experience. An extraordinary nation, noble, humble, kind. Very cultured people, who went to the cinema, listened to music. I discovered music in Poland. In Łódź itself, but I also took many trips to Warsaw, for example, I saw a play by the Warsaw student theater called *Dear Mr. Ionesco*, written and directed by Stanisław Tym. I asked him to act in my third-year film and in my graduation film.

I also went to Kraków, a city that I thought was very beautiful, where you could mostly listen to jazz, but which I finally never filmed.

The jazz cellar that I did film was that of a Warsaw band in the old part of town. The conductor was the husband of the singer Wanda Warska. They appeared in the film gratis, I think they never even saw it.

During three months of vacation I studied with Lagtaa
for our exams in the countryside. We drank vodka together. He was
a poet. He wrote in the magazine *Souffles*.[4] He's very cultured.

At Mostafa's

ABDELKADER LAGTAA I lived with Idriss Karim at the
university residence. We were in the same room, and so we were in
constant discussions, obviously. Meanwhile, Mostafa Derkaoui, who
was married and had a son, was entitled to an apartment in town,
and so we met at his place. Krimou was also in residence. Mostafa's
place, as usual—since he continued the practice in Morocco afterwards for a long time—was an open house. It was a welcoming place,
a place where we all felt at home, where we could drink, eat, and
develop our ideas unfettered. We had three extraordinary Syrian
friends with whom we had extensive political discussions.

Bureau de la Poésie

ABDELKADER LAGTAA In the early 1970s, the artist Ewa
Partum had a conceptual-art gallery in Łódź and needed translators,
especially into French. It was while working with her that I discovered another form of expression that was totally unknown to us. It
was obviously an extraordinary discovery because I realized that
there were artists working with other objects, from other perspectives, and that was very important.

As I became more and more immersed in it, I began to
develop some ideas myself. Ewa and Andrzej, her husband, included
me, let me take part in happenings, things like that, and of course I
started to get more and more involved.

For example, I took part in an international exhibition
in Buenos Aires, presenting a work on the [postage] stamp, which consisted in hijacking it. I also took part in an international exhibition

4   While in Poland, Lagtaa published poems in the Moroccan journal *Souffles*,
      edited by the poet Abdellatif Laâbi. In issue 5 (1967), he introduced
      himself as "born in 1948 in Casablanca. Studies. Now in Łódź for film. 1964
      publishes some poems and articles in Arab journals such as *Al Ahdaf, Al
      Moujahid, Attarik*." *Souffles* reached a political turning point in its final issues
      and was banned in 1972, with its founder Laâbi imprisoned for the "crime
      of opinion." For more, see Kenza Sefrioui, *La revue* Souffles *1966–1973: Espoirs
      de révolution culturelle au Maroc* (Casablanca: Editions du Sirocco, 2013).

in Montreal, I think, as well as in a demonstration in northern Poland, where Andrzej [Partum] and I did cinema-screen acupuncture. In the middle of a screening, we arrived, climbed up ladders and hijacked the film projection.   Andrzej had an office in Warsaw called Bureau de la Poésie, in French. It was a tiny thing. He organized exhibitions. He invited some people. The press never talked about it! They started talking about it around 1974. He had no grants, he had nothing. But he received recognition in the artistic world because of his perseverance. He had ideas that seemed disconnected from reality, but he didn't give a damn. He was an outsider.
        With him, I made a poem on the word Coca-Cola. The idea was to hijack, to deconstruct... Unfortunately, I've not kept anything of it, not even the invitation. We organized happenings. [Theater director Tadeusz] Kantor "directed" the Baltic Sea! There was a lot of action. I took part in a conceptual-art biennial that was held in a defunct church, with a projection screen, a bar. It was quite something. A very opportune moment, when there was a way to do a lot of things. There were a lot of small, almost clandestine initiatives.

Adoption
MOSTAFA DERKAOUI *The Adoption*, that was in second year. I had to make two shorts: a documentary and a feature. My problem was that I didn't speak Polish well, I didn't read the newspapers. I could lie for the feature, but not for the documentary. The professor said to me, "People who lean toward documentary also invent. They're filmmakers."
        At that time I was also very much influenced by phenomenology, Heidegger, Husserl.
        Then I came across an institution that cared for unwanted children. I asked the director [of the orphanage] if I could make a film about it without infringing on people's dignity. She told me, "What fascinates me about this *business*—she used that word—are the people who come here, like to a supermarket, they choose the child that suits them. And the child they want has to resemble them."

That's how I found my subject. I said, "I have a subject. I want to make a film about Agnieszka." "Why her?" "She's Black, her mother had her with a medical student from Africa." The little girl was a three-year-old, she was tall, very beautiful. "I'm going to put myself over there, I'll take a shot of Agnieszka's eyes, her gaze, and nothing else." "Nothing else, you're sure?"

I asked two newly married friends [to play adopting parents]. I wrote dialogue, they learned it, and once they spoke it the way I wanted, I did a technical take with Krimou and the sound engineer, who was also a teacher at Łódź, and I took everyone to this orphanage and I filmed Agnieszka listening and watching the parents speak. They talk about how beautiful and intelligent she is, how great she's going to be. At the end, Jurek [the prospective father] says, "You're not going to do this to me! Everyone will say that Jurek got duped by Marysia." And they leave, and I stay on Agnieszka and the credits roll.

One evening, Jurek and Marysia invited us to their house for dinner. And there we found Agnieszka, at their place. They'd adopted her.

But I must tell you, this film was cursed by the school. They were afraid it would convey a racist image of Poland.

35mm
AHMED LALLEM The distribution of film stock [to students] was not systematic. It was only granted for specific projects that were part of the program. In addition, each film project had to be meticulously explained, well argued with those in charge in order to get authorization to shoot. It should be added that each student was in a way protected by a filmmaker who advised and supported them in front of this committee. No budget was allocated. You presented a screenplay, the production director drew up the budget and the estimate for you. He gave you whatever you needed, but no money.

It was up to you, of course, not to ask for the moon, the impossible. There are orders of magnitude that shouldn't be exceeded, naturally. Filming at Łódź was only done using 35mm film. We didn't use 16mm [...] The school was a real field of research. It was the most total freedom. They never tried to impose a style or any kind of academism. [...] The students weren't considered apprentices who had to take everything from the institution, but artists, even if still budding. [...] It was obviously impossible to make a reactionary film. But there was a great deal of freedom in the choice of subjects. I want to emphasize that point. The institute asked students to maintain a certain awareness of what was happening around them. It was very flexible.

The Whole World in Łódź

ABDELKADER LAGTAA Our model was the Czech New Wave: Miloš Forman, Věra Chytilová... The French Nouvelle Vague [films] too... We could see them in Poland. In fact, at the school we saw all films. Whether or not they were bought by Poland or shown to the public, we could see them. The films were not even subtitled. There was a paper with the translation, which was read to us. Once I even improvised a translation for a French film. We managed. The state understood that students needed to be up to date with what was going on in the world.

That was the extraordinary thing about Poland. In each city, there was an artists' club, a journalists' club, an artists' restaurant. Of course it was full of informers. But it still existed.

Political gatherings

ABDELKADER LAGTAA A lot of relationships were forged at that time, which did or didn't last. And then political activity—going to demonstrate against the Vietnam War, for example—and people meeting because of political affinities. Us Moroccans weren't very numerous, but we were very active.

I remember all kinds of meetings, UNEM gatherings... There was also a year when I organized a national symposium on Black Power, and I had to make the inaugural speech in Polish. There was also the one on Palestine with the Union of Foreign and Polish Students. Idriss Karim and I were members. We discussed these issues. We received the *Tricontinental*. As for Palestine, our Palestinian, Syrian, and Iraqi friends were deeply concerned about these things.

REMEMBER MEHDI BEN BARKA

The Brothers Karamazov

ABDELKRIM DERKAOUI In parallel to the school, we protested a lot: we'd go to vigils in front of the Moroccan Embassy on Throne Day [July 30, marking the king's accession], we protested, we contested, we denounced repressions. It wasn't good for us, for our futures, but we were still as committed as when we left Morocco. Every year we commemorated the demonstrations of March 1965 in which we had taken part before our departure for Poland. Mostafa even staged a play at the [Łódź] language school about the events of 1965 and the disappearance of Mehdi Ben Barka that same year [in Paris].

And then in 1971 there was the Skhirat coup, and then the Boeing coup in 1972 [an abortive military coup; the assault on King Hassan II's Boeing 727]. And all the arrests that followed. By then, there was no question of returning. The Moroccan ambassador to Poland told us "Wait till you get back to Morocco, we'll settle scores with you." He called us "the Brothers Karamazov." And so we were afraid to go back and we thought about our future, we considered the possibility of going to Algeria because there it was pure, hard socialism with [former president Ahmed] Ben Bella.

We also wanted to go to Cuba. We had many friends who were studying sociology in Poland. Among them was Miguel Sobrado, whom we had met at the language school. He suggested that we go to Costa Rica to teach cinema and make films. We agreed, it was an interesting proposition for us. After Boeing [the coup attempt], there was really no question of going back to Morocco, we were risking a lot, we would have gone straight to prison.

March 1965

ABDELKADER LACTAA The demonstrations of March 1965 in Morocco, I took part in them like everyone else, if I may say so. We knew the regime was "reactionary," that was our expression at the time, that it didn't care about the masses. And this decree [no high school for those over seventeen, excluding 60 percent of students] proved it. There was a general sick, heavy, deleterious atmosphere, but that decree was the straw that broke the camel's back. Especially since the opposition tried hard to prevent it, which didn't work, and anger mounted, which led to calls for a strike on March 22. I remember the leaflet of the Moroccan Progressive Youth posted on the doors of the lycée, calling for a strike.

"Cut off from the world"
ABDELKADER LAGTAA In Poland, I maintained a regular correspondence with Laâbi. The last letter I got from him was when he got out of prison—he'd first spent a month in prison—to tell me what happened: the banning of *Souffles* and then his arrest. I was following the news in Morocco thanks to Laâbi, more so than UNEM bulletins. Really, we were cut off from the world. The coup—we learned about it by chance from the radio. Of course, we could go and read *Le Monde* at the press club, but we had to go in the evening and wait: it wasn't very practical. Besides, after the invasion of Czechoslovakia, I went to the library and read all the issues of *Le Monde* since the beginning of the Prague Spring. Because there was a rumor that it was a counterrevolution orchestrated by the CIA... even among my friends.

So I read all the articles in *Le Monde* on the subject, which allowed me to read Charter 77, for example. That's what set me against the invasion, while some friends of mine, Castroists, felt that there was a counterrevolution to be waged.

In any case, anyone who was lucid, who'd lived under these regimes, couldn't possibly support them. The lack of freedom was obvious. Little by little, it was recognized that "bourgeois" democracy was indispensable.

March '68
ABDELKADER LAGTAA There were meetings at school about what was going on. I attended one of the peaceful demonstrations in March. I was president of the school's Union of Foreign Students, which allowed me to participate, to stay informed. As an artist you realize you can't trample freedom, freedom is central for artists, and secondary to power.

At the time, I was really caught up in contradictions. I was in favor of socialism, and in fact, when I arrived in Poland, you could see that there were a certain number of acquired rights: healthcare, schooling, work for everyone... Whenever I was ill, I didn't have to worry about treatment: it was free, like education, which was open and of good quality. But another very visible thing was also the lack of freedom. Maybe if I'd been a student in, I don't know, medicine, I would have noticed it less. But as artists, we were aware of the lack of freedom. Already, at that level, at our level, we realized there was reticence about certain subjects... We'd learn that such and such a film had faced problems... At the time, we really didn't understand what justified that attitude on the part of a progressive theory.

Le cinéma s'insurge!

ABDELKRIM DERKAOUI We left by car with José María and Victor to go and film the États généraux du cinéma in Paris a few months after May 1968. It was for Mostafa's third-year film *Cellar People* [1969]. Because in the story, the journalist gets fired from his job because he did a report on the États généraux. We had film from the school, and we managed to get a camera on the spot. We filmed the debates and we also spent a day at [cinematographer] Jean Charvein's. [The director Jean-Luc] Godard didn't want to be filmed. We edited the film, but the rushes stayed in Poland, in the school's editing room.

MOSTAFA DERKAOUI *Les États généraux du cinéma* is a film project that I didn't make. In 1969, I went to Paris and had the chance to meet a filmmaker who had made May 1968 in Paris what it was. It was Jean Charvein, a director of photography. He volunteered to help me make this film about the États généraux du cinéma. But I didn't have the means to do it. There's a shot in my third-year film that's taken from that shoot—that's all.

ABDELKADER LAGTAA And the poster of the États généraux that I use in my film *Shadow among Others* with Mostafa in the lead role, it was Mostafa who brought it back from Paris. There are many things that Mostafa taught us. The press was very quiet about this May '68 movement, as it coincided with the movements in Poland.

Pressure

ABDELKADER LAGTAA There was pressure after March 1968, but everything continued as before. The same freedom of expression as before. In other words, people knew what context they were evolving in. You couldn't make films that questioned the whole system. But look at what [director Krzysztof] Kieślowski did at the time, or [Roman] Polański... There was the possibility of doing critical things, and that was tolerated because it was considered a microcosm that had no influence on the population at large. Those films weren't distributed: if they were screened, it was always within a well-defined framework. No, I didn't see that freedom of action being challenged by the authorities.

The *Do negatywów album*: A Cinema of Negatives

ABDELKADER LAGTAA What kind of cinema should we do then? What kind of cinema corresponds to our aspirations? Those sorts of debates were very common among us. The idea of a politically engaged film was ever-present in our discussions. At school, I tried things. It was a place of experimentation.

Afterwards, we were confronted with reality. There, too, we couldn't just do what we wanted. But taking up a Moroccan subject was no problem at all.

Guerrilla Anthropology

MIGUEL SOBRADO I remember that Mostafa was very aware of the struggles in Morocco and very concerned about the disappearance of Ben Barka. Committed as we were to the development of our countries, we shared dreams of collaboration and cooperation once we had our diplomas. I obtained my sociology degree in 1971 and returned to Costa Rica. In cinema, there was a real interest and possibilities for the Derkaouis to join me, but it didn't materialize.[5]

Fotopan Film Stock

ABDELKRIM DERKAOUI Sobrado left before us to prepare everything for our arrival in Costa Rica. Everything was set: the plane tickets, the apartment, teaching positions. And then Mohammed Ziani arrived in Poland. At the time he was director of the Moroccan Cinema Center. He'd studied cinema in Moscow. He was a friend of [the actor] Gérard Philippe. And so he arrived in Warsaw, after having spent time in Moscow and Czechoslovakia. He was looking to buy film—because Kodak was very expensive, he was looking for something more affordable. There was Sofcolor, and Orwo, the German film, and there was also the Polish Fotopan. He approached us. He told us, "You have to shave off those beards and come work in the old country. There's no more risk, you're under my protection."

And we went home. Because we weren't needed in Cuba or Costa Rica, it was in Morocco that we wanted to be. We came back for a few months to see how things were. Ziani had promised us a job at the Cinema Center but also help on our film. He kept his promise. He gave us the freedom to release journals [film chronicles] about social issues and cultural events while preparing Mostafa's first feature film.

We spent all of 1973 preparing *About Some Meaningless Events*. And during this time at CCM I was going to film King Hassan II for the press, at events such as Fête de la Jeunesse [the Youth Festival] and Fête du Trône [Throne Day], and we were releasing [film] journals. I even filmed the trial of Abdellatif Laâbi. I kept those reels secretly, as a historical document, but then lost them when I moved.

---

5   Few common projects materialized. Exceptions include Gilles Moizon working in Morocco on some Derkaouis films, and the soundtrack commission for *About Some Meaningless Events*, recorded by a Polish jazz band led by Włodzimierz Nahorny.

Direct Cinema

ABDELKADER LAGTAA I wrote my graduation thesis [at Łódź] on documentary filmmaking: the Québécois cinéma vérité. What interested me was the presence of national concerns. From the beginning we always wondered what we were going to do in Morocco after graduation. And it seemed to me that such an approach could be adapted to Moroccan reality. Of course, I was totally mistaken because nobody was interested in documentaries in Morocco. But it had sparked my interest and it taught me a lot of things.

Attitudes Change

ABDELKADER LAGTAA Education at the [Łódź] film school lasted four years, but I stayed for nine years. In fact, there wasn't enough money to make films. So the films were made very late, compared to the theoretical component. In the meantime, we had the scholarship. As for Poles, they made their diploma films in a professional setting, outside the school. Their graduation films coincided with their first professional film produced by a studio.

Foreigners had a choice: go home after the fourth year, make their diploma film at home, and bring it back to Poland to get their diploma. That's what the Europeans did, because they had the opportunity to do so. We Third World students had no guarantee, so we clung on at the school. Sometimes it caused a lot of problems because there was no money, you had to wait and everything: it was very complicated.

All the more so since the perception of foreigners had begun to deteriorate: in some way, we were being used as a scapegoat. But on a microcosmic scale. Not in the overall population. But the idea began to emerge that Poland was making a lot of effort toward the Third World, and that, given the economic crisis...

One-Way Ticket to Algiers

ABDELKADER LAGTAA In the end, I was seen off from Poland. That's how I learned that I wasn't compatible with the prevailing ideology. What happened was that they refused to extend my residence permit. I was supposed to get a return ticket to Casablanca, and they offered me a ticket to Algiers. Of course, I declined. And I had no money to pay for the ticket myself. So I stayed until this was settled, without a residence permit.

And they tricked me. So I go to the ministry to find out about the progress of my situation. They tell me, It's settled, just give us your contact details. And the same evening, the police come to get me to send me to Algiers. It was December 1975, in the middle of the conflict around the Green March [Morocco's incursion into Western Sahara]. It wasn't easy to return to Morocco.

Idriss Karim went through the same kind of episode. Poland didn't honor its commitments. I came as a representative of an opposition party and had refused the Moroccan scholarship. Those who weren't opponents had a Moroccan scholarship: they had both. They were richer than we were. They had no worries, while we were living on a thousand złotys. Once you accepted, your hands would be tied. But [instead] we were going to protest in front of the embassy.

"Shadow among Others"

ABDELKADER LAGTAA We wanted to make modern films. Films that questioned reality. At the same time, we knew that things weren't moving forward in Morocco. We hoped that things would change politically. But we knew that as long as the politics didn't change, we couldn't carry out our projects. In Poland, we learned that social issues are important [and could reach audiences]. We learned that we couldn't ignore the conditions people lived in. We wanted a cinema that asked questions, questioned realities, political, social, and societal taboos, but also showed the subject in an approachable way. We followed examples from Czech and Polish cinema.

It should also be noted that the socialist context was close to the Moroccan context. There was censorship, the authorities exercised public control. How can you insinuate ideas without the authorities finding a way to stop them? Our experience in Poland helped us to find the means to outsmart the authorities.

"Circulated, like in a rhizome"

MOSTAFA DERKAOUI Movement interests me enormously in cinema. In *About Some Meaningless Events*, in a way it was the challenge: close-ups and movement. I hate static takes, I hate moments of unjustified silence, moments of stagnation. When I was at school in Łódź, I wanted to make a film where I'd be as close as possible to faces, words, and gestures. One of my teachers told me that it was impossible, so I decided to make a film only with close-ups. I wanted to make a film that circulated, like in a rhizome. A different kind of cinema, without roots, stems, or flowers. A cinema that is an expressive will, a will to say something. An experience that is our own, that doesn't repeat other experiences from capitalist countries or those familiar in the Third World, like in Algeria, Egypt, and Brazil.

Authenticity

ABDELKADER LAGTAA Authenticity. That was the question of the day. What is the Casablanca School?[6] It's how to access modernity by starting from local knowledge and especially popular culture. For us, cinema was also that. We had progressive ideas, we were convinced that what was needed was to take a critical look at reality. The cinema we were after had to be realistic, because that's how the audience could relate to it, but with a critical eye: questioning the audience while presenting them with something credible and legible. There had to be a common gateway so that exchange could take place.

More Beautiful than Silence

MOSTAFA DERKAOUI It was Mohammed Abdelkrim Derkaoui, my brother Krimou, who gave me my first real cinema lesson: "Mostafa, stay quiet if what you want to say isn't as beautiful as

6   The Casablanca School, founded in the 1960s by the artists Mohamed Melehi, Mohamed Chabâa, Mustapha Hafid (who also studied in Poland), Mohamed Hamidi, Mohamed Ataallah, and others at the School of Fine Arts including the art historian Toni Maraini and the popular-art specialist Bert Flint. They reappropriated artistic traditions as well as urban and rural architecture, and organized exhibitions in public spaces, the best known being in Jamaâ el-Fna Square in Marrakech in 1969. The Casablanca School supported the production of Mostafa Derkaoui's first feature film, in 1974. See *C.A.S.A.–Casablanca Art School Archives*, ed. Maud Houssais and Fatima-Zahra Lakrissa (Paris: Zaman Edition, forthcoming).

silence!" It's an old Arab proverb. It was on the eve of our entrance exam to the film school in Łódź. We were standing, glued together on the train that was taking us to Poland, holding our five old suitcases bound with old belts of our father, Abderrahmane.

What's strange is that Krimou was able to take advantage of the lesson he'd intended for me. Whatever he says or does always tends toward perfection, while I've continued to hobble along in the din the wheels of a train going a hundred and eighty kilometers an hour make on the rails. The train finally stopped in Warsaw; but I kept on talking and talking nonsense until I grew speechless from talking nonsense. I finally shut up at last. Maybe now that I'm no longer speaking, I'll be able to make a success of the film I've been trying to make since 1974, when I shot the first take of *About Some Meaningless Events*.

Sources

Casablanca-Paris-Łódź, itinéraire d'un cinéaste engagé, interviews with Mostafa Derkaoui, Casablanca, October 2014 and June 2015 (Léa Morin)

Pratiques de l'art conceptuel en Pologne, interview with Abdelkader Lagtaa, correspondence, September 2015 (Léa Morin)

Interview with Abdelkader Lagtaa, Paris, October 2015 (Marie Pierre-Bouthier)

Interviews with Miguel Sobrado, 2016 and 2018 (Léa Morin)

"Avant de *Quelques évènements sans signification*," interviews with Mostafa Derkaoui, Casablanca, September and October 2017 (Léa Morin, Marie Pierre-Bouthier)

Interviews with Mostafa Derkaoui, May 2016, Séminaire réactiver, Casablanca and February 2016, *La Serre*, Marrakech (Léa Morin)

Interview with Abdelkrim Derkaoui, January 2017 (Léa Morin)

Interviews with Abdelkader Lagtaa, September 2018, March 2019, and May 2019, Paris and Aulnay-sous-Bois (Léa Morin, Marie Pierre-Bouthier)

"Pour une dynamique du cinéma collectif," Mostafa Nissaboury, *Intégral*, March-April 1974

Ahmed Lallem, interview with Halim Chergui (Guy Hennebelle), *El Moudjahid*, September 26, 1965

"Images du cinéma marocain," France Culture, 1987 (radio broadcast) "Etudes cinématographiques," FNCCM review, July 1985, interview with Mostafa and Abdelkrim Derkaoui by Driss Chouika and Mohamed Kaouti

Translated from the French by Dominika Gajewska.

This list of sources was collected with the help of the researcher Marie Pierre-Bouthier. I am grateful to Khadija Nour Derkaoui for background information she provided, and to the interviewees—the Derkaoui brothers, Miguel Sobrado, and Abdelkader Lagtaa—as well as to the families of Hamid Bensaïd, Idriss Karim, and Abdellah Drissi. This project would not have been possible without the involvement of teams at the Łódź Film School, in particular Monika Sarwińska and Monika Talarczyk, as well as Małgorzata Lisiecka-Muniak, Dagna Kidon, and Michał Benkes of Studio Filmowe Indeks.

Selected photographs curated and digitized for the exhibition "CINIMA 3: Łódź–Casablanca, la Pologne pour devenir cinéaste: Expérimentations artistiques, luttes politiques, tricontinentale et cinéma à l'école de Łódź dans les années 1960 et 1970," held at Le 18 in Marrakech, 2020, and online at www.cinima3.com/Lodz-Casablanca.

Curated by Léa Morin from the photographic archive of Abdelkrim Derkaoui.

1. KAZIMIERZ KARABASZ, IN CLASS, 1967; 2. [FROM L TO R]: PROF. JERZY TOEPLITZ, PROF. ROMAN WAJDOWICZ, PROF. STANISŁAW WOHL, PROF. JERZY BOSSAK, PROF.ANTONI BOHDZIEWICZ, IN CLASS, 1966–72

1. [FROM L TO R]: UNKNOWN STUDENT, JULIUSZ JANICKI, JÓZEF ROBAKOW-
SKI, JOSÉ MARÍA SÁNCHEZ ARIZA, SAO GAMBA, IN CLASS, 1966–72; 2. IN CLASS, 1966–72

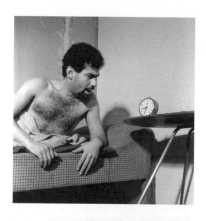

4.–6. MOSTAFA DERKAOUI, ACTING IN A FIRST-YEAR PHOTOGRAPHY EXERCISE SHOT BY HIS BROTHER, ABDELKRIM DERKAOUI, 1966–67

ABDELKADER LAGTAA [SECOND FROM LEFT], DURING A VISIT TO THE HOME
OF THE ROMANI FAMILY FEATURED IN HIS FILM, *BUT HOPE IS OF A DIFFERENT COLOR*, CA. 1971

[FROM L TO R]: ABDELKADER LAGTAA, ABDELKRIM DERKAOUI, MOHAMED REZA, AT STUDENT ACCOMMODATION ON KAROLEWSKA STREET, 1969

[FROM L TO R, BACK ROW]: IDRISS KARIM, ABDELKADER LAGTAA, AZIZ SAYED, MEETING IN SUPPORT OF THE VIETNAMESE PEOPLE ORGANIZED BY THE POLISH BRANCH OF UNEM, NEW AFRICA CLUB IN ŁÓDŹ, 1968

[FROM L TO R]: UNKNOWN STUDENT, IDRISS KARIM, ABDESLEM OUAZZANI, POLITICAL THEATER SHOW ORGANIZED BY MOROCCAN STUDENTS, SJPDC, 1968

365   1. UNKNOWN PARTICIPANT, POLITICAL THEATER SHOW, SJPDC, 1968;
2. MOSTAFA DERKAOUI, POLITICAL THEATER SHOW, SJPDC, 1968

Jakub Barua

THIS-THAT

1989

THE RIDER

(Jeździec)

1990

SABOU

1990

THE WELCOME

(Powitanie)

1990

SHINE

(Blask)

1992

FORGOTTEN PLACES

(Miejsca zapomniane)

1994

Djamel Benkhaled

ANTHROPOLOGY

(Antropologia)

1982

BLINDMAN'S BUFF

(Colin-maillard)

1982

MIRIAM

1984

Hamid Bensaïd

PENSIONERS' HOUSE

(Dom rencisty)

1969

REALISM DOES NOT PAY

(Realizm nie popłaca)

1969 [not preserved]

ZOFIA AND LUDMIŁA

(Zofia i Ludmiła)

1971

TO SERVE TWICE

(Dwukrotnie się przysłużyć)

1973

Juan Caicedo

DE PROFUNDIS PSALM 88

1984

IN CLARO MONTI

1987

Eduardo Coronado Quiroga

THE PROLOGUE

(Prolog)

1979

CHRONICA ANONYMA

1980

CINEQUAN

1981

FACE TO FACE

(Oko w oko)

1983

Mostafa Derkaoui

THE ADOPTION

(Adopcja)

1968

AMGHAR

1968

CELLAR PEOPLE

(Ludzie z piwnicy)

1969

SOMEWHERE, SOMEDAY

(Gdzieś pewnego dnia)

1971

Abdellah Drissi

LESSON 41

(Lekcja 41)

1966

REGISTER 4105

369

(*Matrykuła 4105*)
1970
Oscar Gamardo
IMAGINARIA
1967
Sao Gamba
THE MOON CHILDREN
(*Ogień w oku*)
1970
Ali Abdel Ghayoum
THE NASTAROWICZES
(*Małżeństwo Nastarowiczów*)
1975
Syed Ali Haider Rizvi
MAREK
1978
Fayçal Hassaïri
RESERVED FOR FOREIGNERS
(*Reserve dla cudzoziemców*)
1988
HOPE
(*Nadzieja*)
1989
NORTH-SOUTH
(*Nord-sud*)
1990
JAM Karanja
BORN IN CHAINS
(*Urodzony w kajdanach*)
1983
CREATING TO LIVE
(*Tworzę, aby żyć*)
1983
THE TRAP
(*Pułapka*)
1986

Idriss Karim
MARTA
1969
ELŻBIETA K.
1973
SONG FOR THE DEATHS OF
THE YOUNG
(*Pieśń na śmierć młodzieńców*)
1973
AND EVERYDAY EXILE
(*Et l'exil de tous les jours*)
1975 [not preserved]
Laredj Khader
THE FAMILY
(*Rodzina*)
1982
BELOVED FATHER
(*Kochany tato*)
1983
Abdul Khalik
FOREIGN STUDENTS IN ŁÓDŹ
(*Studenci zagraniczni w Łodzi*)
1961
PLASTIC SURGERY
(*Operacja plastyczna*)
1961
Abdelkader Lagtaa
SHADOW AMONG OTHERS
(*Cień wśród innych*)
1969
WACŁAW A.
1969
BUT HOPE IS OF A
DIFFERENT COLOR
(*Ale nadzieja jest w innym kolorze*)
1972

VOYAGE
(*Podróż*)
1975
Ahmed Lallem
THE LOST ONE
(*L'erreur*)
date unknown
Rolando Loewenstein
GDAŃSK
1978
Beverly Joan Marcus
PATRIK
1979
TOP FLOOR
(*Ostatnie piętro*)
1980
WAIT, WAIT
(*Poczekaj, poczekaj*)
1980
SHADOWS
(*Cienie*)
1982
Chaouki Mejeri
SCHEHERAZADE
1988
AURELIANO
1989
SCENT OF ISLAM
(*Zapach islamu*)
1989
Abdesselam Mezerreg
WHAT NEXT
(*Co dalej*)
1982
90 DECIBELS
(*90 decybeli*)
1983

THE SOURCE
(*Źródło*)
1983
José Morales Perez
ALEKSANDER
1987
Saer Mussa
BUY A NEWSPAPER
(*Kup gazetę*)
1983
HIBERNATUS
1983
Gilbert Nsangata
THE BEST CUSTOMER
(*Najlepszy klient*)
1975
Leonardo Palleja
TRACES
(*Ślady*)
1989
THE PASSAGE
(*Pasaż*)
1990
Roland Paret
BUT STILL, IT'S A PITY...
(*A jednak żal...*)
1971
Kaweh Pur Rahnama
EVENING-CLASS TEST
(*Wieczorna klasówka*)
1966
THE WALLET
(*Portfel*)
1966
NO WAY BACK, JOHNNY
(*Nie ma powrotu, Johnny*)
1969

José María Sánchez Ariza
THE CAT DIED OF HUNGER
(*Kot zdechł z głodu*)
1968
HISTORY OF A SHOT
(*Historia jednego ujęcia*)
1968
Raul Saucedo Zermeño
MEA CULPA
1968
WITHOUT REQUIEM
(*Sin requiem*)
1969
ABOUT-FACE
(*W tył zwrot*)
1970
Sergio Vega
FAN
(*Wiatrak*)
1985
EKOS
1990
Rupen Vosgimorukian
REPORT: SEPTEMBER 1969
(*Raport: wrzesień 1969*)
1970
Samir Zedan
BODY
(*Ciało*)
1984
LAND
(*Ziemia*)
1986
José Luis di Zeo
LETTER TO THE CHILDREN
(*List do dzieci*)
1964

WAKE
(*Velório*)
1965
GUERRILLA
(*Partyzantka*)
1966
CHE
1968
THE MEETING
(*Spotkanie*)
1968

www.etiudy.filmschool.lodz.pl

Abbas, Ferhat 276
Abbazi, Mohamed 259
Abnoudy, Ateyyat el- 199
Abouelouakar, Mohammed 202
Achebe, Chinua 323
Adagala, Seth 297
Adane, Mustapha 73, 74
Adjali, Boubaker 64, 67, 73, 200, 201
Agassiz, Louis 146
Alamgir, Alena K. 158, 159
Alex, Sara 310
Ali, Safaa 310
Allouache, Merzak 278
Amathila, Libertine Inaviposa 65
Amin, Idi 30, 307, 308
Andrieu, Michel 279
Anidjar, Gil 99, 100, 108
Applebaum, Rachel 157
Arnal, Hélène 264
Assare-Addo, Edmund 155
Ayih, Michel 156

Baez, Joan 216, 268, 281
Bakenda, Alina 176
Bakenda, Nicolas 176
Bakenda, Nicolas Jr. 176
Bakri, Mohammed 31
Balázs, Béla 15
Balderas Salas, Ruben 33
Baldwin, James 321
Balogun, Bolaji 23
Barbaro, Umberto 15
Bareja, Stanisław 29
Barša, Pavel 151
Barsaoui, Mehdi 31
Barua, Jakub 23, 29, 33, 214, 225–27, 292, 293, 297, 313, 314, 368
Barua, Stanisław (Stan) 29, 33, 214, 215, 225–27
Bassori, Timité 197
Bauman, Zygmunt 109
Baylon, Gregoire Noe 170–72, 174, 178
Beauvoir, Simone de 281
Belal, Aziz 333
Ben Barka, Mehdi 219, 263–65, 279, 280, 340, 343
Ben Bella, Ahmed 340
Ben Hania, Kaouther 31
Ben Said, Mohamed see Bensaïd, Hamid
Benkes, Michał 349
Benkhaled, Djamel 33, 35, 213, 242, 271, 277, 368
Benmalek, Anouar 70, 71
Bensaïd, Hamid (also Mohamed Ben Said) 29, 33, 234–36, 252, 253, 256, 258, 261, 262, 265, 349, 368
Bensaïd, Nadia see Strzałka, Ewa

Ben Soude, Mohamed 33, 252
Berendt, Grzegorz 102
Bernier, François 145
Bertolucci, Bernardo 272, 318
Bhabha, Homi K. 165
Bierut, Bolesław 79
Bilski, Henryk 91
Bisping, Jean 321
Bjelić, Dušan I. 146
Bloom, Harold 210
Blumenbach, Johann Friedrich 146
Bobako, Monika 23
Bobrowski, Czesław 125
Bogardus, Emory S. 245
Bohdziewicz, Antoni 219, 224, 272, 352
Bondarchuk, Sergei 284
Bongolo, Zounga 70
Borges, Jorge Luis 30
Bossak, Jerzy 15, 20, 31, 209, 217, 290, 317, 323, 325, 352
Bouberras, Rabah 74
Bourtel, Djamel 33, 254, 271
Boutellaa, Abdelcelem 33
Bożena (wife of Abdelkader Lagtaa) 256
Brault, Michel 260
Brecht, Bertolt 73, 331
Brylska, Barbara 238, 254, 366
Brzozowski, Andrzej 234
Buñuel, Luis 32
Burch, Noëll 29
Burton, Eric 68
Busuaechu, Tefferi 203
Bwire, Peter Pages 289
Bwoka, Henry 296

Cabrera, Nestor 33
Caicedo, Juan 33, 237, 240, 368
Capote, Truman 213
Cárdenas, Nancy 19
Carew, Jan 161
Carughi, Ugo 29
Cękalski, Eugeniusz 14, 209
Chafour, Ali 122
Chao Chi, Liou 330
Charvein, Jean 237, 264, 342, 367
Chebâa, Mohamed 266
Cherkaoui, Ahmed 75
Chomentowski, Gabrielle 23, 269
Chraïbi, Saâd 259
Chytilová, Věra 339
Cissé, Souleymane 73
Conrad, Joseph 226
Coronado Quiroga, Eduardo 32, 33, 213, 233, 236, 368

Cortazar, Julio 29
Costa-Gavras 265
Coulibaly, Mamadou Somé 73
Cowles Prichard, James 146
Crow, Jim 157, 163
Cuvier, Georges 146
Czapliński, Przemysław 117

Dam, Aswan 63
Damardji, Djafar 74
Davenport, Charles 146
Davis, Angela 154
Davis, Miles 281
Debray, Régis 238
Derkaoui, Abderrahmane 348
Derkaoui, Mohammed Abdelkrim (Krimou) 24,
          29, 33, 201, 252–54, 256, 259, 264,
          268, 269, 271, 331, 333–336, 338,
          340, 342, 344, 347, 348, 349, 350,
          354, 355, 357, 359, 367
Derkaoui, Mostafa 24, 29, 33, 37, 39, 41, 201,
          205, 219, 237, 238, 244, 252–54,
          256, 258, 259, 261–66, 268, 269,
          271, 276, 281, 285, 330–37, 340,
          342–44, 347, 349, 354, 355, 357,
          358, 365–68
Derkaoui Nour, Khadija "Douja" 253, 254, 330,
          333, 349, 358
Dębska, Tatiana 19, 216
Dia Moukouri, Urbain 199
Diagne, Costa 205
Diakite, Mamadou 182
Diang'a, Rachael 23
Diawara, Caoussou 73
Diop, Majhemout 62
Diop Mambéty, Djibril 294
Djaya, Sjuman 192
Dobb, Maurice 123
Dobrska, Zofia 125
Dostoyevsky, Fyodor 281
Dragostinova, Theodora 149–51
Drissi, Abdellah 30, 33, 243, 252–54, 256, 258,
          266, 271, 275, 349, 368
Du Bois, William Edward Burghardt 20, 320
Dudley, Leonard 182
Dutschke, Rudi 279
Dworczak, Aleksandra 170–72
Dylewska, Jolanta 19, 213
Dymna, Anna 236

Earhart, Amelia 29
Etler, Edward 240
Ezra, Elizabeth 11

Faïcal, H'saïri Ben Khemaïes see Hassaïri,
     Fayçal
Fakihani, Abdelfettah 329
Fanon, Frantz 19, 276, 282, 321
Fassbinder, Rainer (Werner) 318
Fedorowich, Kent 147
Ferber, Abby L. 147
Ferhati, Jilali 259
Fetting, Edmund 217
Feygin, Yakov 153
Fidelis, Małgorzata 149, 152
Fiesch, Jean-Andre 29
Fleischer, Alfred 240
Ford, Aleksander 20, 217
Ford, John 319
Forman, Miloš 339
Freud, Sigmund 9, 298
Fuser, Fausto 33

Camardo, Oscar 33, 271, 276, 369
Camba, Sao (also Seraphinus Otieno) 23, 30,
          33, 43, 289–302, 307–13, 353, 360,
          369
Catlato, Omar 278
Celler, Pierre 264
Cénini, Izza 259
Cetino, Octavio 12, 218, 282–85
Chayoum, Ali Abdel 33, 369
Cibińska, Marta 266
Cierek, Edward 267
Cill, Erasmo 33
Cillabert, Matthieu 23
Cilroy, Paul 21
Cithuku, Ndungi 309, 310
Cleason Carew, Joy 156
Codard, Jean-Luc 30, 224, 272, 317–19, 342
Coldberg, David Theo 146
Comułka, Władysław 94, 111, 113, 267
Cowon, Yakubu 153
Córski, Józef 178
Crabowska, Alina 94
Crabski, August 100, 101
Cramsci, Antonio 238
Creco, Carlos 30
Créco, Juliette 281
Cross, Jan T. 102, 111
Cryczełowska, Krystyna 233
Crzegorzewski, Jerzy 31
Cuerra, Ruy 283
Cuevara, Che 19, 218–20, 264, 277, 279, 280
Cunaratna, Piyasiri 202, 205

Haddad, Moussa 278
Hadouchi, Olivier 23

Haider Rizvi, Syed Ali 33, 234, 369
Haile Selassie 64
Hajdarowicz, Inga 23
Hall, Stuart 87
Halpern, Jan 125
Hamidi, Mohamed 266
Handler, Mario 284
Haneman, Eugeniusz 290
Hani, Chris 21
Hannova, Daniela 150
Has, Wojciech 210-14, 216, 225, 227, 240
Hassaïri, Fayçal (also H'saïri Ben Khemaïes Faï-
cal) 30, 31, 33, 45, 215, 243, 246, 275, 286, 369
Hassan II 269, 340, 344
Haywood, Harry 154
Heidegger, Martin 337
Hemingway, Ernest 320
Hernández, María Rosa 218
Hessler, Julie 157
Hoffman, Jerzy 224, 237
Hong, Young-sun 150, 151
Höss, Rudolf 239
Hughes, Langston 20, 154
Husserl, Edmund 320, 337

Idziak, Sławomir 224
Imbuga, Francis 297
Ionesco, Eugène 335
Issiakhem, M'hamed 74
Ivens, Joris 15, 224
Iyayi, Festus 72, 73

Jagielski, Sebastian 13
Jakubowska, Wanda 15, 32, 209, 217, 218, 221,
    222, 224, 227
Jancsó, Miklós 272
Janicki, Juliusz 254, 353
Jara, Tafesse 203
Jastrzębski, Jan 178, 179
Jennings, Peter 32
John Paul II 161
Johansson, Lars 310
Joyce, James 317
Jutra, Claude 260

Kabera, Eric 310
Kalecki, Michał 125, 127
Kamieńska, Irena 233
Kamissek, Christoph 80
Kamya, Caroline 311
Kaniewska, Maria 290
Kantor, Tadeusz 337
Kapuściński, Ryszard 165

Karabasz, Kazimierz 30, 222, 233-35, 239, 260,
    261, 325, 352
Karanja, John Maina (JAM) 23, 31, 33, 47, 214,
    215, 369
Karim, Idriss 31, 33, 49, 216, 233, 234, 252,
    253, 256, 257, 261-63, 266-68,
    271, 277, 284, 336, 339, 346, 349,
    361, 364, 369
Kasrils, Ronnie 21
Katsakioris, Constantin 23, 84, 158
Kawalerowicz, Jerzy 210
Kaźmierczak, Wacław 15
Kebadian, Jacques 279
Kerouac, Jack 281
Keya, Ingolu wa 296, 297
Khader, Laredj 33, 234, 247, 369
Khaemba, B. 214
Khalif, Omar 156
Khalik, Abdul 33, 242, 369
Khaznadar, Maruf 67
Khoury, Driss 266
Khrushchev, Nikita 10, 11, 62, 84, 86, 195
Kidon, Dagna 349
Kieślowski, Krzysztof 233, 343
Kimathi, Dedan 322
King Jr., Martin Luther 154
Kitchlew, Toufigue 33
Klein, William 224
Kluba, Henryk 30, 217, 227
Konaré, Alpha Oumar 73
Kornatowska, Maria 32
Koudawo, Fafali 60
Koura, Jan 152
Kowalik, Tomira 256
Kowalska, Beata 23
Kreienbaum, Jonas 80
Królikiewicz, Grzegorz 30
Kurosawa, Akira 319
Kurylewicz, Andrzej 238, 268
Kusza, Janusz 216, 268
Kutz, Kazimierz 210

La Guma, Alexa 21
Laâbi, Abdellatif 256, 263, 265, 341, 344
Lagtaa, Abdelkader 24, 31, 33, 51, 53, 201, 219,
    252-56, 258-66, 269, 271, 279,
    281, 285, 329, 330, 332, 333, 335,
    336, 339-43, 345-347, 349, 356,
    359-61, 369
Lakhdar-Hamina, Mohammed 64, 73, 201
Lallem, Ahmed 24, 31, 33, 74, 192, 201, 271,
    278, 334, 338, 370
Langa, Mandla 21
Lange, Oskar 87, 125

Laval, Pierre 197
Lavigne, Danielle 269
Leakey, Louis 321
Lelouch, Claude 224
Lenin, Vladimir 62, 104, 274
Lentin, Alana 155
Leonardo da Vinci 214
Lilpop, Stanisław Wilhelm August 166
Limbrick, Peter 269
Linnaeus, Carl 145
Lisiecka-Muniak, Małgorzata 349
Lledo, Jean-Pierre 74, 204, 205
Lodge, Tom 152
Loewenstein, Rolando 33, 213, 237, 370
Lopez, Eliel 33
Lumière, brothers 30
Lumumba, Patrice 10, 60, 88, 203, 322
Łodziński, Sławomir 9
Łomnicki, Jan 261

Mabinda, Patrik 241
Maciejowski, Jan 266, 267
MacMaster, Neil 149
Madani, Achene 33
Mahi, Ahmed 67
Majewski, Janusz 215, 216, 240
Maleh, Nabil 192, 200
Malek, Ahmed 278
Malhotra, Chander 33
Mancera, Eduardo 33
Mandiou, Touré 191, 193
Mantel-Niećko, Joanna 90
Manyara, Charles 297
Mao, Zedong 150, 284, 330
Marcus, Beverly Joan 19, 33, 213, 241, 242, 245, 246, 248, 370
Marczewski, Andrzej 366
Mark, James 117, 149, 153
Marker, Chris 224, 260, 322, 325
Marx, Karl 330
Masilela, Ntougela 33, 319, 325
Matu, Kavila 310
Matusevich, Maxim 21, 22, 150, 156, 157
Maupassant, Guy de 213
Mazif, Sid Ali 278
Mazrui, Ali 59, 63, 75
Mazurek, Małgorzata 87, 125
Mąka-Malatyńska, Katarzyna 23
McKay, Claude 20, 154
Meddour, Azzedine 74
Mejeri, Chaouki 31, 33, 215, 236, 370
Melehi, Mohamed 266
Mezerreg, Abdesselam 33, 214, 246, 271, 370
Mickiewicz, Adam 109, 140, 141, 275

Mienandi, Hyacinthe 33, 201, 214
Minh, Ho Chi 264, 279, 280
Mĩriĩ, Ngũgĩ wa 292
Mobarak, Mohamed 33
Moczar, Mieczysław 110
Moizon, Gilles 254
Mongo, Alain Richard 175–77, 180
Mongo, Milen 174–77, 180
Mongo, Mrs. 174–77, 180
Morales Perez, José 33, 213, 370
Morek, Jan 169, 174, 180
Morin, Léa 24, 253, 269, 350
Morricone, Ennio 278
Mphahlele, Es'kia 323
Mrożek, Sławomir 215
Mtarasha, Yasinta 310
Muchina, Bob 297
Mulekezi, Everest 154, 156
Mulvihill, Ron 293
Munk, Andrzej 210
Mussa, Saer 33, 214, 234, 370

Nabulaya, Anna 310
Nadrin de Urioste, Armando 33
Nahorny, Włodzimierz 268
Namzhil, Cend 33
Nasser, Gamal Abdel 66, 112, 150
Nayeh, Ameen 31
Ndaliko Katondolo, Petna 309
Negadi, Mustapha 71
Nehru, Jawaharlal 150
Ng'oge, Nangayoma 293
Ngouabi, Marien 63
Ngure, Levis 297
Nichols, Bill 244
Nkomo, Joshua 322
Nkosi, Lewis 21
Nkrumah, Kwame 64, 72, 127, 150, 321
Nowak, Filip 232
Nowicka, Ewa 9, 231, 245
Nowicka, Magdalena 162
Nowicki, Bartosz 23, 160
Nsangata, Gilbert-Ndunga 33, 201, 214, 370

O'Brown, August Agboola 79
O'Casey, Sean 331
Okai, Atukwei 72
Okudzhava, Bulat 217
Olbrychski, Daniel 236
Omburo, Benjamin 156
Ondire, Patrick 226
Oralek, Milan 152
Orłoś, Kazimierz 218
Ōshima, Nagisa 318

Osoba, Segun 72, 73
Otieno, Seraphinus see Gamba, Sao
Ouazzani, Abdeslem 364
Oufkir, Mohamed 331
Ouologuem, Yambo 326

Padmore, George 20
Palach, Jan 216, 268
Palleja, Leonardo 33, 248, 370
Panov, Mitko 239
Papatakis, Michel 202
Paret, Roland 33, 217, 254, 370
Partum, Andrzej 31, 266, 336, 337
Partum, Ewa 31, 266, 336
Pascon, Paul 257, 258
Pasikowski, Władysław 31
Passendorfer, Jerzy 224
Pereira dos Santos, Nelson 283
Pergolesi, Giovanni Battista 263
Perrault, Pierre 260
Petelska, Ewa 219
Petelski, Czesław 219
Petrović, Aleksandar 261
Petrycki, Jacek 360
Philippe, Gérard 344
Picasso, Pablo 317
Pierre-Bouthier, Marie 23, 349
Pineda, Lorenzo 33
Plath, Sylvia 213
Podsiadło, Magdalena 13
Polański, Roman 343
Poniatowski, Józef 236
Popescu, Monica 21
Prashad, Vijay 276
Presley, Elvis 311
Prus, Bolesław 211
Przestępski, Tomasz 237
Przybyło-Ibadullajev, Marta 169, 178, 179
Przylipiak, Mirosław 246
Pudovkin, Vsevolod 15
Pushkin, Aleksander 217

Qāsim, Abd al-Karim 195
Quist-Adade, Charles 158

Rahnama, Kaweh Pur 17, 31, 33, 221–25, 370
Ramírez, Ricardo Torres 33, 271, 275
Rank, J. Arthur 321
Ray, Satyajit 319
Recknitz, Jack 224
Reggio, Godfrey 206
Remin, Katarzyna 19, 213
Renoir, Jean 319
Resnais, Alain 224, 260, 322

Resul, Izzeddin 67
Reza, Mohamed 359
Riza, Salah 33
Robakowski, Józef 353
Robeson, Paul 154
Robinson, Jane 123
Rocha, Glauber 221, 282, 283, 318
Rodriguez, Antonio 33
Rolke, Tadeusz 168
Romm, Mikhail 204
Rosenstein-Rodan, Paul 123, 124
Rosi, Francesco 265
Rostow, Walt Whitman 123
Rouch, Jean 260, 323
Rowden, Terry 11

Saleh Abou, Ziad 139, 140
Sánchez Ariza, José Maria 33, 211, 221, 271, 282, 342, 353, 371
Sandøy, Haakon 254
Sartre, Jean-Paul 281
Sarwińska, Monika 269, 349
Saucedo Zermeño, Raul 32, 33, 55, 215, 219, 237, 271, 279, 281, 371
Sauvy, Alfred 12
Sayed, Aziz 361
Schwenkel, Christina 152
Scott, Brian 160–62
Seeger, Pete 220
Sembène, Ousmane 294, 325
Sen, Amartya 123
Shalah, Abbas al- 204
Shienetar, Vasco 33
Siala, Khelil 33
Siassia, Luc 33
Siefert, Marsha 13
Siekierska, Jadwiga 321
Sienkiewicz, Henryk 117, 166
Siermiński, Michał 116
Simmel, Georg 249
Sissako, Abderrahmane 192
Skolimowski, Jerzy 272
Skórzewski, Edward 237
Skrzynecki, Piotr 236
Slobodian, Quinn 117, 149
Sławińska, Joanna 96
Smihi, Moumen 259
Sobrado, Miguel 24, 254, 264, 334, 340, 343, 344, 349
Solanas, Fernando 12, 217, 218, 282–85
Soldi, Mokhtar 30
Soyinka, Wole 323
Stalin, Joseph 61, 62, 125
Stanek, Łukasz 85, 107, 152

Stejskalová, Tereza 184, 186
Stroop, Jürgen 238
Strzałka, Ewa (also Nadia Bensaïd) 19, 29, 256,
    258
Sugarzhav, Bator 33
Sukarno 150
Sulaiman, Bahjet 215
Sumiński, Tadeusz 178, 180–84
Switat, Mustafa 108
Szacki, Jerzy 108, 116
Szałapak, Anna 236
Szulkin, Piotr 246
Ślesicki, Władysław 235, 236, 261
Śmiech, Witold 90

Zanussi, Krzysztof 237
Zapata, Emiliano 282
Zayani, Moha Ou Hamou 219, 265
Ząbek, Maciej 177
Zedan, Samir 33, 236, 371
Zeo, José Luis di 30, 33, 217–19, 238–40, 271,
    276, 281, 371
Zerouali, A. 257
Ziani, Mohammed 344
Ziarnik, Jerzy 240
Zins, Henryk 320
Zygadło, Tomasz 233, 236
Żukrowski, Wojciech 224

Tadesse, Desta 203
Talarczyk, Monika 23, 242, 269, 349
Telemann, Georg Philipp 237
Telepneva, Natalia 152
Terreken, Getachew 203
Thiong'o, Ngũgĩ wa 292, 322, 323
Thompson, Andrew S. 147
Tinoco, Rafael 33
Titkow, Andrzej 234
Toeplitz, Jerzy 14–16, 20, 204, 209, 217, 290,
    352
Torres, Manuel 33
Toyo, Eskor 72
Traoré, Moussa 73
Tym, Stanisław 238, 254, 335

Van Quynh, Nguyen 224
Varda, Agnès 224
Vaughan, Koyinde T. W. 320, 321
Vega, Sergio 33, 286, 371
Vieyra, Paulin Soumanou 294
Vishwanath, Krishna 184–86
Visone, Massimo 29
Vosgimorukian, Rupen 32, 33, 248, 254, 271,
    273, 371

Wajda, Andrzej 210, 211, 224, 265, 272, 331, 332
Wajdowicz, Roman 290, 352
Wałęsa, Lech 161
Warska, Wanda 238, 268, 335
Waśkowski, Mieczysław 30
Wdowiński, Zbigniew 83
Wimmer, Marian 14
Wohl, Stanisław 209, 217, 352
Wójcik, Jerzy 29
Wright, Richard 22
Wyrzykowski, Paweł 30

Hope Is of a Different Color: From the Global South to the Łódź Film School
This book project originated from a screening program of the same name held at the Museum of Modern Art in Warsaw, November 21–22, 2019. That program, as well as research for this book, was supported by a Lodz Film School internal research grant (N/INS/0520) held by Monika Talarczyk.

Edited by
Magda Lipska
Monika Talarczyk
Series Editor
Meagan Down
Editing
Alan Lockwood
Academic Reviewer
Dr. hab. Dorota Sajewska
Translations
Jolanta Axworthy (text by Katarzyna Mąka-Malatyńska), Dominika Gajewska (texts by Olivier Hadouchi, Léa Morin), Jolanta Scicińska (texts by Beata Kowalska and Inga Hajdarowicz, Monika Talarczyk), Marcin Wawrzyńczak (introduction, biographies, text by Monika Bobako)
Index
Magda Zabrocka (Lingventa)

Design concept and layout
Ludovic Balland Typography Cabinet, Basel
Typesetting and lithography
Marcin Klinger, Studio Temperówka, Warsaw
Typefaces
Ludwig Pro
Jury Regular

Cover photographs
Front cover: Sao Gamba and Ewa Strzałka, photograph by Grzegorz Kędzierski, courtesy Lodz Film School archive
Back cover: *Shadow among Others* [stills], dir. Abdelkader Lagtaa, 1969, courtesy Lodz Film School archive
Insert
Abdelkader Lagtaa, "Point d'interrogation," 1972, courtesy the artist

Copyrights
All texts © Museum of Modern Art in Warsaw, Lodz Film School, and Authors, 2021
All film stills reproduced in this book courtesy Lodz Film School archive

Acknowledgements
The editors would like to express their gratitude to Léa Morin for her help and generosity in sharing research and visual material for this book.
Many thanks to Ania Szczepańska (Université Paris 1 Panthéon Sorbonne) for the inspiration to revisit Mostafa Derkaoui's œuvre.
With special thanks to both Ewa Strzałka and Abdelkader Lagtaa for their engagement, patience in answering numerous questions, and the unquestioned trust they placed in us during the research of this book.

Published by
Museum of Modern Art in Warsaw, Pańska 3
00–124 Warsaw
artmuseum.pl/en

Lodz Film School, Targowa 61/63, 90–323 Łódź
filmschool.lodz.pl/en

Printed and bound by
PASAŻ sp. z o.o.

ISBN: 978-83-64177-87-3
(Museum of Modern Art in Warsaw)
ISBN: 978-83-65501-90-5
(Lodz Film School)

Distributed by
The University of Chicago Press
press.uchicago.edu

Museum of Modern Art in Warsaw
sklep.artmuseum.pl

Available as an e-book edition

The Museum of Modern Art in Warsaw is funded by the Ministry of Culture and National Heritage:

Ministry of
Culture
and National
Heritage of
the Republic
of Poland

The premises and selected projects are funded by the City of Warsaw:

Patron of the Museum and the collection:

Strategic partners of the Museum:

Legal advisor:

more than law

BOOKS

THE MUSEUM UNDER CONSTRUCTION
BOOK SERIES

No. 1 **1968–1989: POLITICAL UPHEAVAL AND ARTISTIC CHANGE**
Edited by Claire Bishop & Marta Dziewańska
Museum of Modern Art in Warsaw, 2009
The texts assembled in this reader are a selective record of presentations from the "1968–1989" seminar, held as a comparative reflection on the artistic significance of 1968, the political transformation of 1989, and methods of communication in art.
ISBN   978-83-92404-40-8

No. 2 **ION GRIGORESCU: IN THE BODY OF THE VICTIM**
Edited by Marta Dziewańska
Museum of Modern Art in Warsaw, 2010
This book is an attempt to read the work of one of the most charismatic and original artists from the former Eastern Bloc, who worked in relative isolation until 1989, and whose art can be viewed in relation to similar positions artists have taken in other parts of the world.
ISBN   978-83-92404-41-5

No. 3 **WARSZAWA W BUDOWIE 2009**
[Warsaw Under Construction 2009]
Edited by Marcel Andino-Velez
Museum of Modern Art in Warsaw, 2010
This book is a record of events that took place as part of the "Warsaw Under Construction" festival's first edition, focused on design, architecture, and town planning, and attempting to capture the spirit and creative energy that had then begun taking over the city.
Book in Polish language.
ISBN   978-83-92404-42-2

No. 4 **AS SOON AS I OPEN MY EYES I SEE A FILM: EXPERIMENT IN THE ART OF YUGOSLAVIA IN THE 1960s AND 1970s**
Edited by Ana Janevski
Museum of Modern Art in Warsaw, 2010
This book is inspired by the first exhibition organized by the museum. It is a journey to a country that has ceased to exist, but which gave rise to the most important art myth in our part of Europe: the myth of radical art.
ISBN   978-83-92404-43-9

No. 5 **ALINA SZAPOCZNIKOW: AWKWARD OBJECTS**
Edited by Agata Jakubowska
Museum of Modern Art in Warsaw, 2011
Seen as a great artist in Poland, elsewhere Alina Szapocznikow (1926–73) has remained relatively unknown. Today she enjoys the status of a discovery, her sculpture entering museum collections worldwide. An artist who always put herself in the difficult position of pioneer heading toward the new and unknown, in 1972, near the end of her life, she confessed: "As for me, I produce awkward objects." Here that life and work is addressed by Griselda Pollock, Sarah Wilson, and Ernst van Alphen, among others.
ISBN   978-83-92404-46-0

No. 6 **LOVELY, HUMAN, TRUE, HEARTFELT: THE LETTERS OF ALINA SZAPOCZNIKOW AND RYSZARD STANISŁAWSKI 1948–1971**
Edited by Agata Jakubowska & Katarzyna Szotkowska-Beylin
Translated by Jennifer Croft
Museum of Modern Art in Warsaw, 2012
The previously unpublished correspondence between Alina Szapocznikow and Ryszard Stanisławski, a woman of increasing importance in twentieth-century art and a man who was an eminent critic and museum director.
ISBN   978-83-93381-86-9

No. 7 **POST-POST-SOVIET?
ART, POLITICS & SOCIETY IN
RUSSIA AT THE TURN OF
THE DECADE**
Edited by Marta Dziewańska,
Ekaterina Degot & Ilya Budraitskis
Museum of Modern Art in Warsaw, 2013
By placing emerging artists in their political and social contexts, this book attempts to confront the activist scene that has arisen in today's art world in Russia. Includes criticism by writers and scholars, and an extensive timeline of the artistic and sociopolitical context.
ISBN   978-83-93381-84-5

No. 8 **OSKAR HANSEN:
OPENING MODERNISM**
Edited by Aleksandra Kędziorek &
Łukasz Ronduda
Museum of Modern Art in Warsaw, 2014
This book analyzes diverse aspects of the architectural, theoretical, and didactical œuvre of Oskar Hansen (1922–2005), a Polish member of Team 10, and chronicles the impact of his theory of Open Form on architecture, urban planning, experimental film, and the visual arts in postwar Poland.
ISBN   978-83-64177-05-7

No. 9 **TEAM 10 EAST: REVISIONIST
ARCHITECTURE IN REAL
EXISTING MODERNISM**
Edited by Łukasz Stanek
Museum of Modern Art in Warsaw, 2014
Team 10 East never existed. This volume develops that term as a conceptual tool to discuss the work of Team 10 members and fellow travelers from socialist countries—such as Oskar Hansen of Poland and Charles Polónyi of Hungary, along with a number of architects from Czechoslovakia and Yugoslavia.
ISBN   978-83-64177-03-3

No. 10 **ANDRZEJ WRÓBLEWSKI:
RECTO/VERSO**
Edited by Eric de Chassey &
Marta Dziewańska
Museum of Modern Art in Warsaw, 2015
One of Poland's preeminent postwar artists, Andrzej Wróblewski (1927–57) created a highly individual and prolific form of abstract and figurative painting. His output reflects the original solutions he devised to address the personal and public issues of his time, in ways that are very relevant today and that continue to inspire artists.
ISBN   978-83-64177-16-3

No. 11 **MARIA BARTUSZOVÁ:
PROVISIONAL FORMS**
Edited by Marta Dziewańska
Museum of Modern Art in Warsaw, 2015
Working alone behind the Iron Curtain, Maria Bartuszová (1936–96) was one of a number of female artists who not only experimented formally and embarked intuitively on new themes, but who, because of a position at odds with mainstream modernist trends, remained in isolation or in marginalized positions. This book deftly reveals how Bartuszová experimented with materials, never hesitating to treat tradition, accepted norms, and trusted techniques as simply transitory and provisional.
ISBN   978-83-64177-26-2

No. 12 **POINTS OF CONVERGENCE:
ALTERNATIVE VIEWS ON
PERFORMANCE**
Edited by Marta Dziewańska &
André Lepecki
Museum of Modern Art in Warsaw, 2017
Always happening in the here and now, and yet implicating past and future, performance is a practice open to the unknown, constantly questioning its own subjects, materials, and languages. This book explores these ideas, potentials, and capacities of performance, stimulating new discussion between theorists and practitioners on the genealogies of performance, on unexpected lines of influence, and on off-center historiographies.
ISBN   978-83-64177-38-5

No. 13 **OBJECT LESSONS:**
ZOFIA RYDET'S SOCIOLOGICAL
RECORD
Edited by Krzysztof Pijarski
Museum of Modern Art in Warsaw, 2017
In 1978, Zofia Rydet (1911–97) began work on a monumental project that would come to be known as *Sociological Record:* photographing the people of Poland at their homes, she produced an extraordinary archive of around 27,000 negatives. The images include faces, interiors, furnishings, and more. *Object Lessons* aims to dispel the myths that have formed around the project in recent years. The essays here contextualize and interpret the *Record* from different perspectives, opening up the work to further inquiry as both an object of interpretation and a subject of theoretical interest. A celebration of Rydet's work, this book reminds us of photography's incredible power to provide a visual way of thinking and a provocative method for archiving the world.
ISBN   978-83-64177-37-8

No. 14 **THE OTHER TRANS-ATLANTIC:**
KINETIC AND OP ART IN
EASTERN EUROPE AND
LATIN AMERICA
Edited by Marta Dziewańska,
Dieter Roelstraete & Abigail Winograd
Museum of Modern Art in Warsaw, 2017
The Other Trans-Atlantic is attuned to the brief but historically significant period between 1950 and 1970, when the trajectories of the Eastern European and Latin American art scenes converged in a shared enthusiasm for kinetic and Op art. As the established axis of Paris, London, and New York became increasingly dominated by a succession of ideological monocultures—such as the master concepts of gesture and expression, Pop, or minimalism—another web of ideas was being spun, linking Warsaw, Moscow, and Zagreb, with Buenos Aires, Caracas, and São Paulo. These artistic practices were dedicated to a different set of aesthetic concerns: philosophies of art and culture dominated by notions of progress and science, the machine and engineering, construction and perception.
ISBN   978-83-64177-42-2

No. 15 **PAST DISQUIET: ARTISTS,**
INTERNATIONAL SOLIDARITY,
AND MUSEUMS-IN-EXILE
Edited by Kristine Khouri &
Rasha Salti
Museum of Modern Art in Warsaw, 2018
The 1970s saw artists, curators, and militants gathering international collections of art, donated by artists, that traveled to established museums, galleries, and community spaces. These museums-in-exile were intended to incarnate the solidarity of artists with political causes and mobilize a wider public. *Past Disquiet* explores the histories of three such museums, plumbing the networks of artists who worked together to make them a reality. Starting with the forgotten *International Art Exhibition for Palestine*, the authors' research uncovered a global map of artists protesting the Pinochet dictatorship in Chile and the apartheid regime in South Africa, and supporting liberation struggles including that of the Palestinian people and the Sandinista revolution.
ISBN   978-83-64177-44-6

No. 16 **MIRIAM CAHN: I AS HUMAN**
Edited by Marta Dziewańskai
Museum of Modern Art in Warsaw, 2019
A rebel and feminist, Swiss artist Miriam Cahn is one of the major artists of her generation. Known for her drawings and paintings, she also experiments with photography, moving images, and sculptures. Cahn's diverse body of work is disturbing and dreamlike, filled with striking human figures pulsing with an energy both passionate and violent. *MIRIAM CAHN: I AS HUMAN* looks at the artist's prolific and troubling œuvre from a variety of vantage points. It is an attempt to bring words and images together—an attentive contemplation of work that is heterogeneous, restless, and full of extreme emotions that coincide with our everyday lives: us, as humans.
ISBN   978-83-64177-55-2

BOOKS

MUZEUM
sztuki   museum
nowoczesnej of modern art
w warszawie in warsaw

ZOFIA KULIK

METHODOLOGY, MY LOVE

BOOKS
N°17

EDITED BY AGATA JAKUBOWSKA

No. 17 **ZOFIA KULIK: METHODOLOGY, MY LOVE**
Edited by Agata Jakubowska
Museum of Modern Art in Warsaw, 2019

Zofia Kulik's rich artistic career has a dual nature. Between 1970 and 1987, she worked alongside Przemysław Kwiek as a member of the duo KwieKulik, after which she began to develop a successful individual career. While KwieKulik's work has been well established as central to the East European neo-avant-garde art lexicon of the 1970s and 1980s, Kulik's solo work has yet to be examined in depth. This monograph, prepared in partnership with the Kulik-KwieKulik Foundation, analyzes the themes of her rich and complex œuvre, addressing the (post)communist condition, artistic labor, intermediality, and the conditions of working as a female artist.

ISBN   978-83-64177-59-0